James Beard
Beard on Food

Other books by James Beard

Hors d'Oeuvre and Canapés

Cook It Outdoors

Fowl and Game Cookery

The Fireside Cookbook

Paris Cuisine
(with Alexander Watt)

James Beard's New Fish Cookery

How to Eat Better for Less Money
(with Sam Aaron)

The Complete Book of Outdoor Cookery
(with Helen Evans Brown)

The James Beard Cookbook

James Beard's Treasury of Outdoor Cooking

Delights and Prejudices

James Beard's Menus for Entertaining

How to Eat (& Drink) Your Way Through
a French (or Italian) Menu

James Beard's American Cookery

Beard on Bread

James Beard's Theory & Practice of Good Cooking

The New James Beard

Beard on Birds

Beard on Pasta

James Beard's Simple Foods

Love and Kisses and a Halo of Truffles:
Letters to Helen Evans Brown

The Armchair James Beard

James Beard
Beard on Food

છે

Assisted by José Wilson

Illustrations by Karl Stuecklen

RUNNING PRESS
PHILADELPHIA · LONDON

9   8   7   6   5   4   3   2   1
Digit on the right indicates the number of this printing

Library of Congress Cataloging-in-Publication Number 00-132690

ISBN 0-7624-0688-7

Editorial consultant: John Ferrone
Cover illustration by Peter Fiore
Cover design by Toby Schmidt
Interior design by Bill Jones
Typography: Goudy Oldstyle

This book may be ordered by mail from the publisher.
Please include $2.50 for postage and handling.
But try your bookstore first!

Running Press Book Publishers
125 South Twenty-second Street
Philadelphia, Pennsylvania 19103-4399

Visit us on the web!
www.runningpress.com

Editor's Note (for pages 5, 236–237, and 291):
Cooks should be warned that there is some risk in eating raw or undercooked egg yolks and ground meat. The USDA goes so far as to say that all ground beef should be cooked to an internal temperature of 160°F, which obviously is not possible in recipes calling for raw meat.

Contents

છ્ર

Introductory Note

⧉

It is wonderful for all of us who treasure James Beard to know that his works are being kept alive for everyone to enjoy. What a pleasure for those of us who knew Jim to read him again, and what a treasure and happy discovery for new generations who will now know him. He reads just as he talked, and to read him is like being with him, with all his warmth, humor, and wisdom.

Beard appeared on the American culinary scene in 1940, with his first book, *Hors d'Oeuvre and Canapés*, which is still in print more than fifty years later. Born in Portland, Oregon at the beginning of this century, he came from a food-loving background and started his own catering business after moving to New York in 1938. He soon began teaching, lecturing, giving culinary demonstrations, writing articles and more books (eventually twenty in all). Through the years he gradually became not only the leading culinary figure in the country, but "The Dean of American Cuisine." He remains with us as a treasured authority, and the James Beard Foundation, housed in his own home on West 12th Street in New York, keeps his image and his love of good food very much alive.

Beard was the quintessential American cook. Well-educated and well-traveled during his eighty-two years, he was familiar with many cuisines but he remained fundamentally American. He was a big man, over six feet tall, with a big belly, and huge hands. An endearing and always lively teacher, he loved people, loved his work, loved gossip, loved to eat, loved a good time.

I always remember him for his generosity toward others in the profession. For instance, when my French colleague, Simone Beck, came to

New York for the publication of our first book, my husband and I knew no one at all in the food business, since we had been living abroad for fifteen years. Nobody had ever heard of us, but our book fortunately got a most complimentary review from Craig Claiborne in the New York Times. Although we had never met him before, it was Jim who greeted us warmly and introduced us to the New York food scene and its personalities. He wanted friends to meet friends, and he literally knew "everyone who was anyone" in the business. He was not only generous in bringing them together, but eager that they know each other. It was he who introduced us to the late Joe Baum of the then-famous Restaurant Associates and The Four Seasons, among other famous restaurants. He presented us to Jacques Pépin, at that time a young chef from France who was just making his way in New York, and to Elizabeth David, England's doyenne of food writers, as well as to many others.

It was not only that he knew everyone, he was also a living encyclopedia of culinary lore and history, and generous about sharing his knowledge. So often when I needed to know something about grains, for instance, I would call him and if the information was not right in his head, he would call back in a few minutes either with the answer or a source. This capability and memory served him well in his books and articles, as well as in conversation and in public interviews.

James A. Beard was an American treasure, and his books remain the American classics that deserve an honored place on the shelves of everyone who loves food.

—*Julia Child*
April 1, 1999

Foreword

༚

When I recall James Beard, which is often even fifteen years after his death, the vibrant man you meet in this lively book comes into clear focus: teacher, food historian, inveterate traveler, unabashed enthusiast, caring cook, and, in this volume, journalist as well.

In 1974, when *Beard on Food* was first published, I wrote, "The genuineness of James Beard's lifelong passion for food and cookery is reflected throughout the volume." That seems even more true when the book is viewed today in its handsome new edition.

It's startling, for instance, that a man who knew so much about the subjects of food and cooking was never condescending, though he spent much of his time communicating with people who knew very little about the subjects or had no confidence in the knowledge they did possess. At the same time, he was a world-famous gastronome who made no apology for American cooking, nor for American wine, and kept on his pantry shelf cans of tuna fish and corned beef hash as well as white truffles.

During the years I was executive food editor of the Washington Post and editor-in-chief of Food & Wine magazine, Jim was a fountain of information, an invaluable sounding board, and a source of pithy, on-target quotations. He was more than the sum of his meals, however. I learned during his visits to Washington that he had passionate opinions about politics and politicians; he was keenly attuned to music and theater (fields in which he had sought a career earlier in his life); and he read voraciously. I have a hazy memory that he might have played bridge, but his favorite sport was gossip.

One day, having met him for lunch near his Greenwich Village home, I was shushed to silence as he (and I) tuned in on the conversation between a couple at a nearby table. It was a joint confessional of infidelity, seemingly multi-layered. Soon they left. "Wasn't that juicy!" said Jim with a grin, and we immediately returned to discussing the fine points of preparing daube of beef.

There are juicy steaks and chickens in *Beard on Food*, but no juicy, off-color stories. What awaits you instead is a portrait of James Beard's world of food sketched in words rather than paint. This may strike you as a very broad topic, but Jim was a very broad man who did his research thoroughly, bite by bite.

He begins with the hamburger and leaves us, between meals, musing about curious food names including "Scotch Woodcock" and the German potato and sausage dish "Himmel und Erde" (heaven and earth). In between, he shows his teaching voice as he explains the feeding and control of a barbecue grill; takes us to dine in France, England, Germany, and the eastern Mediterranean; and counsels readers on cooking without salt.

He shares his enthusiasm for all manners of meats, fish, vegetables, and fruits, singing a hymn to hash, cooking potatoes for breakfast, bemoaning the "tragic decline" of the tomato, and reviving a favorite version of tartar sauce from his childhood. He is bewitched by a huge "pancake sandwich" filled with a thick slice of ham and topped with fried eggs, but he is equally appreciative of micro foods such as sardines and finger sandwiches.

In a time when many home cooks are content to grill, sauté, or merely reheat, he reminds us of the joy of poaching fish and meat, of cooking vegetables à la Greque, and of preparing fish as seviche or escabeche. There are essays, too, on themes he also took up at book length—bread, pasta, and outdoor cooking. Along the way, the man shows himself to be a master of the declarative sentence:

> "I love every part of the pig, from the ears to the feet!"
> "Beets can be beautiful."
> "Ham isn't what it used to be."

You want to read on, and, at the conclusion of an essay you probably will want to cook. Here, too, the reader is in luck. The recipes in *Beard on Food* are appealing and easy to use because Jim hated and avoided superfluous ingredients and show-off techniques. He also had a knack for presenting directions clearly and conversationally. It is as though he is talking to you at the stove.

One's appreciation for the breadth and depth of this material can only be heightened with the realization that it is a compilation of syndicated newspaper columns Jim wrote weekly, assisted by Jose Wilson, in the early 1970s.

Is *Beard on Food* dated, then? While most of the restaurants he mentions are gone and some of the recipes he loved are more likely to be chewed over at a culinary seminar than cooked for family or company, a vast majority of the victuals are as aromatic and fresh as the produce at a farmers' market.

—William Rice
July 13, 2000

Since the publication of *Beard on Food* in 1974, a number of restaurants and other institutions referred to by Beard may have ceased to exist, and the reader is well advised to check before planning a visit. Though less useful, Beard's comments on these restaurants and the food they served are still worth preserving.

Introduction

༚

Beard on Food is my selection of the weekly syndicated newspaper columns that I have written over the last four years. I have picked those that express most vividly my beliefs, my pleasures, my memories, and occasionally my prejudices. I feel pretty strongly about certain things and my column gives me the opportunity to be honest and outspoken about my likes and dislikes; to share my impressions, my discoveries in restaurants here and abroad and at other people's tables; and to give recipes that I think are worthwhile. If I write about hamburgers or chili, which might seem rather mundane foods, there's a reason. Both are very American, a part of our traditions, and I happen to think nothing is better than a properly cooked hamburger or a bowl of really good chili. To perfect a recipe, however simple, is the secret of success in cooking.

People often say to me, "How can you get fresh ideas all the time? Isn't it hard to find something to write about every week?" To me it isn't. Writing a column keeps me constantly aware, interested, curious, and experimental. Fortunately, I'm blessed with keen taste and sight memories, which are easily awakened; I find myself reliving so intensely how something tasted when I was a child—or a young man, or ten years ago, or just last week—that I have the urge to write about it, to share that memory, and perhaps play around with the taste I recall and develop a recipe every bit as good as the dish I remember. Then I am always intrigued by new foods, new equipment, new developments in cooking, and the column gives me a place to talk about them. When I wander into a market (one of my greatest weaknesses, wherever I go), I may see a different cut of meat or an unusual vegetable and think, "I wonder how it would be if I took the recipe for that sauce I had in Provence and put the two together?" So I go home and try it out. Sometimes my idea is a success and sometimes it is a flop, but that is how recipes are born. There are really no new recipes, only millions of variations sparked by somebody's imagination and desire to be a little bit creative and different. American cooking, after all, is built on variations of old recipes from around the world.

Travel is an important part of my food life. I have eaten in great restaurants, in fledgling restaurants, in tiny bistros, at roadside stands, in people's homes, and in markets. I remember the first time I went to the Nice market and tasted socca, a wonderful sort of pancake of chickpea flour and oil. How I reveled in it! I couldn't find a published recipe so I experimented until I found how to duplicate that special taste and texture and then told my readers how to make it.

Food is our common ground, a universal experience. My column has brought me floods of mail and a great sense of intimacy with all of you. Many of you have written about your own taste memories in a very nostalgic and touching way, or sent me your family recipes. Often one of these letters becomes the inspiration for a column. I find it stimulating to have this constant exchange of thoughts and opinions and ideas, and I am gratified to know that I can give you pleasure and perhaps help you to become more critical as well as more appreciative of food, because constructive criticism is mighty important.

I hope you will not only read and enjoy this book, but also take it into your kitchen, try the recipes and maybe add your own touches. If I can share with you the delight and excitement food has given me throughout my life, then I will have achieved what I set out to do.

—JAMES BEARD

CHAPTER 1

My Ways With Meat

୬

... in which we discover how the hamburger took over America ... encounter the steak of the Tartars, cannibal sandwiches, and a nice piece of London broil ... raise the devil in cooking ... learn how to be canny about beef cuts ... experience the pleasures of pot-au-feu and Irish stew ... are told the secrets of good grilling ... have our meat hot and cold ... track down a good ham, create our own "charcuterie," become friends with bacon ... make a hash of things and talk turkey.

Hamburger Can Be Great

Hamburger is so firmly established in America's culinary Hall of Fame that it comes as rather a shock to discover it didn't originate in America at all. The city where it was probably first eaten—Hamburg, Germany—disavows any connection between their kind of hamburger and ours. There, for centuries, chopped beef and onions have been formed into patties and cooked in a little fat on top of the stove, then served, sometimes with gravy made in the pan, as a main course. According to all the great French cookbooks, Germany gets the credit for this dish, which the French call bifteck à la hambourgeoise. It is very often served *à cheval*, or with an egg on top, and very good it is too.

There are all kinds of theories about how hamburger landed on a bun, the way we mostly eat it today. One school claims that it all started in a New York delicatessen, another that it was first served in that fashion at the St. Louis Fair, while various and sundry persons all claim to know the secret of the original hamburger.

Wherever and however the hamburger made its debut, it has certainly taken over the country. Chains like McDonald's, which sell millions of hamburgers a year, have made a billion-dollar business out of it. When I was growing up, there was a chain in the West that served the most elaborate and delicious hamburger imaginable—a four-ounce patty on a toasted and buttered bun, smothered with mustard, mayonnaise, relish, sliced dill pickle, tomato, onion, and lettuce. It was wrapped, diaper fashion, in a paper napkin and slipped into a glassine envelope to prevent the lovely juices from dribbling down your front as you ate. These hamburgers were extraordinarily good, and as I remember, they cost all of fifteen cents.

      I have a *Favorite Hamburger* recipe that I've used for years. It's subtle, it surprises a great many people, and I happen to think it's one of the best ways to cook hamburger. You take 2 pounds of top-quality chopped round or chuck, spread it out on a board, and grate 2 to 3 tablespoons of onion into it—use a fairly fine grater so you get just the juice and very finely grated raw onion. Now mix in about a tablespoon of heavy cream and some freshly ground black pepper. Form into patties —I like a 6- or 8-ounce patty for an average serving.

As to the cooking, it is my firm belief that a hamburger is best cooked in a heavy skillet with a combination of butter and oil, which prevents the butter from burning when you cook at high heat. I think this gives a crustier, juicier hamburger than broiling, unless you happen to have a really good broiler that browns the meat fast. So take your trusty old black iron skillet or your best copper one or your pet aluminum frying pan, Teflon-coated or not (with a Teflon coating you won't need much fat, just a little bit for flavor), and cook your hamburger in the butter and oil over fairly high heat, giving it 4 to 5 minutes a side, depending on how well done you like it. I like mine crusty on the outside and very rare in the center. Salt this creamy, oniony, peppery hamburger before serving it on a buttered bun or English muffin, or as a main course with sliced tomatoes and onions or some home-fried potatoes.

With that creamy, oniony flavor running through the meat you won't need any ketchup or condiments. Mind you, the addition of cream means that the meat will not be as pinky-red as usual, but if you want a hamburger that is out of the ordinary, this is it. With a good salad it makes a most satisfying meal.

I'm also very fond of hamburger au poivre, an offshoot of the steak *au poivre* (steak with coarsely crushed peppercorns pressed into the surface) you find in many French restaurants. I don't advise this for a hamburger sandwich, but *Hamburger au Poivre* makes a good main dish.

Form ground beef into 6- or 8-ounce patties (I prefer a generous 8-ounce serving). Grind or crush 1 to 2 tablespoons of black peppercorns (use a coarse pepper mill or a blender, or crack them with a weight), and press a goodly amount into both sides of the patties. Broil, if you like, or sauté according to the method given in the previous recipe. When done to your taste, salt the hamburgers on both sides. Then, if you want to be opulent, flame them. Pour a little bourbon or brandy into the hot pan, ignite, and shake the pan until the flames die down. Serve these sensational hamburgers on very hot plates, with the pan juices spooned over them.

I like to accompany them with a baked potato or lyonnaise potatoes (potatoes mixed with a little onion and cooked until crisply brown) and salad. The hamburger may be a humble food, but it takes kindly to being elevated to a more exalted plane of eating. Just try it.

Beef in the Raw

I well remember, when I was a young man, walking into a London brasserie and ordering steak tartare, without having the vaguest notion of what I would get. When the patty of finely chopped lean raw beef with the raw egg yolk and all the other trimmings was put in front of me, I took one look at it and thought someone must be playing a joke on me. The waiter asked if I wanted it mixed, and I said I did. He mixed it, I ate it, and ever since I've been a devotee of this unusual dish, which is so much more appetizing than it sounds. Much later I discovered that in New York and other parts of the United States it was considered a superb hangover cure. People in Prohibition days who were wont to wake up with a pretty heavy head from bootleg liquor swore that if they could just get up, and get down a large order of steak tartare, all their symptoms would be cured. Although I doubt this very much, steak tartare does give one a lift. It's the kind of thing to order when you feel there is nothing you really want to eat.

There's a rather amusing, if unsubstantiated, story about how steak tartare got its name. It seems that the Tartars, the fierce nomadic tribesmen of Mongolia who were followers of Genghis Khan, were supposed to have carried hunks of raw meat under their saddles, to "cook" by friction as they galloped. Traveling merchants from Middle Europe picked up this primitive penchant for uncooked meat, and our version—very lean beef or other red meat, scraped, chopped, or finely ground—is said to have come from them, via France and England.

When you order steak tartare in a restaurant in this country, you'll find it is served with all kinds of things—raw egg yolk, little mounds of chopped onion, green onion, or shallot, salt, freshly ground black pepper, capers, and sometimes anchovies, mustard, ketchup, Tabasco, and Worcestershire sauce. The Four Seasons and the Forum of the Twelve Caesars in New York mix in a little cognac, as well. The service of steak tartare in either of these restaurants is a truly remarkable tableside feat. Using two dinner knives, your capable captain or waiter scrapes the seasonings into the meat, reshapes it into a flat patty, and then works everything else in separately, first the egg, then the onion, the capers, the anchovies, each time raking the meat mixture with the knife blades until the final texture is so fine and smooth it is almost a pomade. In most restaurants you do the mixing yourself, which can be fun, too.

To me, French mustard is a necessity in steak tartare, for it gives a lovely, creamy quality, but I've never felt ketchup added much. It makes the whole thing rather sweet. Of course, there's nothing to prevent your eating the raw beef with only salt and freshly ground pepper. Provided your beef is impeccably fresh and impeccably lean, and chopped, ground, or scraped within minutes of the time you eat it, so it keeps its color and freshness, it is extremely good eating without any added embellishments. Be sure always to buy sirloin, top round, or fillet cuts which have the necessary leanness, tenderness, and flavor.

Germany makes a great hors d'oeuvre with steak tartare. The meat, seasoned only with salt and pepper, is spread diagonally on half a toast square. Fresh caviar goes on the other half, with lemon on the side. You don't mix the meat and caviar, but eat them together. *(See Editor's Note, copyright page.)*

⁚ The French make a greater ceremony of *Steak Tartare* than anyone else. Not long ago I watched a waiter in a Cannes restaurant prepare steak tartare. He began with an egg yolk and about ⅓ to ½ cup of olive oil in a soup plate, stirring it very rapidly with a fork until it emulsified, forming a thin kind of mayonnaise. To this he added freshly ground pepper, chopped parsley, chopped onion, capers, and other seasonings, working the mixture constantly with the fork. Finally, he worked in the raw beef, making a very loose, rich, flavorful, and highly seasoned mixture. With French bread, thinly sliced rye bread, or hot unbuttered toast, this makes a most glorious spring or summer luncheon.

As a matter of fact, I know people who still make mayonnaise this way, in a soup plate with a fork, stirring the oil into the egg yolk a very little at a time and working very fast. The mayonnaise has a thicker, stiffer texture than that made in a blender or with a rotary or electric mixer and some regard that thicker mixture as more authentic, more truly French.

I like to serve a big bowl of steak tartare with cocktails, mixing in some finely chopped garlic and onion and an egg yolk (for cocktail food, you don't want too thin a mixture). I sprinkle the top with chopped parsley or a little rosemary and serve it with plain or Melba toast, or small slices of pumpernickel or rye bread, with little knives for spreading. This is great with drinks, because it provides something substantial for the stomach. If you have friends who swear they'll never eat raw meat, you can fool them by rolling the mixture into tiny balls and rolling these in coarsely chopped toasted pecans, walnuts, or hazelnuts.

⁚

The Way It Was

One of the pleasantest things about writing a column is the mail I get. Some of the things I write about seem to strike a universal chord, and I get floods of letters. Often I hear from people who just want to share their own food experiences with me—and how evocative some of their reminiscences are. In response to my column on steak tartare, I got one of the most delightful and nostalgic letters I've had in a long time, filled with an appreciation of food and good living. It came from a Mr. Alexander Shaw, an architect in Bel Air, Maryland, and I'd like to quote some of it because I think you'll enjoy it as much as I did.

"I've just finished reading your appetite-whetting article on beef Tartare and besides making me drool, it has stirred many wonderful memories of a glorious small-town boyhood only Mark Twain could have described, and my own introduction to beef Tartare. Mine was no sudden British surprise, though Overton's and Simpson's and many others in Europe were to come later, but one of pure evolution—right from the start.

"Back in the days of Taft, Teddy and Woodrow, yes, back when Bel Air had dirt streets, tree-lined, deep shade patterned with brilliant sunshine, and a population of about eight hundred, we had services you couldn't find in Utopia itself today, such as door to door sales and deliveries. Each day started out early with the milk man—he furnished the cow, you furnished the container. He dipped it warm and frothy from a big can right into your own brown stone bowl, and all you had to do was put a cover on it to keep the cats out. Next came the ice man hawking big chunks of dirty pond ice dug out of mounds of straw. The wagon had canvas sides painted white, lettered with 'ICE' on each side, looking like a big block of melting ice with four wheels on it. Then in rapid succession came other wagons: the bread man, fruit and vegetable gypsies and, on Fridays, old Skinner all the way from Havre de Grace on the Susquehanna, 17 miles away, with 'fresh' fish.

"But most of all I awaited alternate days for the arrival of the butcher wagon. This I will never forget—it was a large wagon with a rigid top, lots of hooks hanging from the bows, dangling whole, half and quarter carcasses of beef, lamb, veal, and pork. The driver/meat cutter, an unforgettable colored man named Ike, who seemed to always have a thumb or two on the scales with his sales, used to always hand my dog a bone and me some nice scraps of round or sirloin (they didn't sell it ground in those days). And that's how I became an aficionado of raw beef.

"A few years later Bel Air started to grow up and sported a new diner featuring the first hamburgers, which I ate raw with hot horseradish. And then off to college and the wonderful Christmas holidays with all those cook chicks, peach brandy and needled beer. That's when I met my first real, honest-to-God steak tartare face to face—raw egg, chopped onion, fresh pepper, the works. It had to be at the Rennert, Momenthy's or the Metropolitan Smoke Shop, a 'speak' up on Howard Street. But I could never forget those lunches at the Merchants Club beginning with a dozen Ocean Coves followed by—you guessed it—superb tartare. I think they used chopped sirloin and I have always liked very hot horseradish with it.

"As I have grown older I have had the good fortune to be able to travel around a bit, and have savored our old friend in many forms from San Francisco to Salzburg, but I certainly must make mention of the huge mounds of ground round at the Optimist Club's oyster roast at the Pikesville Armory each February—served with pumpernickel, salt, pepper, and sliced Bermuda onions and gallons of beer. No fancy name here, just plain Cannibal Sandwich and it justly rivals the oysters in popularity."

My thanks to you, Mr. Shaw, not only for sharing your memories with me, but also for awakening my own. I, too, remember the vegetable man and the ice man, the traveling butcher, and a man who sold fat luscious tamales and drove through the streets calling his wares. One of the most picturesque vendors we had in the West was the hominy man, who came twice a week with big tins of fresh whole hominy and freshly grated horseradish.

Hominy (not to be confused with ground hominy grits, for which I have very little affection) is corn steamed with lye to remove the seed germ and hull and swell the kernels. Whole hominy is difficult to find now, except in cans, but it is worth searching for. One of the simplest and best dishes I know is sautéed hominy with cream; it's magnificent with fried chicken (or most any chicken dish), with roast pork or pork chops, even roast turkey or duck.

To make *Sautéed Hominy with Cream:* A can of hominy will serve two persons well, or three skimpily, so for four to six, wash the contents of two 1-pound, 13-ounce cans of whole hominy slightly. Heat it in 6 tablespoons butter, shaking the pan and tossing the kernels gently so they don't break up. Season well with salt and a good deal of freshly ground black pepper—pepper really enhances hominy. When heated through, add ⅓ to ½ cup heavy cream, and let it just cook down and blend with the lovely, soft, delicately flavored kernels. Taste to make sure you have enough seasoning, particularly pepper, and serve in a hot vegetable dish sprinkled with a little chopped parsley.

If you've never tasted whole hominy, you have a new treat in store.

Steak with a Difference

One of the most common restaurant luncheon items these days, to be found everywhere from the greasy spoon to the very elegant and high-priced establishments, is London Broil. Exactly what is London broil? Ask a butcher today and you'll get all kinds of answers. Some will hedge, some will tell you the truth, and others will just offer you any old cut of beef.

Up until the last few years, London broil meant just one thing— broiled flank steak. This is a thin piece of meat with very noticeable long coarse graining that comes from the flank, the part of the animal below the loin section. The fat is torn off and the meat trimmed, leaving a tri-angular steak about three-quarters of an inch thick in the middle and thinner at the ends. The flank used to be considered a tough cut, and so it is in the lesser grades, but if you buy prime or choice, the two top U.S. Department of Agriculture grades, the flank is an excellent broiling cut with the advantage of being much less expensive than the more glamorous upper-echelon steaks like porterhouse and sirloin.

London broil, which is very lean and therefore much favored by dieters, has become immensely popular of late, and the demand for flank steak has risen accordingly. So now supermarkets and butchers are beginning to mar-ket all sorts of different cuts under the name of London broil — sirloin butt or rump steak, rib eye steak, even top round. Don't be taken in or fobbed off. It is the thin, fibrous flank steak that makes the best and most authen-tic London broil, provided it is cooked and carved correctly.

&. For *London Broil*, a flank steak weighing 2 to 3 pounds will serve four nicely. Rub it with salt, pepper, and maybe a touch of Tabasco, and broil it close to the broiling unit for just 3 to 4 minutes per side, until the outside is nicely charred and the inside juicily rare, as London broil should be. Carve it on the diagonal with a very sharp knife in long thin slices, and serve it with its own juices on well-buttered toast, or alone with a spicy sauce — pungent tomato sauce, a mustardy sauce, or a zesty sauce diable.

&. For *Sauce Diable*, put ½ cup tarragon vinegar, ¼ cup white wine, 1 finely chopped shallot or green onion, and 1 teaspoon dried tarragon in a heavy pan and cook until reduced by half.

Stir in 1½ cups brown sauce or a good canned beef gravy, a dash of Tabasco, and 2 teaspoons dry mustard. Bring to a boil and simmer 3 minutes. Season with several grinds of black pepper and strain the sauce. Serve with a sprinkling of chopped parsley or chopped fresh tarragon, if available.

Another great way to serve London broil is on the lines of a hero sandwich. Split and toast a long loaf of French bread, butter it well, brush it with Dijon mustard and a touch of Tabasco, and arrange thin, thin slices of the broiled steak on the bottom half. Top with the other half and cut it downward in chunks, to be eaten out of hand. The bread must be crisp, the meat rare, and the seasonings zippy.

Some people like to marinate the steak before broiling. I sometimes use a *Teriyaki Marinade*, a mixture of ½ cup soy sauce, ½ cup sherry, ¼ cup peanut oil, 1 to 2 finely chopped garlic cloves, 1 teaspoon grated orange rind and 1 to 2 tablespoons grated fresh ginger root (or a 1-inch piece of finely chopped candied ginger). Leave the steak in this marinade for several hours, turning frequently, before you broil it.

Another steak that was once rarely seen, but is now appearing more and more in supermarkets, is skirt steak, a very thin steak that comes from the forequarters of the animal, below the rib section. Although it resembles flank steak in many ways and has a good flavor, skirt steak is less tender. A top grade, broiled quickly and seasoned well, then served very rare with mustard or a hot sauce makes another interesting departure from the expensive, thick, well-marbled steak cuts.

Both flank and skirt steaks may also be braised, advisable if you can't get a top grade. Brown them first on both sides, either under the broiler or in hot fat in a skillet, then add some liquid, such as broth, red wine, water or beer, salt, pepper, garlic and herbs, cover, and cook on top of the stove just long enough to tenderize the meat. The steak will not be rare, but the taste and texture will be delicious. Slice thinly on the diagonal, and serve with the pan juices, baked potatoes, and green beans boiled until just bitey-tender, then smothered with crumbled crisp bacon and a few peanuts, and you'll have an appetizing, economical meal, not as hearty as a pot roast, but equally good.

What the Devil Is Devil?

Have you ever wondered just what the devil is devil? So many dishes have the word attached to them that it *is* rather baffling. Classically speaking, in France a deviled food is one that is grilled, dipped in crumbs, and grilled again until it is brown and crisp and then served with a sauce diable, or devil sauce. In England—and this I take from Escoffier, who cooked there for a great part of his life—most deviled dishes have a very high seasoning as, for instance, deviled roes and deviled sardines, which are not crumbed but seasoned with cayenne, mustard, and Worcestershire sauce and served on toast. As a matter of fact, Escoffier produced a *Sauce Diable*, a bottled adaptation of the classic devil sauce, which can still be bought in the better food shops, although it is more difficult to find than it used to be.

Here in the United States our deviled eggs are quite different from those of the English. Theirs are fried in slightly browned butter, then the surface is sprinkled with bread crumbs that have been fried in butter with a little dry mustard. The eggs are slid onto a plate, and a drop of vinegar is added to the browned butter, cooked for just a minute, and then poured over the crumbed fried eggs. Ours, of course, are hard-boiled eggs with the yolks removed, mixed with various seasonings, and returned to the whites and served mostly as a cold luncheon dish or an hors d'oeuvre with cocktails.

Then there's another version of deviled—deviled ham or chicken—and how *they* got to be called deviled the devil only knows. Basically, this is ground ham or chicken, usually with some sweet pickle mixed into it with mustard and other seasonings. It's usually served as a sandwich or cocktail spread and is about as far from the English or French fashion of deviling as one could possibly get. The famous make of deviled ham sold in little cans which you and I have known since our childhood is anything but highly spiced—in fact, it tastes mostly of salt and little else, and why it is labeled "deviled" I've never been able to figure out.

There are other deviled dishes, though, which combine the English and French methods. One is deviled beef bones, of which I am inordinately fond. You usually find these in restaurants where a great deal of roast beef is served, because after the roast beef has been sliced off the bone there are all those rib bones left with tasty bits of meat on them. These meaty bones are dipped in a barbecue sauce or other pungent sauce, broiled, or put in a very hot oven until they are well cooked through, then rolled in crumbs, brushed with butter or oil, and broiled or baked again until lightly browned. They come to you sizzling hot, crunchy with crumbs, and spicy with sauce.

Chewing on these delicious morsels of recooked meat is one of the most satisfying gastronomic experiences I know, and the very thought of it sets my taste buds quivering. It is awfully difficult to resist the temptation of taking them up in your fingers and munching on them. If you are well known in the restaurant, they may not regard you askance, but there are times when, for propriety's sake, you have to content yourself with a knife and fork. Just try to scrape every bit of goodness from those beautiful bones. It's well worth the effort.

You can easily make *Deviled Beef Bones* at home. Just accumulate the bones from two or three roasts (you can freeze them in the interim) until you have a good batch. The bones should have some meat around them, something to chew on. Cut them into ribs, and if you have a meat saw, you can cut the ends off so they look a little neater.

Have ready on a deep plate or pie plate 1 cup (¼ pound) melted butter flavored with 2 tablespoons tarragon vinegar (or vinegar plus dried or fresh chopped tarragon), and on another plate put 2 to 2½ cups sifted bread crumbs. This will be enough for 8 to 10 ribs. Dip the ribs first in the melted butter, turning them well, then in the crumbs. Press the bones in so the crumbs will adhere. Place them on the broiling rack or on a foil broiling pan, very useful for this kind of thing where the crumbs drip, and broil about 6 to 7 inches from the heat unit so they cook very slowly and the crumbs don't burn. Watch them carefully and keep turning the bones so you get a rich brown coating on all sides. If you are cooking them on an outdoor grill, have them at quite a distance from the coals. Turn them often with tongs and treat them very gingerly, as you don't want all those lovely crumbs to fall off. The cooking time will be 15 to 20 minutes, and the crumbs should get very brown and crispy. Serve the deviled bones with sauce diable (see page 8), and you'll have some of the most delicious eating you've ever known.

You can devil small broiling chickens, too. Broil them three-quarters done before pressing them in the butter and crumbs, then finish them off under the broiler. Or you can dip squares of honeycomb tripe in the butter and crumbs and broil on both sides until beautifully brown and crisp. So you see there are more ways than one to raise the devil in cooking.

Tasty, Thifty Oxtail

A number of years ago, in one of the most gloriously self-indulgent episodes in my life, I literally ate my way through a book I was working on, *Paris Cuisine*, for which I tasted and collected recipes from sixty fine Paris restaurants. There was one bistro near where I lived that once a week served a most glorious dish of boned, stuffed oxtail. I begged the patron for the recipe, and finally he let me go into the kitchen and watch it being prepared.

After this book was published, people in various parts of this country went to their butchers and asked to have an oxtail boned. You can imagine the reaction! I really think it is a minor miracle that those butchers didn't form a posse, hunt me down and string me up for daring to suggest they might bone an oxtail. Two or three, I believe, did undertake the job, and they are probably still regretting it, for boning an oxtail not only takes deft hands and good knives, but an incredible amount of patience. It's probably just as well that *Paris Cuisine* is no longer in print.

Now, I'm not going to propose that you undertake this Herculean task. Oxtail unboned makes a very succulent dish, for while there isn't a lot of meat on the joints, what's there is richly gelatinous. When braised, it yields a beautiful, lip-smacking broth or sauce. While there are many different ways to prepare the tail, I enjoy an oxtail ragout most of all. This is not exactly the kind of dish you can eat with delicacy, so I only serve it when I know my guests will revel in it and not be bashful about picking up the bones, gnawing on them and getting the last little bit of goodness.

    🥢 To make 6 or 8 servings of *Oxtail Ragout* buy 2 or 3 whole oxtails and have them disjointed—cut into sections. Put the pieces on the broiler rack and broil until they are nicely colored and crispy around the edges, salting and peppering them as they brown, and turning them once.

Alternatively, you may sprinkle them with flour and brown them all over in a heavy skillet in 4 tablespoons oil and 4 tablespoons butter or beef drippings, seasoning them as they cook—but to me, the broiler method gives a better flavor. Remove the oxtails to a plate.

If you browned them in a skillet, add to the pan drippings 3 large onions, thinly sliced, and sauté until limp and golden. (If you broiled the oxtails, sauté the onions in a skillet in 6 tablespoons oil and butter or beef drippings.) Transfer the onions to a deep braising pot or Dutch oven, add 3 or 4 halved carrots to the fat in the skillet and sauté them lightly, then add these to the braising pot along with 5 whole peeled garlic cloves. Add the oxtails and a bouquet garni—a celery rib, a leek, 2 or 3 parsley sprigs, 2 bay leaves, and 2 teaspoons thyme in a little cheesecloth bag, all tied together so they can be fished out easily later. Add just enough warm water and red wine to barely cover. Bring to a boil over high heat, skim off the scum, reduce the heat, cover and simmer for 3 to 3½ hours, adding more liquid if needed. Test the meat for doneness and taste the broth for seasoning, adding salt, pepper, and maybe a touch more thyme if you think it needs more herb flavor. When the meat is really tender, remove the oxtails and vegetables to a hot platter, discarding the bouquet garni, and let the broth cook down over high heat for 2 or 3 minutes.

I like the broth just the way it is, but you can thicken it, if you prefer. Knead together 2 tablespoons butter and 2 tablespoons flour, form into small balls, stir these into the broth and cook, stirring, until thickened. Or, for a more translucent sauce, blend 2 tablespoons cornstarch with ½ cup water and stir in just enough to thicken.

Pour the broth or sauce over the meat. Serve with boiled potatoes (my preference) or rice, braised small white onions or turnips, or cooked rutabagas mashed with plenty of butter, crusty bread and red wine.

To vary this recipe, use 3 cups canned Italian plum tomatoes in place of part of the cooking liquid, add a teaspoon of dried basil and, if you can find one, a split pig's foot. The sweet flavor of the tomatoes and the gelatinous quality of the pig's foot add yet another dimension to the dish.

Beef, Plain and Fancy

Whenever I read the weekend supermarket ads in the newspapers, I become more and more amazed by the odd names that are given to cuts of beef these days, like "California roast" and "fillet roast" or "fillet steak" with, in parentheses, "chuck." Now while there are certain basic cuts that have been with us for a long time, these names seem to have become part of supermarket jargon during the last few years, and I, for one, consider them to be most misleading. By custom, the fillet of beef is the tenderloin—and chuck is about as far from tenderloin as anything can be.

If you were to look at a butcher's chart of wholesale beef cuts, you'd see that the upper part of the animal is divided into chuck, rib, loin, and round; the lower part into shank, brisket, plate, and flank. The tenderest cuts, for roasting and broiling, come from the center portions, the rib and loin (separated into the short loin and the sirloin). It's from here we get our rib and sirloin roasts and our well-marbled, juicy steaks. Beef fillet or tenderloin, a boneless piece which extends the full length of the loin, is sold whole, as a roast, or as steaks. These range from the little filet mignon, cut from the triangular tip of the fillet, to larger, thicker center cuts like tournedos, tenderloin steak, and châteaubriand. Cuts from the fillet are meltingly tender and very expensive, as there are but two tenderloins to each animal. Chuck, the shoulder section of the animal, from neck to rib; and rump and round, the leg section, are naturally less tender and are usually braised or pot roasted.

While wholesale cuts are fairly easy to grasp, once you start trying to sort out the many retail cuts for roasting, pot roasting, broiling, and stewing, confusion sets in. Names differ according to the part of the country you are in and the local usage, and many of them bear no linguistic relation to the part of the animal from whence they come. Who would know, for instance, that Delmonico roast is the eye of the rib, a Boston cut a section of chuck, and a New York or Kansas City cut a synonym for a loin strip steak, also known as a shell steak? Buying beef can be baffling, unless you can find out exactly where a certain cut comes from. If you get a good meat chart, which most butcher shops can supply, or the helpful little booklet on basic beef cuts put out by the National Cattlemen's Beef Association in Chicago, you'll be much better equipped to cope with the odd terminology of the supermarket meat section.

Now, I'm not saying that chuck and round can't be roasted. They can, provided you buy prime meat, or treat the meat with meat tenderizer. While a top grade of rump or round won't be as butter-tender as the finest rib or sirloin, it can be very good eating. There used to be a cut of round served in big restaurants called a steamship roast that was tender and delicious when thinly sliced, and you'll sometimes find in delicatessens sliced roast beef that has been cut from the choicest part of the round and roasted rare.

    ➣ However, if you're buying an average piece of round or chuck in the supermarket, you're better off turning it into *Braised Beef*. Let's say you have a nice 5-pound boneless roll of chuck, which has been covered with some extra fat and well tied. First, brown it on all sides in very hot melted beef fat, or remove the extra fat and brown the meat under the broiler, turning it often, until the outside is slightly charred and richly colored.

Then transfer it to a braising pan or Dutch oven or a large heavy enameled iron pot in which you have put a little melted beef fat. Salt and pepper the meat to taste, and sprinkle with an herb—the favorite is thyme, because it has a pungency that is most effective with beef, but you could use rosemary or summer savory, which would give an entirely different quality. Add a bay leaf, a tiny sprinkling of cinnamon, 1 or 2 onions, each stuck with 2 cloves, 2 to 3 garlic cloves, 1 or 2 sprigs of parsley, and a leek. Pour in 2 cups of wine, beef stock, beer or water, and let this come to a boil. Reduce the heat, cover the pot, and either simmer on top of the stove over very low heat, allowing 30 to 35 minutes per pound, or cook in a 300-degree oven, allowing 35 minutes a pound, until the meat is quite tender. Add more liquid if needed.

Remove the meat to a hot platter and skim the fat from the pan juices. If you want more gravy, pour additional liquid into the pan, bring to a boil, remove the vegetables and bay leaf, and thicken the juices with little balls of butter and flour, kneaded together. Let it cook down.

Serve the meat sliced, with onions which have been braised separately with a little beef fat and red wine or Madeira, or with crisply cooked buttered carrots, plain boiled potatoes, the glorious gravy, and red wine.

If you have some beef left the next day, either make it into sandwiches or serve it cold with a mustard dressing and a good green salad.

☙

The Pleasures of Pot-Au-Feu

One of the greatest of the homely dishes in the repertoire of French cooking is the pot-au-feu, which most Americans would probably call boiled beef. It's simple, certainly, but it is precisely the simplicity of preparation and the honest, appetizing flavors that make this one of the outstanding gastronomic treats of all time. On restaurant menus throughout France you'll see it listed in various ways—*pot-au-feu*, *pot-au-feu à l'ancienne* (which means the old-fashioned kind), or *pot-au-feu riche*. They are all much the same dish with embellishments. The beef cuts vary from time to time and province to province. Sometimes a chicken is popped into the pot midway in the cooking, or an enormous piece of fresh side pork or salt pork may go in, or even a sausage for the last hour or so. These variations in style make it all the more fun to cook and to eat.

    I have found that in making a *Pot-au-Feu* you get a better result if you make the broth a day ahead.

Put in a pot 2 large marrow bones, an onion stuck with 2 cloves, 2 leeks, a carrot, a bit of fresh or dried thyme, a sprig of parsley (if you can buy Italian parsley with the root still on, use the root as well as the leaves—it gives great flavor), and a head of garlic—not a clove, a whole head. Don't peel it—just take off the papery outer skin and throw it in the pot. Add water to cover, and bring to a boil, then reduce the heat, cover, and cook very slowly for several hours. Taste for salt, and add what you think it needs, then strain the broth, discarding the bones and vegetables, and chill overnight, so you can skim off the fat before adding the meats next day.

About 3 hours before you are going to serve your pot-au-feu, put the broth in a 12-quart pot with 1 onion stuck with 2 cloves, a 2½-pound piece of brisket, a 3-pound piece of bottom round, and 2½ to 3 pounds of short ribs with the bone in, each piece of meat tied so it will keep its shape during cooking. Soak 8 leeks well, removing sand from between the leaves. Cut off the green tops, and tie these in a bundle with 4 parsley sprigs, 3 or 4 sprigs of fresh thyme, and any other herbs you want, such as tarragon, rosemary, or summer savory. (If you can't get fresh herbs, add 1½ teaspoons dried thyme and a pinch or two of other herbs to the broth.)

Bring to a boil, skim off the scum and any little bits of fat that rise to the surface, then cover and simmer for about 2 hours.

Meanwhile, prepare your other vegetables. For eight servings peel 8 small white onions, and peel and quarter 8 small turnips and 12 to 14 medium-sized carrots. Wash and cut in sixths a curly Savoy cabbage (if you can't get a Savoy, a firm green cabbage will do). After the meats have cooked for 2 hours, add the leeks and cook for 15 minutes, then add the onions, turnips, and carrots, skimming the surface every time you add anything to the pot. In a separate pan, boil 8 well-scrubbed small new potatoes in their jackets.

When the vegetables are almost tender, test the meats. If they are done, remove and keep warm. Add the cabbage to the pot and cook for 5 or 10 minutes more, until all the vegetables are tender. Season the broth with salt and freshly ground black pepper to taste, and skim off as much fat as possible, before removing the vegetables. Pour off a good part of the broth, to which the vegetables will have given a lovely sweet flavor, and serve it first in bowls with slices of French bread, cut ¾ to 1 inch thick and dried in the oven. Pass a hunk of Parmesan cheese and a grater so everyone can grate cheese directly into his broth, which adds a certain zest. Reserve some of the remaining hot broth in another bowl to serve with the meat.

Slice part of the meats and arrange on a hot platter with the vegetables. Serve each person a cut of each kind of beef, some vegetables, and a potato. Ladle the hot broth over the meat and hand around some spicy accompaniments—good mustard, coarse salt, grated fresh horseradish, and the tiny sour French pickles called cornichons.

Drink a fruity red wine with your *pot-au-feu*, and have a fruit dessert— perhaps crêpes filled with sautéed apples, glazed with sugar under the broiler, and served with heavy cream.

With its remarkable combination of flavors, *pot-au-feu* is a very interesting dish to serve guests for Sunday luncheon or supper, and once your meats and vegetables are ready to go, the cooking is no effort. One of the greatest virtues of this meal in a pot is that you can cook more than you need, reheat the beef next day, and serve it up with crisp home-fried potatoes (you can cook a chicken in the broth, too, and have that next day) or turn the cold boiled beef into a glorious salad or hash.

Potluck of the Irish—Stew

In the last year or two I seem to have visited restaurants in many parts of Europe, Canada, and the United States, and one of the things I find most fascinating is seeing what other people order to eat. I can't help watching them and listening to them come to their decisions, some of which are a puzzle to me. Why, I wonder, would anyone order some elaborate dish like lobster à l'Américaine or beef Wellington in a tiny restaurant far from civilization, where it is bound to be a disaster, instead of picking something good but simple that is within the restaurant's range? They do, though. There is no accounting for tastes.

I've also been surprised to find how many things have become universal menu standards. Shrimps, for instance, are eternally popular. Chopped beef is a best seller no matter what name it goes under—chopped sirloin, chopped fillet, or plain old hamburger—and whether it is served quite plainly or rather fancily, on a plank with watercress and sliced tomatoes or bordered with duchess potatoes and topped with a broiled mushroom or tomato. It's by all odds America's pet luncheon dish.

Another luncheon favorite is eggs Benedict, which can be really delicious provided the ham is good, the eggs properly poached, and the hollandaise sauce freshly made. Incidentally, there are a couple of variations on this dish, and though neither can rightfully be called eggs Benedict they are rather fun for a change. Little sausage cakes replace the ham in one, in the other cheese sauce stands in for hollandaise.

Something that seems to be popular on two continents—and this I do find amazing—is Irish stew. Not only the British but also the French dote on it. It has, in fact, for more than a hundred years been one of the few English dishes regularly ordered in France. Even that great French chef Escoffier had a very special version, made with tiny lamb chops cooked gently in broth with vegetables.

Perhaps the best Irish stew I've ever tasted was in a London restaurant called Lacy's. It broke with tradition in some ways, which is why I feel it is newsworthy enough to give as a recipe. The chef used shoulder of lamb instead of the usual breast, and cooked the meat in a flavorful lamb broth rather than in water.

❧ To make *Lacy's Irish Stew*, buy 3 to 3½ pounds lamb shoulder and about 1 pound neck of lamb. Have the butcher bone the shoulder, or do it yourself, but in any case, keep the bones. Put bones and neck in a deep saucepan with 2 quarts water. Bring to a boil, and boil for 5 or 6 minutes, skimming off the scum from the surface. Add 1 medium onion stuck with 2 cloves, 1 large bay leaf, 2 large garlic cloves, 1 tablespoon salt,

½ teaspoon freshly ground pepper, ½ teaspoon thyme, and a parsley sprig. Bring to a boil again, reduce the heat, and simmer 2½ hours to a strong broth. Strain, and put the broth in the refrigerator overnight. Next day, skim off the fat.

Remove all fat from the lamb shoulder and cut it into pieces 1 inch wide and 2 inches long. Put the meat in a heavy pan with 3 thinly sliced medium onions, 3 leeks, split in half, washed well, and cut in small dice, 1 bay leaf, ¼ teaspoon nutmeg, ½ teaspoon thyme, and enough lamb broth to come 1 inch above the meat. Bring to a boil, skim off any scum, reduce the heat, and simmer, covered, for 1 hour, then test the meat for tenderness. If it still seems a bit tough, give it another 15 minutes. Then add 4 medium potatoes, finely diced. Cook for 30 minutes, until the stew is slightly thickened by the potatoes, then taste for seasoning. You will probably find it needs salt (1 to 2 teaspoons should be sufficient), a few grinds of pepper, and a touch of nutmeg. Let this cook a little to blend with the stew, and then add 2 tablespoons finely chopped parsley and cook just 1 minute more. This is the kind of stew you serve in bowls or soup plates and eat with a spoon and fork.

Lacy's added a nice touch—they put a good thick slice of toast in the bowls before filling them with stew. You could also serve the toast separately, and let your guests dunk. Hot biscuits would be good instead of toast.

I've also found that the stew gets a good flavor and a marvelous color if you add ¾ pound coarsely chopped spinach about 15 minutes before the end of the cooking time. I warned you that this is a totally untraditional Irish stew, but it's all the better for that. It's different and good enough to serve at a buffet party or Sunday supper.

Barbecuing Is an Art

Walk down the streets of any town, large or small, on a summer evening when dinner is cooking in many a patio and back garden, and the smell of the scented smoke that wafts on the air will give you an idea of how good the various outdoor chefs are. While some are grilling their meat to juicy, mouth-watering tenderness, others are merely shrinking it to a charred, hard hunk that would be shunned by anyone with a decent palate.

Grilling, broiling, barbecuing—whatever you want to call it—is an art, not just a matter of building a pyre and throwing on a piece of meat as a sacrifice to the gods of the stomach. For while barbecuing is a very old and primitive way of cooking, it is also one of the most appetizing methods of dealing with meat known to man, and it deserves to be done with some semblance of technique, accuracy, and care.

One of the greatest mistakes is adding too much fuel. Charcoal briquets, which have become the almost universal fuel for outdoor cooking in this country, are efficient and simple to use, but all too few people realize that they give the best results when used economically. If you have a little hibachi, you don't really need more than 12 to 14 briquets (or at the very most 20 to 24) to cook a normal amount of meat for two or three. Even with the big wheeled grills that can do enough for a large family, certainly 30 or 40 briquets will suffice. If you are spit-roasting a turkey, a very large beef roast, a suckling pig, or a whole baby lamb, all of which take longer to cook, you may need more than 40 or 45 briquets, but the extra amount may be added later on as required. Always start your fire in ample time to let the coals form and the briquets burn down to the point where they are veiled in a lovely white ash and exude an even heat. I build my briquets in a pyramid, and if I don't have an electric starter, I use briquets that have been soaked in some form of liquid fuel. I let them burn up, and as they catch, I spread them out over the fire bed, touching, which makes for better coals than if you let them burn up in the pyramid and try to spread them out later.

The secret of good grilling is to have an even distribution of heat. If the briquets are allowed to form the right kind of bed of heated coals and ash, the whole grill will be evenly heated with a surface temperature between 350 and 375 degrees, the ideal medium for cooking.

Four inches below the grill, midway between it and the coals, the temperature will be around 600 degrees, and if you were to check in the coals themselves with a pyrometer, which measures the heat in a fire, you might find it was as much as 1,200 to 1,400 degrees. This is the perfect distribution of heat. From the fiery coals to the midway point the temperature cools off so that by the time the heat reaches the grilling surface it cooks the food steadily and well instead of charring it to a black and horrible mess that is still almost cold inside when you cut into it.

For properly cooked meat, time the grilling. First measure the meat. If a steak is 2 inches thick, give it 10 minutes a side if you like it very rare. Let it brown gradually on one side, turn, and cook until browned on the other. If you want to char the outside, let it cook to the point of doneness you like, then increase the heat either by bringing up the firebox or by adding more briquets on the outside of the fire, letting them catch and then building them up under the meat so the heat increases all at once. Turn quickly to char both sides.

While we all like a good thick grilled steak, don't overlook some of the less expensive cuts like flank or skirt steak which grill quickly and well. Another of my favorites is leg of lamb, boned and butterflied, or spread flat, then grilled like a thick steak after it has been salted and peppered and given some garlic and perhaps rosemary. I also like a succulent pork steak, cut ¾ to 1 inch thick from the leg with the round bone in. I rub it well with prepared mustard and brush it while it grills with just enough honey and additional mustard to give it a nice crispy glaze— smoked ham steaks can be done in the same way. Ducks, if they are not too fat, can be split and flattened slightly with a blow from the cleaver and grilled—first bone side down, then on the skin side. Watch them carefully to see that the fat that drips into the coals doesn't create a fire that will scorch the delicate skin. If it does drip, there are several things you can do to take care of the flaring up, such as quenching the flames with a spray gun filled with water, but I prefer to put a dripping pan— either a narrow ice-cube tray or a double fold of aluminum foil—in the center of the firebox and push the coals around it. If you are dealing with meat, you would, of course, trim off most of the excess fat first, which isn't always possible with poultry.

That's just about all there is to outdoor cooking—a good fire, good coals, and patience, for this is one endeavor in which patience, rather than speed, should be your watchword.

The Cool Delights of Summer Meals

I happen to think that most foods taste better if they are allowed to cool before being eaten. I purposely plan to cook certain dishes and let them cool to room temperature, without refrigerating, before I serve them. Others I find benefit from being chilled overnight. To me, one of the great joys of summer eating is that I can vary my menus by having a meat hot one night and cold the next.

Take pork, for instance, that most neglected of summer delicacies. A roast loin of pork with a beautiful apricot or apple glaze makes a glorious hot dinner and an even more glorious cold one, after being refrigerated, then brought to room temperature and served thinly sliced with mustard mayonnaise and a string bean salad. You can serve this for a company dinner with great aplomb, and it needs nothing more save bread, fresh fruit to follow, and perhaps a bottle of chilled champagne, for no other wine so complements the rich succulence of pork.

Then, again, what could be better than a plump chicken, roasted until the skin is deliciously crisp, cooled to room temperature, and served forth with a good old-fashioned potato salad? Or chicken marinated in a mixture of soy sauce, chopped garlic, a little sherry, oil, a tiny touch of grated orange rind, and grated fresh or chopped candied ginger, then broiled, cooled, and served with thin onion sandwiches and a tomato salad?

Another old summer favorite of mine is veal Mediterranean, which can appear first hot and then cold, in the guise of vitello tonnato.

    For *Veal Mediterranean*, make little incisions with the point of a sharp knife in a 4- to 5-pound boneless rump roast of veal. Cut 3 or 4 garlic cloves into thin slivers and stuff these into the holes, then insert 10 to 12 anchovy fillets, pushing them in very deeply with the garlic. Rub the meat with a little dried basil, and brown it on all sides in a deep pot in 5 to 6 tablespoons olive or peanut oil. Add 3 good-sized onions, peeled and thinly sliced, 1 carrot, 1 leek, and a few sprigs of parsley. Let the vegetables cook a bit, then add a veal knuckle (if you can't get one, two small pig's feet will do, but the veal knuckle is by far the best), 1½ cups white wine, 1 cup water or stock, a good teaspoon of freshly ground black pepper, and about ½ teaspoon salt—there's a good deal of salt in the anchovies, but you'll need this little bit extra.

    Bring to a boil, reduce the heat, and simmer on top of the stove or in a 300-degree oven for 1½ to 2 hours, or until the meat is tender—but not soft and mushy, or it won't slice well.

With this succulent hot veal have buttered noodles with a good sprinkling of grated Parmesan cheese and a cucumber salad dressed with vinaigrette sauce or a mixture of mayonnaise and sour cream flavored with dill.

For *Vitello Tonnato*, refrigerate the leftover meat. Strain the pan juices and chill them in the refrigerator overnight so the fat rises to the top and the stock becomes a firm jelly. Next day, remove the fat and put the jelly in the blender with a 7-ounce can of tuna, 1 garlic clove, and 2 or 3 anchovy fillets. Whirl until blended. If you don't have a blender, melt the jelly, flake the tuna finely, chop the anchovies and garlic, and mix them all into the melted jelly, then return to the refrigerator and chill until thick and syrupy.

Take the leftover veal from the refrigerator and slice very thinly. Spoon the tuna sauce over the slices, and decorate with capers. Chill a little, and serve with chopped parsley, chopped fresh basil, if available, and a mustard mayonnaise.

Even without the jellied stock, you can make a delicious tuna sauce for cold veal by mixing a 7-ounce can of tuna, flaked, 6 or 7 finely chopped anchovies, 1 or 2 finely chopped garlic cloves, and 1 tablespoon each of chopped fresh basil and parsley into 1 cup mayonnaise mixed with ½ cup sour cream. Blend thoroughly, spoon over the cold sliced veal, and garnish with capers and chopped parsley.

You might serve the vitello tonnato with *Spaghettini Estivi*, which is best made in summer when you can get beautiful sun-ripened tomatoes. Peel and slice tomatoes and combine with thinly sliced raw onion and a touch of chopped fresh basil or dried basil, then mix with French dressing made with 6 tablespoons olive oil, 1½ to 2 tablespoons wine vinegar, and salt and freshly ground black pepper to taste. Chill until very cold.

Just before serving time, cook 1 pound very thin spaghettini (to serve four people) in boiling salted water until just tender to the bite— don't let it get mushy. Drain it well. Toss the hot spaghettini with the ice-cold tomato salad, sprinkle with a little chopped parsley, and serve this fantastic hot-and-cold combination with the vitello tonnato.

With Italian whole-wheat bread or crisp rolls, a good white wine, thoroughly chilled, and a dessert of fresh raspberries, strawberries, or figs, I can think of no more enticing summer supper.

A Good Ham Is Hard To Find

Ham isn't what it used to be. Once you could go into a market and find specially cured smoked country and Smithfield hams, but nowadays you seldom encounter a commercial ham that has firm meat with a rich, salty, pungent flavor. The majority palate in this country belongs to the children and younger people who aren't accustomed to the old-style ham we knew. They like something pinky, with only a slight flavor of curing and no definite taste. So most of our hams have a toned-down flavor because water is added to the cure and they are cured quickly. The packers have found that quickly cured hams also sell well because they come "ready to eat," requiring no soaking, preboiling, or baking, no work for the housewife.

However, you don't have to be deprived of good ham if you are willing to go to the trouble of tracking it down. There are farms all through the United States that sell country hams by mail, some of the better meat and delicacy stores stock them, and you can often find them advertised in magazines. The South has peach-fed, peanut-fed, even artichoke-fed (Jerusalem artichokes, that is) hams which are cured in a brine, smoked, treated, and aged about three months. Throughout New England, the Middle West, and the Northwest you will find good country hams, and even though some are tenderized and precooked, they still carry a hint of that smoky, salty, old-fashioned flavor.

I'm lucky enough to have a choice of five or six places near me where I can get excellent hams, one within two hours' drive of New York. There's a fine place in Vermont, others in Virginia, Maryland, and Pennsylvania. Many of the country hams I have liked best have come from Virginia and Kentucky. They are cured, smoked, rubbed with coarse pepper, and sewn up in muslin, which keeps out any insect life, and hung from the rafters.

There's another type of Virginia ham that is totally different from the country hams, and that's the Smithfield, the most distinctive and distinguished ham in America and one of the world's greatest. Years ago, when a ham fair was held in Paris at Easter, the Smithfield was the only American ham shown. Smithfield is a tiny village close to Hog Island, where the first Jamestown settlers kept their pigs, and it is here that the famous ham originated.

To qualify as a Smithfield, the hams must come from a lean type of hog, part razorback, which has been partially peanut-fed. They must be cured in Smithfield, or within a certain radius, in a way that gives them this extra-special flavor, then aged. An aged Smithfield ham becomes quite moldy, and this mold has to be scrubbed off with hot water and a stiff brush before the ham is soaked, boiled, and briefly baked to give it a glaze.

Smithfield ham comes both cooked and uncooked and, to my mind, is much better served cold than hot, very thinly sliced, with beaten biscuits or some kind of bread to enhance its rich, nutty flavor.

While other Virginia hams may be cured and treated in the same way, they cannot be called Smithfield. Some of these other hams are aged for two, three, or four years, and people have been known to keep them for as long as twenty, perhaps curing the ham when a child is born and saving it for the son's or daughter's wedding party. These hams are very dry and need a lot of soaking and cooking, but they are interesting and well worth trying.

Ham is one of our most fascinating and varied native foods. It differs so widely that there is always a new flavor to discover, and one never tires of eating it. I serve a great many country hams during the year for big cocktail or breakfast parties, and I have my own way of cooking them, which I find works very well for any kind of raw country ham, but not for one that is ready-cooked or ready-to-eat.

To cook a *Country Ham*, put it in a roasting pan, fat side down, and add 1 to 1½ quarts liquid, either water seasoned with 1½ cups wine vinegar, 1 bay leaf, and 1 teaspoon thyme, or pure apple cider seasoned with 2 cloves, 1 bay leaf, and 1 teaspoon thyme. For festive occasions I sometimes use a good California sherry or port, which gives the ham a remarkable flavor and finish. No seasonings; the wine has enough aromatics of its own.

Cover the pan completely with aluminum foil, crimping it around the edges to seal the ham airtight. Bake in a 350-degree oven, allowing 20 to 25 minutes a pound. At the end of the cooking time, take off the foil, remove any skin, and brush the fat with sieved brown sugar or equal quantities of brown sugar and crumbs, then put it in a 450- to 500-degree oven for 10 minutes to glaze.

The Splendors of Charcuterie

For the first time in forty years, New York has a real charcuterie shop, like every town and almost every village in France, and I am delighted once again to have these delicious pork tidbits at my command. The word "charcuterie," as my friend Jane Grigson explains in her excellent book *The Art of Charcuterie*, is derived from *chair cuit*, the cooked meat of the pig. The closest thing we have to a charcuterie in this country, outside of New York, is the Italian pork store which sells fresh sausages, sausage meat, and various cuts of fresh and cured pork.

The killing of pigs and curing of the meat dates back centuries, especially in France. Two thousand years ago the Gallic hams were prized and praised by Roman epicures. The Chinese, too, were partial to the pig. It was, as a matter of fact, a crossbreeding of the small, plump Chinese porker with the skinny, long-legged boarlike beast of Europe that produced our own domestic pig.

When I was a youngster, we'd have a pig or two slaughtered each year at a little farm we owned in the country, and the farmer would make various and sundry things for us. We always had our own smoked hams, bacon, and sometimes our own sausage, so sampling the good things of the recently-opened charcuterie in New York brought back all kinds of happy memories. This new charcuterie has two of my favorite sausages, *boudin blanc*, made with pork and pork fat, and *boudin noir*, a French blood sausage. *Boudin noir* is magnificent roasted or broiled and served with applesauce and mashed potatoes; it makes my mouth water just to think of it.

Two other types of sausage the charcuterie makes for sale are *andouillettes* and *crépinettes*. *Andouillettes* are tripe sausages, which you either like or don't like. I happen to think they are a great delicacy, but I have friends who are violently opposed to them on the grounds that this is too intimate a part of the pig to eat. *Crépinettes* consist of coarsely chopped sausage meat wrapped in caul, the fatty, delicate, almost lacy membrane from the pig's interior. Broiled or sautéed and served with a sauce, or perhaps mashed potatoes and applesauce, the little 3-inch-long crépinettes make delectable eating.

There are, of course, other kinds of charcuterie you don't have to cook. One is *rillettes* (see page 246), a smooth rich pâté of pork preserved in its own fat, to be spread on toast or French bread. Another is *jambonneau*, a mildly cured little ham from the hock, like a picnic ham, which has been rolled in crumbs and cooked. *Jambon persillé* is a jellied mold of pieces of well-cooked ham mixed with a lot of chopped parsley, so you get a brilliant green marbling through the pink of the ham.

I love every part of the pig, from the ears to the feet. After being soaked in brine for several days, the ears are cooked very slowly until tender (there should still be a nice little bite to the center), then rolled in butter and crumbs, broiled or baked until crisply brown, and served with a piquant vinaigrette sauce.

    Pieds de Porc Panés are cooked in a similar fashion. These are not hard to make, provided you can find the feet at your nearby pork butcher. To serve four, buy 4 meaty pig's feet (8, if they are very small), and wrap each one very tightly in muslin, several thicknesses of cheesecloth, or an old pillowcase. Tie very firmly. Cook the feet in a rich bouillon of 4 cups water, an onion stuck with 2 cloves, a carrot, a bit of celery, a bay leaf, 2 or 3 garlic cloves, a few sage leaves, salt, and peppercorns or freshly ground black pepper, until very tender, from 2½ to 3½ hours. Cool in the bouillon, or remove to a dish to cool.

When cool, remove the wrappings, roll the feet in toasted crumbs, dribble melted butter or pork fat over them, and either brown under the broiler or cook in a 475-degree oven, turning them several times, until brown and crisp on the outside.

Serve the pig's feet with a well-flavored vinaigrette sauce and the traditional accompaniments of French fried potatoes and a bowl of watercress. Although you may find it takes a bit of work to remove all the little foot bones and get at the edible part, if you like foods that are gelatinous to the bite and palate, you'll love these tasty little morsels.

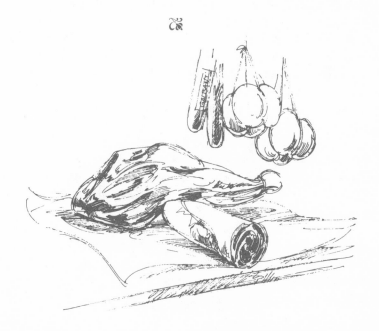

The Friendliest Meat

I've long said that if I were about to be executed and were given a choice of my last meal, it would be bacon and eggs. There are few sights that appeal to me more than the streaks of lean and fat in good side bacon, or the lovely round of pinkish meat framed in delicate white fat that is Canadian bacon. Nothing is quite as intoxicating as the smell of bacon frying in the morning, save perhaps for the smell of coffee brewing.

While bacon doesn't always taste as good as it smells, for there are many grades and varieties, many ways to cook it—and many ways to ruin it—by and large this is probably one of the most satisfactory of our traditional meats. Our ancestors practically lived on it. For the homesteader, a side of bacon was a treasure, for it meant meat, if not variety, a meat that could be eaten for every meal, with the fat used to fry fish or potatoes, or to make biscuits.

Bacon has probably more palate appeal than any one other meat. Think of the ever-popular "BLT down with mayo," a toasted sandwich of bacon, lettuce, tomato, and mayonnaise. Add some sliced turkey or chicken breast, and you have the noble club sandwich. Then there's that earlier popular snack, the cheese dream, a great combination of Cheddar cheese, bacon, and sliced tomato. Bacon has also figured in the annals of the hamburger. A great favorite of mine at the New York restaurant Maxwell's Plum is a large hamburger with crisp bacon and melted cheese on a well-buttered bun, a superb merger of flavors and textures. You bite into the cheese, and as its smooth melting quality flows into the juicy hamburger, you suddenly hit the crisp bacon—a royal pleasure.

Recently I was sent a beautiful side of Canadian bacon, an excellent loin, that was just delicious baked in a piece, like a small ham. There was this gorgeous bacon, with all the attributes of fine ham, and an even more tender, luscious texture, so, I reasoned, why not use it instead of ham in a Croque Monsieur, that deliciously crisp, crunchy French sautéed sandwich?

    For a Variation on *Croque Monsieur*, I lightly buttered 2 slices of homemade bread with the crusts on, put between them 2 pieces of Canadian bacon, which I had previously broiled lightly, topped them with 1 healthy slice of Swiss Gruyère cheese (you could use Emmenthaler, Fontina, or even Münster, but I like Gruyère best for this), pressed the top slice down firmly, buttered the outsides of the bread, and sautéed the sandwich until it was crisp, brown, and buttery on each side, with the melted cheese lovingly embracing the bacon.

Garnished with parsley and a few olives or pickles and eaten hot with a glass of chilled white wine or beer, this is a classic luncheon or snack that can't be bettered, utterly seductive to the bite.

Bacon is a most adaptable meat, whether you buy the paper-thin packaged type or the kind that comes in a slab and is cut medium-thick or thick. Personally, if it is a good smoky bacon, I like it cut thick and broiled. With eggs fried in butter and home-fried potatoes, what a breakfast it makes! Medium-thick bacon I sometimes bake in a 350-degree oven until it is not too crisp and not too limp, just in between. To me, bacon that is too crisp loses its quality and flavor and becomes quite disagreeable. For this reason, I recommend broiling paper-thin bacon. You can experiment with timing until you get the texture you prefer.

Even more popular than bacon and eggs in England and Canada is bacon with fried or broiled tomatoes, rather like having a bacon and tomato sandwich without the lettuce and mayonnaise, and with the toast on the side. Four rashers of bacon, four slices of fried tomato, crunchy rye or whole-wheat toast—that's a fine way to start the day.

Bacon adds so much flavor to other foods. I love to bard a roasting chicken with bacon slices, draping them over the breast and sides, removing them for the last third of the cooking so the bird can have its final browning and basting. I lace kidneys with bacon on skewers, broiling them together until it is hard to divorce one flavor from the other. Who could imagine sautéed liver without its ally—strips of bacon? And what fisherman doesn't revel in bacon and fresh-caught trout, rolled in cornmeal and cooked in the bacon fat until the outside is crispy brown, the inside moist and tender? Bacon is perhaps the most friendly of all meats because it combines so freely and easily with other foods.

Glorious Hash

I doubt if there are many dishes that can be as great—or, if badly made, as horrendous—as hash. It's kind of a universal dish. Just about every cuisine in the world features hash in one form or another. The French do things with chopped meat cooked in various fashions and call it *haché*. The Poles hash veal and turn it into a toothsome meal. Even the Chinese have mixtures of two or three kinds of finely cut meat and vegetables that, while we might not dare to call them by as plebeian a name as hash, follow the same basic principle.

We in these United States, with our mixed culinary background, have done the most to make hash a glorious thing to eat. I remember a number of years ago stopping at a small country hotel in Minnesota and getting one of the best hashes I ever tasted. It was made with cold roast beef, excellent roast beef to begin with, diced rather coarsely with bits of the fat and cooked in beef drippings with finely chopped onion and chopped cooked potatoes, then seasoned with salt, pepper, and a dash of Worcestershire sauce. The hash came out brown and glazed, crispy around the edges and tender and moist inside, and it was so delicious that I almost ordered another helping.

Then, of course, one of the pleasures of having corned beef is that if you buy enough, there is a nice chunk left for hash. Years ago, when I was in the food business and had a little shop where we featured hors d'oeuvre and other goodies for the table, we made a specialty of corned beef hash on Saturdays and charged a very fat price for it—in those days, an astonishing price—but we made our hash with good corned beef, not too finely chopped, which is the trouble with much hash, and we chopped everything by hand—meat, onions, and potatoes.

When I make hash, I like to use two-thirds meat to one-third potatoes, or half and half, with onion to taste and only salt, pepper, and nutmeg for seasoning. You can add a bit of Tabasco or Worcestershire or garlic, but basically it's that wonderful blend of onion, potato, and beef that makes a great hash.

Chicken hash has always been a favorite in America, too. There must be a million different versions. Some are merely cut-up chicken in a rich cream sauce with maybe a little onion or tarragon, served with rice or potatoes. In the old days, the Ritz in New York used to make a very famous, very rich chicken hash, served in a border of puréed green peas.

The other night, I dined on a perfectly beautiful sautéed chicken that had been lightly floured and cooked in butter with white wine, salt, pepper, and a touch of rosemary. I purposely bought more chicken than I knew I could eat, because I wanted to make chicken hash. I served half the chicken and let the rest cool in the pan, then removed it, added ½ cup white wine to the pan juices, heated them, scraping up the brown bits, and poured this over the cold chicken, which I'd put in a bowl.

 Next day, to make *Chicken Hash* I cut the leftover chicken into rather large dice, which gave me about 2½ cups light and dark chicken meat, and added 2 or 3 finely cut-up gizzards. I boiled 5 smallish waxy white potatoes, let them cool, and diced them. I skimmed the chicken fat from the bowl, saving the little bit of gravy at the bottom to add later on, put the fat in a skillet with some butter, and gently sautéed 1 finely chopped large onion until it was pale yellow. Next I added my potatoes and cooked them with the onion, seasoning them with a touch of rosemary, salt, and freshly ground black pepper, then added the chicken and the gravy, mixed everything together well, and let it cook gently for 5 minutes. I then poured in ⅓ cup heavy cream and let that cook down. By this time the hash was nice and brown, so I quickly folded in ½ cup chopped parsley and served it good and hot with a green salad.

It was so tasty that next morning I reheated what was left, popped a poached egg on top, and had myself one of the best breakfasts I've ever eaten.

There are all kinds of ways to vary this simple recipe. Sometimes I add ½ cup finely chopped sautéed mushrooms, or put in some toasted almonds at the last minute. Or I may leave out the heavy cream and mix in a couple of egg yolks instead, sprinkle the top with grated Parmesan cheese and run it under the broiler for a few minutes to set the egg and brown the cheese, watching it very carefully. Whatever you make it with, a good hash is a joy, and one of the best ways I know to make a simply wonderful meal out of leftovers.

Turkey Any Time

Can you remember the days when you tasted turkey only once or twice a year? Then it was the bird featured as the Thanksgiving treat, looked forward to as something very special. All that has changed. Turkey is now an everyday meat, so much so that it has almost replaced chicken in restaurants and lunch counters, for turkey breasts yield more meat per pound and are more practical to use.

Even I was amazed to discover the other day just how many ways you can buy turkey. Whole, fresh or frozen, ready to stuff or stuffed, basted and nonbasted (basted turkeys are those injected with fat to lubricate the breast and keep the meat moist and tender). Smoked and frozen, ready to serve. Then there are frozen turkey breasts, turkey hips, turkey thighs, or the turkey hindquarter, which consists of the leg, thigh, and oyster, the most luscious little morsel in the whole bird. Apparently the producers think so, too, because they brag about including it. If you are a white-meat or a dark-meat fan, you can buy all-white or all-dark boneless frozen pan roasts, or a combination of the two, packed in a disposable aluminum pan.

Ground turkey meat, which I first encountered and used in the West, is now generally available and very good to add to a meat loaf or a pâté. The flavor is excellent. Some of the best buys are the whole turkey fillet, the choicest part of the breast, sold frozen and ready to cook; turkey steaks, cross-cut from the breast; and turkey cutlets, boned and skinned breast meat, sliced about ¼ inch thick, which makes a great substitute for scaloppine in these days when veal is in short supply and enormously expensive. Cooked quickly and sauced like scaloppine, you'll have a hard time distinguishing them from the best-quality veal.

I'm very partial to the frozen turkey breasts, with the skin and bone left on. I like to roast them and serve them for one hot meal, then use the leftovers for turkey in lettuce leaves (see page 251) or turkey salad. Recently, at the suggestion of my old friend and fellow writer Helen McCully, I used the breast for a turkey version of the Italian vitello tonnato.

To make *Turkey Tonnato*, buy an 8- to 9-pound turkey breast. This is a pretty large piece of meat, so I'd advise you to use only half of it for your turkey tonnato. Cut it in half. Loosen, but do not remove, the skin on the half-breast, and slip 5 or 6 anchovies under the skin. Make incisions in the meat with a small knife, and stud with little slivers of garlic, as you would do for leg of lamb.

Roast the flavored turkey in a 350-degree oven, allowing about 20 minutes a pound, or until it reaches an internal temperature of 160 to 165 degrees, basting during the cooking with a mixture of half melted butter and half white wine. When the turkey is cooked, let it cool at room temperature.

When it has cooled sufficiently, remove the whole piece of breast meat from the bone and check it for salt. The anchovies under the skin practically eradicate the need for salt, but taste at any rate.

Now make 2 cups of your favorite mayonnaise and add to it 1 cup finely flaked tuna, preferably the dark chunk style, which is better for this than the firm solid-pack white meat. Break the tuna into tiny flakes with two forks before combining it with the mayonnaise, 1 very finely chopped garlic clove, and 2 tablespoons finely chopped parsley. If you have some anchovies left, you might chop them and incorporate them with your sauce.

Cut the turkey meat in nice thinnish slices, and dip each slice in the tuna mayonnaise. Arrange on a serving dish, and garnish with sliced or quartered hard-cooked eggs. Make a rice salad with cold cooked rice, adding olive oil and vinegar in proportions of four parts oil to one part vinegar, chopped parsley, chopped scallion, and very finely chopped anchovy. Toss well, heap in the center of your serving dish, and garnish with cherry tomatoes or watercress. Serve with the remaining sauce (you can vary the sauce by using 1 cup mayonnaise and 1 cup sour cream, if you wish) for a delicious, inexpensive luncheon.

To use the other half-breast, you could roast it and, when cold, cut it into thin slices or dice, toss it with toasted walnuts, finely cut celery, and a mixture of half mayonnaise, half sour cream. Serve this turkey salad on greens with hard-boiled eggs and black olives, and thin rye bread and butter sandwiches. With either of these dishes, a chilled white wine is extremely pleasant.

CHAPTER 2

A Good Catch

ॐ

... in which we extol raw fish and deplore overcooked ... run into the salmon season ... sample salt fish and sardines ... appraise the anatomy of a lobster ... crave the crayfish ... pot the shrimp ... delve the depths of bouillabaisse and clam chowder ... and cultivate a taste for gastropods.

How to Cook Fish without Meat

Centuries ago the Polynesians devised a way of cooking fish without fire that was gradually adopted along the Pacific coast of South America and in through Mexico. How it got there we'll never know unless records are unearthed at some future time to tell us how foods migrated from the Orient and South Pacific. In South America and Mexico this preparation of fish is called *seviche*, sometimes spelled *ceviche*, and it's so delicious and utterly simple that I can't understand why people in other parts of the globe didn't think of it. Probably because few people had limes and lemons at their disposal in the past as they do nowadays, and without them seviche couldn't be, for the fish is marinated in lime or lemon juice and the citric acid "cooks" it. Strictly speaking, it should be lime juice, which has the greatest flavor and does the best job, but lemon juice will do the trick.

Although different countries use different fish, for my taste you want a delicate white fish or seviche—sole, flounder, sand dabs, red snapper, most any of the white-fleshed fish from the ocean or the whitefish from the inland waters of the Great Lakes. The fish should be filleted, which means you can use frozen fillets if you can't get fresh.

For six servings of *Seviche*, put 6 medium-sized fish fillets in a flat dish and barely cover with fresh lime juice, lemon juice, or a combination of the two. Refrigerate for 5 to 6 hours, at which point you'll find the whole texture of the fish has changed and the translucent uncooked flesh has turned white, firm, and almost flaky, the way it does when the fish is cooked, a miraculous metamorphosis. Drain the fish and reserve the juice.

There are different ways of dressing the marinated fish for the table. I like to add 3 tablespoons finely chopped canned peeled green chilies, 1 small onion, very finely chopped (if you like garlic, use 2 or 3 finely chopped garlic cloves instead), 2 tablespoons chopped parsley, and 3 or 4 tablespoons olive oil. Sprinkle the top with 1 tablespoon fresh herbs, coarsely chopped—you can use tarragon or basil or, if you live where there are Spanish-American or Chinese markets, fresh coriander, otherwise known as cilantro or Chinese parsley.

Taste the fish to see if the flavor is sharp enough. It should be after the long marination. If not, add 2 or 3 spoonfuls of the reserved lime juice. Season with salt and pepper to taste.

Serve the seviche well chilled as a first course or luncheon dish. You can leave the fillets whole or cut them in thin strips and arrange them on greens. Some people put them in scallop shells, a very pretty and appropriate form of presentation.

Another very good seviche is made with tiny raw bay s[...]
are marinated and dressed in the same way as the fish, or th[...]
mixed, after marinating, with peeled and chopped ripe tomato[...]
and basil, and lots of chopped parsley. Served in scallop shells [...]
make a perfectly delightful, light first course.

There's a good reason for the popularity of seviche south of the border. It's cool and refreshing with a hint of spiciness, marvelous for hot weather when appetites flag.

If you shy away from the idea of fish that hasn't been cooked in the usual way, there's another Latin American dish, first cousin to seviche, that is rather different and equally pleasant.

~ It's called *Escabeche* and to make it, take 6 fresh or frozen fish fillets (use the same types mentioned before), salt them lightly on both sides, and marinate in lime or lemon juice barely to cover for ¾ to 1 hour. Pour off the marinade and reserve, dry the fish well, and dust very, very lightly with flour, a little more salt, and some pepper. Melt 4 tablespoons butter and 2 tablespoons oil in a skillet. Sauté the fish very quickly on both sides until heated through and delicately browned. Remove to a serving dish. Sprinkle with 2 to 3 finely chopped garlic cloves, 1 tablespoon paprika, 1 teaspoon dried cumin seed, 1 teaspoon oregano, 3 or 4 canned green chilies, cut in thin strips, 1 large red Italian onion, sliced paper-thin, and about 2 tablespoons chopped parsley. Add about ½ cup olive oil and 1 to 2 tablespoons of the reserved juice, or to taste, and refrigerate, covered, for 24 hours, until the fish is imbued with the various flavors. Remove the dish and garnish with shredded lettuce, sliced stuffed olives, and perhaps some little green onions, cut in long shreds. Serve with good bread or hot rolls and a cucumber salad, or, if you want a hot vegetable, fresh peas or corn on the cob, for a summer luncheon or supper. You can change the flavor by adding orange juice with the olive oil and lime juice and scattering a little bit of grated orange zest on top just before serving.

allops. They
ey can be
onion
hey

...oking fish that few people seem to know about. Maybe
...t as popular in this country as it deserves to be—it is
...ked. How often have you been served, in a home or
..., overfried fillet that tastes like a shingle with crumbs
...salmon that is dry, grainy, and flavorless? It all boils
...hing—overcooking.

The Japanese, as you know, eat a lot of raw fish, which means it has to be superfresh. A market in Cambridge, Massachusetts, where Julia Child buys most of her fish, caters to the Japanese colony in Cambridge, and if you go late in the afternoon, there is practically nothing left.

Now, I'm not suggesting you switch to raw fish, although for an interesting taste experiment you might try the sashimi served in Japanese restaurants—thin, delicate slices of raw tuna, striped bass, or similar saltwater fish accompanied by a little bowl of soy sauce and green Japanese horseradish for dipping. Once you discover the tenderness and flavor of fish in its natural state, you'll see why overcooking is nothing short of a crime.

The Canadian Department of Fisheries and their Home Service Bureau have made extensive tests on the fish that they (and we) catch in the oceans, lakes, and rivers and have found that they all have something in common. Regardless of the fish or the cooking method there is one uncomplicated rule of thumb that can be followed. Measure the fish, whether it be whole, in steaks, or in fillets, at its thickest point. Then cook exactly 10 minutes for each measured inch of thickness. For frozen, unthawed fish, double the cooking time.

Actually, this remarkably simple approach was started some years ago at the University of Washington by Evelyn Spencer. She did a great deal of work on the subject of fish and came up with a method of quick, high-temperature cooking which was tested and adapted by the Canadians. I use their method constantly in my cooking classes and demonstrations and have found it to be infallible.

So if you are baking fish fillets or steaks, or even a whole stuffed fish, all you have to do is measure the thickness, put the fish in a buttered dish with seasonings, and cook in a 450-degree oven, allowing 10 minutes per measured inch (20 minutes for frozen fish).

If you are baking them en papillote—that is, in an aluminum foil package with the edges sealed—allow a little extra time for the heat to penetrate the foil, 5 minutes more for fresh fish, 10 for frozen.

To broil fillets, arrange them on a piece of buttered foil on the broiler pan and use the same rule to gauge the cooking time. Fresh fillets should be cooked 2 to 3 inches away from the heat unit, frozen ones 4 inches away. Be sure to buy thick fillets for broiling. Very thin ones have a tendency to dry out. These are better sautéed or pan-fried. To pan-fry, salt and pepper them, dip them lightly in flour, and fry in about ¼ inch of hot, but not smoking, fat or oil.

A poached fish, which should never be allowed to boil but merely be simmered gently in hot court bouillon or flavored and seasoned water, also gets the same timing of 10 minutes per inch measured at the thickest point, usually behind the head.

 Poached Trout with Horseradish Cream can be made with small fresh brook trout or frozen rainbow trout. Make a simple court bouillon by bringing to a boil in a pan ½ cup dry white wine, 1 pint water, a sprig of parsley, a slice of lemon, 1 onion stuck with 2 cloves, ½ teaspoon salt, 2 or 3 peppercorns, ½ bay leaf, and a pinch of thyme. Reduce heat, simmer 20 to 30 minutes, then strain the liquid. Pour into a shallow pan (such as a skillet) enough of the hot court bouillon to cover the trout. Bring to a boil, reduce the heat, add the trout, and let them simmer gently until done, allowing 10 minutes per inch of thickness (or 20 if frozen). When cooked, the flesh should flake when tested with a fork. Remove the trout from the liquid and serve with *Horseradish Cream*, made by combining 1 cup sour cream with 1 cup freshly grated horseradish or bottled drained horseradish to taste.

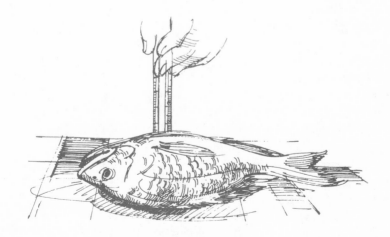

Salute to Salmon

When I was a child, I spent a great deal of time close to the mouth of the Columbia River in Oregon, so salmon has always been an important part of my food life. Salmon, with its delicate pink flesh and brilliant silver skin, is not only one of the most decorative but also one of the best fish we have. Alas, because of pollution and the damming and blocking of rivers, much of the salmon that used to come to the East Coast is gone, probably forever, although I did hear some heartening news the other day. Experiments are going on in New England to breed small salmon weighing no more than about 2 pounds, an ideal size for salmon lovers. A whole fish could be cooked in practically any pot, without needing a fish boiler or a specially large pan.

Such a revival would have great meaning for New England, for here in summers past, when salmon was at its peak in the rivers, the traditional Fourth of July dinner was boiled or poached salmon with egg sauce and the first new potatoes and green peas of the year. It's touching to think that in the days when our country became independent this significant meal celebrated three of the gifts of the waters and the land. Now, of course, salmon from various sources is available for the greater part of the year, new potatoes for nine months, and peas all the time.

Salmon has always been popular in Europe. Wherever you go, you find poached salmon with plain, green, or mustard-flavored mayonnaise, and cucumber salad. In England it is often served at big party suppers. I remember giving a dinner party years ago at a private eating club in London where the first course on the menu, written by the owner-manager, was "poached young grilse." This caused a few people to ask what manner of fish this was, since it tasted like salmon. Well, it was salmon. Grilse is a virgin salmon, supposedly with a finer texture and flavor than any other.

In Oregon, when I was young, there was a great profusion of salmon in the Columbia River, and if you went to Astoria, at the river's mouth, during the season, you found hundreds of people fishing and hundreds more in the canneries. I vividly remember stopping at a cannery with friends and buying for 50 cents a large measure brimming with salmon cheeks—literally, the cheeks from the salmon heads. Sautéed in butter and oil or broiled with crumbs and butter they are the most delicious morsels, with a very different texture from the body of the fish. Nowadays, salmon are scarcer and salmon cheeks have become practically as expensive as caviar.

The salmon we had is the Pacific salmon, the royal Chinook, a large fish with a goodly amount of oil, a brilliant color, and superb texture and flavor.

Recently, while spending a nostalgic summer at the Oregon beach, I bought and broiled some fillets of Chinook which were exceedingly thick and practically boneless. With salmon fillets, you must be very exacting about the cooking time. Give them 10 minutes for every inch, measured at the thickest point. As there may be as much as half an inch difference in the thickness of the piece you buy, you should cut and broil it according to thickness. Should your fillet be thicker at one end than the other, it is best to undercook it a bit, because if you broil the thinnest part for as long as the thick, that end of your fish will be extremely dry and tasteless.

One thing I enjoy most about *Salmon Fillets* is that the skin on one side becomes a delicious morsel when broiled. I like to rub the fillets quite well with coarse salt, let them stand for 15 to 20 minutes, then place them skin side up on a broiling pan covered with oiled cooking parchment or aluminum foil. I broil them for the required 10 minutes per inch of thickness, 6 minutes of the time on the skin side and 4 minutes on the flesh side, turning the fish very carefully with a pancake turner or large spatula. When you turn the fish flesh side up, you can, if you wish, sprinkle it with a few buttered crumbs, but be careful not to let them burn. You can easily tell when the fish is cooked because the color changes from its raw reddish pink to a paler shade, a lovely deep pink. Broiled fillets should be served piping hot, on hot plates, and if you are like me you'll start by attacking that beautiful crisp skin, which tastes so good.

Serve these fillets with lemon butter, hollandaise, or Béarnaise sauce, or with what we westerners call tartar sauce, one which is in many ways different from the classic.

To prepare *Tartar Sauce*, take 1 cup mayonnaise and add to it ⅓ cup finely chopped dill pickle, ⅓ cup finely chopped onion, 1 teaspoon finely chopped capers, and a touch of mustard. Blend well and add a dash of lemon juice or tarragon vinegar if it seems to lack sharpness. Let the sauce stand an hour or so before you serve it, and it will gain a great deal in quality as the flavors have time to merge and mellow.

I know I will probably get a load of letters from all of you telling me that you have a different recipe for tartar sauce. Well, I realize that there are as many different versions of this sauce as there are versions of fried chicken. I've had tartar sauce with chopped fresh dill and parsley plus a touch of garlic, and tartar sauce with chopped fresh tarragon and shallots, but this is the one I remember from my childhood, and to my mind it is the best, so I think you should give it a whirl and see how you like it. Add a bit of chopped parsley to the sauce just before you serve it, and garnish your salmon with parsley sprigs.

With these delectable broiled salmon fillets, nothing is better than crisply fried potatoes, be they homemade French fries or sautéed potatoes. Or, if you can find little new potatoes, leave the skins on, cutting a belly-band from around the middle, and boil or steam them. This gives you a summer meal that couldn't be bettered anywhere.

Another great Oregon delicacy of my childhood was the local smoked salmon, which was more kippered, or hot-smoked, a method typical of the early Indian way of preparing the fish.

As I grew older, I learned to appreciate the Atlantic smoked salmon from Nova Scotia, Scotland, Ireland, and Scandinavia with its gentle curing, lovely pale color, and beautiful texture, so delectable when cut with a very sharp knife in long paper-thin slices more or less across the grain, the way you find it in restaurants and food shops where the greatest care and tradition are maintained. Then, as I traveled more, I discovered Scandinavia's gravlax, a superb dish for salmon lovers.

⌒*Gravlax* is not hard to make, although it takes patience. To serve six to eight, buy 3 to 3½ pounds center cut of fresh salmon. Ask the fishman to leave the skin on but to split the salmon and remove the backbone and the little bones surrounding it. Place one half, skin side down, in a bowl or casserole, and rub it very, very well with a mixture of ¼ pound coarse salt, ¼ cup sugar, and 1 to 2 tablespoons coarsely ground peppercorns. Rub well into the fish, then place a very large bouquet of fresh dill on top. Rub the second half of the salmon with the seasoning mixture and place over the dill, skin side up. Cover with foil, then weight down with canned goods. Set the bowl on a platter, as the salmon will give forth liquid, and refrigerate for 36 to 48 hours, turning each day to cure evenly and basting with the liquid that accumulates. Weight it down again each time. At the end of the curing time, remove the fish, scrape away the dill and seasonings and dry on paper towels. Place on a carving board (I like to put a bouquet of dill at one end, parsley at the other) and slice thickly on the diagonal, detaching the flesh from the skin as you do so. Serve as an appetizer or a main course for luncheon or supper or with other fish dishes as you would in a Swedish smorgasbord.

The curing condiments and the dill give the salmon a most exciting flavor, which is perfectly complemented by rye bread and a sweet mustard sauce.

To make *Mustard Sauce*, combine 4 tablespoons seasoned German mustard (not hot, but very spicy), 1 teaspoon dry mustard, 3 tablespoons sugar, 2 tablespoons wine vinegar, ⅓ cup vegetable oil, and 3 tablespoons finely chopped dill plus a little finely chopped parsley. Whisk well until it has the consistency of a thin mayonnaise. Refrigerate, covered, for 5 hours before serving.

Traditionally, gravlax should be served with akvavit and maybe beer, both freezing cold. In summer, when salmon is at its best and most plentiful, try this marvelous way of serving a superlative fish.

Try Salt Fish for Breakfast

In our present-day pattern of eating, we have almost forgotten a most important part of our food heritage—salt fish, one of the earliest American products to travel back to Europe. Fishermen from Spain, Portugal, Italy, France, England, and the Scandinavian countries ventured far into the Grand Banks of Newfoundland to catch cod, mackerel, and herring which they preserved for the long voyage home by salting and drying. The Norwegians, of course, had long used salt herring from their surrounding waters as a winter food, but it was the Mediterranean countries, where salt cod became a staple of the diet, that cooked the fish most imaginatively. In Portugal alone, it's said there is a salt cod recipe for just about every day of the year, and France and Italy also have dozens of unusual recipes.

One of the greatest is the French Provençal *brandade de morue*, which at one time you could buy on Fridays throughout the south of France. In fact, certain delicatessens, noted for making the best brandade, would ship it by bus and train to other towns each Friday. Brandade is traditionally made in a mortar and pestle, although these days a blender or the food processor makes much shorter work of it. Cooked salt cod, heavy cream, olive oil, garlic, and freshly ground black pepper are pounded in the mortar until they become a creamy paste with the texture of fine mashed potatoes. Eaten warm, with little fingers of fried toast, a garlicky creamy brandade is one of the most exciting foods I know.

In this country, potatoes and salt cod have long been regarded as natural partners—creamed codfish with boiled potatoes, codfish balls, and, finest of all, codfish cakes.

     I was brought up on this simple but wonderful version of *Codfish Cakes* created by Mother's Chinese chef in Portland. Soak 1½ to 2 pounds boneless salt cod overnight in water. Next day, change the water, then place in a pan in fresh cold water and bring to a boil. Lower heat and simmer until cod is just tender and flakes easily when tested with a fork. Drain well and shred with two forks.

Combine the flaked cod with an equal quantity of cooked potatoes, freshly mashed with plenty of butter so they have a rich texture, 1 or 2 eggs, 1 teaspoon ground ginger or 1½ to 2 teaspoons finely grated fresh ginger, and freshly ground black pepper to taste. Mix well and form into cakes about 3 inches across and 1 inch thick—they are very delicate, so handle them carefully. Sauté the cakes in plenty of butter in a heavy skillet until crisply brown on both sides. Garnish with a little chopped parsley and serve with freshly made toast and, if you like, with strips of bacon or salt pork, for one of the best breakfasts you've ever eaten.

As the westward trek of the pioneers opened up this country from coast to coast, and the great native salmon of the Atlantic and Pacific oceans became a part of American eating, salt salmon, as well as salt cod, was quite a common product. One of the most famous of the Hawaiian pupus or appetizers, lomi-lomi, salt salmon almost literally massaged to softness with the fingers, arose because of the New England missionaries, who introduced salt salmon there as a replacement for the salt cod for which they nostagically yearned.

While I was summering in Oregon I found to my delight that one can still buy salt salmon bellies and sometimes the delicious fat tips, which are cut from around the head of the salmon and salted. Here's a good way to serve them, in case you are lucky enough to find salt salmon in your fish markets.

Soak the *Salt Salmon* in cold water for several hours, then poach in cold water or half cold water and half cold milk until the fish flakes easily. Pour off liquid, keep the fish warm on a hot platter, and top with 1 or 2 pats of butter. Combine in a saucepan 3 tablespoons melted butter and 3 tablespoons flour, cook several minutes, stirring, until golden and bubbling, then stir in 1 cup hot milk and stir until thickened. Add freshly ground black pepper (no salt), stir in ½ cup heavy cream and 1 or 2 more pats of butter, and simmer 5 to 10 minutes. Taste for seasoning. You may, if you like, add several tablespoons coarsely chopped hard-boiled egg or 2 tablespoons chopped parsley to the sauce.

With boiled potatoes or crisp toast and a good hot cup of tea or coffee this makes a magnificent Sunday morning breakfast.

The Sardine, a Small Miracle

Every summer, around the beginning of August, one of the most mouth-watering events of the year takes place in New York—the Fancy Food Show. This is a show basically for the trade, which means buyers who come from various shops and stores all over the country to find new and interesting foods. It's a breathtaking spectacle, row after row of booths displaying all the great delicacies of the world. There are untold yards of sausages and other cured meats, caviar, cheese, dried and preserved fruits, just about every kind of canned food you can think of, biscuits, cookies, and enough candy to satisfy the sweetest tooth.

Having been in Norway recently, I stopped to look at the Norwegian products, and the innumerable cans of sardines made me realize how important the tiny sardine, the young of a fish belonging to the herring family, is in our eating pattern. I can't remember a time when we didn't have Brisling sardines, which are the best known of those from Norway, or sild, another kind not as commonly found. What a boon they have been over the years. One inexpensive little can will provide a snack, a sandwich, or even a salad, and they are great to carry along on an outing. One of my favorite sandwiches is homemade bread, well-buttered, spread with mashed sardines, a few drops of lemon juice, and a thin slice of onion, eaten with a glass of beer or wine.

Brisling sardines are rather different from French, Portuguese, or Maine sardines. They are very small—one can may hold anywhere from six to twenty-six of them, and their good fishy flavor is increased by the slight smoking they get when they are prepared for canning, before being packed in their natural oil or olive oil. When I was in Norway, I discovered the following unusual and delicious way to serve these tiny marvels.

Wined Sardines on Toast: melt 2 tablespoons butter in a skillet, and cook 1 small onion, coarsely chopped, and 2 crushed garlic cloves until wilted. Add a 3-inch strip of lemon peel, 1 cup dry white wine, and 1 bay leaf. Simmer over low heat for about 10 minutes. Carefully turn two 3¾-ounce cans of Brisling sardines into a small bowl, draining off the oil. Strain the hot wine mixture over them, and marinate at room temperature for 1 hour. Serve these winey sardines on hot buttered toast, topped with a spoonful of sautéed mushrooms, as a snack, or a luncheon or supper dish for six.

*Another sardine dish that has become almost a tradition at holiday time in Scandinavia is what I call *Scandinavian Special.* This recipe makes quite a lot, but if you refrigerate it in glass jars or a mold it will keep well—omit the onion juice, though, if you're going to keep it.

Mash 4 to 5 cans Norway sardines very finely, and season with ½ teaspoon salt and 1 teaspoon paprika. Blend 1 pound cream cheese with 2 tablespoons lemon juice, ½ cup chopped parsley, and a little onion juice. Season to taste with salt. Whip the sardines and cream, cheese mixture together really well until light and well blended. Taste. You may need to add a little more lemon juice. Put into a decorative oiled mold. Chill a little, then unmold onto a serving platter, garnish with watercress, and serve with crackers as a first course, or a cocktail spread.

Sardines are wonderful with drinks, as a snack. Sometimes I combine ½ cup cottage cheese with ¼ cup sour cream, ½ cup minced green onion, and 3 tablespoons chopped parsley, blend it well, add 1 teaspoon dried dill or some chopped fresh dill, mound it on a serving dish, and arrange a wreath of Brisling sardines around it and some chopped parsley in the center. Very crisp toast or good Melba toast goes around the mound—or I may put party rye in the oven to dry out until it is curly and crisp and use that.

Another of my standbys over the years is a *Potato and Sardine Salad.* Cook 6 medium-sized new potatoes in their jackets until just tender. As soon as they can be handled comfortably, slip off the skins and slice them into a bowl. Add 3 tablespoons olive oil, 1 tablespoon wine vinegar, and a touch of salt and pepper. Cool. Meanwhile, coarsely chop 1 red Italian onion. Add this to the cooled potatoes, and season with salt and pepper to taste and 1 to 2 tablespoons chopped parsley. Toss with oil and vinegar and arrange on a bed of greens. Open and drain two 3¾-ounce cans of Brisling sardines, carefully remove from the can, and arrange on top of the-potato salad, alternately with quartered hard-boiled eggs. Serve with mustard mayonnaise—1 cup mayonnaise mixed with ⅓ cup Dijon-style mustard, a dash or two of German mustard, and 1 tablespoon chopped fresh dill or 1 teaspoon dried dill.

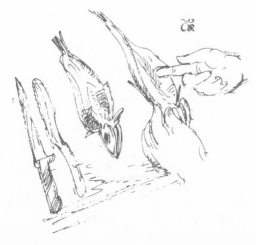

Lobster, Aristocrat of the Ocean

Few things in the world of food are as fascinatingly constructed, as curious to look at, and as delicious to eat as a lobster. For some reason, lobsters have always been considered luxury food, classed with caviar, squab, game, and all those delicacies one eats at elaborate dinners and on special occasions. I can't imagine why. True, lobster is expensive, but what isn't today? It's worth every penny it costs. Nothing tastes quite like a lobster, and nothing is as succulent when it is properly prepared—and as far as I'm concerned, the simpler the preparation the better.

Lobsters abound in East Coast waters from Long Island to far north in Canada, and although they are not as plentiful off the Massachusetts and Maine coasts as they used to be, there are still plenty to be had in Canadian waters. Lobsters are sold in different sizes, all the way up from the delicate little 1-pound ones called "chicken" lobsters, which yield 4 or 5 ounces of meat, to enormous monsters weighing up to 20 or 25 pounds. These heavy ones make exceedingly good eating, but you won't find them very often. Lobsters just under 1¼ pounds are called "heavy chickens," those weighing 1¼ to 1½ pounds are known as "quarters," and a 2-pound lobster is referred to in the trade as a "deuce" or 2-pounder. At 2¼ to 2½ pounds they are "small jumbos," and larger ones up to 5 pounds are called "jumbos."

If you live far away from lobster country, there are several lobster "farms" in Maine and Canada that will air-ship lobsters packed in seaweed that arrive live and kicking for you to cook. Many airports in New England now have shops where you can purchase live lobsters and have them specially packed to take back on the plane with you.

A live lobster is a dappled, dark-green, sort of underwater-camouflage color. When boiled or broiled, it turns a brilliant red, so distinctive that "lobster red" has become a recognized color term.

Some people have tender feelings about cooking live lobsters, contending that because they thrash about and carry on when boiled they should be killed before they are put in the pot. Others say a lobster has practically no feeling in its nervous system, which I think is probably true. However, if you are squeamish about plunging a lobster in boiling water, put it in cold water, cover the pot, and bring the water to a full boil so the lobster just wafts away in a dreamy state. If you have no scruples, grasp the lobster behind the head, dip it head first in boiling salted water, cover the pot, and cook it. I find you get the best result if, after the water returns to the boil, you allow 5 minutes for the first pound and about 3 minutes for every other pound.

I don't cool the lobsters in the water because I find they then become overcooked. I take them out and cool them. Cold lobster, with well-seasoned mustardy mayonnaise and lemon, is my favorite, but I know many people who feel equally strong that nothing beats a lobster hot from the pot.

To tackle a boiled lobster, first cut off a little piece at the head and drain the liquid from the inside. Then divide the lobster in half, either by cutting the shell with shears or splitting it with a heavy knife and mallet. Inside is a rather weird anatomy. Most of the meat is in the body, along which runs a long black intestinal vein, which should be removed. In the head, behind the eyes, is the tiny stomach sac or craw, which again should be removed. You'll also see in the head little bits of meat, some green matter (this is the liver or tomalley and absolutely delicious) and, if the lobster is female, ruby-red "coral," the undeveloped spawn or roe. Interestingly enough, the spawn is much better raw than cooked, with a remarkable flavor, different from anything you've ever known. When cooked, it is rather dry and is best combined with the tomalley or worked into mayonnaise.

When you serve hot lobster, supply large napkins or bibs, shears, lobster crackers, and picks for getting the meat from the claws, plenty of melted butter and lemon, good bread, and either cold beer or chilled dry white wine. From there on, it's every man for himself. Everyone has his own particular fashion of eating a hot lobster, all equally satisfying.

I have always thought that broiled lobster was a much overrated dish, but many people, I know, feel it is the greatest. It must be carefully cooked, or the meat will be dry, tough and tasteless.

For broiling, the lobster must be split alive. The trick is to make a very deep incision with the point of a heavy knife where head and body meet, which severs the spinal cord and kills the lobster immediately. Then cut right through the entire length of the lobster with the knife and a mallet or with shears, drain it, and remove the vein and stomach. If you want to make a sauce with the tomalley and coral, remove them and fill the head cavity with seasoned bread or cracker crumbs (which may be mixed with shrimp or crabmeat). Salt, pepper, and butter the lobster halves well, put them flesh side up on the broiling pan, and broil about 4 to 5 inches from the heat for 12 to 15 minutes, basting frequently with melted butter, and a sprinkle of salt, pepper, and paprika if you wish.

Serve your broiled lobster with melted butter, which you may mix with the tomalley and coral, a touch of lemon juice, and a hint of garlic. Again, bread and foaming cold beer or chilled white wine are all you need with it.

First Catch Your Crayfish

When I was growing up in Oregon, we children would organize fishing parties at the beach in summer and trek up the Necanicum River with little nets, lots of string, and bits and pieces of fresh liver or part of an ear of corn, which we would put on string as bait. We would sit on the riverbanks and drag in crayfish by the dozen. Our catch was proudly hauled home to be cooked in a red wine court-boullion with plenty of seasonings and eaten for dinner that night with salad and good bread and butter. I can still remember how tasty those juicy little shellfish were.

Alas, in these days of industrial pollution and dirty streams in the Northwest—and many of the European countries, too—crayfish seem to have all but disappeared from our lives, and from menus. Only rarely now do you get crayfish in the Pacific Northwest although in Louisiana and the Delta country they are still eaten in vast quantities, with great gusto.

The people of Sweden and other Scandinavian countries think so highly of crayfish that they hold annual festivals, albeit some of the countries can no longer supply their own needs but have to depend on imports. August is the traditional time for the festivals, a time of merry uninhibited feasting, with two or three gulps of akvavit and swallows of beer along with every crayfish, so that by the time you get through with a couple of dozen you have done a pretty good job of both drinking and eating.

While summering in my native Oregon, I was surprised and delighted to receive a call from my friend John Bennett, a chef in San Francisco. John told me he had been getting marvelous crayfish and asked if I would like some. Would I! Before we knew it a parcel of crayfish had arrived alive and kicking by Greyhound bus. We immediately put on a court bouillon, tossed in the crayfish, and sat down to a superb and nostalgic luncheon of these little delicacies, with Finnish rye bread from the local bakery and ice-cold beer.

The crayfish came from two men who have formed the Burkhim-Tate Crayfish Company and are sending them to the San Francisco area, so there is new hope for all western lovers of crayfish. They can now feast on these succulent shellfish during the May to September season. The traps are now yielding a daily catch of 30 to 40 crayfish each, and it is hoped that the scope of the catches will increase as the business grows.

In San Francisco, John Bennett serves the crayfish à la nage, which means they are cooked in a rather elaborate court bouillon and either served warm in the liquid or allowed to cool in it and served cold. In another version, the famous gratin d'écrevisses that one finds in so many great restaurants in France, the cooked crayfish are taken out of the shells and served in a rich sauce, similar to Nantua sauce, made with the bouillon.

To my mind, one of the simplest and most delicious ways to cook these succulent shellfish is as *Crayfish à la Bordelaise*. For four, you'll need 36 to 40 crayfish. Make a *mirepoix* by cutting 2 carrots, 2 onions, and 2 ribs celery into fine julienne strips or dice. Melt 5 tablespoons butter in a large kettle, and cook these vegetables in the butter until just wilted. Season with salt and freshly ground black pepper. Add 2 cups dry white wine, let it cook for a few minutes, then add the crayfish and cook them just until the shells turn red, about 8 to 10 minutes. Mix in 1½ cups tomato purée or puréed Italian plum tomatoes, bring to a boil, and let the tomato blend with the other ingredients. Correct the seasoning, and pour the fragrant, steaming mixture into a large tureen or bowl. Serve with saffron rice, a green salad, crisp bread, and plenty of cold beer.

If you can find or order crayfish in your locality, they are something to hail with joy and treat with reverence. If you can't, you might try substituting a few small lobsters in this recipe, or jumbo shrimp.

Crayfish can also be turned into a very good and pretty salad. Remove the cooked meat from the tails and large claws, and serve on a bed of lettuce with some quartered hard-boiled eggs and two or three of the little red crayfish, in the shell, as garnish. Top with a rich mayonnaise, a rémoulade sauce, or a Louis dressing.

Shrimp in the Diminutive

Years ago, when I was writing *James Beard's Fish Cookery*, I learned a lot about shrimp, among other things that no other shellfish even approaches it in popularity. You can find cooked or raw shrimp in supermarkets in the smallest villages as well as fish markets in big cities. Shrimp, especially the ubiquitous shrimp cocktail (with a sometimes pretty badly flavored sauce that I have heard called "the red menace"), has become one of the more dominant aspects of American cuisine. In restaurants across the country you can order shrimp cocktail, shrimp salad, broiled shrimp, and shrimp masquerading under the name of "scampi", which they are not. Scampi belong to another family of shellfish, *Nephrops norvegicus*, known in France as *langoustines* and in England as Dublin Bay prawns.

The shrimp we eat come from all over the world—from Panama, the Indian Ocean, France, Denmark, and Norway as well as our own Atlantic and Pacific waters and the Gulf of Mexico. Although we have a wealth of shrimp in this country, all too few people know the delights of the very tiny shrimp from the coasts of Alaska, Maine, California, and Oregon, as delicate and delicious as any seafood can be. Maine, I'm happy to say, is making great strides in promoting these little beauties, marketing them frozen in the shell; frozen, shelled, and deveined, both cooked and uncooked; shelled; deveined, and breaded. If you buy these shrimp (the French call them *crevette rose*) in the shell with their heads on, they are great fun for a cocktail party. Just put out a huge pile of cooked shrimp and let everyone shell for himself. Of course, for a salad or creamed or curried shrimp, it is much easier to buy the shelled shrimp meat and save yourself the trouble, for it takes a lot of these tiny babies to make a pound, and the shelling is a pretty tedious job. One time in Alaska I saw a roomful of thirty or so Indian women, all wearing white cotton gloves to protect their hands while they shelled the shrimp—it was really quite a sight.

There are two vital points to remember when cooking shrimp. First, there is no reason to ruin the taste and texture by overcooking, no matter how large they are. Plunge them into rapidly boiling salted water, and after it returns to the boil give them no more than 3 to 5 minutes, according to size (for tiny shrimp, 1 minute is enough), then drain them immediately. Do not let them cool in the liquid, or they will continue to cook and get soft and mushy.

Second, always salt the water well—otherwise you won't get a good-tasting shrimp. I know shrimp live in salt water, but that doesn't salt them enough. For a subtler flavor, try cooking them in court bouillon instead of water. Combine water with white wine or a little wine vinegar, add your favorite herbs and spices, salt, and pepper, and let it cook for 4 to 5 minutes before adding the shrimp. It gives them a delicate and very pleasant taste. You can use the leftover court bouillon to make soup or a sauce for fish, first cooking it down to intensify the flavor and then straining it.

Before you cook shrimp, I think it is rather nice to devein them, although the Shrimp Association says there is no reason save aesthetics to remove the black vein—it certainly won't harm you if you don't. So take your choice. You can easily remove the vein when you peel the shrimp by cutting through the curve of the shell with scissors and washing the vein out. If you buy frozen shelled, deveined, and cooked shrimp, you won't have that problem.

Tiny shrimp make one of the world's greatest shrimp dishes, potted shrimp, which hails from England and is as commonly served there as shrimp cocktail is here. If you try it, I think you might well switch allegiance, for potted shrimp have a definite buttery spicy quality that is quite addictive. You can make this dish, at a pinch, with the tiny shelled canned Icelandic shrimp, but it is infinitely better with the little fresh ones.

To make enough *Potted Shrimp* to serve four as a first course, melt 6 ounces butter and pour off and reserve the clear part, discarding the sediment. Toss 1 pound tiny cooked and shelled shrimp in the hot clear butter, seasoning with ¼ to ⅓ teaspoon freshly grated nutmeg and a pinch or two of cayenne pepper as you do so. Add the seasoning little by little, and taste to see when it is to your liking. The nutmeg flavor should be noticeable but not overpowering, for the butter will absorb the spice as the shrimp chill and the butter solidifies. Ladle the buttery shrimp into small pots, and seal the top with a thin layer of more clarified butter (this will keep them for about a week). Chill in the refrigerator until cold.

Serve potted shrimp with cocktails or as a first course with thinly sliced buttered brown bread or homemade Melba toast, or, in the English manner, with thin slices of smoked salmon, which is a most luxurious and elegant way to start a dinner party.

You can also eat these sweet, delicious little shrimp without any kind of seasoning or sauce to enhance their flavor. I remember years ago that one of the international steamship lines served huge bowls of tiny shelled European shrimp on the bar at cocktail time, and people dipped in and ate them like peanuts.

Whenever I am on the West Coast, I eat my fill of the baby Pacific shrimp. In Vancouver I had them stacked high on half an avocado and bathed with a wondrous Louis sauce. I was served them skewered, four or five to a pick, with Dungeness crab legs, and tartar sauce as a dip. While I was staying at the beach in Oregon I made sandwiches of shrimp mixed with good homemade mayonnaise, and I had them for lunch in a spinach roll, which is actually a spinach soufflé baked in a jelly-roll pan. While it is not hard to make, it looks and tastes delicious.

For the *Spinach Roll*, you will need either 3 pounds fresh spinach or 4 packages frozen chopped spinach. Thaw frozen spinach in a pan over very gentle heat or pour boiling water over it. Drain extremely well, since frozen spinach has a high water content. Fresh spinach should be washed and well picked over, placed in a kettle with no water other than that clinging to the leaves, tightly covered. and wilted down. This takes a very few minutes. Drain it well and chop it coarsely.

Put the very well drained chopped fresh or frozen spinach in a bowl. Mix in 6 tablespoons melted butter, 1½ teaspoons salt, ½ teaspoon freshly ground black pepper, and 2 or 3 good dashes of nutmeg (nutmeg and spinach have a great affinity). Beat in 4 egg yolks, one by one, then beat the 4 egg whites until they hold soft peaks and fold them thoroughly into the spinach mixture. Taste for seasoning.

Lightly butter an 11-by-14-by-½-inch jelly-roll pan, line it with waxed paper, butter the paper, and coat it with bread crumbs. Spread the spinach mixture in the pan, even it with a rubber spatula, and sprinkle with a little grated Parmesan cheese. Bake in a 350-degree oven for about 15 minutes or until just firm when touched lightly with the fingers.

While the roll is baking, sauté ⅔ cup finely chopped onion or green onion in 4 tablespoons butter until just limp. Blend in 3 tablespoons flour, and cook for 2 or 3 minutes. Mix in ½ cup dry vermouth or white wine, stir well, and season to taste with salt and pepper, a dash of Tabasco, and 1 tablespoon chopped fresh tarragon or 1 teaspoon dried tarragon. Gradually stir in 1½ cups light or heavy cream or evaporated milk, cook, and stir until nicely thickened. Taste for seasoning. Mix in ½ cup chopped parsley and 1½ to 2 cups cooked tiny shrimp.

Remove the baked roll from the oven, cover it with a piece of buttered foil, and invert on a board. Peel off the waxed paper. Spread with two-thirds of the shrimp mixture, then very carefully roll up like a jelly roll onto a flat serving plate, using the foil as a pusher. Spoon the remaining shrimp over the center and serve at once to six people.

You can fill the roll with other mixtures—creamed seafood or asparagus tips or scrambled eggs. It is equally good hot or cold.

The World's
Most Famous Fish Stew

During a recent vacation in Provence, I spent a morning at one of the local fish markets, where stall after stall was crammed with a splendid display of Mediterranean fish. This led me to muse on the one dish which, more than any other, signifies to most people Provence and its coast, and that is bouillabaisse.

Later, I happened to be leafing through some magazines, and in one called *Gastronomie* I came across a whole issue dealing with many different versions of how bouillabaisse first came to be. It was utterly fascinating, and though I'm not sure which version I believe, or even if I believe any of them, I'll tell you a couple and let you decide.

A major error in one version was the statement that the first bouillabaisse, described as a discovery of the ancient Greeks that traveled to Rome and eventually to Marseille, included tomatoes. Now, as we all know, tomatoes were not introduced to Europe until after the discovery of America and didn't really come into common use until the middle of the eighteenth century, and thus were not even dreamed of in ancient Greece. It's perfectly possible, of course, that the forerunner of this great fish stew did originate in Greece, because the same fish are found there that are available in Provence and southern Italy, but it seems fairly certain to me that it was the Provençaux who, throughout the years, developed their own pattern for it, a pattern far removed from the original.

There's another, rather charming version that intrigued me because I have spent some time in the port of Les-Saintes-Maries-de-la-Mer in the Camargue, named for the saints who supposedly set sail for Marseille to escape from the Holy Land after the crucifixion—St. Mary Magdalene, St. Mary Jacob, St. Mary Salome, St. Mary of Bathsheba, St. Martha, and St. Trophine among others. The story goes that they ran into a terrible storm that almost tore the boat to pieces and were washed ashore on a deserted beach where, after sleeping for almost two days, they awoke to find fishermen with great pots of this fragrant stew. At this tiny little port in the Camargue, the arrival of the Marys is still celebrated every year at the end of May.

Anyway, I'll go along with the idea that bouillabaisse is one of the oldest seafood dishes known to man. It really cannot be prepared anywhere but around or near the Mediterranean, because to give a bouillabaisse the quality it needs, one must have certain traditional fish such as conger eel, rascasse, and St. Pierre, plus a variety of other ingredients—some people put in one thing, some another.

Perhaps the finest bouillabaisse I know is served at a restaurant that has long been a favorite of mine, l'Escale, 27 kilometers west of Marseille in the village of Carry-le-Rouet. Next to this I'd put the bouillabaisse at the Brasserie des Catalans, in Marseille.

Since we can't make a true bouillabaisse here, we have to be satisfied with our own fish stews or soups—clam and fish chowder and the cioppino of California, which is probably our finest effort.

To make *Cioppino*, first steam 1 quart clams or mussels in 1 cup red or white wine until they open (discard any that don't) and remove from shells. Strain broth through a fine cloth and reserve. Heat ½ cup olive oil in a large pot, add 1 large chopped onion, 2 finely chopped garlic cloves, 1 chopped green pepper, and ¼ pound dried mushrooms, soaked in water until soft. Cook 3 minutes, then add 4 peeled, seeded, and chopped tomatoes, and cook 4 minutes. Add the strained broth, 4 tablespoons Italian tomato paste, and 2 cups California red wine, preferably Pinot Noir. Season to taste with salt and freshly ground black pepper. Simmer 20 minutes, then taste for seasoning. Add 3 pounds sea bass or striped bass, cut in serving pieces, or thick fillets of firm-fleshed fish, cut in pieces. Cook just until done, then add the clams or mussels, 1 pound crabmeat (or 2 Dungeness crabs, in pieces and sections), and 1 pound raw shelled shrimp. Simmer just until shrimp are cooked. Sprinkle with 3 tablespoons chopped parsley and serve to six, with crisp French or Italian bread.

A rather simpler shellfish stew, one that I have been teaching my students for over fifteen years and never tire of, is *Seafood Mediterranée*. This is a perfect party dish, quick to make, and invariably popular.

Heat ½ cup olive oil in a large sauté pan or skillet. Add 3 chopped garlic cloves and 6 rock lobster tails, shelled and cut in thirds, and sauté them very quickly. Add 1 cup white wine, 2 cups Italian plum tomatoes, 1 teaspoon oregano, 2 bay leaves, 1½ teaspoons salt, and ½ teaspoon freshly ground black pepper. Arrange 12 cherrystone clams around the edge of the pan, hinged side down, bring to a boil, reduce the heat, cover, and cook 5 minutes. Add 1 pound shrimp, shelled but the tails left on, cover, and cook 3 minutes, or until the shrimp are pink and the clams open. (Sometimes clams are a little recalcitrant. Steam any that have not opened for a few more minutes, after removing the other shellfish, then discard any really stubborn ones that have not opened.) Sprinkle the fish stew with 1 cup chopped parsley, and serve in soup plates or bowls, with plenty of French bread to mop up the juices. Serve to six.

Clam Chowder, Northwest Style

One of the most famous of the dishes considered to be all-American is clam chowder. Chowder, as you may know, is derived from the French word *chaudière*, and it came to New England by way of the French Canadian fishermen who drifted across the border and were wont to cook up their fish stew or soups in a big pot, or *chaudière*. The New Englanders picked up other recipes from French Canada—for example, long before Yankee pot roast was ever heard of, they were making various versions of *boeuf à la mode*.

Chowder is a basic theme that has known all sorts of variations. New England clam chowder is made with salt pork, potatoes, milk, and quahogs, cherrystones, or littlenecks. Some New Englanders will tell you that there is only one type of clam you can use, while others recommend a different one. Then we have Manhattan clam chowder, considered by many to be a "bastard" chowder. Certainly it must have had a Mediterranean base, because it includes tomatoes and is redolent of herbs that scream Italy or Greece, while the flavor, texture, and quality are entirely different.

On the West Coast, especially the Northwest where you have razor clams, the chowder is similar to the New England version, although at times light or heavy cream will be used instead of milk, so this becomes, in a way, a much more formal soup. You also find bacon included, rather than salt pork, probably because people here had their own smokehouses.

I'm going to give you my family recipe for *Oregon Clam Chowder*, which I think is damn good. It is easy to do and can be made, if necessity bids, with canned razor clams.

Drain 1½ cups chopped or ground clams, preferably razor clams, and reserve meat and liquor. If you grind the clams yourself, be sure not to throw away the liquor that comes from them. If you don't have much clam liquor, you can add a bit of bottled clam juice, though there is usually enough.

Cut 3 slices of salt pork or thickly sliced smoked bacon into small shreds, and cook in a skillet over medium heat until quite crisp. Remove and drain on paper towels. Add to the fat in the pan 1 finely chopped medium onion, and brown lightly. Thinly slice 2 medium potatoes, and cook in 2 cups boiling salted water until just tender. Add the bacon, onion, clam liquor, and salt and pepper to taste, and simmer 5 minutes. Add 3 cups light cream and bring to a boil. Correct seasoning, add ground clams, and just

heat through. Serve with a dollop of butter in each bowl, a mere
pinch of thyme, and a little chopped parsley. Serves four to six.

While this is not the traditional New England clam chowder, it is
awfully good.

Gastropods for Gastronomes

I can remember when people referred to the French with great disdain as "snail eaters," and anyone going to France was warned that he might, all unawares, be served snails in a restaurant without knowing what he was getting. Snails were regarded as highly suspect, something to be avoided at all costs. That attitude has changed with the times. In my travels across the country during the last ten years I've found *escargots à la bourguignonne* on the menus of restaurants where I certainly didn't expect to discover anything as sophisticated as snails. I've been even more amazed to find that the children of some of my friends just love to eat these mysterious little morsels. There's no doubt about it: snails are becoming ever more popular here.

According to a charming legend that goes back a great many years in American gastronomy, someone of French origin who loved snails brought a few to this country—I believe to California—and from that small beginning they spread far and wide.

There are, of course, different types of edible snails—the sea snail, or periwinkle; the small snails from North Africa that we occasionally see fresh in our markets; the *Helix asperse*, or common garden snail; and its superior relative *Helix pomatia*, the larger vineyard snail that is cultivated in France on special snail farms. Some people think those repulsive slimy slugs we find in the garden are edible snails. They are not, although they, too, are mollusks. The edible snail has a beautiful striped shell and a head with delicate feelers that it can tuck back into the shell, shutting itself in. It feasts fastidiously on grass and the leaves of trees and vines.

Fortunately, we don't have to go out into the vineyards to catch our snails, nor do we have to go through the processes of preparing them— soaking them in several changes of tepid water to make them cleanse themselves, boiling them for 5 minutes, taking them out of the shells and removing the inedible parts, rinsing them, and cleaning the shells. The Dutch, the Belgians, and the French have done all that for us. They clean, cook, and can the snails and package them for sale with the sterilized shells in an acetate tube, box, or plastic bag, grading them according to size—super extra, extra large, and very large. All you have to do is open a can of these imported snails, rinse them, make the snail butter, and pop them back in the shells to be heated with the butter in the oven to an aromatic, irresistible succulence.

When the snails are heated in the shells, they are usually put on metal or pottery snail plates, about the size of a shirred-egg dish, that have small indentations, one for each shell. Or the shells may be put on small baking dishes on a bed of rock salt, although this is not customary.

Instead of heating the snails in the shells, some people prefer to use the enchanting little snail pots sold in cookware shops. These measure about 1½ inches in diameter at the widest point, just large enough to tuck in one or two snails with a good dollop of snail butter.

⟫ *Snail Butter* can vary a great deal, but for, let us say, 4 dozen snails, enough for four to eight people (a good snail eater can easily get away with a dozen), cream ¼ pound soft but not melted butter with 2 to 3 tablespoons finely chopped shallots, 2 to 3 finely chopped garlic cloves (or more, if you like the flavor), about ¼ cup chopped parsley, and a little salt and freshly ground black pepper. Some people like very parsleyed snails, while others prefer a rich garlic flavor or the delicacy of shallots. By changing the proportions of these ingredients in the mixture, you can develop a snail butter that is yours alone.

Slip the snails into the shells, and cover them well with the snail butter. Leave in the refrigerator for a number of hours so the butter penetrates and flavors the snails. To heat, arrange the shells on the hollows of the plates and pour a tablespoon of white wine over each one. Bake in a 450-degree oven for 7 to 8 minutes, until the butter, melting and mingling with the wine, gives forth an almost unbearably delicious smell.

Now if you want to be very correct, you'll serve the snails with the special little snail tongs made to pick up and hold each shell, and the rather long, two-pronged forks for fishing them out. Actually it isn't necessary to buy these contraptions. You can use an oyster fork and, protecting your fingers with paper napkins, hold the very hot shells. You will need plenty of French bread to mop up the lovely melted butter. Real snail lovers often sip the last drop of juices from the shell after removing the snail and most of the butter. Drink some red or white wine with your snails—either one goes rather well.

Snails aren't always served in shells or pots. I once had them in mushroom caps that had been half-broiled with lightly garlic-flavored butter. One or two snails were put in each mushroom cap, finely chopped walnuts were sprinkled over them, and a little dab of snail butter put on top. These were popped in a hot oven for 8 minutes and then served on little rounds of fried toast—bread cut in circles and sautéed in butter until brown and crisp. They were, I can tell you, exquisite.

However, to the average American, snails in the shell with snail butter, the classic *escargots à la bourguignonne*, are the thing. You can even buy them ready-prepared and frozen in the shell, butter and all, so you only have to heat them, a sure sign of their widespread popularity and, to me, a mark of great progress for the American palate.

⁊ CHAPTER 3 ⁊

Earthy Subjects

☙

... *in which we squeeze, shred, spit, and roast a variety of vegetables ... bring out the vegetable plate...learn new ways with asparagus, radishes, lettuce, and cucumbers ... lament the decline of the tomato ... admire avocados ... bank on mushrooms ... ponder potatoes, onions, and the sweet beet ... meet the cabbage family and its salty sister ... economize with chickpeas and lentils ... go on a bean binge ... and hear a tale of two salads.*

Please Squeeze the Vegetables

The longer I cook vegetables, the more I learn about them. In the last year I have discovered a great deal about purées and shredded vegetables, which are among the most delicate and delicious of preparations. I've also found out the advantages of squeezing certain vegetables before cooking them. Why squeeze vegetables? Mainly to remove most of the excess liquid they contain, which makes them much pleasanter to eat.

Zucchini, for instance, becomes a totally different vegetable when it is shredded and squeezed. I like to use a Mouli julienne, a marvelous gadget with three interchangeable disks that you can find in the better kitchen shops. By simply turning the handle, you can shred vegetables from extremely fine to fairly coarse. After shredding the zucchini, I put it in a clean dish towel and squeeze until the water oozes out. Then I quickly sauté the zucchini in a mixture of oil and butter, maybe with a little garlic and grated cheese, either cooking it until it browns on one side, turning it, and browning the other side, or covering and steaming it. Either way it comes out wonderfully crisp and bitey, with none of that soggy, droopy quality one usually associates with zucchini.

Another vegetable that takes well to this treatment is the cucumber. Thoroughly squeezed, then steamed in butter with a touch of chopped fresh dill or tarragon and some lemon juice, it is an unbeatable accompaniment to fish, veal, or pork.

Squeezing also benefits chopped mushrooms. If, after chopping, you squeeze the mushrooms well in a dish towel, you'll find they cook more quickly and don't leave a soupy residue in the pan. This is true of any dish that calls for chopped mushrooms, like *duxelles* (see page 88), and don't, for heaven's sake, throw away those squeezed-out juices—they are just great for flavoring soups, broths, or sauces.

Chopped parsley for a garnish will be much nicer and fluffier if you give it a good squeeze after chopping. Squeezing also benefits tomatoes, which today seem to have much more water content than they used to, whether they are those semi-red cannonballs we get in winter or the luscious garden-ripened ones of summer.

Peel the tomatoes, cut the top slice off, then grasp them firmly in your hand and squeeze, so the seeds and most of the liquid dribble out, leaving only the firm flesh to be chopped for a tomato purée or a sauce. Sauté the chopped tomatoes in butter, letting them just melt down, and you'll find they take on another quality completely.

    I have a standard *Tomato Sauce*, which I use for all kinds of dishes. For this you scald 3 pounds tomatoes in boiling water, then peel them, cut a slice off the top, and squeeze out seeds and juices. Chop the flesh rather finely, and put to drain in a colander. Heat 4 tablespoons butter and 2 tablespoons olive oil, or 6 tablespoons olive oil, in a heavy skillet, add the tomatoes, and let them just melt down over medium heat. As they begin to heat through, add 1 crushed garlic clove (it need not be peeled—all you want is to impart the flavor) or 2 or 3 garlic cloves, if you like garlic extremely well. Season with 1½ teaspoons salt, 1 teaspoon dried basil or several leaves of fresh basil, and a few grinds of black pepper. If the tomatoes are very acid, you can add a tiny fillip of sugar, which will give them a better flavor.

Cook the sauce very slowly for ¾ to 1 hour. Then, if you feel it is too liquid and needs strong binding flavor and texture, add a 6-ounce can of tomato paste, which will give you a very thick sauce. (Be careful it doesn't splash on you when it boils up.) Taste for seasoning before using.

If you can't get decent tomatoes, you can use the 35-ounce can of Italian plum tomatoes, cooking them down well to eliminate the excess liquid before adding the tomato paste. They don't have quite the same flavor as fresh tomatoes, but the quality is excellent.

This is a good, honest, basic tomato sauce, perfect for seafood such as lobster, shrimp, or crab, for cooking chicken, or with vegetables, rice, or pasta. Add a little fish broth, and you have a richly flavored fish sauce. Or add meat broth, or mushroom broth and some chopped cooked mushrooms for enrichment. You might also try this perfectly wonderful luncheon or supper dish, a very great favorite of mine:

✎ Poach big fat Italian sausages in water or white wine, drain, then smother them in the tomato sauce and let them cook a little. Serve with rice or pasta, or put them on top of polenta, that Italian cornmeal delight, cover with the sauce, grate Parmesan cheese or a mixture of Parmesan and Gruyère over the sauce, or put some slices of mozzarella on top, and put in the oven until melted.

☙

Vegetables and the Outdoor Menu

The Greeks have a word for and a way with fresh young vegetables that is just right for the summer months when the passing parade in the markets and gardens is too tempting to resist. Many people neglect vegetables because they don't know what to do with them. When I go to the markets here and in Europe, I buy just about every one I can find at the peak of its growth, then turn my haul into large batches of vegetables à la Grecque.

Vegetables à la Grecque are as old as time, but surprisingly enough not too well known, although this is one of the simplest and most delicious ways of cooking seasonal vegetables. Little green beans and wax beans, whole green onions or tiny white onions, small firm mushroom caps, halved celery hearts, artichokes, leeks, fingers or cubes of eggplant, sliced or halved zucchini—nearly all the vegetables in our ken except peas— lend themselves to this style of preparation. Since they are eaten cold rather than hot, they can be made in quantity, refrigerated in containers for weeks, and brought out as you want them. It's a great way to take advantage of the seasonal drop in price and to enjoy vegetables all summer long with a minimum of effort. Fall and winter vegetables can be treated in the same manner—halved or quartered fennel bulbs, cauliflowerets, broccoli buds.

 For *Vegetables à la Grecque*, you must make a poaching liquid or court bouillon. For 1 pound string beans or 1 large eggplant cubed, or 8 artichoke bottoms or 4 artichoke quarters, combine in a large shallow pan or deep skillet ½ cup olive, corn, or peanut oil, ⅓ cup vinegar, ⅓ cup dry white wine or vermouth, 1 teaspoon salt, ½ teaspoon freshly ground black pepper, 1 bay leaf, 1 or 2 cloves garlic, a dash of Tabasco, and 1 teaspoon thyme, tarragon, oregano, or basil, whichever you prefer (if you have fresh basil in your garden, so much the better). Let's say you're using green beans, in which case you'd leave them whole but cut the ends off. Place them in the mixture and add water to barely cover. Bring to a boil very slowly, then reduce the heat and poach until they are just crispy tender. Remove from the heat, taste the liquid for seasoning, to see if it needs more salt, then let the beans cool in the liquid. When they are well cooled, transfer to a serving dish and chill lightly in the refrigerator or in a cold place. Serve sprinkled with chopped parsley.

For a big party, you might cook three or four different vegetables, giving each one an appropriate herb—thyme for beans, oregano for eggplant, basil for zucchini—and serve them as a first course, a salad, or a vegetable course. Or team a couple of them with a grilled steak or hamburgers, some good bread, and fresh fruit for a wonderful outdoor dinner.

🔊 Little white onions can be given a slightly different treatment. This version is not called à la Grecque but *Onions Monegasque*, after the principality of Monaco. To the à la Grecque poaching liquid add a healthy pinch of saffron, and when the onions are just starting to get tender, mix in 2 tablespoons tomato paste and ½ cup seedless raisins. Cook until the raisins are puffed and the onions barely tender but still crisp and crunchy. Cool them in the liquid.

I make a lot of these, using about 45 to 50 peeled white onions, refrigerate them in jars, and serve them all summer because my guests love them so much. The saffron gives a distinctive flavor and, blended with the tomato paste, the prettiest color imaginable. You can also cook wax beans in the same manner.

Another good way to prepare summer vegetables is to cook them in beef, chicken, or mushroom broth with salt and pepper until they are crisply tender. Cool them in the liquid (don't overcook—they will continue cooking as they cool), and chill them in the refrigerator until you are ready to use them. Drain, transfer to a serving dish or salad bowl, and give them a generous covering of vinaigrette sauce (3 parts oil to 1 part vinegar with salt and pepper to taste) and some chopped fresh herbs and parsley. Serve these vegetables vinaigrette as a salad or with grilled foods, as part of a cold buffet, or for a picnic. Vegetables cooked in this way do not need to be eaten icy cold, just at room temperature. Remember, the poached vegetables should not be cooked to death. They should still have a slight bite to them and be well marinated so the flavors of the poaching liquid or dressing mingle with and enhance their own natural goodness.

One of my favorite outdoor meals starts with an hors d'oeuvre table substantial enough to be a full course as well as an accompaniment to drinks, followed by an entrée grilled over charcoal, a hearty vegetable dish, then fruit and cheese. I might have little patties of chopped meat, or a tiny club steak, or a ham slice basted with mustard and honey, or grilled fish, with a gratin of potatoes. By serving less meat, a menu can actually be more festive and much more interesting.

A day ahead, make your vegetables à la Grecque or vinaigrette and chill them. Then bring them out in attractive serving dishes along with crusty bread, sweet butter, and some chilled white wine—I like the good, inexpensive California jug wines, or the country wines from France that you can now buy in economical half-gallons.

If you can buy those unwaxed English-type hothouse cucumbers, the kind that need no peeling, simply slice them paper-thin, sprinkle with salt, and toss in a mixture of half mayonnaise, half sour cream. Leave to wilt for several hours, then sprinkle with chopped parsley or chives. Tomatoes are at their best in summer. Peel and thinly slice several ripe tomatoes, dress them with olive oil and wine vinegar, and sprinkle with chopped fresh basil or chives, or maybe some finely chopped green onions.

So now you have your vegetables à la Grecque or vinaigrette and your tomato and cucumber salads. Round out your hors d'oeuvre table with any of these other foods: thinly sliced prosciutto and salami; anchovies; herring tidbits; Norwegian sardines, nicely arranged with halved hard-boiled eggs and sprinkled with chopped parsley; Polish sausage, heated in red wine, sliced, and served hot; cold asparagus; cole slaw; potato salad; stuffed eggs with Russian dressing; fresh shrimp or crabmeat with mayonnaise.

The number of things you can have for an hors d'oeuvre table is endless, and if you don't feel like getting the grill going, a hearty hors d'oeuvre table alone can serve as your Sunday lunch or supper.

Vegetables, Spitted and Foiled

In summer, I'm very often asked what to serve with grilled meats, poultry, and fish. Naturally, one can always count on casseroles and vegetable dishes prepared indoors, but it is rather more fun and a lot more unusual to serve vegetables cooked right on the barbecue grill or spit. I don't know how many of you who have grills with electric rotisseries have tried spit-roasted vegetables, but I can assure you they make pretty exciting eating. While you can't do every sort of vegetable that way, some just seem to be made for it.

Take potatoes. Huge Idahos, spitted and revolved for about an hour in their well-scrubbed skins, taste superlatively good with lamb chops or steak. Big fat yams, which require about the same time as Idahos, take on a wonderful flavor when spit-roasted over charcoal, as do big unpeeled onions. Let the onions revolve for 45 to 50 minutes if you like them very soft, about 25 for crisply soft. Serve with grilled steaks and roast beef. They will be hot and crisp all the way through, neither strong-tasting like a raw onion nor as sweet as one that is fully cooked.

Whole green peppers, so delicious with lamb or pork, are also good for roasting. Don't seed them before spitting, or it will leave too big a hole; seed them when they are done, which takes about 20 minutes. A combination of the peppers and the crispy roasted onions tastes awfully good with, perhaps, a sliced tomato salad.

A whole large eggplant, spitted and roasted, will be creamy and delectable after about an hour, the skin enticingly charred. Split and serve to be seasoned to taste and eaten from the skin. Or try roasting whole acorn or banana squash over medium heat for an hour, then split, seed, and serve. The huge Hubbard squash should be cut in big hunks, speared, and revolved for 50 minutes to an hour over medium heat. I think you'll find that this novel approach to vegetable cookery introduces a whole new world of flavor.

You can foil vegetables too, which to my mind is often more satisfactory than spit-roasting. For this you take a square of heavy-duty aluminum foil big enough to envelop whatever you want to grill. Put the vegetables and seasonings in the center, bring up the top and bottom edges, fold them together, overlap the folds, and then fold the sides.

 ␛These neat, compact little packages of *Foiled Vegetables* which don't take up much space, can be tucked around the chicken or meat, at the sides of the grill. To go with chicken, combine fresh green peas and tiny young carrots, not too thick. Wash the carrots well (if they are crisp there is no need to peel them) and place on the foil. Allow 3 to 4 carrots per serving and add ½ to ⅔ cup peas, a pat of butter, and salt and pepper to taste. Grill about 30 minutes. Tiny boiling onions, peeled, put in foil with a dab of butter, salt and pepper, and, if you like, a touch of grated Parmesan cheese, also take 30 minutes. Shake the packages once in a while so they don't stick to the foil, and they will come out all steamy and fragrant, even better if you have added a tablespoon of sherry or Madeira before sealing the package.

For a favorite of mine, *Foiled Ratatouille*, arrange on each foil square a slice of smallish eggplant, a slice of onion, a slice of tomato, a tiny bit of chopped garlic, salt, pepper, a touch of basil, 2 tablespoons olive oil, and, if you wish, 1 or 2 mushroom slices. Seal well and cook about 30 minutes. Serve with roast lamb, lamb chops or hamburgers.

Whole tomatoes, peeled or not, cook beautifully in foil. I find they are better if you first gently squeeze out juice and seeds. Place the tomato on the foil with butter, pepper, salt, fresh or dried basil, and the merest hint of chopped garlic, if you like it. Seal securely, and cook on the grill from 20 to 25 minutes. I take mine off at 20 before they get too mushy; at 25 they will be semistewed. These are always extremely popular, so make a few extra for seconds.

Then there's that summer favorite, corn, which emerges tender, buttery, and mouth-wateringly good when cooked in foil. Husk young fresh ears, brush well with melted butter, season with salt, seal, and cook over the coals for 10 to 15 minutes, turning two or three times. Once in a while you might add a sprinkling of chili powder, which gives the corn a sprightly quality, or a small amount of chopped green pepper for complementary flavor.

When you remove your foil packages from the grill, pop them in small baskets or other containers and serve one to a person, to be unfolded or opened with scissors at the table. It's a simple, effective, and efficient way to cook vegetables outdoors.

Peel That Pepper

Probably one of the most versatile and varied vegetables we have, and one that is often overlooked, is the pepper. Peppers belong to the *Capsicum* family, and are relatives of the eggplant, tomato, and potato. They are believed to have originated in tropical America (they were cultivated more than 2,000 years ago by pre-Incan tribes), spreading to Europe, Asia, and Africa at a fairly early date, so that now they are firmly entrenched in the cuisines of many different countries.

Most familiar to us are the big round or tapering sweet or bell peppers, which are green to start with and then, as they mature, change their face and turn red. Then there are the pale green or light yellow sweet chili peppers, the pimiento pepper, and various and sundry hot chili peppers of all shapes, colors, and sizes, some of them extremely colorful and exotic. These often seem to increase in fieriness as they decrease in size. Such seasonings and spices as Tabasco, paprika, chili powder, cayenne, and crushed red pepper, all made from different hot peppers, are a very important part of our cooking.

I like the green and red bell peppers for garnishing and as a raw vegetable, but I find that more and more I prefer them when they have been grilled or broiled until the skin can be scraped off, a process in which the flesh becomes slightly cooked and much more flavorful. I find the skin of most bell peppers, either raw or cooked, to be rather disagreeable, so now I always grill my peppers before using them, which can be done on a charcoal grill in summer, under the broiler, or over a gas flame. I lay the whole peppers on the grill over the coals, or on the broiling pan close to the broiler, and let the skin scorch and blacken—and I do mean blacken. You must keep turning them from side to side until the entire skin surface is pretty well charred and blackened, and then scrape it off with the back of a silver knife or some sort of scraper. You don't want to tear the flesh, merely to scrape off the skin, which you will find comes off quite easily.

Then remove the stem and the seeds, because in even the sweetest of sweet peppers the seeds sometimes tend to be hot. Cut the peppers in strips or quarters, and you are ready to turn them into a delicious salad or appetizer.

    For *Sweet Peppers with Anchovies*, remove the skin, stem, and seeds from 12 to 15 bell peppers, and quarter or halve them. Arrange in a flat serving dish. Dress with 8 tablespoons olive oil, 1 to 2 tablespoons wine vinegar (I find the sherry wine vinegar sold in specialty food shops is especially good—it has a lovely, full, nutty flavor), 1 teaspoon or more of salt, and a few grinds of black pepper. Let the peppers marinate in the dressing for several hours. Remove to a serving plate, combine with 2 cans anchovy fillets, drained, and 2 tablespoons chopped parsley, and serve as an appetizer. Or you may serve them in the dish in which they marinated and pass the anchovies and parsley separately. Add tuna fish and capers to this combination for a more substantial dish, or serve just the marinated peppers with capers and parsley as a delightful salad or hors d'oeuvre.

You can use your basic marinated peppers as a salad, add them to a green salad with some sliced raw mushrooms, or use them to garnish a rice or potato salad. There is no end to the ways peppers can add gusto and flavor to your everyday meals. Skin and seed them, cut in ½-inch strips, and sauté them quickly in olive oil, adding a dash of wine vinegar just before taking them off the heat, and you have an unusual and inexpensive vegetable for outdoor meals, to accompany roast or barbecued pork chops, or other barbecued meats.

Don't think for one moment that your favorite stuffed pepper recipe won't be twice as good if you take the trouble to skin the peppers before stuffing them. The difference in texture and taste is well worth the effort, and you'll probably be able to cut down a little bit on the baking time. I have a stuffed pepper recipe I use in my classes that you might like to try.

For *Peppers Stuffed with Anchovies and Raisins*, remove the skin from 8 green peppers as previously directed (otherwise, parboil them for 10 minutes in salted water). Split in half lengthwise, and remove seeds. Arrange in a baking dish or two baking dishes. For the filling, combine ½ cup raisins, ½ cup pine nuts, 16 chopped anchovies, 2 finely minced garlic cloves, 2½ cups bread croutons (previously sautéed in oil and butter until golden brown), 2 teaspoons chopped parsley, 2 teaspoons dry vermouth, and salt and pepper to taste (go easy on the salt, as the anchovies are salty). Mix well. Fill peppers with this, put 1 teaspoon olive oil on the top of each one, and bake in a 350-degree oven for 30 minutes. Serve as a first course.

Harvest of Good Eating

The months of harvest bring some of the greatest of all treats fr(den and countryside. I'm thinking especially of the big luscio yellow tomatoes, sweet peppers, and chili peppers in glowing green, red, and yellow. Tomatoes and peppers, with eggplant and squash, onions, and garlic, are the makings of the French ratatouille, a dish that is the epitome of the wonderful flavor of the fall vegetables.

Recently I have found that in making *ratatouille*, the secret is to use equal quantities of everything except garlic, herbs, and seasonings. If you haven't prepared *Ratatouille* in some time, you might like to try it this way. First, heat ½ cup oil—it can be olive or peanut oil, but olive oil definitely gives the best taste—in a heavy skillet and very gently sauté 5 finely chopped garlic cloves. Add 1 ½ cups chopped onion, and let that melt down and blend with the garlic, then put in 1½ cups coarsely chopped green or red pepper, 1½ cups rather coarsely diced eggplant with the skin on (it doesn't need to be soaked or salted before- hand), and 1½ cups zucchini, sliced and quartered, or, if you prefer, shredded on the coarse side of a grater and squeezed in a dish towel to rid it of excess water.

Blend these vegetables together well by mixing them with a wooden spatula and shaking the pan. Then add your seasonings—1 tablespoon salt, 1 teaspoon freshly ground black pepper, and 2 or 3 tablespoons chopped fresh basil or 2 teaspoons dried basil. You can also add a touch of cayenne pepper or Tabasco. Cook for about 10 minutes over very brisk heat, stirring almost constantly, then add 1½ cups peeled, seeded, and chopped ripe tomatoes, or if you can't get really good fresh tomatoes, 1½ cups canned Italian plum tomatoes. Let the tomatoes blend in, and cook the ratatouille down to the consistency you like. Some want their ratatouille extremely crisp and chunky, and other prefer it cooked to a thick, soft mixture—it all depends on your personal taste. If you feel it is too dry, you can add a little additional liquid, such as tomato juice, water, or broth, let it blend and cook down, and correct the seasoning.

Ratatouille is a theme that has infinite variations. You can add all kinds of other vegetables, according to taste, mushrooms, perhaps, sliced fennel or celery, a few leftover beans, and even a few Greek or Italian olives, or a little grated lemon rind or a squeeze of lemon juice, which gives a lovely fresh, zippy flavor. This is just about the most versatile of vegetable dishes, and one in which you can use your imagination. Served

., ratatouille is one of the best of all accompaniments to roast lamb or chicken or hamburgers, or you can have it cold, with the addition of a little oil and vinegar and chopped parsley, as a first course, or a light luncheon dish.

If you are looking for a way to stretch meat—and who isn't these days?—bake *Lamb Shanks with Ratatouille*. Say you have bought half a dozen nice meaty lamb shanks. Trim off the excess fat, dust them with flour seasoned with salt and freshly ground black pepper, and sear them well on all sides in 4 tablespoons butter and 2 tablespoons oil until they are nicely browned. Add 2 finely chopped garlic cloves, 1 bay leaf, 1 teaspoon dried oregano or tarragon, and 2 cups stock. Cover and simmer for 1 hour. Meanwhile, cook your ratatouille and transfer it to a baking dish. Top with the lamb shanks, and pour the pan juices over them. Cover and bake in a 350-degree oven for 20 minutes, then take off the cover and bake 15 to 20 minutes longer, or until the shanks are tender and a luscious golden-brown.

Or, how about *Leftover Pot Roast with Ratatouille*? Put a layer of ratatouille in the bottom of the casserole, then a layer of cold sliced pot roast, then another layer of ratatouille. Cover, and heat in a 350-degree oven for 35 minutes, or until the meat is heated through and the ratatouille bubbling. You can sprinkle the top with grated Gruyère cheese during the last 10 minutes. This, with steamed rice and a carafe of robust red California jug wine, makes a delicious, satisfying, and cheeringly inexpensive dinner.

The Vegetable Alternative

Every now and then I get a letter from one of my readers that is so interesting, or contains such a good idea, that I want to share it with all of you. A few weeks ago I had a letter from Mrs. Theodore R. Roberts of Eugene, Oregon, who wrote, "In this garden-conscious time, it would be pertinent to revive a once-standard item on restaurant menus, the vegetable plate. As with anything, it can be delectable or appalling, but last evening I discovered a refinement that abolished the problem of having the yolk of the poached egg run into the vegetables.

"Because of a European trip, our garden was planted late, and just yesterday I picked the first cucumbers and a handful of bush beans of a small size. The beans needed nothing but seasoning and butter, and the cucumbers were served with vinegar, sour cream and chopped chives. I'd been wanting to try a recipe for *tortilla de patatas*, which we had liked in Spain, and that was the substitute for the poached egg. The potatoes and onions that were cooked and folded into the omelet were not from our garden, but the chopped parsley was. Since I picked enough ever-bearing strawberries to top part of the baking-powder biscuits I baked, for a shortcake, we had a meal that was both enjoyable and economical."

I don't know how many of you can remember when every restaurant had a vegetable plate—a collection of various cooked vegetables with a poached egg in the middle. Sometimes it was extremely good eating, and sometimes absolutely miserable. Anyway, Mrs. Roberts's solution is a very attractive one that I think bears adopting.

As a matter of fact, I have been experimenting more and more this year with vegetables, both hot and cold. Often I combine them, perhaps having two or three different vegetables at a meal. I happen to enjoy them, but I also think it gives a menu a refreshing feeling and a change of pace. If you take pains with vegetables—and there are just heaps of ways to do them—they can be one of the most satisfactory of all courses.

For instance, when beautiful red peppers are in season, I char them under the broiler, scrape the skin off, and cut the peppers in very thin strips. I put them in a dish, dress them with salt, pepper, oil, and vinegar, and let them stand and marinate, sometimes for several days. They can be served alone, or with a little onion, or with any combination of vegetables, and they are good either cold or hot. I also like to cook green beans until they are crisply tender, have them with butter or olive oil and chopped garlic or basil, save what is left over, and serve them the next day as a cold vegetable with the addition of a little vinegar.

The other night I had cold green beans with the peppers, and cold beets with sour cream and a little lemon juice. With these two cold dishes

I served something which is rather like Mrs. Roberts's Spanish tortilla of potatoes, only this happens to be an Italian version.

   To make a *Frittata of Potatoes*, first melt 6 tablespoons butter in a large, heavy skillet. When it is just foaming, add 6 well-beaten eggs and 1½ to 2 cups sliced cold boiled potatoes (or you can use cold sautéed potatoes if you happen to have some left over), spreading the potatoes around the pan. Add to this 2 or 3 finely chopped garlic cloves, 1½ teaspoons salt, 1 teaspoon freshly ground black pepper, and a little chopped parsley—about 1 or 2 tablespoons. Turn the heat down very low and let the egg set around the potatoes, which will take about 10 or 12 minutes. Then sprinkle the top quite lavishly with grated Parmesan cheese, or a mixture of grated Parmesan and grated Gruyère, and run it under the broiler for a couple of minutes to set the top and brown it lightly.

Run a spatula around the bottom of the pan, slip the frittata out onto a platter, and serve it with the vegetables I mentioned.

You'll have a perfectly delicious and satisfying meal, and I warrant you won't miss meat one little bit. This frittata can be made with practically any vegetable you want—artichoke bottoms, zucchini, onions, peppers, peas, beans, tomatoes, cucumbers—according to what you have in your garden or can find in the supermarket.

Spring Brings Asparagus

In early spring my market is filled with big, beautiful bunches of asparagus, which must surely be one of the most precious members of the vegetable kingdom. Anyone who has ever grown asparagus in the garden knows the thrill of finding the first tender little green shoots sticking up through the ground. Cutting that first crop, rushing it to the kitchen, and feasting on early, home-grown asparagus makes spring a reality.

For my money, asparagus is one of the greatest gifts of the Old World to the New, and the developments over the last thirty or forty years have made it an even more delicious and varied vegetable. Now we have the jumbo or colossal variety, the slim and succulent stalks, and occasionally a very thin kind similar to wild asparagus that is extraordinarily good if properly handled. I well remember that when I was a child in Oregon we had practically nothing but the giant white asparagus that was grown in California, primarily for canning, for these huge white spears take much more graciously to processing and have a luscious flavor quite different from fresh asparagus.

When I lived in Europe, I ate a lot of the fresh white asparagus which is grown widely there and sometimes reaches enormous size. The stalks are peeled carefully, and the cooked asparagus is served either hot or cold, just like the green kind. I recall a restaurant in the countryside of France where the owners grew white asparagus. In season you could have a glorious meal of asparagus, cooked to order, followed by a roast baby chicken, tiny new potatoes, cheese, and dessert. Would that we had asparagus farms where we could get such a service.

The green asparagus sold in our markets, especially the medium stalks, has to my mind the greatest charm and flavor. To prepare it, first snap the stalks at the point where they break easily, then scale them with a vegetable peeler or a knife, peeling more deeply as the stalk gets coarser to take off a good deal of the skin. Then, if you wish, tie the asparagus in bunches and cook in boiling salted water until crisply tender. Some people like to stand the bunches upright in a deep asparagus cooker, so the stalks cook in the water and the delicate tips steam, which is a good way to treat large asparagus, provided it doesn't get overcooked. I find most people tend to overcook asparagus, and I wish they wouldn't.

I like mine very crisp to the bite, so I lay it flat in a large aluminum or Teflon-lined skillet in boiling salted water and cook it very quickly until it is barely tender, removing the stalks with tongs as they are ready— because some stalks are thinner than others, there may be a variation of a minute or two.

You can tell when the stalks are done by pinching them, or by shaking the pan to see if the tips bob back and forth. Depending on the thickness of the stalks, asparagus will take from 7 to 12 minutes to cook. This is something on which you can't give a definite rule—you must watch carefully and cook until it is done to your taste and bite.

∽To me, hot asparagus needs no saucing but salt and freshly ground pepper, or this simple *Butter Sauce*: Blend about 2 teaspoons flour and ¼ cup water to a smooth paste, stir in 6 tablespoons butter, bit by bit, cook for a few minutes, and season to taste with salt, pepper, a little lemon juice, and grated nutmeg. You can vary the seasonings as you will. Many people fancy hollandaise on their hot asparagus, but I prefer to have mine cold with good mayonnaise flavored with mustard and lemon juice, a sublime combination of flavors. I've known people who put grated Parmesan cheese and a fried egg on top of asparagus, some like it wrapped in thin slices of prosciutto and sprinkled with Parmesan, others like a cream sauce on the spears, while there are some who cover asparagus with a tomato and garlic sauce, which I think absolutely smothers the delicate and distinctive flavor.

∽There's a Chinese way of cooking asparagus that is especially good for thin stalks or the very tiny ones you get late in the season. To *Stir-fry Asparagus* cut the stalks in diagonal slices about 2 inches long, put them in a sieve, lower them into rapidly boiling salted water, and cook 3 to 4 minutes, then drain. Melt ¼ pound butter in a large skillet, season with salt, freshly ground pepper, a little lemon juice, and 1 or 2 tablespoons soy sauce, put in the blanched asparagus, and toss as you would a salad, letting it cook for several minutes, until buttery, tender, and tasty. I've had asparagus cut in very small pieces, boiled rapidly, and dressed with melted butter, or hollandaise, or cream sauce, which is known as "asparagus in the style of green peas." You can also cook it, dip it in egg and bread crumbs, and deep-fry it in hot fat until it is crisply brown on the outside and deliciously unctuous inside.

With so many ways to prepare and serve fresh asparagus, it is a crime not to take advantage of its seasonal abundance, rather than using frozen or canned asparagus which is another vegetable entirely, with a much stronger taste. I remember, many years ago, a very fashionable restaurant that was the talk of Los Angeles and Hollywood where asparagus was served with a vanilla sauce, for dessert, which only goes to prove how infinitely accommodating this delectable vegetable can be.

A Rave for Radishes

From my earliest years I have adored the crispness, colorfulness, and spicy tang of radishes. I can recall my first feeble efforts at gardening, when I planted little rows of radishes and was so thrilled when they came up, and even more thrilled when it was time to pull them and eat them fresh from the ground. Very few things in life have ever tasted better to me.

Then I remember that on my first trip to France I was introduced to that perfect combination of good bread, sweet butter, and the firm, brilliantly red radishes the French always include on their hors d'oeuvre list in the spring, when the radishes are at their finest. I found the contrast of flavors and textures very interesting and satisfying to the taste buds. In England one sometimes finds radishes on the breakfast plate with toast and butter, and that's extremely good, too. I often serve a plate of early spring radishes with their leafy bright green tops still on (I like to eat the tops if they are fresh and tender—there's a lovely bite to them), accompanied by homemade bread and butter, as a first course.

As my palate and I grew more sophisticated, I went to a cocktail party where I encountered a delicious hors d'oeuvre of an anchovy fillet wrapped around a red radish, which I thought was something really extra special.

Although we are most familiar with the tiny red globe radishes or the more elongated ones we buy in the markets, radishes do vary considerably in color, shape, and size, and in flavor from mild to peppery hot. The long white icicle radishes, less strongly flavored, are wonderful eaten freshly pulled and crisp, with a sprinkling of salt. Then there are the huge black radishes which, peeled, grated, and mixed with chicken or goose fat, make a delectable spread for bread. The Japanese use an enormous white radish called *daikon* which grows 2 or 3 feet long and has a sweet and tangy flavor unlike any other. These radishes are usually served as a garnish, thinly sliced in soups, or grated and served in a tiny bowl to be eaten with or stirred into the dipping sauce for sashimi, those tender little slivers of raw fish; or tempura, batter-dipped, deep-fried vegetables and fish.

Radishes have been cultivated for thousands of years in the Far East, and they are one of the most flavorful of vegetables. As a salad material, their pungent, peppery taste gives piquancy to otherwise dull fare—and it's always nice to know that 3½ ounces of radishes are only about 17 calories.

While radishes are a familiar ingredient in a mixed green salad, recently I found an exciting new way to use them when I attended some classes in Middle Eastern cooking given on the West Coast by my great friend and co-worker, Philip Brown. He made a salad with oranges, I believe Moroccan in origin, that I have since adapted and served to many people. It's very good with lamb, and sensational with curry or other dishes that have a hot seasoning or are rather rich in butter or oil.

Nothing could be simpler and more beautiful to look at than his *Radish and Orange Salad*. Peel 4 good-sized navel oranges, and either section them or slice them very thinly, being sure to remove all the bitter white pith. Arrange these on a bed of washed and dried salad greens—I prefer the crisp leaves of romaine or iceberg lettuce. Now wash, trim, and shred 1 bunch red radishes. I use a Mouli shredder, a little gadget with a handle that cuts vegetables into lovely, long shreds, but you could use the shredding side of a hand grater. Then kind of drape the radish shreds around the fruit, so you get a glorious color contrast of deep orange, bright green, rosy red, and snow white. Or you can make a wreath of radish shreds around the oranges, or pile them in a mound in the center—here's where you can give your artistic instincts free rein.

Although the original dressing for this salad is made with lemon juice, sugar, and salt, I like to use a vinaigrette, made with 8 tablespoons olive oil to 1 tablespoon lemon juice, 1 teaspoon salt, ½ teaspoon freshly ground black pepper, and 1 to 2 tablespoons orange juice. Taste the dressing before adding it to the salad and tossing—you may need more lemon juice, or lime juice, which is excellent with it. You'll find this vinaigrette has a quite different flavor that enhances the mixture of fruit and vegetables.

Sometimes I vary the salad by alternating sections of orange and grapefruit, or orange and grapefruit sections and avocado slices, which combine with the crisp piquancy of the radish in a most subtle way.

Legendary Lettuce

With its long crisp leaves, shading from brilliant light green to pale yellowish white, romaine is not only one of the most distinctive of all lettuces, standing out noticeably in any mixture of salad greens, but definitely one of the greatest, with a delicious flavor and a texture that stays crunchy in a salad longer than any other. Fortunately for us, it is also one of the few greens apart from iceberg that can be bought just about anywhere in the country.

Romaine has a very ancient and quite fascinating history. The name by which we know it, an adaptation of "Roman" lettuce, is a misnomer. Originally it was known as cos lettuce (and still is, in England) because it was native to Kos or Cos, one of the Greek Dodecanese islands in the Aegean. Classical mythology has it that Adonis was concealed by Venus in a bed of cos lettuce, where he was killed by a foraging wild boar, and because of this, lettuce was eaten at funeral repasts in ancient Greece and Rome.

The Latin name for lettuce is *Lactuca sativa*, derived from lac, or milk, presumably because of its rather milky juice, and this gave rise to yet another legend. According to Apuleius, the eagle obtained its perspicacious vision by touching the juice of a wild lettuce leaf to its eyes before soaring on high, which began an age-old belief that lettuce makes one eagle-eyed.

Legends apart, it's an amusing coincidence that it is to the classical romaine lettuce we owe Caesar salad, which has nothing to do with that great Caesar who conquered Gaul, but was named for one Cesar, a restaurateur of Tijuana, Mexico, who invented it in the 1920s, capitalizing on romaine's ability to hold its crispness through frequent tossings. Now I'm going to tell you the trick to making a true Caesar salad—toss the leaves first with the olive oil, before adding the lemon juice, anchovies, egg, grated Parmesan cheese, and croutons. The oil forms a protective coating that prevents the leaves from wilting when they are tossed with the other ingredients.

In England, cos lettuce was considered a great delicacy for many years, and often the crisp inner leaves were rolled and munched with thin bread and butter as a teatime delicacy. Romaine cooks very well, too. You can braise it in chicken broth until just tender, then brown it lightly in butter, as you would celery hearts, and serve it as a vegetable.

Or, for your next bread stuffing for turkey or chicken, try adding some shredded romaine—it gives a delightful lightness.

Recently, at a class given by Philip Brown in California, I came across a completely new and different way to cook romaine—in a soufflé. This is one of the most delicious romaine dishes I've ever had. The soufflé is light, with an unusual flavor, and the little bits of chopped romaine give a pleasant crunchiness. This is really a complete vegetable course in itself. With a roast of lamb or beef, or a chicken casserole, you need no potato or green vegetable or salad to complete the meal.

While *Philip Brown's Romaine Soufflé* does take a little time to prepare, the recipe is not involved, and it's a great addition to your repertoire of things to serve for dinner. Another nice thing is that this soufflé can wait. You can make it and fold in the egg whites an hour before you bake it. Just hold it in the refrigerator and transfer it to a preheated oven half an hour before serving time, and you'll find it rises perfectly.

Cut off the bottom of 1 head of romaine. Wash thoroughly and chop coarsely. Put into a heavy saucepan with a little water and cook until wilted. Drain well and chop finely. Melt 1 tablespoon butter in a skillet, and cook 3 chopped green onions until soft but not brown. Add romaine and cook, stirring, until moisture has evaporated. In a saucepan, melt 3 tablespoons butter, mix in 3 tablespoons flour, and cook for 2 to 3 minutes, stirring. Add 1 cup extra-rich milk, heated, and cook until thickened. Separate 4 eggs. Beat the yolks into the sauce, one at a time, then add 1 cup shredded Cheddar cheese and cook until smooth. Stir in the romaine mixture until well blended. Season with 1 teaspoon salt, ½ teaspoon Worcestershire sauce, and 2 or 3 dashes of Tabasco.

Lavishly butter a 1½-quart soufflé dish, sprinkle with grated Parmesan cheese, coating bottom and sides, and shake out excess. Beat the egg whites until they hold soft peaks, and stir about one-third of them into the romaine mixture, blending thoroughly. Fold in the remainder lightly; if small lumps of egg white remain, that's fine. Pour mixture into the soufflé dish, and smooth the top. Sprinkle with a little grated Parmesan cheese, and put into a preheated 400-degree oven. Immediately reduce the heat to 375 degrees and bake for 25 to 35 minutes, according to whether you like your soufflé a bit runny in the center, in the French manner, or rather firm. Then rush it to the table, for soufflés wait for no man.

A Vegetable that Keeps Its Co

Recently, I read a most amusing news story in the paper. It
Michigan, after experimentation of six months to a year, a se
has finally been perfected. It's made, naturally, from a seedless cucu
one that produces a crunchier, crisper, better result.

This started me thinking about cucumbers and all the different types
we have—the little pickling cucumbers, the tiny gherkins and burr
gherkins, so delicate and bitey, and the kind that are unfortunately most
prevalent in our markets—a watery, overgrown variety, laden with big
seeds, that are dipped in wax before they are shipped. These, for the most
part, are a quite unattractive vegetable, coarse, seedy, and unpleasant to
the bite. In the West you find a different variety, lemon cucumbers, which
hardly look like our accepted idea of a cucumber at all. They are about the
size and roughly the shape of a duck or turkey egg with a yellow skin and
a kind of fresh, lemony overtone that tastes so good you want to munch
on them like an apple.

In the last several years there has been a great surge of the Chinese
cucumber—or English hothouse cucumber, as it is often called—a long,
slender type often found in the better markets at a special price. These, I
consider, are the best of all cucumbers generally found in markets today,
and I believe you can now get them all across the country. They are
lightly seeded, crisper than the usual kind, and perfect for salads and
sandwiches. Slice them paper-thin, salt them lightly, rinse briefly under
cold running water, pat dry, and put in a sandwich with salt, freshly
ground black pepper, and a flick of mayonnaise, and they are blissfully
good for tea, picnics, or even—the way a friend of mine likes to eat
cucumbers in summer—for breakfast.

If you can buy only the big, waxy, coarse cucumbers, they have a much
better texture if you peel them, split them in two, scrape out the seeds with
a teaspoon, slice them very thinly, salt them slightly, put them in a colander and run cold water over them, then let them drain and give forth their
own water for an hour or so before using them. Most cucumbers, except the
lemon and Chinese, fare best if cut and seeded before being sliced in the
usual manner or cut in long thin strips, whichever you prefer.

In summer, there's nothing quite as cool and refreshing as cucumber
sandwiches, cucumber soup, or cucumber salads. Because the cucumber is
about as universal a vegetable as there is, you'll find different versions of
cucumber salad all over the world, from the Orient to the deepest part of
Central Europe and the Middle East.

In our country, cucumbers are a traditional part of our eating pattern.
For instance, who could think of salmon, hot or cold, without cucumbers?

ith hot salmon they may be cut into little lozenges, steamed, and served with melted butter and a little chopped fresh dill. With cold poached salmon, they should be sliced paper-thin in the French manner, tossed well with vinaigrette sauce, and sprinkled with fresh chopped tarragon, dill, or parsley. As a first course, this cucumber salad is delicious alone or combined with just a hint of peeled and seeded ripe tomato, finely chopped. One of my favorite salads as a child was thinly sliced cucumber, salted, drained, and washed, combined with the thinnest slices of sweet onion, either the red or the Bermuda, dressed with vinegar, oil, and seasonings or just vinegar, salt, and pepper and left to marinate for several hours before being eaten. The onion added a tangy briskness to the delicate cucumber. Now I often make a Syrian cucumber salad, cutting the cucumbers in long thin shreds and dressing them with yogurt, salt, pepper, a little lemon juice, and a sprinkling of finely chopped fresh mint and parsley. This, too, should marinate several hours before serving.

◈ One of the most famous of all ways to use cucumbers is in a *Scandinavian Cucumber Salad*, which is just as common there as cole slaw is here and is the accompaniment to many different dishes. First, make a sweet-sour dressing by combining ½ cup vinegar (I like to use cider or white wine vinegar), 2 tablespoons water, ½ teaspoon salt, 3 tablespoons sugar, about ⅛ teaspoon freshly ground black pepper, and 3 to 4 tablespoons finely chopped fresh dill or half dill, half parsley. This will be enough for 2 medium-sized cucumbers or 1 Chinese cucumber, which should be sliced as thinly as possible or cut in long julienne strips, according to choice. Pour the dressing over the sliced cucumbers, cover with plastic wrap, and let stand for at least 3 hours before serving, undrained, in the marinating dressing, true Scandinavian style.

So there you have an international cross section of ways to use one of the most pleasing of all vegetables—one that will keep its and your cool on the hottest day. And if you've never tried this little trick, when you peel a cucumber lay the cut side of the peel on your forehead or cheek on a sweltering day and let its dewy moisture soothe and refresh your skin.

೭

The Decline and Fall of the Tomato

The tomato, one of the greatest food gifts of the New World to the Old, was not eaten in North America until the eighteenth, possibly the nineteenth, century. For some reason it was considered a decorative plant, and the fruit was allowed to go to waste. Thank goodness someone finally had the courage to eat one of those little golden-red globes and proclaim it for its delicious acidity and wondrous texture.

Europeans were not so laggard. By the time the North Americans took up "love apples," Europeans had been using them for almost a century and a half. If one goes by the fact that many tomato dishes in the French and other cuisines are labeled "à la Portugaise," it seems likely that the Portuguese were the first to cook with tomatoes in any quantity, followed by the Italians and the southern French. One of the notable departures from the rule of classic cuisine in France came when lobster à l'Américaine made its appearance at the Great Paris Exposition of 1861. Ever since there has been much controversy about the antecedents of this famous dish. Some claim it should be spelled "Armoricaine," but Armorique is Brittany, and no less an authority than Prosper Montagné proved that at the time the recipe was created the Bretons shunned the tomato. So perhaps the name was merely a graceful acknowledgment of the tomato's origin.

By now, the tomato has become our most universal fruit. It goes into the club sandwich, the bacon and tomato sandwich, tomato juice and paste, soup, spaghetti sauce, just about everywhere. Recently I even saw a recipe for a tomato ice cream, not a sweet one, but a frozen mixture of tomato purée and heavy cream, highly spiced and seasoned, which might be rather fun served with seafood, after the style of that undying tradition of American buffet tables, the tomato aspic ring filled with seafood, rice, or chicken salad.

Tomatoes have such a variety of uses and fit into so many different parts of the menu that it is hard to see how people ever cooked without them. I did a great deal of research on tomatoes while I was working on my big American cookbook, and I discovered that some of the early tomato recipes were for sweet dishes: compotes, jams, and marmalades—one recipe from the early nineteenth century was for a tomato custard, sweetened, and spiced with cinnamon and nutmeg.

Tomatoes were very different then. Naturally ripened, red, and luscious. Lately, this most glorious of fruits has gone into a tragic decline in the United States because it is being produced on a scale and in a manner that makes it an almost total gastronomic loss.

In England, you can get delicious tomatoes from the Channel Islands. In Italy, France, and Spain, tomatoes are raised properly, for quality and flavor, and they are a joy to eat. But in New York, indeed in most parts of the country, save for a few weeks in summer when local vine-ripened tomatoes are in season, the tomato situation is dismal indeed. We now get tomatoes that are grown for shelf age instead of for the delight of the eye and the palate, tomatoes grown in soil which is not right for them and gives them a woolly texture and an unyielding rocklike consistency. The growers in certain states where the climate favors year-round crops seem to have asserted themselves in a most dictatorial fashion, with a total disregard for public taste, and have persuaded the authorities that their tomatoes alone should appear in our markets. Unless we can grow a few plants in a garden plot or indoors in flower pots, this looks like the end of the line for all of us who have some regard for good tomatoes. I think all tomato lovers should unite and make a forceful presentation of the case for the ripe, flavorful tomato, or we may be forever condemned to that tasteless, colorless little red cannonball that remains unchanging beneath its plastic shroud, until it finally gives up and rots away.

For a time it seemed as if the saving of the tomato was to be the cherry tomato, which when it first appeared had excellent flavor, texture, and color. Recently this, too, seems to have gone the way of mass production, with a corresponding deterioration in quality. However, should you be able to find, or grow, good cherry tomatoes you'll find they lend themselves to cooking as well as to eating raw. For a new vegetable idea, steam or bake them, and serve them with steak, chicken, or other meats.

For *Steamed Cherry Tomatoes*, it is worthwhile, if tedious, to peel them first. Pour boiling water over 1 pint firm cherry tomatoes, let stand 1 minute, then plunge in cold water, and the skins will peel off easily. Place them in the top of a double boiler with 6 tablespoons butter, 1 teaspoon salt, and 1 teaspoon finely chopped fresh dill. Cover and steam over hot water until just heated through. Serve topped with more chopped dill.

To bake, melt the butter and toss the unpeeled tomatoes in it until coated. Sprinkle with salt and pepper and put on a baking sheet in a 300-degree oven for 10 to 15 minutes, or until just cooked through but still firm.

Another favorite trick of mine, when I can get really ripe cherry tomatoes is to make a *Tomato Preserve*, which harks back to those old nineteenth-century recipes.

Remove the stems from 2 pints very ripe cherry tomatoes, leaving the stem end intact. Pour boiling water over them, let stand for

2 seconds, then slip off the skins.

Boil 4 cups sugar and 1½ cups water with 2 slices lemon over medium heat for 5 minutes, scraping the sugar from the sides of the pan with a rubber spatula. Add the tomatoes to this heavy syrup and cook gently at a bare simmer until just cooked, about 15 to 20 minutes. They must stay whole, not break up. Skim off any scum and ladle the cooked tomatoes carefully into a dish. Cool, cover, and chill. These make a delicious cold dessert with heavy cream or over ice cream, or an unusual breakfast preserve.

The All-American Avocado

Although they are a standard item in supermarkets today, I can remember when avocados—then called alligator pears—were a very expensive delicacy. They were usually the purple-skinned variety rather than the glossy green soft-skinned ones and the dark type with hard skins that we see now at different times of the year.

The avocado is indigenous to this hemisphere, and it gave rise to the one great sauce of the Americas that will go down in gastronomic history, the Mexican guacamole. Guacamole (pronounced gwok-ah-moh-lay) is 100 percent American because the principal ingredients are native to these shores—the avocado, the green chili, and the tomato. From Mexico it spread to North America via California, and now it is made and served all over the country, as a dip, a spread, a salad, and a sauce. In certain areas you can even buy a ready-made frozen guacamole in supermarkets.

⁓There are innumerable versions of *Guacamole*. Here is my favorite. First buy avocados that are soft enough to be mashable but not so soft that they have turned dark. Mash 2 good-sized avocados well with a fork. Add 1 or 2 chopped green chilies, the kind that are sold in cans as "peeled green chilies," removing the tiny seeds that sting your tongue unless you like a pretty hot, zesty flavor.

(For a really spicy guacamole, use 1 very finely chopped jalapeño or serrano chili instead.) Mix in about 2 tablespoons lime juice and 1 to 1 ½ teaspoons salt, depending on the avocados. You should add enough to bring out the mixture of flavors. If you are not using the guacamole immediately, put the avocado pit in the mixture or cover tightly with plastic wrap to prevent it from darkening.

That's my recipe for a basic guacamole. You can vary it by adding all kinds of bits and pieces. Peeled, seeded, and chopped ripe tomatoes and finely chopped onion are traditional. Not so traditional but very good are crumbled crisp bacon, chopped roasted peanuts, or chopped salted almonds or coarsely chopped toasted filberts or thin, thin strips of flavorful ham.

You can also beat in a touch of olive oil or some cumin or finely chopped garlic, and certainly the herb cilantro (fresh coriander) belongs here. A good sprinkling of chopped cilantro with its distinctive, strangely dark flavor (some dote on it, others can't abide it) is a wonderful counterpoint to the smooth, buttery blandness of the avocado.

Guacamole is as versatile as it is delicious. Everyone knows it as a positively addictive spread or dip with tortillas or tostados or corn chips, but try it sometime in salads—seafood salads, chicken salads, vegetable salads. I like to put it in a green salad that contains thinly sliced raw onion and maybe a few slices of green pepper and cucumber, or to slather it over cucumbers, topped before serving with sour cream and a healthy powdering of chopped cilantro or fresh parsley. I also love it as a sauce for chicken that has been dusted with flour mixed with a little bit of chili powder and fried. Then it is sensational on hamburgers or charcoal-broiled steaks and chops, and if you add lashings of chopped green pepper, it tastes wonderful on fish.

There is a very similar sauce with the delightful name of *Mantequilla de Pobre*—poor man's butter. Mash your 2 avocados, add 2 chopped, peeled, and seeded tomatoes, 1 tablespoon oil, and 2 to 3 tablespoons lime or lemon juice or wine vinegar with salt and pepper to taste.

This dates back to the pre-Hispanic days when there were no cattle, and therefore no butter, and it was used as a spread or added to dishes to give the soft texture and rich flavor that butter would. The famous cookbook writer Elena Zelayeta serves it in her home as a dip for *carnitas*, a great little appetizer of crisp, seasoned pork.

To make *Carnitas*: Cut 2 pounds very lean pork into small pieces, sprinkle with salt and pepper, and let stand an hour or so. Bake very slowly in a 300-degree oven on a fine mesh rack, to allow the fat to run off, until the little bits of pork are crisp and brown, about 1½ hours. Serve with *mantequilla de pobre*. The contrast between the hot pork and the cold, suave avocado sauce makes a really unusual and exciting cocktail appetizer.

Mushroom Magic

I can remember that when I was very young there was a big field about 200 feet from our house in Oregon where in season, especially the fall, mushrooms popped up by the hundreds. Often someone would rise early to gather a five-gallon bucket of these field treasures. They would be quickly sautéed and served on toast for breakfast, and my, how good they were! Our field mushrooms were mostly the little buttons, the wild variety of the mushroom now cultivated commercially on a vast scale in cellars in Pennsylvania and other states. I was told not long ago that the yield in 1970 was 194 million pounds, which would make a tremendous mountain of mushrooms.

While increasing amounts of the creamy tan, almost golden mushrooms are now appearing in American markets, more in the West than the East, the majority of the mushrooms we buy are the white button kind. In New York they come in 3-pound wooden baskets lined with blue paper, and when you open one the sight of the freshly picked, glistening, snowy-white caps nestling in a field of azure is a feast for the eyes.

Mushrooms are an indispensable part of hundreds of the world's greatest dishes, prized for the delicious flavor, color, and bouquet they impart. Yet though they occur in some of the richest recipes of the *haute cuisine*, mushrooms are incredibly low on the calorie scale—a whole pound adds up to less than 100 calories—so they can be indulged in with absolute abandon. Weight watchers will find raw mushrooms sprinkled with salt and pepper make a perfect, hunger-appeasing munchable. For years I have been an advocate of eating mushrooms raw. Thinly sliced, tossed with olive oil, vinegar, salt, freshly ground pepper, and a touch of tarragon, they make a most joyous salad, and a few raw mushrooms sliced into a green salad will give it a wonderfully fresh, delightful taste and texture.

If you prefer your mushrooms cooked, they may be broiled or sautéed, stuffed with all sorts of things, or finely chopped and made into one of the most marvelous mixtures known to man, *duxelles*, a highly concentrated mushroom paste named for the Marquis d'Uxelles, for whom it was created. In my cooking classes I give my own version of this famous, classic French recipe, one of the most rewarding ways to use a basketful of mushrooms bought at a reduced price when they are a bit past their prime.

≈ While you don't need pristine white mushrooms for *Duxelles*, you do need time, patience, and a really large chopping knife to make the preparation easier and speedier. Take 1½ to 2 pounds mushrooms, wipe them well with damp paper towels, and chop them very finely, stems and all. Place in a dishtowel and twist the towel until all the liquid has been squeezed out. The liquid may be used to flavor sauces or soups. Melt 10 tablespoons butter in a very heavy skillet (a black iron one is ideal) over low to medium heat. Add the mushrooms and 2 tablespoons finely chopped shallot or onion, and stir until well mixed with the butter. Cook over the lowest heat, stirring every 10 or 15 minutes to move the mushrooms from the bottom of the pan to the top and adding more butter if necessary, until all the moisture has been drawn from the mushrooms and they have become completely dehydrated and considerably reduced—this will take from 1½ to 2 hours. At the end of the cooking time you should have a thick dense mass of mushrooms, very dark, almost black in color. Add 2 teaspoons salt, mixing it in thoroughly, and remove the mixture to a bowl to cool. This *duxelles*, stored in a screw-topped jar, will keep for at least two weeks in the refrigerator, or it may be frozen.

There are all kinds of ways to use this glorious mushroom mixture. Sandwich it between French crêpes, stacked eight or nine high, dot the stack with butter, heat it through in the oven, and serve sliced in wedges. Or swirl the *duxelles* in scrambled eggs and serve on a platter for breakfast with bacon, frizzled ham, or sausages on the side. I had this combination once in a vol-au-vent, a huge patty shell filled with golden scrambled eggs marbled with the black of the mushrooms, and it was one of the most elegant dishes imaginable, perfect for luncheon or supper.

I also like to blend *duxelles* with cooked mashed yellow turnip or potatoes or celery root for a dramatic blend of flavors. You can make a sandwich of it, between slices of well-buttered toast, spoon it over hamburgers, or make it into tiny hot canapés by mixing 4 or 5 tablespoons shredded Gruyère or Cheddar cheese into ½ cup *duxelles*, spreading the mixture on small rounds of toast and putting them under the broiler until the cheese melts. *Duxelles* gives a terrific lift to sauces—try swirling it into a cream sauce, a brown sauce, or a brown gravy.

Potatoes for Breakfast

I love potatoes for breakfast. They are a marvelous enhancer of bacon and eggs, or ham and eggs, or sausages, or whatever you enjoy eating in the morning, and they happen to be one of my small indulgences when I travel. I usually breakfast very simply at home, but when I'm away I let myself order fruits and ham or sausage or whatever I feel like and really revel in it. It's too bad that we are all so rushed these days we can't find time to savor the first meal of the day. We just grab a glass of juice or a piece of fruit, some toast, and a cup of coffee or tea and call it breakfast. How nice it is to sit down to platters heaped with good hearty food and take one's time, then get up from the table with a feeling of warmth and well-being that makes it easy to face the day's problems.

Breakfast potatoes aren't much effort to make. You can use precooked potatoes or the frozen, ready-shredded potatoes for hash browns. However, to my mind, the old-time boiled potato, not overcooked, works best. I remember years ago sitting in small diners and little country restaurants and watching the cook fry peeled, boiled potatoes in butter on the griddle, chopping them up with a one- or two-pound coffee can as they fried. It was a very deft trick. I've tried it a few times, and I can do it if I really put my mind to it, but I'm not advising that everyone attempt it.

Finding the right potatoes for hash browns can be a problem. Buying potatoes is no simple matter these days. Potato dealers and, to a great extent, potato producers don't take the trouble to sell and grow all the various potato varieties there used to be in the markets. Now you mainly get two types—new potatoes, both the little round red ones and the long white ones, and Idaho baking potatoes. There are usually some local potatoes which you will be told are Oregon potatoes or California potatoes, or Maine or Long Island potatoes, but no one ever tells you what variety they are or how they boil or bake or if they are good for salad. That's something you have to find out for yourself, and it's too bad because the difference between the waxy potatoes for boiling, salads, and refrying and the floury ones that are best for baking is so great that you could save yourself a lot of trouble if you knew more about what you were buying. Maybe we'll have to go back to growing our own potatoes.

⊷For *Hash Brown Potatoes*, take the best boiling potatoes you can find, the kind that have a little firmness and waxiness. New potatoes are good, or medium-sized potatoes that do not seem too floury. Boil them, without peeling, in a small amount of salted water in a heavy pan, covered, until they are just barely pierceable. For hash browns, they don't have to be completely cooked, nor need you fry them right away;

they can rest overnight.

Peel the boiled potatoes carefully and chop fairly coarsely. For 6 to 8 potatoes, melt 5 to 6 tablespoons butter in a Teflon-lined or black iron skillet, adding a tablespoon of oil if you like. Press them down rather well, and cook over fairly brisk heat until a beautiful brown crust forms on the bottom. Then, for a doubly luscious treat, invert the pan on a plate and slide the potatoes out in one big cake. Return the pan to the heat, add 1 or 2 more tablespoons butter, slide the unbrowned side into the pan, and cook until browned on the second side. Salt and pepper both sides well during the cooking. Then slide the cake out onto a hot plate and serve immediately—these potatoes won't wait.

If you want, you can make separate potato patties in small 5- or 6-inch skillets, using about 2 tablespoons butter and 1 tablespoon oil for each one. Shake the pan gently while browning.

You can also use raw potatoes of the same waxy type. Shred them on a shredder into cold water so they won't discolor. For 5 to 6 potatoes, which will serve four to six people, melt about 5 tablespoons butter in a heavy skillet. Dry the shredded potatoes thoroughly on paper towels, press them down in the pan, and cook in the same manner as the chopped boiled potatoes, or as a shortcut, use the ready-prepared frozen potatoes which come in long shreds.

⋙ Then there's another version, more like the *Swiss Rösti Potatoes*. Boil potatoes for about 10 minutes, until they are about half-cooked, or peel baked potatoes. Shred the cooked potatoes and cook as before. Turn out on hot plates, and serve with ham and eggs, bacon and eggs, sausage and eggs, finnan haddie, or codfish cakes.

I have been known to breakfast on nothing but these delicious, crispy-brown potatoes, liberally salted and peppered, with fruit, toast, and tea.

Naturally, you don't have to limit breakfast potatoes to breakfast. They are just as good for lunch or dinner with broiled steaks, chops, or hamburgers. In fact, they are my idea of one of the greatest ways to eat potatoes at any time of day, and that's saying a lot, because I'm really enamored of the potato in all its guises.

꙳

The Well-fried Potato

French fries must be one of the most popular foods in the world. Everyone seems to adore them. In Holland you can buy them on the street, with mustard mayonnaise. The Germans like them with mayonnaise, too. In Canada and Britain they are sprinkled with white vinegar. Most Americans smother them with ketchup, but personally, I like mine *au naturel*, just a well-fried, crisp strip of potato with no flavoring other than salt and pepper.

Considering the universality of French fries, it's odd—and rather sad—that you so seldom get them as they should be, 100 percent crisp, tender, and freshly made. Mostly, you are presented with a dismal pile of soggy, smelly French fries without enough salt and pepper—so dismal, in fact, that if I see them coming on a plate I usually ask to have them removed.

There are a few little tricks about making French fries that you might like to know. First, the question of the potatoes. Some people like the mealy Idahos, others the boiling potato that has a slightly waxy quality when cooked. I like either, if they are properly done. You might, just for fun, do a little research with different types of potatoes and see which gives you the most satisfactory result. Try the long white California potatoes, the Idaho, the Maine, all those that come in at various times of year.

❧ To make *French Fries* to serve four, 4 medium to large potatoes should be ample. If you want a lot of French fries—some kids do—throw in an extra one for the pot. Peel them and cut into long strips from ¼ to ½ inch wide and thick—or you can cut them in rounds. Or in little wedges if the potatoes are small. One restaurant I know uses wedges of small potato with the skin on, well scrubbed, of course. Potatoes are better if peeled and cut just before you cook them. If you can't do that, put them in cold water, take them out just before you fry them, spread them on a double layer of paper towels or a terry towel, and dry thoroughly. Line a baking sheet or jelly-roll pan with paper towels, and put it in a 200- or 250-degree oven to keep the potatoes hot and crisp as they are fried.

For frying, you can use a very large deep skillet with a frying basket, an electric French fryer, or one of the French pots with a basket that can be drained by hooking it onto the handles at the sides. Or you can use a deep saucepan and a sieve.

Unless you use an electric fryer, you'll need a good frying thermometer. The temperature of the fat is tremendously important, and the return to the temperature between each batch is even more important.

There are two methods of deep-frying potatoes—the one-fry method and the two-fry method. It might interest you to know that the double-fry method was a serendipitous accident that created soufflé potatoes, the very puffy slices you get in fancy restaurants. It seems there was a big party that depended on a train arriving. The train was late, so the chef dropped the basket of already fried potatoes into the hot fat a second time, and, to his surprise, they puffed up. Now I'm not going to guarantee that if you fry potatoes twice they'll turn into soufflé potatoes, but it's an amusing story.

To make *French Fries*, vegetable oil or vegetable fat is probably best for deep frying. Heat it to 375 degrees, and heat the basket in the fat. (If you put a cold basket into hot fat, it will naturally cool it off.) See that your potatoes are thoroughly dry, lift the basket out, toss the potatoes in it, and lower the basket slowly into the hot fat, being careful it doesn't splatter. The thickest French fries will take 8 to 10 minutes to cook, those of matchstick size considerably less. Lift the basket and shake the potatoes around once or twice during the cooking so they don't stick. Nothing is worse than a whole mess of potatoes stuck together. When they are nicely browned, remove the basket from the fat, test to see if the potatoes are crisp and tender to the bite, then turn them onto the paper-lined pan to drain. Put the pan in the oven, reheat the basket, check the temperature of the fat, and cook the rest of the potatoes in batches. Sprinkle them with salt and freshly ground black pepper just before serving.

For the two-fry method, you proceed as for the one-fry method, except that you heat the fat only to 300 to 325 degrees (remember to heat the basket, too). Cook the potatoes in this fat, a few at a time, for 5 to 6 minutes, until they get rather flabby-looking and not brown. Drain on paper towels and leave at room temperature anywhere from 1 to 1½ hours, until you are ready to do your second frying. Then reheat the fat (with basket) to 375 to 380 degrees, toss the pre-fried potatoes into the hot fat by handfuls, and fry for 2 or 3 minutes, until they are the shade of brown you prefer. Be sure to bring the fat back to the proper temperature for each batch or they will be soggy. Keep warm in the oven and season just before serving.

They'll be crisp, golden-brown, piping hot, and perfectly delicious. I don't think you'll want another thing with them, least of all ketchup.

Potatoes Without Meat

It can be both a challenge and fun to seek out things that are substantial and good enough to replace meat. There's pasta, of course, beans, lentils, and split peas—and also potatoes. How often does one think of potatoes without meat? Yet they are a great food in their own right.

᪥ I have a dish that I dearly love, made with baked potatoes scooped out of their shells (save the shells, cut them in strips, crisp them in the oven, and you have a most delicious hors d'oeuvre) that goes by the romantic name of *Potatoes Byron*. Bake 6 potatoes, scoop the pulp from the shells—don't mash it, just break it up coarsely—and mix in ½ pound butter (with all that butter you can see why this is a meat substitute), salt and freshly ground black pepper to taste. Put in an 8- or 9-inch round glass baking dish or pie dish, pour over a good ½ cup heavy cream, and leave for 30 to 45 minutes so the potatoes absorb the cream, butter, and seasonings. Sprinkle ½ to ¾ cup coarsely grated Swiss or Gruyère cheese over the potatoes, and place in a 375-degree oven until the potatoes heat through and the cheese melts, forming a golden crust. Serve these rich, creamy potatoes as a main dish with wilted spinach or mustard greens, an interesting salad, and bread and butter, and you'll never miss the meat.

᪥ Then there's that old Irish standby, *Colcannon*, a real country-style dish. Peel, boil, and mash 6 potatoes. Shred 1 medium head of cabbage. Render all the fat from ¼ to ½ pound bacon in a big skillet, remove, and toss the cabbage in the fat. Cover and steam the cabbage in the fat until just crisp, remove the lid, and add ½ cup stock, cover again, and simmer until the cabbage is very tender. Toss the bacon back in and cook it through completely, then remove both cabbage and bacon, drain well, and chop rather coarsely. Combine with the mashed potatoes and taste for seasoning, adding salt and pepper to taste. I like to put this in a baking dish, dot it with butter, and run it into the oven for a minute or two, so it gets a brown crust on the top.

We seldom think of potatoes in relation to Italian cooking, but one of the exceptions is potato gnocchi, the Italian member of the great family of gnocchi, some of which are made with semolina, some with cornmeal, some with cottage cheese, and some with cream-puff dough.

For *Potato Gnocchi,** bake or boil 6 large baking potatoes until tender. Peel, mash well, and chill overnight. Next day mix in 3 egg yolks and 2 teaspoons salt. Turn out onto a lightly floured board, make a well in the center and put in 1 cup flour. Knead thoroughly, adding more flour as needed to make a smooth, elastic dough—2 to 2½ cups in all, depending on whether you use all-purpose or unbleached hard-wheat flour. The dough should not be too firm, but it must have an elasticity almost like bread dough. Roll it into long, sausage-like shapes, and slice each one into 1-inch segments. Press your thumb into each segment to curl the edges of the dough—you can also do this with a pencil or a cooking chopstick.

Drop these little gnocchi into 4 quarts of rapidly boiling salted water. Lower the heat and cook them gently, uncovered, for about 3 to 5 minutes, or until the gnocchi rise to the surface. Remove with a slotted spoon to a serving dish, and serve with melted butter and freshly grated Parmesan cheese, or with a good pasta meat sauce, and pass additional Parmesan.

Team this with a salad of watercress and thinly sliced onion, drink red wine, and finish off with a crème caramel.

*This recipe comes from one of the most enchanting books I have read in a long time, *The Potato Book*, by Myrna Davis, published by William Morrow, 1973.

Consider the Onion

I happen to be crazy about onions, so I can never understand why they are so unpopular with certain people who banish them from their lives on the grounds that they are disagreeable—to the taste and on the breath. I don't see how the kitchen could have survived without onions, for they have been cultivated since prehistoric times. Throughout the world, no vegetable is as indispensable, raw or cooked, as a flavor ingredient in innumerable dishes, or as a pickle.

No other vegetable is as legendary, either. Onions, we are told, were part of the cargo on Noah's ark. The Egyptians regarded them as a symbol of the sun they worshiped as a god, with the concentric rings of the sliced onion representing heaven, hell, earth, and the universe. If you've never studied the inside of an onion, cut one in half sometime and really look. It is one of nature's most amazing works of art.

Onions were the backbone of many diets in the past. The Egyptians fed vast quantities of them to the builders of the pyramids to give them strength, and Alexander the Great stuffed his armies with onions to give them courage. I also read somewhere that the wives of Irish fishermen used to prepare for their husbands a breakfast of sliced onions, rum, and stout, which taken at dawn would certainly enable one to face the coldest seas.

The onion is a many-faceted vegetable. There are the tiny pearl onions which we pickle and the Dutch, Belgians, and French eat as a vegetable, although peeling these babies is a pretty monotonous task. Then we have the rather larger white onions that we cook whole for creamed onions, onions à la Grecque, or any number of hot and cold specialties and relishes, medium-sized yellow onions for boiling or to chop and slice and use in different dishes, the mild red Italian onions, the big delicate Bermudas, and the enormous Spanish variety that are in season from fall to late spring. Just the other day I was enchanted to receive a box of these giant golden globes, perfectly matched in size and contour, that flourish in the volcanic soil of Oregon and Idaho. They make absolutely superb eating. I love them raw, thinly sliced, with a hamburger or cold meats or in a hearty, flavorful onion sandwich.

The day my gift box arrived I happened to have some slightly stale homemade bread, about two or three days old. I sliced this very thin, buttered it well, covered it with paper-thin slices of Spanish onion, sprinkled them with some coarse salt, and pressed another slice of bread firmly on the top—and there was my supper.

I can easily make a whole meal of onion sandwiches, for to me they are one of the greatest treats I know, and they are awfully good with cold chicken or cold roast beef, too.

Think about onions when you are cooking outdoors on the charcoal grill, in spring or summer, for there is nothing quite as good with spitted roast meat, especially beef or lamb, or with steak.

  Put the onions, either unpeeled or peeled and foil-wrapped, just at the edge of the fire to roast. Remove the charred outside, or the foil, and eat this most pungent and delicious of vegetables while it is hot, crisp, and tender, adding some salt, freshly ground pepper, and butter. Onions cooked this way are so much better than those uninteresting French-fried things that are more batter than onion.

  You can also take thickish slices of raw onion, butter them, and grill them over the coals until they are crisply done and slightly glazed. Or you can simmer them in water or bouillon until tender but still firm, then put them on a baking sheet, dot them with butter, sprinkle them with bread crumbs and grated Parmesan cheese, and brown them under the broiler.

  I like an onion salad with grilled meats. When beefsteak tomatoes are in season, dip them briefly in boiling water to loosen the skins, then peel them, slice rather thickly, and alternate with hearty slices of Spanish onion. Dribble over this a little olive oil and wine vinegar, sprinkle with salt and freshly ground black pepper, and you have an extraordinarily good accompaniment to your steak. I also take Spanish onion slices, break them into rings, and put them in a bowl, covered with water and ice cubes and about ½ cup vinegar to each 2 cups water, with some salt and pepper. Leave these, covered, in the refrigerator for several hours, then drain them, toss with your favorite French dressing, and serve icy cold for an unforgettable salad.

  Onions and potatoes combine marvelously. Sauté onion rings in butter, and add an equal quantity of boiled, peeled, and sliced potatoes. Continue sautéing until the potatoes are delicately browned and the onions slightly caramelized, then sprinkle them with some chopped parsley.

This tasty, satisfying onion and potato sauté is great with meats grilled over charcoal.

Beets Can Be Beautiful

It always amazes me how people tend to forget or ignore one of the most delicious and versatile vegetables we have—the beet. While beets are most plentiful in summer, they remain in good form all year round, with a color and flavor few other vegetables can equal. When you buy beets, look for the small ones. Older beets take long cooking and are often rather woody.

    Fresh beets must be cooked with a couple of inches of the stem left on, and never peeled before cooking, or they will bleed away much of their beautiful ruby color. Don't even scrub or brush them, as this may puncture the skin; just wash them gently.

Cook the beets in boiling water, tightly covered, and let them simmer slowly until tender, which, according to size, takes from about 30 to 45 minutes. Don't pierce them with a fork until you are sure they are tender. Plunge them into cold water, and as soon as they are cool enough to handle, slip off the skins, trim off the root and stem ends, and slice, dice, or cut in julienne strips. Very small beets may be left whole; larger ones should be cut up.

Sliced, and dressed with butter, salt, and freshly ground pepper, perhaps a touch of lemon juice if you like, or seasoned and tossed with sour cream, hot beets are so good it seems unbelievable that they are not more popular. Try them, too, with a little grated orange rind and orange juice (which you can thicken with a bit of cornstarch, if you like) for a very interesting flavor combination. I sometimes shred the beets or cut them in thin julienne strips and toss them with finely chopped spinach or their own beet tops, cooked just like spinach, then give them some salt, pepper, butter, lemon juice, and just a touch of nutmeg.

Cold beets are another story. The French love beets in salad. In fact, in all their markets you find beets cooked in their skins, ready to be peeled, something I have never seen in this country and would like to.

    I love a salad of shredded cooked beets, chopped hard-boiled egg, and thinly sliced onion dressed with homemade mayonnaise, or half mayonnaise and half sour cream, piled on greens, and served with finely chopped parsley or dill—beets and dill have a lovely relationship. Another of my favorites is thinly sliced beets and thinly sliced onions dressed with a vinaigrette sauce with finely chopped tarragon in it.

Did you ever try shredding a little of the sweet beet and tossing it with what I call the bitter salad greens, like endive and chicory and arugola or even watercress, and vinaigrette sauce? It tastes just marvelous. Sometimes I throw in a little finely chopped garlic or thinly sliced onion.

❧ Beets have a natural affinity for herring and smoked fish. A *Scandinavian Salad* is a good, hearty buffet or main dish salad, beautiful to look at and to eat, and the longer it marinates the better it gets. Take a 12-ounce jar of herring tidbits and cut them very thinly, then combine them with 1 to 1½ cups diced cold meat (tongue is good, veal is excellent, or cold beef will do, if you cut it in thin strips), 1 crisp apple, diced with the skin on, 1 cup diced cooked potatoes, and 1 cup diced or julienne beets. Toss well with mayonnaise, or mayonnaise and sour cream, and pack into a mold. Unmold on a bed of greens and sprinkle with chopped fresh parsley or dill (or dried dill). Garnish with quartered hard-boiled eggs and a few tiny beets.

I've always had a fondness for pickled beets, which my mother did in a number of ways. While the cooked beets were still warm, she sliced them and put them into jars with alternating slices of onion, then covered them with good cider vinegar or wine vinegar. These were allowed to mellow a week or so before being eaten. Sometimes she popped sprigs of fresh dill in the jar, or put the beets down covered in vinaigrette mixed with dill and a touch of garlic. We used to drop shelled hard-boiled eggs in the ruby-red vinegar from the pickled beets, let them sit for several days, and use them in salads or as a garnish for various dishes.

One of the most famous old American dishes is red flannel hash, which has come to be thought of as corned beef hash with chopped beets mixed into it. There's a story to the effect that this was the hash that was made the day after a New England boiled dinner. A writer friend of mine put this in an article once and received a rebuke from an old-time New Englander who said that red flannel hash had not come about that way; the original boiled dinner had been boiled cod with various vegetables, beets being one. Next day's meal, made of vegetables and bits of fish, was the true red flannel hash. Then I read in an old cookbook that only the vegetables from the boiled dinner were made into hash, and since meat was often scarce, the vegetable hash was served with a slice of cold meat. So I guess all we can be sure of is that the beet always played a role in the history of New England eating.

❧

Cabbage and Its Cousins

Has it ever occurred to you how many different members of the cabbage family we eat? First, there's the common green or white cabbage that we find in the markets all year round, the splendid Savoy cabbage with its dark-green textured leaves, and occasionally the very young spring cabbage with crispy, brilliant gray-green leaves that look just as if they had been painted. Then there's the red cabbage, which is so beautiful if you slice through its heart and gaze at the intricate red and white marbled interior, a vegetable work of art. There's Chinese cabbage, with long leaves of palest greenish white and a texture quite different from other cabbages, and the Oriental bok-choi, which you'll find in Chinese markets looking more like a rather eccentric version of Swiss chard than a cabbage.

Brussels sprouts are tiny members of the cabbage family that flourish in fall and winter, and then there's cauliflower, which is actually a somewhat freakish variant of the same cruciferous family as the cabbage. Other relatives are good old-fashioned kale, which lasts all winter long, collard greens, the familiar green broccoli, and the less familiar purple broccoli that I find in New York's Italian markets. This is a most spectacular vegetable, purple on top and pale green underneath. When you cook it, just as you'd cook cauliflower, the purple blanches out, leaving a delicate greeny mauve color, but either cooked or raw it tastes wonderfully good.

Another type of broccoli, called broccoli rabe or rape or broccoli di rapa, is sort of a cross between broccoli, mustard greens, and turnip greens. This, too, can be found in Italian markets in the fall and winter, and you'll recognize it by the long, rather coarse stems with leaves and funny little clumps of buds that look almost like a stunted broccoli.

> To cook *Broccoli Rabe*, first soak it well, then cut off the top part with the leaves and flowers and part of the thick stems. Steam them in water for just a few minutes until barely wilted down, then chop them. While you're doing this, melt about 4 tablespoons olive oil (for 3 pounds broccoli rabe), add 2 finely chopped garlic cloves, salt, and freshly ground black pepper, then toss the wilted vegetable in the hot oil, just as you would toss a salad. Add a squeeze of lemon juice, a hint of dill or thyme or basil, and toss again. Serve very hot.

I had this the other night with roast duck, and it was delicious. It makes a great change from the usual cabbage. Actually, I happen to love cabbage, provided it is properly cooked. I think it is so often maligned because most people were brought up to cook it in the old way, boiling it in lots of water until it was soggy and smelly and quite horrible.

To know the true joys of cabbage, just quarter it or cut it thinly, toss into salted water, and cook for only a few minutes until it is barely tender and still crisp. Drain it, drench with butter, salt and pepper it, and give it a bit of lemon juice and a touch of chopped dill or tarragon. Serve it forthwith, and you'll have one of the finest vegetable dishes known to man.

I also like to shred cabbage as if I was making cole slaw, then render 5 or 6 slices of bacon, cut into tiny pieces, and toss the shredded cabbage in the fat, turning it quickly several times until it braises to a light delicate brown and wilts down with the bacon flavor all through it. I then add a finely chopped garlic clove and a little white wine, cover the pan, and simmer for about 10 minutes, seasoning the cabbage with salt and pepper just before I dish it up.

While I prefer all the simple, easy ways of cooking cabbage to a lovely bitey crispness, there still lingers in my mind the memory of some cabbage I once had for lunch in a French farmhouse. The cook had taken an old cabbage, shredded it very finely, and cooked it covered in a small amount of fat from the pork roast and a touch of white wine over very low heat for several hours, very, very slowly, until it was almost a purée. She then seasoned it well with salt, pepper, more white wine, a drop or two of lemon juice, and a pinch of sage. She served it on the same dish with a loin of pork that had been perfectly roasted with the skin left on until it was crunchy on the outside and juicy inside. If you don't think this sounds like one of the most exquisite versions of cabbage one could eat, do me the honor of trying it.

Finally, I'd like to tell you my way of cooking *Brussels Sprouts*, yet another vegetable many people dislike because they've usually had them cooked on and on until they go all soft and mushy. I put mine in a bare minimum of boiling water, after trimming and washing them, and cook them rapidly for 5 minutes. Then I drain them well, melt about 4 tablespoons butter in a saucepan, and toss them around in it until the butter turns a deep brown and the smell of the butter and the sprouts mingles in a way that intoxicates the nostrils. With a dash or two of salt and some freshly ground black pepper you have sprouts fit for the gods. Or I might cook them in the same manner and then toss them in olive oil with quite a bit of chopped garlic and a little lemon juice—and I do mean toss, until each one is coated with the fruity oil and an overtone of lemon. Grind some pepper on them, sprinkle with some chopped parsley and dill, and, once more, you'll have really delicious Brussels sprouts. Another of my tricks—and you can use this for broccoli rabe, too—is to toss the sprouts with the oil or butter, garlic, salt and pepper, and a good handful of pine nuts or, if you can't get them, walnuts that have been toasted in butter or oil until they are crisp and crunchy.

A Plea for Sauerkraut

It distresses me to learn that less and less sauerkraut is being eaten in this country. How can this crisp, pungent, versatile vegetable, so long a part of our gastronomic heritage, have fallen from favor? I can't remember a time when I haven't eaten sauerkraut; I couldn't live without it, and I hope I never have to. When I was a child, the man who ran a little farm we owned in the country used to bring us a barrel of sauerkraut right after its fermentation, and we had it all winter long, taking up bowlfuls, washing it thoroughly, and eating it raw or cooked in all kinds of ways.

Sauerkraut, you know, not only goes with hot dogs but also with turkey, goose, duck, pork, beef, even fish. The tradition of sauerkraut with turkey on the Thanksgiving menu in Maryland, Delaware, and Pennsylvania dates well back into the beginning of the nineteenth century, possibly even the late eighteenth. Goose and duck are tremendously improved by sauerkraut—the tart, fermented quality balances the fattiness of the bird. It's amazingly good with boiled beef, too. Instead of cabbage, try cooking some sauerkraut in a little bit of the stock from the beef for 30 to 45 minutes—it makes a much more interesting accompaniment. Then there's that great dish of sauerkraut and pork products you find in Germany, France, Switzerland, and the Tyrolean section of Italy under such names as *Berner Platte* and *choucroute garnie*.

I well remember going many years ago to a small brasserie or beer restaurant in Alsace after a very disappointing dinner where I had eaten nothing. I was with an equally disgruntled fellow guest, and we sat down and ordered a special *choucroute à l'Alsacienne*. What an impressive and appetizing sight it was—a great platter heaped with a steaming mound of sauerkraut surrounded by paper-thin slices of pink ham, sliced garlic sausage, and salt pork, garlanded with tiny Strasbourg sausages (which we would call frankfurters) and perfectly cooked potatoes, all piping hot. We drank steins of beer and ate for at least an hour until we were soothed and satisfied.

    It's easy enough to make *Choucroute Garnie*. First look in your local meat markets for various types of hearty sausages—knockwurst, frankfurters, Polish kielbasa, or Italian cotechino. For six persons or more, wash 3 pounds fresh or canned sauerkraut very well and put it in a deep kettle with 3 cups homemade or canned chicken broth. (If you like, use beer or white wine for part of the liquid.) Add a big chunk of rather lean salt pork, soaked in water to remove the excess salt, 1 or 2 cloves garlic, and about 2 teaspoons freshly ground black pepper. Bring to a boil, cover, and simmer for 45 minutes to 1 hour. For your major piece of meat, buy a 3-pound piece of smoked pork loin (sold in most markets nowadays) and roast it in a 325-degree oven for 25 minutes per pound, or until it reaches an internal temperature of 170 degrees. (There is also a ready-to-eat smoked pork loin that only needs heating through in the oven, so be sure to ask if it needs to be cooked or not.) Put 12 frankfurters or 6 knockwurst in with the sauerkraut for the last 20 minutes to heat through and also a ready-cooked Polish kielbasa if you can find one. Boil 12 potatoes in their jackets separately, then peel.

When it comes time to assemble the dish, drain the sauerkraut and mound it in the center of a big platter. Slice the pork loin and arrange around the sauerkraut. Garland with the sliced kielbasa and salt pork, the whole frankfurters or knockwurst, and the peeled potatoes. Serve with hot mustard—the Dusseldorf or German-type mustard or the French Dijon mustard.

You can do a party for as many as twenty people simply by adding more sauerkraut, sausages, and some sliced ham. With dill pickles, rye bread, and beer or Alsatian white wine you will have mighty good eating from this simple fare. If you have only eaten sauerkraut spread on a hot dog, this classic dish will be a pleasant surprise. Or you might try raw sauerkraut with French dressing, surrounded with thinly sliced onion marinated in the dressing and, perhaps, tomato wedges, as a salad with your next grilled steak or with a rack of barbecued spareribs, which take to sauerkraut like peaches take to cream.

The Versatile Chickpea

One of the most interesting of our dried legumes, the vegetable family that includes beans, peas, and lentils, is the chickpea. Chickpeas are comparatively unknown in this country, although they are a very old vegetable, having been grown in India many centuries ago. The Asian, European, and Middle East countries have all absorbed chickpeas into their cuisines—in India they are known as "gram," in Italy as "ceci," in Spain as "garbanzos," in France as "pois chiches," and in the Middle East, with variations in spelling, as "hummus." At one time they were widely used in Turkey to feed horses, and probably camels, too, for they were called "camel corn" there. Chickpeas do make a very nourishing horse feed, and I well remember traveling around the countryside of Portugal one day in a carriage and watching the driver, who was very fond of his horses, feeding them vast quantities of chickpeas.

If you don't know a chickpea when you see one, it is hard and round with a deep yellow color. Dried chickpeas take a good bit of cooking. Soak them overnight and then put them in water to cover with a garlic clove, a sprig of thyme and some salt and bring them to a boil. Then, for ½ pound chickpeas, add ½ teaspoon bicarbonate of soda, which helps to tenderize them, and cook them until they are very soft, which can take anywhere from 2 to 5 hours. Sometimes you can find them in Italian markets presoaked and ready to cook, but if you don't want to go to all the bother of soaking and cooking them, canned chickpeas work extraordinarily well. Drain them, wash them, and drain again before using. In some Middle Eastern and specialty food shops you may find roasted salted chickpeas in bottles or jars. They are crisp and salty, with a surprisingly pleasant flavor, and make an unusual cocktail nibble.

I like to use chickpeas because there are so many interesting things you can do with them. They can be heated and served, in equal proportions, with spaghetti, sauced with your favorite tomato sauce or simply butter and cheese, a great change from the usual pasta because of the two different tastes and textures. They are also good in vegetable soups, or in salads. For a salad, cook them with plenty of seasoning, drain, cool, and mix with a little finely chopped onion, a touch of minced garlic, olive oil, vinegar, salt, and pepper. The texture, crunchy but soft, is delicious with cold meats like corned beef and pastrami or with sausages.

Chickpeas combine well with canned beans in what I call a *Ranch Salad*. Mix equal amounts of chickpeas, kidney beans, and the white beans called cannellini with sliced onion, garlic dressing, and a little finely cut celery.

If you're bored with the usual starchy vegetables, try a *Chickpea Purée*. For eight servings, purée 3 cans drained and washed chickpeas in a blender or food mill or push them through a sieve with a wooden spoon. Combine the purée with a good knob of butter, a tiny bit of finely chopped garlic, salt and pepper to taste, and enough heavy cream to give a consistency like mashed potatoes. Heat through and serve with pork, lamb, turkey, or duck.

Even more delicious is a cold chickpea purée which is treated in rather a different way, a Middle East specialty called hummus bi tahini. Tahini is a sesame-seed paste with a wonderful nutty flavor, and you can buy it in jars or cans in Middle East stores, specialty food shops, health-food stores, and even in some supermarket chains on the East Coast.

 For *Hummus bi Tahini*, use ½ pound dried chickpeas, cooked according to previous directions and cooled, or 2 cans chickpeas, drained, washed, and drained again. Put them through a food mill or sieve or whirl them in the blender with the juice of 2 lemons and possibly ½ cup water, until you have a creamy paste. Finely crush 2 to 3 garlic cloves with 1 teaspoon salt and pound into the chickpeas thoroughly. Then gradually mix in ½ cup tahini and, if you have not already added lemon juice, the juice of 2 to 3 lemons—the paste should have a good strong lemony flavor, and it should be about as thick as mayonnaise. If too thick, thin with a little water. Let it rest for 20 to 30 minutes, then taste to see if you have enough garlic, salt, and lemon juice. If you like spicy mixtures, add a good slug of Tabasco as well.

To serve, put the hummus bi tahini in a bowl, pour a little olive oil on top and sprinkle with a fair quantity of paprika and chopped parsley, or just use the oil and a dusting of finely chopped fresh mint.

Serve as a cocktail dip or a first course with bread sticks, Melba toast, raw vegetables, or heated pita, that marvelous flat Middle East bread so many stores seem to carry these days. Tear the bread in bite-size pieces for dipping in the paste.

Look to the Lentil

When you dip your spoon into a bowl of steaming lentil soup, you may well be eating a culinary descendant of the "pottage of lentiles" for which Esau sold his birthright. These tiny bean-like seeds, from one of the first plants used for food, are a very ancient form of sustenance. The Egyptians and Greeks cooked these small legumes, and so did the Romans—in fact, Pliny the Elder, the Roman naturalist, recommended them as a food that produced mildness and moderation of temper. Remarkably, they are just as popular throughout the world today as they were all those centuries ago.

The lentils we use most in this country are the brown ones from Oregon and Washington, but there are others, like the red variety of Egypt, the green lentils of France, the yellow lentils of India, and some that are almost black. The only real difference in the many varieties of lentil is the size. Compared to ours, those of Egypt and France are quite small.

Lentils might have been devised for winter meals. They are a marvelously nutritious, satisfying, and economical food, and to me, their flavor is more interesting and distinctive than any of the beans, except perhaps the fava. In the old days lentils, like other dried legumes, required long soaking and long boiling, so they were rather tedious to prepare. Now, thanks to the processed packaged lentils we buy in our supermarkets, no presoaking is required and cooking takes very little time.

For six to eight servings, put 1 pound lentils in a 4- or 5-quart pot with 5 to 6 cups water, an onion stuck with 2 cloves, a bay leaf, and 1 tablespoon salt. Bring to a boil, reduce the heat, cover, and simmer for about 30 minutes. The important thing with lentils, as with beans, is not to overcook them until they get mushy and have no character. After you have cooked them for 30 minutes, taste to see if they are tender. If not, cook a little longer. Drained, buttered, and served with a sprinkling of chopped parsley, cooked lentils make a pleasant switch from the usual starchy vegetable. For a variation, after draining the lentils, sauté them quickly in a skillet in butter, olive oil, or bacon fat with 1 cup finely diced green onions, 1 cup crisp little bits of bacon, and ½ cup chopped parsley, tossing them together.

This makes a delicious accompaniment to spareribs, pork chops, roast duck, roast lamb—almost any meat, in fact.

For a one-dish meal on an icy winter's day, could there be anything quite as warming and heartening as a big pot of *Lentil Soup?* Put a ham or pork bone in a deep pot with 1 pound lentils and twice the usual amount of water or stock—about 2 to 3 quarts—for in this case the lentils need to be cooked until quite, quite soft, about 1 hour. When cooked, put them through a sieve or food mill, taste the purée for seasoning, and add freshly ground black pepper and salt to taste (you won't have to add much of the latter if the meat bone was very salty). Add 1 cup finely chopped onions, 2 finely chopped garlic cloves, 1 teaspoon thyme, ¼ teaspoon nutmeg, and enough additional water or stock, if needed, to make a good thick soup. Cook this down for another 30 minutes, at a simmer. You can make the soup even heartier by adding thinly sliced frankfurters or knockwurst for the last 5 to 10 minutes of cooking time, and richer by stirring in ½ to ¾ cup heavy cream for the last 5 minutes, blending well. Taste once more for seasoning, and serve topped with a sprinkling of chopped parsley and crisp croutons.

One of my great joys is a lentil salad. This is something you are seldom served, and I really don't know why, because it is excellent with cold meats such as ham, boiled beef, or chicken. This type of salad is ideal for a picnic or a covered-dish supper because it is no problem to carry and holds up well. In fact, if you don't finish it all the first time, it can mellow in the refrigerator for one or two days.

For *Lentil Salad*, put 1 pound lentils in a heavy saucepan with 5 cups water and 2 teaspoons salt. Bring to a boil, reduce the heat to a simmer, cover tightly, and cook for just 28 minutes—check by tasting to see that the lentils are tender but still firm. Drain well, then put the lentils in a big bowl and toss. them lightly with 3 or 4 tablespoons olive oil or salad oil. Let cool thoroughly. When the lentils are cold, add 1 large onion, finely chopped, 1 or 2 ribs celery, cut in fine dice, and, if you wish, ½ cup finely chopped green pepper or pimiento, and fold in gently. Make a dressing with ½ cup olive oil or peanut oil, 2 tablespoons good wine vinegar (or to taste), ⅔ to 1 teaspoon freshly ground black pepper, and 1 teaspoon salt, or to taste, depending on the amount of seasoning you like. Pour this over the lentils and toss lightly, until well blended. Allow to mellow in the refrigerator for several hours. Just before serving, garnish with chopped parsley and perhaps some finely chopped hard-boiled egg.

Bean Salads for All Seasons

I always welcome the advent of summer because it offers such an infinite variety in the dishes one can eat, many of which can be prepared ahead and kept in the refrigerator for several days. It's a delight to be able to bring forth an instant source of a good meal, something that can be added to or dressed up for an appetite-tempting lunch or supper.

For instance, take beans. I love beans in all their colors, shapes, and varieties, and I find them as delicious cold as hot, truly an all-season food.

The red kidney bean is known to us all through the ranch salad that has been so much a part of our menus for the last few years, and so is the chickpea. I find few people are as familiar with a great favorite of mine, the Italian cannellini, a white kidney bean that you usually find in cans in the Italian food section of supermarkets, so I'm going to give you a couple of recipes for this bean. If you can't find cannellini, you can use white pea beans or Great Northern beans, cooking them according to the package directions until they are just tender, but not mushy. Add an onion stuck with a cloves, a bay leaf, and 2 or 3 cloves of garlic so that they become delicately imbued with these aromatic flavors. Drain them well and add a touch of oil while they are still warm to stop them adhering to each other, then chill until ready to use.

༄ For a simple *White Bean Salad*, use either 1 pound pea beans, cooked, or 2 cans well-drained cannellini (these would be 1-pound 4-ounce cans). Make a vinaigrette dressing with 8 tablespoons oil, 2 tablespoons wine vinegar, 1 teaspoon salt, freshly ground black pepper to taste, ½ teaspoon dried basil or a little chopped fresh basil, and 2 cloves garlic (crushed and put in a little cheesecloth bag if you want to discard them after they have perfumed the dressing, otherwise finely chopped). Mix into the beans, chill them, then take them out of the refrigerator, and let them warm almost to room temperature before serving. Add extra dressing, if you think they need it, and sprinkle chopped parsley or chives on top for color.

This is an excellent, standard bean salad that goes with everything, especially such cold foods as stuffed breast of veal, roast chicken, or meat loaf. Add a mixed green salad, too, if you wish.

༄ A particular passion of mine—and I think of everyone who tastes it—is a *Cannellini Bean and Tuna Salad*. To serve four to six persons, depending on their appetites, use 2 cans well-drained cannellini beans, or 1 pound white pea beans, cooked. Mix them with a vinaigrette made with 6 tablespoons oil, 1½ to 2 tablespoons wine vinegar, ½ to 1 teaspoon salt (if your cooked beans have not been previously salted), ½ teaspoon freshly ground black pepper, and ½ teaspoon dried basil or some chopped fresh basil. Let this sort of melt into the beans, without tossing them too much, which breaks them up. Arrange in a serving dish and top with 1 cup finely chopped onion and two 7-ounce cans white-meat tuna, flaked. Top with additional chopped fresh or dried basil and a goodly portion of chopped parsley, and pour more oil and vinegar—about 3 tablespoons oil and 2 teaspoons vinegar—over the tuna and onions at the last minute.

This makes a perfectly delicious main-dish salad, with the smooth mealy texture of the beans blending with the crispness of the onion and the flaky tuna. Or, for a summer buffet, you might serve it with a mousse of some kind, ham or chicken perhaps, a green salad, and crusty French bread.

⌁For another good hearty salad, combine two 1-pound cans of well-drained red kidney beans with 1 to 1½ cups leftover boiled or rare roast beef, cut in thin strips, ½ cup very finely cut celery, and 1 minced garlic clove.

Toss well with 8 tablespoons oil, 2 tablespoons wine vinegar, with salt and freshly ground black pepper to taste, and garnish with thinly sliced red Italian onion, separated into rings, halved hard-boiled eggs, and some black olives, preferably the Greek ones. Sprinkle with chopped fresh basil and chopped parsley or chives, and serve as a main dish for luncheon.

Or, if you are going on a picnic, pack the salad in a bowl and take it along as part of your *al fresco* meal—it's more fun and more filling than sandwiches.

The Bean that Won the West

Nothing could be more American than the pinto bean, that exquisite pale pink bean speckled with brown that is common to the western states and Mexico. This was one of the vegetable crops the conquistadors found when they invaded Mexico, and as they progressed north they came across many pinto beans growing in the part of America that is now California, New Mexico, and Arizona, for this was one of the standard foods of the Indians. They dubbed it "pinto," Spanish for "spotted", because of its coloring.

Pinto beans can be bought in many of our markets, and if you have never cooked them, you should quickly add this colorful member of the dried legume family to your repertoire. You can use pinto beans in all sorts of bean casseroles, in place of white beans or red kidney beans, for they combine felicitously with roast pork or chops, ham, lamb, duck, or sausage, and they make a good hearty accompaniment to steak or hamburgers. In these days of sky-high meat prices, beans are a boon, not only as a way to stretch the meat you buy, but also as a supplementary source of protein. Pinto beans are especially rich in vitamin B-1, another mark in their favor.

For those of you who love Mexican food, if you don't know the *frijol pinto*, which, along with the *frijol negro* (black bean) and *frijol rojo* (red kidney bean), is one of the mainstays of Mexican cuisine, I think it's high time you rushed out and bought a package and cooked yourself some *frijoles*, or *frijoles refritos*, or *frijoles con queso*.

꙼Let's start with basic *Frijoles*, beans Mexican style. Put 2 cups (1 pound) pinto beans in a saucepan, and cover with warm water. Bring to a boil, cover, reduce the heat, and simmer very slowly—and I do mean simmer; simmering keeps the beans whole, but if you boil them they are apt to break up—until they are very, very tender, which can take 3 hours or more. (Because pinto beans grow in a very dry climate they take longer to cook than some of the other dried legumes.) Add more water if it cooks away, but not too much—there should not be a lot of liquid left when the beans are done. When the beans are almost cooked, season them with about 1 tablespoon salt, or to taste. Always salt beans after they have cooked, not before.

Melt ½ cup lard or bacon fat or ham fat in an earthenware casserole or a large heavy skillet. Mash a few of the beans into the fat, then add a little of the bean liquid and more beans. Continue adding and mashing until all of the beans are used, stirring from time to time, and cook until they have the consistency you like. They shouldn't be too dry, but neither should they be soupy—just moistly dry is what you are aiming for. Serve to six, with broiled meat or hamburgers or Mexican food.

For *Frijoles Refritos*, or refried beans, allow ½ cup lard or bacon fat for each 3 cups cooked frijoles. Melt some of the lard in a heavy skillet and mash some beans into it (it is best to do this in stages, first a couple of tablespoons of lard, then a few tablespoons beans, adding more lard as the beans get dry, more beans as the lard is absorbed, this will give you a nice creamy consistency). Stir over low heat until the beans are very hot and crispy around the edges. To my mind it doesn't hurt if you depart from tradition and mix a little chili powder or chopped green chili pepper into your frijoles refritos—it gives them a delicious spiciness.

Frijoles con Queso, beans with cheese, is just *frijoles refritos* with little cubes of Jack or Cheddar cheese popped on top and allowed to melt over the beans before they are served. This is wonderfully tasty, even better if you sprinkle it with chopped fresh coriander leaves, the cilantro the Mexicans love and use so much in cooking.

For a good satisfying casserole made with pinto beans, one of my favorites is *California Beans with Cognac.*

Soak 2 cups pinto beans overnight. Drain. Put in a saucepan with 2 finely chopped garlic cloves, 1 onion stuck with 2 cloves, a bay leaf, 1 teaspoon thyme, and boiling water to cover. Cover and simmer gently until very tender. Drain, reserving 1 cup of the bean liquid.

Melt 6 tablespoons butter in a pan, add 1 small onion, finely chopped, and sauté until golden. Add 2 cups tomato sauce or canned Italian plum tomatoes, ⅓ cup cognac, 2 teaspoons salt, ¼ cup chopped parsley, and the 1 cup reserved bean liquid. Bring to a boil, reduce heat, and simmer 30 minutes. Mix with the beans, put in an earthenware casserole, and bake in a 325-degree oven until just bubbly. This will serve six. To turn this into a one-dish meal, you can add 1 cup diced cooked ham and 1 pound cooked sausages to the beans and sauce before reheating, or brown 4 thickish pork chops on both sides, place them in the bottom of the casserole, cover with the beans and sauce, and bake until chops are tender.

The Salad Born at the Waldorf

When the crisp fall apples appear in the markets, I am always tempted to try out all my favorite apple recipes. I love apple dumplings and apple crunch and apples bonne femme, and I have always had a weakness for a Waldorf salad made with those tart and juicy fall apples, a very American dish that was created at the old Waldorf Hotel, which opened in 1893 at Fifth Avenue and 34th Street, where the Empire State Building is now.

I remember when I was about nineteen years old marveling at the massive beauty and utter luxury of the old hotel. The great columns and beautiful ironwork, the exquisite furniture and luxurious fabrics, and the wonderful collection of Victorian art were unforgettable. I also remember the first time I had lunch there. I had had a tooth pulled that morning, and I was being very good to myself, so after taking a long walk I decided to treat myself to lunch at the Waldorf. I called and reserved a table by the window facing 34th Street, and I sat there feeling rather awed, because I had never lived in New York until that year and I had heard and read so much about the Waldorf and this was my debut. I've no idea what I ordered except I recall thinking I should have some Waldorf salad. When it came I'm afraid I was a little bit disappointed because it was late for the tart apples, and while the salad was attractive and flavorful, it didn't excite me the way it would have done had the apples been the right type. However, the glamour of the room and the occasion and the overwhelming pleasure of eating in such an elegant atmosphere more than made up for it.

I've been doing a bit of research about the salad called Waldorf, and I've come across some rather interesting facts. Although we always think of a new dish as having been created by a chef, it was the then young maître d'hôtel of the Waldorf, Oscar Tschirky, who originated the Waldorf salad. The name of Mr. Oscar later became synonymous with the Waldorf, and when the hotel moved up to its present site at Park Avenue and 50th Street, he was one of its greatest attractions. I knew Oscar over a period of years, not only in the hotel but away from it. A very good friend of mine had been a longtime patron of the Waldorf and, in fact, kept an apartment there. When she gave a party, Oscar would come up to see that everything was as it should be. He was a very simple man and a man of enormous charm and great appreciation. Whenever I go into the Waldorf, I remember him wandering through the various rooms, smiling and checking to see that things were right.

Soon after the Waldorf opened, it became a favored center for the enormous and elegant parties given by New York society. When Mrs. William K. Vanderbilt had a benefit concert for St. Mary's Hospital for

Children, it was held at the new hotel, which had all the facilities she needed. It was a very large and important social occasion. Walter Damrosch conducted the New York Symphony Orchestra, and there was a great supper at which Oscar introduced the light, delicious, and different Waldorf salad, at that time a revolutionary combination of foods because most people didn't eat fruit salads as they do now. This may, as a matter of fact, have started the fruit salad vogue.

No one kept the original recipe, made up on the spur of the moment as many other things have been in culinary history, because no one, least of all Oscar, ever dreamed that this would become a household salad across the country, and something served in every restaurant. We do know that the original salad was different from the one we have now, which includes chopped walnuts. The early version was merely equal parts of diced tart apple and celery bound with mayonnaise and served on greens. Since then, it has seen many variations, some good, some not so good. I happen to think the addition of walnuts was inspirational. It gives another texture and flavor that is most pleasing. I've had it with pecans, which are all right, but don't have the flavor of English walnuts, and I have seen it gussied up with maraschino cherries and a gob of whipped cream on top, and other horrors that make it something absolutely revolting.

&Here is the version of *Waldorf Salad* that I like. Combine 1½ cups diced apple (if the apples are beautifully colored, you might keep some of the brilliant red or green skin on) and 1½ cups diced celery, and bind them with about ⅔ cup of good mayonnaise, flavored with a touch of mustard. The quality of the ingredients is important. The apple must be tart, crisp, and juicy, with a good bite, the celery cut very, very thinly, not in great chunks, and the mayonnaise homemade and well seasoned with mustard, but no sugar, please. Arrange on a bed of greens, garnish with coarsely chopped walnuts, putting one perfect walnut half on the top, and serve at once.

Nothing is worse than a Waldorf salad that sits until the apples become brown and awful. It should always be made and served at the very last minute. It goes extraordinarily well with game, chicken, and turkey and is delicious with cold meats.

If for nothing else, Oscar of the Waldorf will always be remembered for his very original salad.

The Tomato Salad Test

One of summer's greatest joys is to pick a sun-warmed, sun-ripened tomato from the vine, dust it off on your sleeve, and eat it like an apple. Savor the wonderful taste of the juice and the seeds on your tongue, and you realize that in a tomato, ripeness is all.

A great French restaurant critic who has been known to write blistering reviews of any he finds faulty says that he tests a new place by ordering a *salade de tomates*, or tomato salad. This ranks as one of the most frequently eaten hors d'oeuvre in French restaurants, and it can be extraordinarily good or extraordinarily bad. The tomatoes must be ripe, peeled, thinly sliced, and not salted until the very last minute. They may be sprinkled with coarsely ground pepper and chopped herbs, but no salt or oil should touch them until the salad is served at table. Tomatoes that are dressed beforehand form a sort of slimy, gooey sauce that is most unpleasant to eat. To enjoy this classic, simple tomato salad at its best, just take a really good garden-ripened tomato, peel and slice it, and serve it at room temperature with no more enhancing than perhaps some chopped parsley and fresh basil, freshly ground black pepper, then salt, a little olive oil, and, if you wish, a touch of vinegar or lemon juice.

There are, of course, other approaches to a tomato salad. You may slice the tomatoes thickly without peeling them, give them plenty of pepper and basil and a dressing of oil, a tiny bit of vinegar, and some finely chopped garlic. Or core the tomatoes, cut them in wedges, combine them with good healthy slices of red Italian onion or Spanish onion, and toss with freshly ground black pepper, salt, olive oil, and a touch of wine vinegar. With good crusty French bread you'll have one of the great summer eating experiences.

If you can buy or grow big, beautiful, round, ripe tomatoes, scoop out the shells and you can fill them with all kinds of good things.

≈One of my favorites for a summer luncheon in the garden or to take on a picnic is *Tuna-Stuffed Tomatoes*.

Fill 6 large scooped-out tomatoes with a mixture of 1 large can solid-pack white-meat tuna, ½ cup coarsely chopped onion or scallion, 1 teaspoon salt, ½ teaspoon freshly ground black pepper, 1 or 2 tablespoons chopped parsley, 1 or 2 tablespoons chopped fresh basil (or 1 teaspoon dried basil), 4 tablespoons olive oil, and 1 tablespoon lemon juice. (If you like garlic, add 1 or 2 chopped garlic cloves, mix with the oil and lemon juice, then toss with the tuna mixture.) Sprinkle chopped parsley on top of the stuffed tomatoes, and garnish with sliced olives or soft black Greek or Italian olives. For a special party touch, crisscross 1 *y* fillets on each tomato. Place on greens for a first or main *i* additional vinaigrette sauce. Serve with crisp toasted rolls *i*, and, if it's a hot day, ice-cold beer.

so like to fill the big tomato shells with crisply cooked green *i* Toss 1 pound cooked green beans with 4 tablespoons oil, 1 *i*spoon lemon juice, 1 teaspoon salt, ½ teaspoon freshly ground pepper, and ½ cup finely chopped onion. Fill the tomatoes, and top them with a tomato slice and some chopped parsley.

This makes an easy and filling vegetable-cum-salad course—for instance, with a grilled chicken or teriyaki steak you might just have a big tray of the stuffed tomatoes with French bread and chilled wine or beer and some fresh fruit for dessert.

Another combination that makes a pleasant lunch or snack is something I discovered at a small, very successful soul food restaurant in Montmartre run by two black Americans. It was known as Greased Pig Salad and it became a very popular hors d'oeuvre with the French.

For each serving of *Greased Pig Salad*, arrange on a plate a few very crisp leaves of Boston, romaine, or Bibb lettuce. Top with slices of really ripe tomato and maybe a slice of red onion. At the last minute, add 3 or 4 slices of crisp bacon. Serve this with a good mayonnaise, and you have what is really a bacon and tomato sandwich without the benefit of bread.

Dutch Treat

I love to get mail from people who really enjoy food, like the man in Baltimore who described in the most eloquent terms his early food memories and the beginning of his life-long passion for steak tartare. Recently I received another fascinating letter from Max Dekking of La Jolla, California.

"I, being a born Dutchman," he wrote, "naturally think the Dutch 'Huzarensla' is the greatest of all salads. Huzarensla literally means 'Hussar salad,' named so because when the Hussars, the fierce Russian soldiers, invaded the Netherlands centuries ago, the dish they most of all demanded when stopping in a village or settlement or farmhouse was the Dutch salad-meat dish, which subsequently therefore became known as 'Huzarensla' and is still one of the most famous and most beloved Dutch national dishes. I hereby give you the family's 400-year-old recipe. I would be greatly pleased and honored if sometime soon you would try it and give me your honest opinion of this wonderful meal-in-one salad."

Well, Mr. Dekking, I did try your salad, and it's a great meal, just as you said. I have eaten many beef salads, but this one has a quality that is quite different. When I make a beef salad, I use quite chunky pieces of meat and potato, but for this everything has to be chopped very, very fine, so be sure your chopping hand is in good condition when you make it, because you'll have to do a lot of chopping before you finish. This is the kind of salad that should be prepared well in advance and left to mellow in the refrigerator in a bowl or mold for three or four hours before being served. The Dutch unmold it onto a bed of greens and surround it with large chunks of bread (we can't get the bread they eat, which is very good indeed, but you should have the best bread you can buy or bake). Provide plenty of sweet butter for the bread, and a robust Dutch beer or whatever fine beer is available, and finish your meal with a selection of cheeses. This is the kind of salad, incidentally, that is really great for a buffet party. It's hearty, with interesting contrasts of flavor and texture, and it looks most attractive on a platter on its bed of crisp salad greens.

&For *Max Dekking's Beef Salad*, I'm giving you the proportions he prefers, but I think you might try it his way first and see how you like it and then maybe make your own little variations on the theme.

To start with, you will need 3 cups very finely chopped cold rare roast beef. Add to this 2 cups very finely chopped cold boiled potatoes (new potatoes, if possible, otherwise the rather waxy type), 1 cup very finely chopped cold cooked beets (you can use canned beets, if you like), ½ cup very finely chopped tart apples, 2 large onions, chopped very fine (and I really mean large onions), ½ cup very finely cut celery, 1 finely chopped shallot (if you can't get shallots, you could use a clove of garlic), and 3 small Dutch sour gherkins or, if not obtainable, 1 large kosher sour dill pickle, chopped very finely.

Make a vinaigrette dressing, using 3 parts olive oil to 1 part white wine vinegar (or rather less, if you don't like the vinegar flavor to be too pronounced), salt and freshly ground black pepper to taste, and perhaps a little Dijon mustard. It's hard to say exactly how much dressing to use, because it should be just enough to bind the salad. I happen to think that it is a good idea to add a tablespoon of mayonnaise to each cup of dressing to make everything hold together better. The salad shouldn't be sloppy, because you want it to be firm enough to hold its shape nicely when unmolded on the platter, so be sparing with the dressing—it's better to serve additional dressing on the side than to use too much in the salad. Mix everything together well, pack into a bowl or mold, and leave in the refrigerator for three hours before serving.

When you are ready to serve, unmold the salad on greens and garnish it with 2 hard-boiled eggs, sliced. I like some parsley, too, for garnish, but then I like parsley with everything.

If your platter is big enough, surround the salad with chunks of bread, or serve the bread separately, as you wish.

After the salad, bring on a tray of cheeses. Since you are going Dutch, you might have a Dutch Edam or Gouda, with a good Cheddar and some Swiss Gruyère or Emmenthaler. Follow the cheeses, if you like, with crisp cookies or a cake, and coffee, and you'll have had a simple but excellent meal, the kind of good, hearty, everyday fare we can all eat with appreciation and relish. I think a beef salad is one of the best dishes there is, and I'm very grateful to Mr. Dekking for having reminded me of it, and for giving me a new and different version.

⚜ CHAPTER 4 ⚜

Whims of Taste

ॐ

... in which we select the essential herbs and spices ... make a little saffron go a long way ... catch the scent of the vanilla bean ... caper in the kitchen ... salute salt ... unleash the power of pepper ... muse over mustard, olive oil, and olives ... get into a pretty pickle ... and distinguish true flavor from false.

My Six Essential Herbs

If I had to pick six herbs I couldn't cook without, I'd settle for basil, bay leaf, rosemary, savory, tarragon, and thyme. Parsley too, of course, but that is so universal it goes without saying.

Basil grows so readily in most parts of this country that, come spring, anyone with a patch of garden or a sunny windowsill should invest in a couple of plants. The matchless flavor of fresh basil is a natural ally of tomatoes and the prime ingredient in the Italian pesto, a dark-green paste made from basil leaves pounded with garlic, pine nuts, olive oil, and cheese that is spooned on pasta and rice and into soups. Pesto freezes well, so you can keep it year round. Fresh or dried, basil is exceedingly good with veal and many fish dishes.

Bay leaves have a delicate pungency that enhances all kinds of cooking. They are as appropriate a flavoring for a custard or arrowroot pudding as for a stew or sauce. The French pop a couple of bay leaves on top of a pâté while it is baking (if you try this, cover them with foil to keep them flat). In Italy, crumbled bay leaves are fried in olive oil with chopped onion, garlic, celery leaves, and tomato to make soffritto, a seasoning for sauces, soups, and stews.

Rosemary, asserted the great writer-cook Marcel Boulestin, is not for remembrance—it's for cooking veal. Lamb and beef as well. Put two or three sprays of rosemary on a just-cooked steak, pour on a little warm brandy, ignite, and let burn out to give a terrific flavor to the meat. The French custom of dipping a rosemary sprig in oil and brushing a steak, chop, or fish with it during the broiling is a very subtle flavoring trick indeed. Always pulverize rosemary's needlelike leaves in a mortar before adding them to a sauce or stew.

Savory, or *sarriette* as it is known in France, where it grows wild in the hills of Provence, is little known and little used in this country. The French often roll little goat's milk cheeses in its tiny, spiky dried leaves. Savory is an excellent herb for lamb, pungent enough to take the place of both salt and pepper if need be, which anyone on a salt-free diet might bear in mind.

Thyme is an herb without which no self-respecting cook can exist. It goes in ragouts, sauces, and stocks. There are several varieties of thyme, of which the most familiar is the tiny-leaved French thyme. The lemon thyme is very pleasant, too. An unusual and effective way to use thyme is to blend it with four ounces of cream cheese, a couple of tablespoons of heavy cream, a touch of minced garlic, and a soupçon of salt. Use about a teaspoon of the fresh leaves, half that amount of the dried. Chill and serve as a snack or a non-sweet dessert.

And then there's tarragon, a most exceptional and helpful herb. The unique flavor of its pointed leaves belongs with fish, is an absolute must for Béarnaise sauce, gives vinegar a glorious taste, and is the best friend a chicken ever had.

One of the greatest—and simplest—chicken dishes I know is *Poulet Sauté à l'Estragon*. To serve four, have 2 broiling chickens cut in quarters. Melt 4 ounces of butter with 2 tablespoons of oil in a large heavy skillet with a cover. When quite hot, add the chicken pieces and brown them skin side down first, then turn and brown the other side. This will take about 10 minutes. Salt and pepper them well. Add 8 to 10 finely chopped shallots or 10 to 12 green onions. Lower the heat, cover the pan, and simmer very, very slowly for 15 to 18 minutes, 20 minutes if the chickens are on the large side. Remove the cover, increase the heat slightly, and add 1 cup dry white wine with 4 tablespoons chopped fresh tarragon or 2 tablespoons dried tarragon, and 4 tablespoons chopped parsley. Turn the chicken pieces again, cook briskly for 3 or 4 minutes, turning once, and serve on a hot platter with some crisp toast as garnish and, if you like, tiny new potatoes.

The whole process takes less than 30 minutes, and you have a dish you could serve with confidence to the most critical group of food buffs. All you need to complete the meal is a salad or green vegetable and a very simple fruit dessert, with possibly some good cheese before the dessert. The same wine you used in the cooking will go well with the chicken.

Some final advice. Dried herbs cannot be used for ever and ever. They don't last that long. Keep them in a dark place, tightly sealed in glass jars, tins, or polyethylene bags, and smell them now and then to see if they are holding their strength. If not, throw them out and get some more. There's no economy in cooking with a spent herb.

Know Your Spices

So often we tend to buy a different spice because a recipe calls for it, use it once, and forget it. Seldom if ever do we try to figure out other dishes that might be enhanced by that particular spice—or even by the good old standbys like cinnamon, nutmeg, cloves, and paprika.

Take cinnamon, for instance, one of the most standard of all spices. I'm sure most people never think of putting it in anything but desserts and coffee cakes, yet there are hundreds of Greek, Middle East, North African, and Mexican dishes to which the distinctiveness of cinnamon adds a new dimension of flavor. The Greeks put cinnamon in meatballs and moussaka, the Moroccans and Tunisians use it in exotic meat pies made with layers of paper-thin pastry. and the Mexicans add it to *picadillo*, a kind of ground meat hash, and *mole*, that highly unusual sauce compounded of fiery chilies, spices, and unsweetened chocolate.

Even in our own country, cinnamon crops up in main dishes. My housekeeper, Clay Triplette, who is an expert at southern cooking even though he isn't southern, always adds a good bit of cinnamon, as well as salt and pepper, to the flour in which he dips chicken before frying it, which gives his fried chicken the most haunting, subtle, and delicate flavor. Cinnamon has this trick of bringing out unsuspected nuances in everyday foods. If you're having sliced oranges for breakfast, try sprinkling them with a little powdered sugar and cinnamon. The flavors are most compatible. A dash of cinnamon is excellent in lemon-flavored dishes and a perfect complement to anything involving chocolate.

Next, let's consider cloves, those aromatic little buds that look like tiny brown nails. Cloves are probably the most overused and misunderstood of all spices. While they are invaluable in cooking, they should always be used with great care and discretion, or their strong flavor can become overpowering and coarse. I, for one, think the habit of studding a ham with dozens of cloves to make a pretty pattern is a great mistake. If you must have cloves with ham, a light dusting of ground cloves is much better.

On the whole, cloves tend to be used here in traditional but rather unimaginative ways, such as in the mixed ground spices for pumpkin pie. Instead, I feel they should be put where they really make a contribution. If you stick a couple of cloves in the onion with which you are flavoring a pot roast or a stew or beef stock for a soup or sauce, they really give a great lift and change the usual taste to something quite delicious.

I also find that a clove stuck into a baked apple or pear, or a suspicion of ground cloves in the syrup used to poach dried prunes, can turn a rather run-of-the-mill dessert into something special.

Nutmeg is so common that we often forget how versatile it is. I own two enchanting little silver nutmeg graters, which elegant people were wont to carry in their pockets in the eighteenth and nineteenth centuries in order to grate fresh nutmeg on their food and drink, rather the way it is considered smart nowadays to carry your own small pepper mill. Nutmeg belongs in so many things. A pinch in a béchamel sauce, in creamed chicken or chicken fricassee, or in a cheese soufflé heightens the flavor and introduces a piquant overtone. The marriage of spinach and nutmeg, if well adjusted, is remarkably successful, and I find that there are certain cakes, such as spice cakes, in which the assertiveness of nutmeg is a necessity.

Then there's mace, actually the red netlike covering of the nutmeg in its natural state, which turns orange when dried. Mace, removed from the seed and sold either ground or in small pieces, or blades, tastes very similar to nutmeg, but milder and subtler. Ground mace should be carefully checked before use, for it can get rather rancid. Like nutmeg, it is marvelous in spinach dishes, especially creamed spinach and spinach soufflé, or in the stuffing for a turkey or chicken. I put mace in pound cake, where its fragrant freshness is a good counterpoint to the rich, heavy, vanilla-ish quality of the cake. I like to pop a blade or two of mace into pickles or other foods preserved in vinegar or vinegar and oil because I've found it gives a pleasing and interesting taste, and I have even been known to use a touch of ground mace, just a dusting, on pot roast.

Lastly, there's that universally popular spice, paprika, which I honestly believe many people buy only to sprinkle on food for color, rather than appreciating it for what it really is—one of the world's great flavors. Paprika is a spice of great charm, with infinite possibilities, and to look on it merely as something to make a dish colorful is to neglect its true culinary qualities. There are so many different kinds of paprika, from hot to sweet, from bright orange to rich red. The finest paprika is Hungarian, and the Hungarians are lavish with it. A goulash may have a whole tablespoon of paprika, sometimes sweet, sometimes part sweet and part hot. Paprika will turn the sauce for a fricassee of chicken to a creamy rose, and it also does something quite wonderful to the flavor of a tomato sauce.

It pays to know your spices. Take regular inventory, smelling, tasting, and throwing out those that have gone stale and flat from age. Then get out of the spice rut and learn how to use spices intelligently, adventurously, and with a very personal flair.

The World's Most Precious Seasoning

I have always been fascinated by the lore of spices, those mysterious and magical seasonings that have been an important part of our culinary practices for centuries. I have written about some of the more familiar—cinnamon and cloves, nutmeg and paprika. Now I'm going to discuss a spice that some of you may not know as well—saffron, which according to an old herbal quoted by the great English food writer Elizabeth David, is a "useful aromatic of a strong, penetrating smell and a warm, pungent, bitterish taste." Saffron is one of the most ancient and esteemed of all spices. Those wily traders, the Phoenicians, introduced it to the south of France and to England, where it still persists after hundreds of years in the saffron buns of Cornwall and old place names like Saffron Walden.

As a flavoring, a dye, and a medicine, saffron was highly prized in Europe in the fifteenth and sixteenth centuries, and even today it ranks as the costliest spice in the world. The minuscule vivid red threads are actually the dried stigmas of the *Crocus sativus*, a fall-blooming purple crocus that is cultivated in Spain, Portugal, and Italy, and it takes 75,000 flowers, picked by hand, to yield one pound of saffron. One of those little tins you buy for 65 cents contains only about eight-tenths of a gram of saffron, about a teaspoon. It would take 35 of these boxes to make just one ounce, which works out to around $364 a pound. However, to quote Elizabeth David again, "One grain or 1/437th of an ounce of these tiny fiery orange and red threadlike objects scarcely fills the smallest salt spoon, but provides flavoring and coloring for such a thing as a paella or a risotto or a bouillabaisse for four to six people." So, you see, a very little goes a long way.

Saffron occurs in the cuisines of Spain, Italy, southern France, Iran, and India and, oddly enough, in that of our own Pennsylvania Dutch country. How it became a part of that thrifty Germanic farmhouse cooking is rather an interesting story. In 1734 it was brought over by the Schwenkfelders, a group of Silesians, some of whom owned saffron warehouses in Holland. To this day, you'll find a recipe for their traditional wedding cake, colored and flavored with a goodly amount of saffron, in Pennsylvania Dutch cookbooks, and my friend Betty Groff, who lives in Lancaster County, Pennsylvania, can recall the days when people there had their own saffron beds.

The saffron sold in stores and supermarkets is mostly imported from Spain and comes in tiny packets or glass vials, or boxes that look like aspirin tins. For best results, buy the threads, which have the true, intense saffron color and flavor. There's a powdered form of saffron with a lot of color but little strength, and in Spanish groceries you may see something called "paella seasoning," which doesn't taste much of saffron either.

Always use saffron with discretion. A mere pinch lends an unbelievably delicious quality to such rice dishes as the paella and arroz con pollo of Spain, Iranian polo, Indian biryani, and the classic Risotto alla Milanese of Italy, for which I'm going to give you my recipe.

To make *Risotto alla Milanese* for four, you'll need 1 cup rice, or maybe a little more, either long-grain rice or the imported Italian Arborio rice. If you use long-grain rice, it's a good idea to wash it first, and dry it on a towel.

Now melt 6 tablespoons butter in a large, deep and heavy skillet, either iron or Teflon-lined. When it bubbles, add 1 small onion, finely chopped. Sauté until just wilted down to a delicate pale gold. Add the rice and toss it around with a wooden spoon to coat it well with butter, but do not let it brown. Add ½ cup dry white wine, and let this almost cook away. Have ready in a saucepan 2 pints hot homemade chicken stock (or canned chicken broth or chicken bouillon cubes dissolved in water). Start adding the stock, about 1½ cups at a time, and let each addition cook away rather briskly, stirring the rice often. As the rice absorbs the stock, add more. Continue stirring and adding stock until the rice starts to get tender, then add a good pinch (about ¹⁄₁₆ teaspoon) of saffron, which you have pounded in a mortar and pestle and then steeped in about ¼ cup hot stock. Stir this into the rice very well, so it dissolves and distributes its lovely flavor and color.

When the rice is tender to the bite and almost dry, stir in 3 tablespoons butter and ½ to ¾ cup freshly grated Parmesan cheese. The grains of rice will be soft, creamy, yet separate, quite different from other rice dishes.

Serve the risotto in four heated soup plates, with melted butter and more grated Parmesan for your guests to add as they wish.

In Italy, risotto alla Milanese is usually offered as a first course, or with certain meats such as osso buco—braised veal shank. I like to serve it as a main course for luncheon or supper, with a rather hearty salad of mixed greens and onion with a hint of garlic in the dressing, and a white Italian wine, followed by a simple dessert of fresh fruit.

Capers in the Kitchen

Few things in the gastronomic world seem to baffle the average person as much as capers. In my cooking classes, eight out of ten students ask, "What are capers and where do they come from?" Some think they are pickled nasturtium buds, and, as a matter of fact, they aren't too far off. Nasturtium buds can be pickled in vinegar and used like capers, the main difference being that they have a more peppery taste. However, capers are the pickled buds of a completely different shrub called *Capparis spinosa*, a plant ancient in origin that grows both wild and in the cultivated state from the Mediterranean area to southeast Asia. The caper plant may even be the hyssop so often mentioned in the Scriptures.

Capers grow on low trailing bushes, very similar to those on which you find wild blackberries, and they like a dry and rocky habitat. The green buds are carefully picked and sieved to separate the sizes, from small to quite large, and then preserved in mild vinegar or occasionally in salt, the way you sometimes find them in Italy or in Italian food shops. These capers are often extraordinarily large, much larger than those we are accustomed to buying in the small narrow green bottles, and they should be transferred to a larger jar and kept in vinegar or white wine. Capers vary a good deal. Some, like the Italian and Spanish, are very big. Others, like the firm round capers grown around Provence in the south of France, are quite small. These have by far the best color and are usually considered the choicest.

I use capers a lot. I like their distinctive, herby flavor and the additional bite imparted by the vinegar which makes them a most piquant and interesting condiment or seasoning.

Certain dishes just wouldn't be the same without capers. They are one of the traditional seasonings for steak tartare, along with onion, mustard, pepper, and salt, and for smoked salmon, and they are used extensively in cold dishes, particularly salads. These tasty little buds add color and a nice spiciness to a beef, crabmeat, or lobster salad, and to the famous *Salade Niçoise* of France (see page 289). Then there's a most unusual and delicious salad from Greece which consists of nothing but shredded carrots and capers tossed with a mustardy vinaigrette sauce.

While it is logical for capers to crop up so often in Mediterranean cooking, surprisingly enough you find them used extensively in Mexico, Latin America, and the Spanish-speaking islands of the Caribbean—especially Cuba, where they are often combined with olives. At a Cuban-owned grocery store near my house I buy a mixture of tiny green olives and huge Spanish capers all in one bottle, delicious in salads.

In England, capers are always to be found in a famous and rather unusual cream sauce, to which the pickled buds are added at the last minute, as the traditional accompaniment to boiled leg of mutton or lamb. A badly made caper sauce can be as grim and awful as library paste, but when it starts with a base of a good béchamel sauce, with the piquant acidity of the capers coming through, it is a marvelous complement to boiled or poached meats—boiled beef as well as lamb or mutton, and poached chicken.

Here is my recipe for *Caper Sauce*. Melt 3 tablespoons butter, preferably in a glass or enameled cast-iron saucepan (it is inadvisable to use metal because of the acidity of the capers), add 3 tablespoons flour, and blend well together. Cook 2 or 3 minutes, until the flour is well absorbed by the butter and gently frothing, then add 1 cup boiling chicken or veal broth and stir vigorously over medium heat until thickened. Reduce heat, and simmer 5 minutes, stirring occasionally. Season with ½ teaspoon salt, a touch of freshly ground black pepper, and a healthy pinch of nutmeg. Remove from the heat and stir in ½ cup warm heavy cream. Return to the heat and simmer (do not boil) for 3 or 4 minutes. Taste for seasoning.

Just before serving, stir in ⅓ cup well-drained capers, or more if you like them, and merely heat the capers through. You may also add 1 tablespoon chopped parsley if you like—it gives the sauce a nice color. Serve with any of the meats mentioned.

Salt, Sovereign of Seasonings

Salt is one of our greatest culinary gifts, an incomparable condiment, an everyday necessity and perhaps the most precious and invaluable of our kitchen staples. It goes into all our foods, even desserts, for a pinch in a cake batter, a pie crust, or the poaching syrup for fruit adds immeasurably to the finished product.

The very word has become synonymous with excellence. We talk of people being the salt of the earth, or of a man being worth his salt, a phrase that comes from the Latin *salari*, salt money or pay for work. When we say someone is worth his salt, we mean he is worth his salary.

Salt comes from two sources. One is the sea and the great salt beds or flats that form as the water evaporates. The other is rock salt, found in the earth in a crystalline form. You can buy sea salt in different grinds, but if you are spending the summer by the sea, you might like to make your own. Just fill very flat pans with sea water and leave them in the sun until the water evaporates, leaving a grayish white crust of pure sea salt. It may not be as attractive to look at as the packaged type—which is snow-white, fine, and pours easily because it has magnesium carbonate added to prevent it from clogging in damp or humid weather—but it will be just as salty and good.

Then there is coarse salt, available in different-sized crystals. For use in the kitchen and as a flavoring I like kosher salt, a free-flowing, rather coarse crystallized salt you find in many supermarkets now. It has a good saltiness that appeals to me very much. Other people like the really coarse salt the French call *gros sel*. You often find a little dish of this served with certain dishes such as boiled beef, as a crunchy, delicious condiment. (It's good with raw vegetables, too.) Even larger salt crystals go into salt mills (these resemble pepper mills except that the crusher, the interior mechanism, and the little handle that operates it are made of noncorroding wood, rather than metal) to be ground fine at the table by those who like their salt freshly milled.

Coarse salt is an essential part of one of my favorite fish dishes which is supposedly Oriental but has become quite common here.

For this *Salmon Orientale* you will need, for four persons, 4 fillets of salmon. Ask to have a piece of salmon cut toward the tail, not from the thickest part, filleted, and cut lengthwise into 4 pieces of practically the same thickness, each one with skin on the flesh. Measure the thickness by standing a ruler upright beside the fillet—it will be cooked for 10 minutes per inch measured at the thickest point. Rub both sides of the fish quite generously with coarse salt, and let stand for at least 30 to 35 minutes before broiling. Place on a piece of foil, skin side up, on a broiler rack about 4 inches from the heat, and broil for two-thirds of the time on the skin side, one-third on the flesh side. (If your fillets are 1 inch thick, you broil them for 6 minutes on the skin side, then turn and broil 4 minutes flesh side up.) Remove from heat, brush the flesh lightly with oil or butter, and broil ½ to ¾ minute more. Remove to a hot platter and serve with dill butter.

 For the *Dill Butter*, cream 6 tablespoons butter with 1 teaspoon dried dill or 2 teaspoons chopped fresh dill and ½ teaspoon lemon juice. Beat well together and chill for a few minutes. Put a good spoonful of the butter on each serving of salmon.

If you are cooking outdoors, you can grill the salmon over charcoal, following the same method and cooking time. Brush the grill with oil (or put the fillets in a basket grill which makes it easier to turn them) and cook skin side down first, then turn and grill flesh side down. With the broiled or grilled salmon you might have boiled new potatoes, or cucumbers which have been peeled, seeded, cut into long strips or small squares, and cooked in boiling salted water until they are just translucent—not soft, they should still be slightly bitey. Drain well and toss with a little butter and freshly ground pepper.

This makes a most unusual and pleasing main dish for a summer dinner or luncheon, salt-flavored but not salty. It bears out my theory that salt is a flavor as well as a condiment.

Doing Without Salt

Many people these days are forced to go on a salt-free diet—or perhaps it would be more correct to call it a salt-restricted or low-sodium diet, for almost everything we eat contains some natural sodium; it's the salt we add in cooking that is the problem. I'm always getting letters asking what can be done to alleviate this gastronomic plight, which is one of the most difficult anyone who loves good food must face.

While nothing really takes the place of salt, or high seasoning (for again, many people on a low-sodium diet can't have much seasoning, either), there are a number of things that help enormously. As one who has been from time to time among the salt-deprived (and I happen to like a lot of seasoning in my food), I've discovered a few tricks that really work.

I remember well being on a salt-free diet for several weeks in a French clinic. My daily intake was rigidly controlled, with all my food weighed out. Fortunately, at mealtimes we were given a plate with a pepper mill, a small pot of Dijon mustard, half a lemon, and sometimes fresh parsley, basil, or thyme. I can tell you that when all else fails to stimulate the taste buds, the spicy perfume of freshly ground pepper will do the trick. The proper seasonings, I found, go a long way toward making food so palatable and delicious that you can almost forget the lack of salt.

Just a squeeze of lemon juice on meat, chicken, vegetables, practically any dish, seems to enliven the natural flavor. Season artichokes with a little lemon juice (and, if you're not forbidden it, a touch of olive oil), and you'll never miss the salt shaker. Coarsely ground black pepper and lemon juice bring out all the nuances of a baked potato. So does a spoonful of sour cream or yogurt, or unsalted butter, but over the years I've learned to do without even these. Now I savor the simplicity and earthy goodness of a well-baked, crisp-skinned potato with nothing more than a sprinkling of aromatic, freshly ground pepper.

Here's another little hint for cooking vegetables without salt: add a teaspoon of sugar to the cooking water. It won't make the vegetables sweet, but it will give them a more finished flavor, and when you serve them you can add some chopped herbs and freshly ground pepper, too.

Fresh herbs, with their matchless pungency, are one of your best allies. One day for lunch in Iran I was served a beautifully grilled chicken with a plate of fresh herbs in lieu of salad. The chicken had a good flavor and a nice crispy skin, and the contrast of the herbs, which you munched along with it, did something quite extraordinarily exciting to the palate.

It's well worth growing your own herbs. Basil, chives, thyme, summer savory, tarragon, dill—all have a definite, appetite-provoking flavor of their own, an interesting texture, and when picked in little sprigs or leaves, they give food a delightful visual quality. Take as your flavoring palette little branches of thyme, with their infinitesimal leaves and sharp fragrance; the soft plumy sprays of dill with its delicate bouquet piquant tarragon with those long arrow-shaped leaves, so good on sliced tomatoes; flat Italian parsley, with a form and flavor completely different from the curly type; and fresh coriander, also known as cilantro, which has a taste like nothing else on earth and evokes memories of the cooking of China and Mexico, the Middle East and Portugal.

One of my favorite salt-free dishes is *Herbed Broiled Chicken*, done in a rather different way that transfers the flavors to the meat. For four persons, get 2 split broilers. Finely chop ⅔ cup green onions and 1 to 2 garlic cloves, depending on how much you like garlic. Combine with ½ cup finely chopped mushrooms, 2 tablespoons chopped parsley, and freshly ground pepper to taste (I often add 1 or 2 dashes of Tabasco as well).

Cream 1½ sticks (6 ounces) unsalted butter (or, if you are on a strict diet, margarine), combine it with the chopped mixture, and then, with your fingers, loosen the skin of the chicken, being very careful not to break or pierce it, and insert the butter mixture under the skin, distributing it well over the flesh. Starting with the chicken bone side up, broil to the degree of doneness you prefer, turning it midway in the cooking and broiling it skin side up until done. Baste the chicken during the broiling to give it more flavor. In summer, I like to make a mixture of creamed butter and chopped fresh herbs and stuff this under the skin, which gives a really fantastic flavor.

It takes inventiveness to make a saltless diet enjoyable, but it can be done.

ॐ

Pepper Power

For years I have routinely prescribed freshly ground pepper in all my recipes, because I wouldn't dream of using anything else. If you have ever doubted that it is superior to the ready-ground, compare the two for yourself. You will find that ground black pepper packed in jars or cans tends to go stale quickly, and it never has the potent fragrance of crushed peppercorns. For those who care enough about the difference in flavor a pepper mill is essential, and pepper mills are so inexpensive these days that anyone can afford to own one. If you don't have one you can crush peppercorns with a small mortar and pestle or with a rolling pin, or you can grind them in an electric blender.

Many people ask me what the difference is between white pepper and black. White pepper is simply ripened more and is stripped of the black outer crust. It is somewhat more intense in flavor than the black but lacks its delightful aroma. Most of the good black peppercorns available in our markets is the variety known as Malabar. Look for jars containing peppercorns of uniform size rather than a mixture of large and small. Some people feel they must put white pepper into white sauces, to keep them chaste, and reserve black pepper for dark sauces. I consider this a lot of nonsense. I prefer flavor to prettiness and use black pepper in whatever I choose.

A third form of pepper, from Madagascar, is making its appearance in specialty food shops. It has been popularized by the French, who call it poivre vert—literally, "green pepper." To describe it I can't do better than quote from Elizabeth David's *Spices, Salt and Aromatics* in the English Kitchen. "Poivre vert," she writes, "is exactly what it says it is; pepper which is green in both senses—green because it is unripe, fresh peppercorns, and green in color. Soft as a berry, poivre vert can be mashed to a paste in a moment. . . ."

While we customarily add pepper to our food in moderate amounts, used boldly as the dominant flavor, it can give a dish great distinction. This is the case with one of the most popular of all steak preparations—steak au poivre. Primarily a French dish, it has become thoroughly Americanized and can be found in almost any steak restaurant, where it is sometimes known as "peppered steak" or "steak with crushed peppercorns." At home you can make it with any good cut of steak, and it needn't be the most expensive. I frequently use club steaks or small shell steaks from my local supermarket. Or I may do one large steak and carve it into slices.

⤷ Traditionally *Steak au Poivre* is cooked quickly in a very hot skillet, although it can be broiled. Use a 6- to 8-ounce steak, ¾ to 1 inch thick, for each person. Trim off excess fat. Very coarsely grind or crush 1½ to 2 teaspoons pepper for each steak. Press the pepper into both sides of the steaks, and salt well. For 4 steaks heat about 3 tablespoons each of butter and oil in the skillet, or melt down some of the fat trimmings and add a bit of butter and oil. When the fat is quite hot and about to sizzle, put in the steaks. For rare meat, cook over fairly high heat about 3 minutes on each side, turning once or twice. For medium rare or medium, turn the heat down very low and cook 1 or 2 minutes more. The skillet will remain quite hot for that amount of time.

Remove steaks to a hot platter or directly to hot plates. Serve just as they are, or rinse the pan, scraping the bottom and sides, with 3 or 4 tablespoons of red wine, sherry, or Madeira, and spoon over the steaks. Or if you want to be very grand, when the steaks are done add about ⅓ cup bourbon or cognac to the skillet and ignite, keeping your face averted from the flame. Let the alcohol burn out.

Remove the steaks to a platter, add a little extra liquor to the pan, and pour the juices over the steaks. For a finishing touch sprinkle with chopped parsley.

Serve with watercress or a good salad. If you want starch as well, serve mashed potatoes or a baked potato. This makes an extremely satisfying family or company dinner.

Roast duck can be given the same peppery treatment as steak. Press very coarsely ground peppercorns into the breast of a roasting duck 30 minutes before it is done, then run it under the broiler for a few minutes to give it a crusty finish. This produces duck with an exciting and unusual flavor. It is excellent served with turnips and a nice cold dish of applesauce.

Make Mine Mustard

I'm an inveterate collector, and over the years, almost without knowing it, I've amassed quite a collection of mustard pots, both the commercial ones and the kind made of silver and glass you find in antique shops. I have a pot that resembles a snail, another shaped like a champagne cork, and several different types from the famous mustard-producing house in Dijon, France, where the mustard is put up in stunning blue-and-white pots. Looking at my pots started me musing on mustard, one of the most versatile flavorings and seasonings we have.

Mustard is made by grinding or pounding black or white mustard seed (you're probably familiar with the white seed, used in picklemaking) and discarding the husks. What remains is mustard flour or dry mustard. The word has an ancient origin—it comes from *must*, the leftovers from the wine pressing, with which the Romans mixed the pungent pounded seed to a paste. The Italian *mostarda*, which preceded mustard in pots, is a kind of relish made from fruits preserved in sugar syrup to which a great deal of mustard has been added. When you taste these beautifully colored, deceptively innocent fruits you'll be surprised by their pungency and hotness. They can be bought in Italian stores or food specialty shops, and they make a perfectly delicious relish to use in place of mustard with cold meats or chicken, or with boiled beef dishes like the Italian bollito misto, the French pot-au-feu, and our own boiled beef.

You can buy mustard in various strengths and flavors. The simplest form is the dry mustard which the English, who like their mustard very hot indeed, mix with water, making a fresh batch whenever needed. They like it with all manner of meats, especially sausages and roast beef. ("Meat," says a popular British slogan, "needs mustard.") In France, mustard flour is mixed with white wine for the famous Dijon mustard sold throughout the United States in little glass jars or the more attractive blue-and-white pots. Then there are herbed mustards from France and Germany, some mixed with tarragon, and one that contains crushed mustard seeds. The type most used in America for hot dogs, hamburgers, and sandwiches is a darkish brown. It's pungent and spicy but not very hot. Another one, called salad mustard, is light in color and has practically no bite.

You can use either dry or prepared mustard in cooking, and you'll be amazed how just a touch brings bland food to life. Cream sauce for broiled fish or veal cutlets, for example, is infinitely better if you add some mustard and a few drops of lemon juice. You can also make a remarkably good and piquant sauce for cold foods (fish, shrimp, crab, chicken, and practically all poached vegetables, particularly asparagus and leeks) by mixing mayonnaise with mustard to taste—this can be any type you prefer, as hot or as mild as you like it. This mustard mayonnaise gives extra zip to sandwiches, too. Then here's another simple trick. Split a loaf of French bread lengthwise, spread with butter and brush with mustard, sprinkle with some chopped green onions and parsley, and heat through in the oven as a change from garlic bread.

I well remember, some years ago, visiting one of the great gourmets of France. While I was there, every hour on the hour, he brought in from his apartment windowsill a dish of pieces of hare which he carefully brushed with mustard so it would absorb the spicy flavor before being cooked the next day. A mustard coating on hare, rabbit, or chicken, which is more to our taste, gives the meat a really interesting and unusual flavor.

To make *Mustard Chicken* for four, dust 4 half chicken breasts lightly with flour, and sauté in a heavy skillet in 4 tablespoons butter and 2 tablespoons oil until nicely browned on all sides. Remove, spread each piece liberally with mustard (Dijon or herbed mustard or a paste of hot mustard or whatever you like), and put in a shallow baking dish.

In the fat remaining in the pan sauté 1 finely chopped medium onion for a couple of minutes, and add another tablespoon of butter if needed and about ½ cup finely chopped mushrooms. Sauté with the onion, then add 2 tablespoons chopped parsley, and salt and freshly ground pepper to taste—you won't need much pepper because of the mustard. Then blend in 1 cup heavy cream and let it just heat through. Pour the mixture over the chicken, and bake in a 350-degree oven for about 30 to 35 minutes, or until the chicken is tender when tested with a fork. Taste to see if the sauce needs more salt, and add a few drops of lemon juice. Serve at once with fluffy rice.

This is a simple but splendid dish—the cream gives the sauce a lovely texture, and as it cooks with the mustard it thickens a little more.

Olive Oil to Taste

You've probably been to wine tastings and cheese tastings, but you have to be around Provence, or a similar olive-producing area, to know the importance of an olive oil tasting. Oils differ so much in quality, color, taste, and texture.

I was in Provence at the beginning of the year, the season when the olives are gathered from the trees in the neighborhood of Grasse, Cannes, and Opio. Not far from where I was staying was a wonderful old oil mill, which must be one of the few really old ones still going. Tastes in oil have changed, and in these last few years oil has become quite different from the way it was before. Many more oils are blended, and many people have switched to oils other than olive, but to a true olive oil user and lover, which I am, there's no joy to match that of watching the olives being crushed and then tasting the various oils that come forth.

My friends and I wanted to buy oil for the kitchen and the Provençal dishes and salads that depend for their flavor on the essence of the local olives, so one day we went to the old mill and watched the olives being pressed. The mill is run by water power, with a big wheel outside that turns the presses. These are not too big, just about 6 feet in diameter. There's a large cone with a stone wheel that revolves and crushes the olives so the oil flows into the vats below. After this the oil is poured through woven jute mats that look like huge table mats, and pressed to filter it completely. The oil from the first pressing, the virgin oil that brings a premium price in stores, is of the finest quality and a beautiful, brilliant greenish gold. While oils from other pressings may have a very good flavor, they are not as high in quality. Incidentally, in some countries you will find a very green oil, which comes from pressing some of the leaves with the fruit, to give color.

After the pressing we briefly and lightly tasted some of the oils, and I found one that was very fruity, with a superb bouquet like a great wine, and a magnificent, round, full olive taste—the type of oil I love most. I know many people who find a fruit oil rather disagreeable to their palate and prefer one that is lighter, or has been blended with a tasteless olive oil so there is only a faint hint of the characteristics of the olive, but I want the full flavor or none at all.

We came home with our prize and the first night used it for a salad made with four parts of oil to one of lemon juice and a great deal of garlic, because the local garlic is very delicate in flavor. You pound it in a mortar and add it to the dressing, and it makes a brisk, wonderful contrast to the rich fruitiness of the oil.

The dressing was tossed with curly endive, Belgian endive ing of cooked beets from the local market. (The natural swe beet takes away the sharp bitterness of the greens and gives esting interplay of tastes.)

If you like, you can add fresh herbs to your dressing—tar and a bit of thyme are all good—but as far as I'm concern lence of the salad depends on the excellence of the oil.

This holds true with many of the dishes of the Mediterranean region such as pizza, whose flavor comes from the oil in the dough and the sauce; pissaladière, the southern French version of pizza; and ratatouille, that inspired Provençal mélange of vegetables.

If you've never tasted one of the simplest and best of all sauces for pasta, I suggest that next time you hunger for a plate of spaghetti you try *Spaghetti con Aglio e Olio*—with plenty of oil and garlic. For four, cook 1 pound spaghetti in plenty of boiling salted water until just tender but still bitey—as the Italians say, *al dente*. While it cooks, heat 1 cup of the best olive oil until barely warm. Add 4 to 5 finely chopped garlic cloves (this may sound like a lot, but it is the garlic that makes the dish) and let them soak in the warm oil for 2 or 3 minutes. Drain the spaghetti well, and toss it with the oil, garlic, and freshly ground black pepper to taste. Don't serve cheese with this. The distinctive and complementary flavors of the oil and garlic are all you need.

For another version of this dish, sauté the garlic in 4 tablespoons oil until lightly colored. Combine with ½ teaspoon crushed dried hot red pepper and ¾ cup heated olive oil and toss with the cooked spaghetti.

Good olive oil isn't hard to find. If you shop in stores that carry a big selection, get a small can or bottle to test before you buy in quantity. There are excellent Italian, French, and Spanish oils to be had. In fact, one finds better Spanish oils here than in Spain because they export their best. I have also had delicious California oils. These are harder to find than they used to be. The market is getting smaller, since so much oil is sold in bulk for other uses, but if you shop around in California, you can find some really well-flavored olive oils.

Buy your oil carefully, use it wisely, and safeguard the flavor. If you don't use a great deal, buy in small quantities and keep the oil in a bottle with a tight cork or ground glass stopper to prevent it from becoming rancid. Never let seasonings such as garlic and herbs stand in the oil for longer than a few hours—they can also turn it rancid. I don't consider it a good idea to refrigerate olive oil. It congeals and is not pleasant to use, although in many restaurants in Provence it is the custom to freeze tiny

ainers of the fruity oil and serve it thick and almost solid, along with
.e hors d'oeuvre. This isn't a practice I recommend, but try it if you like,
as a talking point.

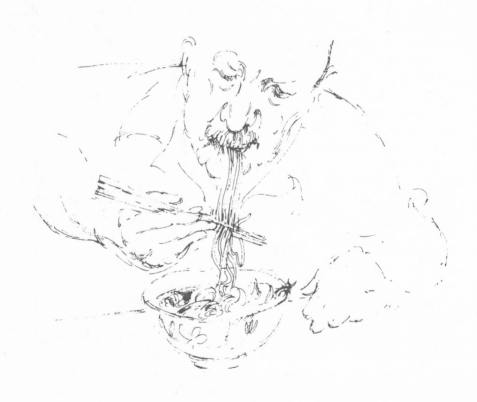

Olives, Anyone?

Olives are one of our original foods, described by author Lawrence Durrell as having "a taste older than meat, older than wine, as old as cold water." They grow in many parts of the world, among them the Middle East, Greece, Cyprus, Italy, the south of France, Spain, Portugal, Algeria, Morocco, and our own California. Wherever they are found, the local people regard them as the ideal food for nibbling, with or without drinks, and they indeed rate as the most perfectly simple and simply perfect hors d'oeuvre known to man.

If you dine at the famous Forum of the Twelve Caesars in New York, the first thing put on the table is a bowl, usually a silver one, heaped high with ten or twelve varieties of olives. There might be tiny black olives from Nice, no larger than a peanut; huge luscious green Spanish olives stuffed with pimiento and the little manzanilla olives stuffed with anchovy; the long, pointed calamata olives from Greece, almost purple in color; green unstuffed olives from Spain and California, sometimes called queen olives; and the soft Greek or Italian black olives preserved in olive oil after they are dead ripe. These have a real bitter salty tang that tantalizes the palate, and they are also the most favored cooking olives for Mediterranean dishes.

In Spain, two types of green olives are gathered for table use, the very large and the small manzanilla. The freshly picked olives are cured by a slow process in which they are first placed in water, changed every day for a fortnight, to get rid of the bitterness, then transferred to old wine or brandy barrels and cured in a strong pickle of sea salt and the softest, freshest of water, in which they will keep for about two years. (There is also a shortcut process in which the olives are first put in a soda solution for a few hours, then in fresh water, and then in the brine.) The green olives you buy in jars are packed in brine, and they can be had in varying sizes, either whole or pitted and stuffed with pimiento, anchovy, onion, or almonds. Once olives have become wet, they should never be left out of their liquid or in the open air more than is necessary, or, as you may have noticed, they tend to shrink a bit and the appearance and flavor are impaired.

Black or ripe olives are left on the tree until they become dark and oily before being given the brine treatment. California ripe olives are not the same as those imported from other countries—they are a different type and are processed differently. Their brownish flesh is firmer to the bite and has a distinctive flavor—not as tasty as other black olives in my opinion, but they are good to look at and make a most beautiful garnish. Then there is another type of imported black olive that has been dry-packed. These are rather wrinkled and not as pleasing to the eye, but they have a fine sharp flavor. They are reconstituted by soaking in oil or used as they are for cooking.

Another type of olive harvested here is the green ripe olive—these are small olives picked just as they are on the cusp of being ripe, and their flavor is something else again.

Next time you are having friends in for drinks you might have an olive tasting—set out bowls of all the kinds you can find; it's great fun. Most good olives can be served just as they come from the jar. However, with black or ripe olives you can give them extra zest by letting them stand in olive oil with a touch of garlic for a day or two, or grating a little lemon peel over them and tossing them in oil—they are extraordinarily good that way.

If you're an olive buff, you'll like this *Cheese and Olive Salad*, delicious for a buffet party, with cold meats for luncheon, or to take on a picnic. You'll need imported Swiss cheese—either the Emmenthaler, with great big holes, or the rich-flavored Gruyère, with very few holes. For six to eight servings, finely shred 2 pounds Gruyère or Emmenthaler cheese. Combine with 2 cups finely chopped green onions or scallions and 1½ cups sliced stuffed green olives, mixing well. Toss with a dressing made from 1 cup olive oil, ¼ cup wine vinegar, 4 teaspoons Dijon mustard (you need a strong mustardy flavor for this), 1 teaspoon salt, and ½ teaspoon freshly ground black pepper. Arrange on a green nest of fresh salad greens—Bibb, Boston, butter or leaf lettuce, or romaine—in a salad bowl, piling the salad up nicely. Garnish with more stuffed green olives.

The Joys of Pickling

For as long as I can remember, mustard pickles and watermelon-rind pickles, sweet pickles and dill pickles, all the various types of relishes that were put up for winter and spring eating, have intrigued me no end. I love to sniff the hot spicy vinegar smell, the turmeric-laden air when mustard pickles are being made, the fragrance of the cassia buds that went into some of the sliced sweet pickles my mother used to prepare. It is no wonder to me that we have a National Pickle Week. I think it might well be a National Pickle Month.

We are surrounded by pickles in our markets and supermarkets, and while some commercial packs are pretty dreary, others are perfectly marvelous. So many foods just scream for a good pickle. Dill pickles, of course, go with ham and corned beef, with sandwiches and sauerkraut dishes, but have you ever tried a thinly sliced dill pickle on a hamburger? It's superb. One of the greatest emotional pleasures imaginable is to wander down the street munching on a big luscious garlic-laden kosher dill, either fresh or brined.

Then there are the little sour gherkins, or cornichons, you get in France with the pâtés and other bits of charcuterie served at the beginning of a meal. I also like these tiny crisp sour pickles with boiled beef or other boiled meats for the delicious flavor contrast.

Pickles are a joy to eat, but an even greater joy to make. In a cooking class I held in Oregon we had a magnificent team of pickle-makers, two women who meet for two or three weeks every year and pickle to their hearts' content. They gave me a jar of last year's parsley pickles, a typical sweet pickle recipe made with gherkins and tiny pickling onions, spices, and a sweet and sour vinegar bath, but the jars were packed with great clumps of parsley which not only looked beautiful but also imparted a very delicate overtone of flavor. The same women make a curry pickle, with turmeric, curry powder, and cloves adding pungency and bright color, that is fine as an ordinary pickle, even better with such things as curries and chilies.

When I was a child, we used to prepare perhaps twenty different kinds of pickles and relishes for the winter. We always had chowchow and mustard pickles, a huge barrel of dill pickles, and some special ones in jars, but those I enjoyed most were oil pickles, or olive oil pickles, which have been favorites in this country for fifty or sixty years. Oil pickles, for my palate and taste, need olive oil, probably because that was the way they were made when I was young.

    To prepare *Oil Pickles* you can use either very small cucumbers, about 3 inches long and 1 inch in diameter, or cucumbers 4 inches long. You'll need about 10 to 12 of the medium, 4-inch size, or about 30 of the 3-inch ones. Wash them well, and slice on a slicer or, if you are deft, with a knife into slices not over ¼ inch thick. Peel and slice paper-thin 4 or 5 medium onions. Mix cucumbers and onions in a large bowl, and sprinkle with a mixture of ½ to ¾ cup salt and 1 teaspoon powdered alum. Let them stand in a cool place overnight. In the morning, drain and rinse them thoroughly and put them back in the bowl, which should also be rinsed. Pour over them enough vinegar (I like to use red wine vinegar) to just cover, and let them stand for 1 to 4 hours—4 hours is preferable.

Drain off the vinegar and measure it into a kettle. For each cup of vinegar add 2 to 3 tablespoons olive oil and ⅓ cup brown sugar. Add 2 tablespoons celery seed and 3 tablespoons mustard seed. Bring the mixture to a boil, and pour it over the cucumbers. Pack into hot sterilized jars and seal. Let the pickles stand a week before you use them.

These are so crispy and good and different that if I were you I would try them out and, if you like them as much as I do, make another batch so you won't eat them all up before the winter is over. Oil pickles are good with cold meats, such as thinly sliced corned beef or roast beef, and extremely good with fish. Sometimes I make a sandwich with the pickles and cream cheese; it's a delightful snack.

Making pickles is great fun. Look up a good pickle book and try all kinds—watermelon-rind pickles, curry pickles, dill pickles, bread-and-butter pickles, mustard pickles, and the many other delights that are well worth your time and effort.

The Fragrant Bean

The vanilla bean comes from the pod of a climbing orchid plant native to Mexico that grows about 40 feet tall and flaunts spectacular flowers. The seed pods, from 4 to 8 inches long, must be picked before they get too ripe—otherwise, they burst and all the goodness that is turned into vanilla extract is scattered to the winds. The green pods are cured until fermentation starts and a magnificent perfume develops. I say perfume because when you are cooking with vanilla a heady fragrance permeates the kitchen and you think: "Oh, if I could just put some of that on my hand or my handkerchief, how wonderful it would be."

Nowadays very few people seem to use vanilla beans as our mothers and grandmothers did; they mainly use the extract. That seems to me a pity because the bean, though hardly cheap, is so much more versatile. If you put just one bean in a jar with sugar to cover and let it stand for a week, you'll have fragrant vanilla-flavored sugar to sprinkle on fruit or to top something you've baked. I always keep half a dozen beans, split down the edge with a sharp knife, in a tightly corked pint bottle of cognac. After it has stood for a couple of weeks I have a marvelously pungent homemade vanilla extract that has taken on some of the flavor of the cognac as well (you can, if you prefer, use rum, bourbon whiskey, or even vodka instead of cognac).

Often a recipe will tell you to put an inch of vanilla bean in the milk you are scalding for a custard. Before you do this, first run the point of a paring knife down one edge so that it will open and spill the minute seeds into the milk, for these are the source of the flavor. Some companies that make high-grade ice cream use these seeds, and anyone who doesn't know about this practice is apt to think there is pepper or dust or some other foreign body in the vanilla ice cream, whereas it is only the infinitesimally small seeds that have spread through it, giving the ice cream, in my opinion, great distinction.

That's only a beginning. An inch of vanilla bean added to the simple syrup in which peaches, pears, or pineapples are poached brings out the best in the fruit. A touch of vanilla added to the batter for dessert crêpes improves it enormously, and if you're making muffins that have a certain amount of sweetness, such as blueberry or pecan muffins, a touch of vanilla helps this batter too. When I make an apple pie, I use butter and vanilla lavishly, and I always put a couple of drops of vanilla with the sugar for baked apples. Try it.

~ If you've never made a *Vanilla Soufflé* for dessert, here is perhaps the finest way to appreciate the flavor of the bean. For this, melt 3 tablespoons butter in a heavy saucepan and blend in 3 tablespoons flour. Stir until smooth, add just a pinch of salt, and cook the mixture for 2 or 3 minutes, to remove the raw taste of the flour. Scald 1 cup milk with 1 inch of vanilla bean. Remove the bean, and stir the milk into the flour mixture until smooth and thick, then let it simmer 2 or 3 minutes. Take the piece of vanilla bean and another inch of vanilla bean and scrape the black seeds from the inside into your soufflé base along with ½ cup sugar. Remove pan from the heat, and stir in 4 lightly beaten egg yolks. Return to very low heat for just a minute or two, stirring until the eggs are just heated through.

Remove to a large bowl and allow to cool while beating 5 egg whites until stiff but not dry. Fold a quarter of the egg whites into the vanilla mixture with a rubber spatula, quickly and thoroughly. Then fold into the rest of the egg whites, but do not overfold. Pour into a 6-cup or 1 ½-quart buttered and sugared soufflé dish—it should be about two-thirds to three-fourths full. Bake in the center of a 375-degree oven for 25 to 35 minutes, according to how you like your soufflé. Allow 25 minutes for a soufflé that is firm on the outside and slightly runny inside, 35 minutes for one that is firm throughout. If you don't have a vanilla bean, use 1 tablespoon vanilla extract instead, but be sure it is the pure extract, not the synthetic type which doesn't have the same unctuous quality.

Serve this delicious puffy soufflé to four persons the minute it comes from the oven with, if you want to gild the lily, some whipped cream.

Flavor—True or False?

I am a great lover of garlic, as I am of onions and of nearly all the herbs. I value the good, natural flavors that make food so much more interesting and acceptable to the palate, and I shall never understand why some people will quite happily accept a substitute for the real thing.

Take garlic, for instance—and then consider those abominations, garlic powder and garlic salt. The honest flavor of fresh garlic is something I can never have enough of. On the other hand, should I be unfortunate enough to bite into something seasoned with garlic powder or salt, I find I can taste it for thirty-six hours. I was once given mayonnaise blended with so much garlic powder that it was almost repulsive. It made me feel quite ill and completely spoiled the meal for me.

I consider both garlic powder and salt and onion powder and salt to be among the more disagreeable of the so-called advances in our eating. To me, it is absolutely pointless to ruin good food with these awful ersatz flavors when it is so simple a matter to use the real thing. Dehydrated chopped onion or garlic I find bearable, but, for the most part, I see no reason to use any form of substitute when the vast majority of us live within easy reach of fresh garlic, onions, shallots, or green onions.

Personally, I have never liked or used a garlic press, because I find it no trouble to chop or mince garlic. A garlic clove is a very easy thing to handle. There are times when you don't even need to peel or chop it, just toss it whole into the pan, where it will spread a delicious seasoning and can be removed at the end of the cooking. Salads take on a marvelous briskness if you rub a clove of garlic on the little crusty button at the end of a day-old loaf of French bread until the crumbs absorb the flavor, and then toss it into the bowl to perfume the greens. The lucky person who gets this little *chapon*, as it is called, for a delicious final bite will savor it greatly.

Fresh garlic is something you can regulate according to your likes and dislikes, from a delicate whiff to a tremendous surge. There are ways to use great quantities of garlic without getting an overpowering flavor, like Chicken with Forty Cloves of Garlic (see page 235) and Julia Child's wonderful *purée de pommes de terre à l'ail* in Volume 1 of *Mastering the Art of French Cooking*, a heavenly combination of mashed potatoes and a sauce containing 30 cloves of garlic. When you tell people how much garlic there is in these dishes, they never believe you, because after the garlic has been cooked slowly for a certain length of time it loses its harsh rawness and becomes something completely delicate and refined. It's hard to say exactly how or at what stage this happens—all we know is that it occurs after a certain application of heat, one of those mysteries which make cooking the most fascinating of pursuits.

This also happens when you make *Garlic Soup*, a very simple but superb soup that tastes even better if you use leftover fat from a chicken, goose, or pork roast. Melt 3 tablespoons chicken, goose, or pork fat in a heavy saucepan over low heat. Add 30 peeled garlic cloves (you can use less or more, as you wish), and shake over gentle heat so the garlic cooks without browning. It should just melt in the fat; letting it brown is fatal as the flavor turns bitter. Add 6 to 8 cups chicken stock and season to taste with salt and freshly ground black pepper. I also like to grate a tiny bit of nutmeg in. Simmer for 15 to 20 minutes, and then force through a sieve or food mill to purée the garlic. Reheat the soup. Beat 4 or 5 egg yolks, and stir in 3 to 4 tablespoons olive oil. Stir some of the hot soup into the egg yolks to temper them, and then stir them very gently into the soup and heat. Do not under any circumstances let the soup come to a boil, or the yolks will curdle. Serve in large soup plates, ladling the soup over pieces of crisp toast, one to a plate. Serves six to eight.

The robust and beautiful flavor of this soup is something that could never, ever be achieved with garlic powder. So leave those substitutes on the shelf, look at them once in a while with distaste—and then forget about them.

✤ CHAPTER 5 ✤

Inspirations and Improvisations

ॐ

... in which we whip up simple dishes for the unexpected guest ... explore the perfection of pasta ... the myriad delights of quiche ... the creation of fabulous fondues ... and concoct a refreshing summer salad.

Impromptu Meals

Have you ever had friends drop in around mealtime and then realized there's practically nothing to eat in the house but eggs and a can of soup? Of course you have. We've all faced those emergencies when one has to do some quick improvisation. I remember reading in the paper about a woman who kept her wits about her during the last great New England snowstorm. Her family was yearning for, of all things, apple pie. Suddenly she remembered the mock apple pies our forefathers made with soda crackers, sugar, spices, and butter, and she produced one forthwith. It was a huge success, and before the storm was over she'd made it again and again. That's what I call intelligent thinking.

My own way of coping with unforeseen situations is to keep a special shelf stocked with things I can reach for when I have to make a meal in a hurry or feed unexpected guests. I always have cans of minced clams, salmon, tuna fish, corned beef, corned beef hash, sardines, pimientos, white truffles, evaporated milk, broths and soups, olives, and a selection of pasta from the tiny orzo to the big macaroni (I find I use the thin spaghettini more than anything else). I usually keep frozen crabmeat in the freezer, also vegetables of various sorts and bits and pieces of leftover ham and chicken.

&.Recently I picked up a new quickie from Philip Brown, an excellent cook who does demonstrations with me from time to time. Let's call it *Philip's Sardine Special*. Open and drain 2 cans of French or Portuguese sardines—preferably the boneless, skinless kind—and wash them very carefully with warm water, being sure not to break them up. Pour ¼ cup olive oil into a small baking dish and top with 1 large onion, finely chopped. Arrange the sardines on the onions and mix in a 4-ounce can of pimientos, cut in thin strips. Season with ¾ teaspoon salt and ½ teaspoon freshly ground black pepper, and pour on another ¼ cup oil. Bake in a 350-degree oven for 30 minutes. Sprinkle with chopped parsley and serve very hot, with toast. With a salad and some cheese, you have a satisfying meal for four.

&.Hash is one of my favorite spur-of-the-moment supper dishes. For *Quick Corned Beef Hash*, heat 3 tablespoons butter and 3 tablespoons oil in a heavy skillet, add 1 medium onion, finely chopped, and sauté until translucent and lightly colored, about 4 minutes. Add 1 can corned beef, coarsely chopped, and 1 can corned beef hash. Blend well. Season with salt and pepper and turn the hash over several times. Add ¾ cup boiling water or ½ cup heavy cream or evaporated milk, and cook it down quickly. Reduce heat, and cover the pan for 3 or 4 minutes to give it a chance to steam. Remove the cover and loosen the hash from the pan with a spatula—it should have formed a crisp bottom crust. Turn it over, omelet fashion, and turn out onto a hot platter. Top with fried or poached eggs or roll scrambled eggs into it before you turn it out.

Serve with heated chili sauce or homemade pickles and hot biscuits, if you have them. For dessert, have ice cream.

Another swift dish that will also stretch to serve a lot of people is *Spaghetti with Clam Sauce*. Open and drain two 7-ounce cans minced clams, saving the liquid. Heat 4 tablespoons olive oil in a small skillet, add 2 finely chopped garlic cloves, and cook for 4 minutes. Add the clam liquid, raise the heat, and cook down. Bring 2 quarts well-salted water to a boil, and cook an 8-ounce package of spaghettini rapidly until just tender but still bitey. Drain and place in a colander over boiling water. Heat the minced clams through in the garlic broth and add some chopped parsley or chives. Dish the pasta into 4 plates and spoon the clam sauce over it. Sprinkle with more parsley—no cheese on this, please; it's better as it is.

With a glass of white wine, salad or sliced tomatoes, crisp bread, and fruit to follow you have a top-notch meal, as good as you'd get in an Italian restaurant.

Perfect Scrambled Eggs

When people invite you in for a quick meal, or if something goes wrong in the kitchen, they are apt to say, "Oh well, I'll just scramble some eggs," as if "just scrambling some eggs" couldn't be simpler. As a matter of fact, scrambling eggs is one of the more complex kitchen processes, and there are various schools of egg scrambling. There are those who believe eggs should be scrambled in a double boiler over simmering water, those who believe they should be scrambled quickly, and those who believe that it takes slow and most accurate timing to make the curds tender, delicious, and of varied sizes. Every person regards his particular fashion of scrambling an egg as a mark of his culinary skill, and so it is. My good friend Julia Child once demonstrated her theory of scrambling eggs on television. She lifted the pan from the burner and then lowered it, to adjust the heat and the scrambling process, then as the final moment arrived, she accelerated her tempo to make the eggs come to just the right point. Hers is an extremely good method, provided you have the patience and dexterity.

Scrambled eggs can be so delicious, so creamy and rich and eggy, if I may use the word, that it is too bad we don't use them more. They combine well with many things—chopped sautéed mushrooms, finely chopped ham, crisp bacon bits, little slices of sausage, freshly grated Parmesan or Gruyère cheese, chopped herbs, finely chopped peeled and seeded tomatoes—as well as being perfectly splendid on their own.

Depending upon the number of eggs to be scrambled, I like to use a small or large Teflon-coated pan. I have a cast-aluminum Teflon-lined 9-inch omelet pan with rounded sides that I use for up to 4 or 5 eggs and a 10-inch pan for larger quantities, which are much harder to make. I disagree completely with those who say you can scramble one egg well. It is an impossibility.

For *Scrambled Eggs* I think you should gauge at least 2 eggs per person. Add salt, freshly ground black pepper, and 1 or 2 dashes of Tabasco, and then beat lightly with a fork. For lighter scrambled eggs, I beat in 1 teaspoon of water for every two eggs. I don't like cream or milk added to scrambled eggs, but if I want them extraordinarily rich, I mix in softened butter, as I will describe later on.

If I am adding ham or bacon, I would use 2 slices of Canadian bacon about 3 inches in diameter and 2 pieces of ham of the same size and ¼ inch thick, precook it lightly, cut into thin shreds, and toss into the pan with a tablespoon or two of butter. Let this warm over low heat, then add, for two servings, 4 beaten eggs and, as you do, increase the heat to medium high. As soon as the coagulation starts, make pushing strokes with a rubber or wooden spatula so you get curled curds. I'm not quite as definite in my movements as Julia Child. I lift the pan off the burner from side to side with sort of a circular motion, while pushing with the spatula. As the heat in the cooking eggs increases, the curds form much faster, and there you have to remove the pan from the heat and work faster with your pushing. That's the ticklish point. You have to know the exact moment to cease applying any heat and rush your eggs from pan to plate, or they will be overcooked, hard, coarse-textured and disagreeable.

Now, if you want very rich eggs, as you push curds in the pan add little bits of softened butter, which will melt in and give you delicious, heavily buttered scrambled eggs such as you have seldom experienced. In some places, they are called "buttered eggs," and that's a very good term.

If you are adding chopped herbs or mushrooms, lace them in as you scramble the eggs so they become a part of the amalgamation of the creamy curds. Of course, there is nothing wrong with adding chopped parsley or chives or other bits and pieces after you have transferred the eggs from the pan to a plate or platter.

If you have never tried the combination, cook scrambled eggs with sliced smoked fish for your next Sunday brunch or luncheon. A platter of smoked salmon, smoked eel, smoked sturgeon, or smoked whitefish, with lemon wedges, good rolls or bagels, and a huge pile of creamy eggs—that's good eating. If you like, you can scramble the eggs at the table in an electric skillet or chafing dish, guiding them to a perfect conclusion as you chat with your guests.

I have had, in my time, memorable meals of scrambled eggs with fresh truffles, scrambled eggs with caviar and other glamorous things, but to me, there are few things as magnificent as scrambled eggs, pure and simple, perfectly cooked and perfectly seasoned.

In Praise of Pasta

It's odd how when you're in Italy no meal seems complete without pasta, yet here we're so apt to forget what a wonderfully simple, variable food it is. In these days of rush and hurry, a dish of pasta can be made in nothing flat, and with an elegant sauce, salad, and maybe cheese and fresh fruit you have an exceptionally good dinner.

For more than six hundred years, pasta, made from the purest and simplest of ingredients—fine wheat and water—has been a staple of the diet of people in many countries, and in all that time its manufacture has stuck pretty consistently to the classic formula and the end result has been something to savor.

Certain things have been added to pasta—artichoke flour; tomato, spinach, and carrot to add color and flavor; eggs to produce the golden noodles of the Central Europeans—but these are incidentals. Generally speaking, pasta is made from hard wheat, the finest from durum wheat, which is high in gluten, or wheat protein, a substance that gives pasta its natural bite and firmness of shape and texture. At various times attempts have been made to produce it from other things, but the results have found little acceptance with lovers of good pasta.

Lately though, there have been disturbing signs that pasta in the future may not be what it was in the past. There's a new FDA ruling that permits a change in ingredient standards, and a major food company is coming out with a type of macaroni for school lunch programs that is "enriched" by the addition of corn and soy flours, with a little more than one-third wheat. To me that just isn't pasta. I find it rather shocking that a food that has been a tradition in our lives for so long can suddenly become something quite different, with a different color, taste, and consistency, no longer the archetypal product. Nothing, as far as I'm concerned, can ever take the place of honest pasta made from honest wheat, and when it comes to adding protein, I'd rather eat my pasta with meat sauce or grated cheese, in the usual way, instead of getting it through soy.

I like to know what to expect from the food I buy, and I have always found our commercial packaged pastas to be steadily dependable in constant use, never varying in flavor and quality, good, inexpensive, and easy to cook, if you follow the directions on the box, although for my taste they tend to overestimate the cooking time. I like my pasta to be what the Italians call *al dente* (to the tooth), or with a little bite to it, not mushy or soft. Test it by fishing a piece from the water and biting to see if it is cooked to your taste.

I love pasta, and I use a great deal of it, from the tiniest pastina and orzo (which is shaped rather like a large grain of rice) up to lasagne and the huge seashells and rigatoni. It's such fun to play around with all the different shapes and sizes—the little wagon wheels and butterflies, the long thin strips of spaghetti and tagliatelle, and the lovely thin broad noodles.

I cook orzo until it is just tender, toss it with butter and sometimes a little grated Parmesan or Romano cheese, and serve it with grilled foods or a stew instead of potatoes or noodles or rice. It has a nice texture, excellent flavor, and makes a great sauce sopper-upper.

I cook a lot of the thin spaghettini, too. Sometimes I have it with a quick clam sauce or one made with fresh tomatoes simmered in butter with a touch of garlic and basil, or that glorious summer mixture called pesto—fresh basil, parsley, pine nuts, and oil ground to a paste that turns the pasta the most beautiful green as you eat it. Or I might sauce it very simply by soaking chopped garlic in warm olive oil for a few minutes and tossing it with the pasta. This is one of my great favorites.

If you are feeling extravagant, canned white truffles, shredded and tossed in butter, are wonderful with fettuccine or spaghettini, but just melted butter and freshly grated cheese tastes awfully good, too. All of these can be done in minutes and make a most satisfying meal. I hold no brief for those elaborate sauces that take forever to cook. When anyone tells me he has a marvelous spaghetti sauce that takes three days to make, I run screaming because I know only too well that it is going to be overseasoned, overtomatoed, and overrich.

To me there's nothing better than to take pasta, be it noodles, spaghettini, seashells, orzo, or what you will, blanch it for about 5 minutes in boiling salted water, drain it, and then cook it in rich boiling chicken stock until done to taste. Serve it in bowls with plenty of the broth, a little grated Parmesan or Romano cheese, and a sprinkling of freshly chopped parsley. It's the kind of dish you'll be hungry for when nothing else in the food line seems to appeal to you.

≫ If you like a good meat sauce for your pasta, probably the most famous is the one the Italians call *Ragú Bolognese*. Cut ½ pound bacon into very small pieces, and cook it gently in a saucepan with 2 tablespoons butter. Add 2 finely chopped or shredded carrots, 2 finely chopped medium-size onions, and 2 finely chopped ribs of celery. Brown lightly, then add 1 pound lean ground beef, breaking it up with a fork so it browns evenly. Then add ½ pound chicken livers, trimmed of all membrane and chopped. Cook for 2 to 3 minutes, then mix in ¼ cup concentrated tomato paste and 1 cup rather dry white wine. Season with 1 teaspoon or more salt, ½ to ¾ teaspoon freshly ground black pepper, and a generous pinch of nutmeg. Add 1½ cups broth (chicken, beef, or broth made with a bouillon cube), cover the pan, and simmer very, very gently for 40 minutes.

Uncover, check the seasoning, and stir in 1 cup heavy cream—this is optional; some people prefer the sauce as it is, others like the cream flavor. Heat for a minute. I always add a good tablespoon of chopped parsley, and I have been known to put in a finely chopped garlic clove. You can add such things to the basic sauce at your discretion.

This sauce Bolognese is good on spaghetti, macaroni, or any pasta, and for lasagne. Alternate in a baking dish a layer of the sauce, a layer of lasagne, a layer of béchamel sauce, well seasoned with nutmeg, some freshly grated Parmesan or Romano cheese, and repeat the layers in that order until the dish is full, ending with béchamel sauce. Top with a heavy grating of Parmesan cheese, and bake in a 350-degree oven until the cheese has melted and the sauce is brown and bubbly.

The other day I went to a luncheon where pasta was featured, and we tasted a tremendous variety of dishes, one of which I'd like to share with you because it was such a lovely flavorful mixture—an adaptation of the Greek *pastitsio*:

To make this version of *Pastitsio*, first cube 1 large (1½ pounds) or 2 smallish eggplants and sprinkle with salt. Sauté in ⅓ to ½ cup olive oil until delicately brown, shaking the pan well and turning the cubes with a wooden spatula. Drain on paper towels. Parboil and slice 1 pound of Italian sausages, such as cotechino or langanicaa, sold in Italian markets and some supermarkets, or substitute good, not too fat, sausage meat, thinly sliced and browned and well drained. (If you can't get highly flavored sausage, add a chopped clove or two of garlic or a little sautéed onion.) Combine the sausage and eggplant.

Cook 1 pound of ziti, a very large version of macaroni, in about 4 to 5 quarts of very well salted boiling water, uncovered. Stir occasionally, because pasta loves to stick to the bottom of the pan. Cook until just tender to your taste, then drain in a colander.

Meanwhile, make the béchamel sauce. Melt ⅓ cup butter in a pan, blend in ⅓ cup flour, 1 teaspoon salt, ⅛ teaspoon nutmeg, and ⅛ to ¼ teaspoon freshly ground black pepper. Cook until it bubbles, to cook the flour thoroughly, then very gradually add 3 cups hot milk. Stir over medium heat until thickened, let simmer for several minutes, and then stir in another cup of hot milk or ½ cup heavy cream.

You will also need three Italian cheeses—grated Parmesan, thinly sliced mozzarella, and a 1-pound container of skim-milk ricotta.

Take a 9-by-13- or 14-inch baking pan, the type you would use for lasagna, and cover the bottom with a layer of sauce. Then add the ziti, half the sausage-eggplant mixture, more sauce, then a little Parmesan, some ricotta, more sauce, the rest of the ziti and eggplant mixture, another layer of sauce, more Parmesan and ricotta, and top it all with slices of mozzarella. Bake in a 375-degree oven from 30 to 40 minutes. Do not overbake. It should have a nice moist quality.

Served with a green salad, this makes a good hearty dinner or supper, or an excellent buffet dish for a party.

Quiche, the People's Choice

I can remember when quiche Lorraine was a great novelty. Now every bride attempts it, most restaurants have it on the menu, and it is considered the chic thing to serve guests. Considering the peasant origin of the dish, that's a pretty rapid rise in status.

Seldom, however, do you find quiche Lorraine made by the true, classic method. Originally, this open-faced tart from the province of Lorraine consisted of bread dough with a filling of eggs, cream, and usually bacon— no cheese. The idea of including cheese probably crept in because fresh cream cheese sometimes replaced the cream.

If you are making bread, you might try the classic crust. Roll out bread dough very, very thinly or else take a small chunk and press it into a tart tin or pie pan with your fists. Add the quiche filling and bake according to the recipe I am going to give you. Or go the usual route and make a pastry shell instead.

&. I personally feel a pastry shell is much better for being prebaked before the filling is added. For *Quiche Pastry*, sift 2 cups all-purpose flour and ¼ teaspoon salt into a bowl or onto a board. Make a well in the center and add ¼ pound butter, cut in very small pieces, and 1 egg mixed with 1 tablespoon lemon juice. Work this thoroughly with the fingertips (or in a mixer with a paddle, not a beater, attachment) until the butter is incorporated and the dough stiff. Add additional liquid if necessary. Form into a ball and chill for at least half an hour.

Roll out the dough between sheets of waxed paper and line an 8-inch or 9-inch pie pan or tart tin (the kind with a removable bottom is good for quiche). Don't pull the dough—just lift it up gently and let it settle in the pan. Trim and crimp the edges, put a piece of foil or waxed paper on the dough, and weight it down with uncooked beans or rice to prevent the pastry from puffing up during baking. Bake in a 425-degree oven for 18 minutes, then remove the beans or rice and paper, brush the inside of the shell with a little beaten egg yolk, and bake 3 minutes longer. This glazes the center so it won't get soggy. Cool a little before filling.

&. For *Quiche Lorraine*, arrange 6 strips of cooked, well-drained bacon in the baked shell. Beat 3 egg yolks with 2 whole eggs, and combine with ⅔ cup heavy cream, ½ teaspoon salt, and a pinch of nutmeg. Blend well and pour over the bacon. Sprinkle with nutmeg and a touch of freshly ground black pepper. Bake in a 375-degree oven for 20 to 25 minutes, or until the filling is delicately browned and puffy and just set in the center.

Remove from the oven, cool for a moment, then cut in wedges and serve. Quiche should be eaten fresh from the oven while it is gently risen and creamy, rather than when it has settled down to flat solidity.

To vary the recipe, you can cook the bacon until crisp, cut it in pieces, and mix into the egg-cream mixture with about ½ cup freshly grated Parmesan cheese and 1 tablespoon of chopped parsley. Or substitute tiny raw bay scallops for the bacon strips, with a teaspoon of chopped parsley and a bit of fresh chopped dill or dried dill.

From Lorraine's neighbor, Alsace, comes *Onion Quiche*, equally good as a first course or as a side dish with roast beef or steak. For this you use finely chopped onions, steamed in butter, and a little grated Parmesan cheese, topped with the egg-cream mixture.

Elizabeth David makes a *Roquefort Quiche* that is glorious eating. Crumble about ¾ cup French Roquefort cheese into the baked pie shell (don't substitute any other blue cheese—only this works properly), and add the egg-cream mixture. Bake at 375 degrees for 15 to 20 minutes, then reduce the heat to 350 degrees and bake a further 5 to 10 minutes, or until just set.

Serve piping hot to quiche lovers, like one friend of mine who is so mad for the dish he vows his theme song should be "Quiche me, quiche me again."

Vegetable Variations on a Quiche

Nowadays all kinds of things get incorporated into a quiche, from shellfish and smoked salmon to asparagus tips and corn. While this is a long way from the classic quiche Lorraine, it's an enterprising and permissible extension of the basic dish that makes good culinary sense.

To my mind, nothing is more inviting, especially in spring and summer, than a vegetable quiche, for this versatile dish lends itself eminently well to a variety of seasonal vegetables. Many of these can be used as accompaniments to roast meats and poultry, or to cold meats, as vegetable and starch in one.

❧One of my favorites is a *Spinach Quiche*, which makes a good luncheon or supper dish. Thoroughly wash 1½ to 2 pounds fresh spinach. Place in a heavy pan with no water other than that clinging to the leaves, cover, and wilt down over medium to high heat. By wilting down I mean you should cook it just until the water comes out of the spinach and the bulk is reduced. Drain it very well, pressing to get out all the water the spinach has exuded. Then chop the spinach coarsely and season it with 1 teaspoon salt, a touch of nutmeg, 1 teaspoon dried tarragon, or 1 tablespoon chopped fresh tarragon, and a few drops of lemon juice. Mix very well and taste for seasoning.

Have ready a baked pie shell, made in the same way as the shell for quiche Lorraine (see preceding recipe), and, before adding the filling, spread the bottom of the shell thickly with Dijon mustard. This is a trick I learned from my friend Simone Beck, which she gives in her cookbook *Simca's Cuisine*, and it gives a wonderful flavor to the finished quiche.

Arrange the spinach in the shell, and sprinkle with ½ cup crumbled feta cheese or shredded Gruyère or sharp Cheddar or finely grated Parmesan. Beat 2 eggs and 2 egg yolks well with 1 cup heavy cream (or use half heavy cream and half plain yogurt, which gives the custard a sharper flavor). Pour over the spinach, using enough to fill but not spill over the shell, sprinkle with 1 tablespoon chopped parsley, and bake in a 350-degree oven for 30 to 35 minutes, or until the custard is just barely set. Let it cool a little and serve just warm to from four to six people.

For variation number one on this vegetable theme, blanch 2 pounds young fresh green peas for 2 minutes in boiling salted water. Drain quickly, and place in the baked shell (don't brush with mustard this time) with 3 tablespoons grated onion or 2 tablespoons finely cut green onions, 1 teaspoon salt, ½ teaspoon freshly ground black pepper, and, if you have it, 2 teaspoons finely chopped fresh mint. Sprinkle with ¼ cup grated Parmesan cheese, add your egg and cream mixture, as before, and bake 35 minutes at 350 degrees.

This goes extraordinarily well with lamb or chicken, or any cold meat that you might be serving. It's surprising what a different flavor peas take on when baked this way.

❧ You can use 1½ cups finely cut green onions, blanched in boiling salted water for 30 seconds and well drained. Toss these with 2 tablespoons melted butter, put them in the baked shell, and top with ½ cup grated Gruyère or Cheddar cheese and the egg-cream mixture, seasoning the custard to taste with salt, and a dash of Tabasco.

❧ A *Carrot Quiche* is rather out of the ordinary, and marvelous with roast lamb or a steak, instead of the usual potatoes. Finely shred 4 to 5 carrots. Blanch for 1 minute in boiling salted water. Drain thoroughly, then mix with 4 tablespoons melted butter, 1 teaspoon salt, a tiny bit of marjoram or oregano, and 2 tablespoons chopped parsley. Brush the baked shell with mustard, put in the carrots, a squeeze of lemon juice, 4 tablespoons grated Parmesan, and the custard mixture. Bake at 350 degrees for 35 minutes, or until just set.

It fascinates me how versions of the quiche crop up in other countries. The British have a bacon and egg tart, first cousin to quiche Lorraine, and the Welsh have a leek tart. Actually, this is really not as remarkable as it might appear. The proximity of France and Britain and the inter-change of the people over the centuries brought about many such culinary transferences.

There are many similarities between the Welsh language and that of Brittany. The Bretons make annual treks across the Channel in small boats after the harvest season, bringing foods to sell—in particular, long braids of beautiful yellow onions—and after they have been in Wales a day or so, owing to the closeness of the languages, they and the Welsh can understand each other and even carry on fairly intelligent conversations.

The leek, of course, has a long history in Wales and great symbolic significance. It is said that at the Battle of Agincourt the Welsh soldiers went into battle with a leek proudly pinned to their tunics to proclaim their nationality.

❧ To make a *Leek Tart*, first bake your pie shell. While the shell is baking, take 3 good-sized leeks, split them in half lengthwise and then in half again, and wash them thoroughly to remove all the sand. Finely mince the white and a little of the green part, and sauté quickly in 3 tablespoons butter, shaking the pan and tossing the leeks with a wooden spoon so they become soft, but not mushy or completely cooked. Then broil 3 to 4 slices lean bacon until cooked through, but not crisp and crumbly or the bacon will lose its flavor when recooked in the tart. Drain on paper towels, cut in small pieces, and combine with the leeks. Spoon the leek and bacon mixture into the pie shell.

Lightly beat 5 medium or 4 very large eggs, add 1 to ¼ cups light cream, half-and-half, or evaporated milk, and mix well together. Season with 1 teaspoon salt, ½ teaspoon freshly ground black pepper, and ¼ teaspoon nutmeg. Mix well with a whisk and taste—there should be enough salt to season the custard and a nice overtone of nutmeg. Then stir in ⅓ to ½ cup grated Parmesan cheese.

"Now hold on," I can hear you saying, "Parmesan cheese certainly isn't Welsh." It isn't, but if you go back as far as the seventeenth century you will find English, Welsh, and Scottish recipes in which Parmesan cheese is called for, and it has been used consistently over the years as the delicate seasoning cheese it is. It won't become sticky, like other cheeses, and it adds a fine basic flavor to whatever dish you put it in.

Pour the cheese-flavored custard over the leeks and bacon, put the pie in the center of the oven, and bake at 375 degrees from 25 to 30 minutes, or until just set like a custard pie, not wobbly or overcooked. Remove and cool. If you are serving it as an hors d'oeuvre, cool for 25 to 30 minutes so it will be firm enough to slice into small squares or wedges that can be eaten with the fingers. For a lunch, brunch, or Sunday supper dish, cool only 15 minutes.

Team it with salad and maybe a fruit dessert, and you have a light but satisfying meal.

Fondue, the Chameleon Dish

Cheese fondue is a Swiss creation that dates back to the sixteenth century when the German Swiss, who had become Protestant, were battling with the Catholics from central Switzerland, whence cheese comes. There is a legend that after a full day's battle the two factions declared a truce to meet for a communal dinner of a certain milk soup, made with cheese, into which pieces of bread were dipped. As the story goes, a bucket was placed on the borderline between the two regions of Switzerland. One group supplied the milk and cheese, and the other supplied the bread. Thus the tradition of dipping bread into a communal dish was established. Eventually fondue became part of the cookery of French Switzerland, which is close to the Savoy district of France, and it is not surprising that it was known to Brillat-Savarin, the great eighteenth-century gastronomic authority, who wrote about a fondue party he gave in Boston in 1795. After introducing fondue to that city, he reported, it became quite the rage there.

It is once again the rage throughout the country, and many variations on the fondue principle have come along. Among these is the fondue bourguignonne or what the Swiss call fondue friture, for which one prepares a pot of hot oil and butter or simply hot oil. Into this bits of meat and vegetables or other ingredients are dipped. There is also a fondue orientale, sometimes called a fondue moderne or a fondue chinoise, which is done with a broth for dipping, very similar to the hot broth dish one finds in parts of China—and, of course, in some Chinese restaurants. Fairly recently a chocolate dessert fondue was invented, into which one dips bits of fruit, cake, crisp cookies, and such items.

As you can see, it is possible to entertain with fondue from beginning to end, as one hostess did for a party in Midland, Michigan, which I attended. For the principal dish she provided two kinds of cheese fondue, one made with Cheddar cheese to which a little bourbon was added instead of the usual kirsch—a stroke of imagination, I thought. (As a matter of fact, I had a very good cheese fondue once that incorporated gin.) So if you are planning to make a traditional cheese fondue—or fondue neuchâteloise, as it is known in Switzerland—don't worry about being authentic if you can't find any kirsch. Improvise. Here, then, is the way to prepare a cheese fondue. I will first give a basic fondue and then follow it with the adjustments that make it fondue neuchâteloise.

☙ This basic recipe for *Cheese Fondue* will serve four persons quite well as a main course and many more than that if used as an hors d'oeuvre. Shred, grate, or dice a pound of Swiss Emmenthaler cheese, and dredge it in 3 tablespoons of flour. Rub the inside of the fondue pot with a cut garlic clove. (The fondue pot itself, which can be made of glazed pottery or earthenware or of enameled iron, is known in Switzerland as a *caquelon*.) Place the pot on medium heat and pour in 1½ cups of white wine. Swiss wine makes it all the better, but any good dry white wine will do. Keep this over medium heat until the wine is warm, but don't let it boil. The recipe calls for a tablespoon of lemon juice, but I seldom find it necessary. Add the cheese by handfuls, and stir it with a wooden spoon until the cheese melts and the mixture has the appearance of a light, creamy sauce. Add a little freshly ground black pepper and a few grains of nutmeg, and let this boil up for a minute. Transfer the pot to low heat—and this can be an electric table stove or alcohol burner—and adjust the heat so that the fondue continues to bubble.

Arrange small cubes of French bread, with the crust on, around the fondue. Invite guests to help themselves, spearing the bread cubes with the fondue forks or the handled skewers now on the market, and as they dip, stirring right down to the bottom. This ritual continues, of course, until the fondue is gone, at which point there will be a crust at the bottom of the pot, which is called a *religieuse*. This is a very special treat, and it can be taken out with a wooden spoon or spatula.

The traditional *Fondue Neuchâteloise* calls for equal portions of two kinds of cheese—Emmenthaler and natural Gruyère. Do not dredge with flour but proceed to heat the wine and add the cheese as directed above. When the fondue is at the boil, add 3 tablespoons of kirsch mixed with a tablespoon of cornstarch. Lacking kirsch, substitute gin, vodka, or bourbon. Stir in the liquid, and allow the fondue to boil up again.

I have had this dish in Switzerland with only bread for dipping and a crisp chilled Swiss wine to drink. However, you can serve any number of items for dippables. At the party I mentioned earlier, in addition to bread there were also cubes of sausage (bologna and mortadella) and ham, and a large tray of raw vegetables—cauliflower, broccoli, cucumber, scallions, carrots, radishes, celery, and turnips.

There are many different versions of cheese fondue beyond those given here, and all of them are delicious and an extremely easy way to entertain.

Rice for a Salad Switch

It sometimes seems to me that we have become such traditionalists in our eating patterns we get in some rather depressing culinary ruts. For instance, take potato salad. In a restaurant, a delicatessen, or the picnic hamper, what do you invariably find? Potato salad. Potato salad made with mayonnaise, with French dressing, with bacon dressing. Hot potato salad, cold potato salad. No matter where you go, even in Hawaii where food is so influenced by the Orient, good old potato salad reigns supreme. Not that it isn't one of the greatest salads ever, I'm not disputing that, but it does become a bit of a bore when you have it over and over again. The same thing is true of cole slaw. We have it with mayonnaise, with sour cream, with celery seeds, sweet and sour slaw, hot slaw, and cole slaw with all kinds of other things—seafood, chicken, peppers, apple, even pineapple, which I happen to think is a pretty revolting mixture.

Yet how often do you ever encounter a rice salad? Even those who love rice with Chinese, Japanese, and Indian food, who serve it as a starch with poached fish, or broiled chicken, or beef Stroganoff, or as a dessert, never seem to think of it as salad material.

The success of a rice salad depends, of course, on the rice. You need fluffy well-drained rice with each kernel separate, rice that can be held over. I'm not going to give you a lesson on rice cookery here—I'm sure you don't need one—but I am going to tell you the great secret of preparing rice for a salad. When it has reached the bitiness you like, drain it, add a couple of tablespoons of oil, and toss it well with two forks (not a spoon, which bruises the grains and makes them sticky and gluey) so that the oil coats the cooling rice grains and keeps them separated and fluffy.

The simplest of all rice salads is the one the Italians often serve with vitello tonnato (see page 23), just plain fluffy rice tossed well with oil, lemon juice or vinegar, salt, and freshly ground black pepper, garnished with a bit of chopped parsley. It's delicious with other cold meats, or with cold meat loaf, cooled herbed chicken, or turkey.

For the next kind of Rice Salad, you mix in crisp diced vegetables. First, cook 1 cup raw rice by your favorite method, then toss gently with 2 or 3 tablespoons oil.

Add 1 cup finely chopped green onion or red Italian onion, 1 cup peeled, seeded, and finely diced cucumber, ½ cup seeded and finely diced green or red pepper, 1 cup peeled, seeded, and chopped tomato, and chopped fresh basil and parsley to taste. Toss well with a vinaigrette dressing made with 5 parts olive oil to 1 part lemon juice or wine vinegar, salt, and freshly ground black pepper. Keep well cooled (not chilled) until serving time. Arrange on a bed of greens and garnish with rings of pepper, strips of green onion, and thin slices of tomato.

This is superb with foods from the outdoor grill—steaks, chops, chicken, or boned and butterflied leg of lamb.

☙ *Salade Orientale* is not just a salad but an elaborate one-dish meal. To serve eight, cook 1½ to 2 cups rice until bitingly tender (not mushy). Drain and season with salt and freshly ground black pepper. Toss gently with 2 to 3 tablespoons oil, using two forks. Leave to cool. Meanwhile, cut 1½ cups cooked shrimp into smallish pieces, leaving a few whole ones for garnish. Combine with 1 cup crabmeat and, if you like, ½ to 1 cup mussels, which have been steamed with white wine and water (or use the canned mussels from France or Scandinavia). For an alternate seafood mixture, you might have bite-size chunks of cooked lobster or lobster tails or raw bay scallops with either shrimp or mussels. To either seafood mixture, add ½ cup finely cut celery, ½ cup finely chopped green or red onion, and ½ cup peeled, seeded, and finely diced cucumber. Toss with the rice and a vinaigrette sauce made with 4 parts olive oil to 1 part wine vinegar, 2 tablespoons chopped fresh or 1 teaspoon dried tarragon, 1 tablespoon prepared mustard, and salt and pepper to taste. Garnish with the whole shrimp, and serve on greens.

With this unusual salad, have Melba toast made from rye bread, or hot French bread and sweet butter.

☙ Or you can make a *Beef-and-Rice Salad*. To the same amount of oil-tossed rice, add 1½ cups finely diced cold boiled or roast beef, ½ cup finely chopped red onion, ½ cup diced celery, 1 cup coarsely chopped hard-boiled egg, and ½ cup peeled, seeded, and chopped tomato. Toss well and dress with a vinaigrette sauce to which you have added 1 crushed or chopped garlic clove, blended well with the oil. Or use instead 1½ cups cold roast pork with ½ cup finely diced celery and ½ cup finely diced crisp green apple. Omit the other ingredients, and don't put garlic in the dressing. Let either salad stand for an hour or so in the refrigerator, toss again, heap on a bed of watercress, and garnish with sliced tomatoes or cherry tomatoes, chopped parsley, and a little chopped thyme.

For a heartier meal, arrange a ring of stuffed deviled eggs around the edge of the salad bowl, and have crisp breads or toast, and perhaps a hot vegetable dish for balance, such as spinach soufflé or green beans with almonds and bits of crisp bacon.

☙

☙ CHAPTER 6 ☙

Sweets and Soothing Drinks

☙

... in which we get in a stew over rhubarb ... fool around
with summer berries and cherries ... turn apple pie
upside down ... cherish our ice creams and sherbets ...
and the richness of syllabub and crème brûlée ... improve
on pound cake...lead the fight for a good cup of tea ...
and get into the heartwarming habit of hot chocolate.

Rhubarb, Herald of Spring

Rhubarb has always meant for me the coming of spring. The minute I see those enormous leaves and red stalks coming up through the ground and taste the first dish of stewed rhubarb, I know that the earth is once more sending forth good things to eat.

In my part of the country, Oregon, rhubarb was one of the first members of the vegetable world to emerge—for it is a vegetable, and not a fruit, although we have treated it as a fruit all our lives, in fact, ever since it came into common use about 1835. Actually, both the plant and its root have been used for centuries—in China, where one type of rhubarb originated; in Tibet, whence came rather rare varieties of rhubarb that are used in medicinal compounds; and in Siberia, which gave us the more common variety we know and grow. In the last thirty years, a lot of rhubarb has been grown in hothouses, the main difference being that the stalks are a delicate pinky red, whereas the field kind are deep, almost ruby red.

The Siberian rhubarb, the old stalwart harbinger of spring that we have had in our gardens for ages, used to be considered a great spring tonic. People took rhubarb and soda tablets, ate rhubarb, and drank sassafras tea in the belief that they were cleaning out their systems, but that habit has all but perished. Now rhubarb is enjoyed mainly as a dessert by those who like its tart acidity—there are many who do and just as many who don't.

Then, of course, there is rhubarb wine. In the Victorian and Edwardian eras, when bars and social drinking were not the customary thing, as they are now, this was one of the many homemade wines prepared and drunk by family and guests. I have friends in Pennsylvania and other parts of the country who still make rhubarb wine in May, when the rhubarb is most plentiful and the stalks big and juicy. One friend got her bottles mixed up one day and put her dry rhubarb wine in Harvard beets, instead of vinegar, which she discovered gave them the most wonderful flavor, so now she uses it that way all the time.

A word of caution about rhubarb—no matter how tempting the crinkly green leaves may look, don't attempt to eat them. They are so full of oxalic acid they can be very toxic.

Though we usually talk about "stewed" rhubarb, the best way to cook these long lovely stalks, to my mind, is in the oven.

   To make *Baked Rhubarb*, take 1½ pounds rhubarb, trim off the leaves and stem end, wash the stalks, and cut them into pieces 2 inches long. Put these in a pottery or porcelain casserole with sugar to taste (some people like their rhubarb sweeter than others, so I think one should sugar it fairly lightly when cooking, then let everyone add sugar at the table), about ¼ cup water, and a dash of salt. Cover and bake in a 350-degree oven for 35 to 40 minutes, until just tender, but not mushy, with delicately pink-tinged juice. This baked rhubarb makes a delicious spring dessert served cold with brown sugar and heavy cream, or a little whipped or sour cream.

Or you can turn your baked rhubarb into that heavenly British dessert called a *Fool*. Bake 2 pounds rhubarb in the oven until it is quite tender, put it through a food mill to get a thick purée, and sweeten to taste. Just before serving, fold the purée into an equal quantity of whipped cream or sour cream and serve very cold in small glass bowls, topped with whipped cream garnished with a little shredded preserved ginger.

Most people are accustomed to eating rhubarb in a pie—in fact for years it was called pie plant, and there are still some who refer to it by that name. This luscious deep-dish *Rhubarb Pie* is a favorite of mine, served warm with heavy cream or whipped cream marbleizing the pink juices.

Mix 4 cups rhubarb, cut into half-inch pieces, with 1¼ to 1½ cups sugar, 4 tablespoons flour or 2 tablespoons quick-cooking tapioca, ¼ teaspoon salt, and ½ to 1 teaspoon grated orange or tangerine rind. Turn into a deep 9-inch pie dish lined with rich pie crust, and dot with butter. Trim the edges of the pastry, moisten them, top with pastry crust, trim the edges, and crimp top and bottom edges together. Cut slits in the top for the steam to escape. Bake in a 450-degree oven for 15 minutes, then reduce the heat to 350 and bake about 25 to 30 minutes longer. Serve warm or cold.

The Fruits of Summer

One of nature's great gifts to us throughout the summer is an abundance of luscious fresh berries. To me these are still the most seasonal of fruits, despite the fact that some of them can be found in our markets year round.

We start with strawberries, from the tiny wild ones you can pick for yourself if you're lucky enough to live near a strawberry patch and have the necessary patience, to the giant berries with stems still attached that are flown from Arizona and California to all parts of the country—and even to Europe. At their peak, these magnificent specimens have a full, round flavor that is as different in taste from the tiny wild variety as the berries are in size.

Then there are raspberries, of which the red are perhaps my favorites of all summer berries. The black, which are much scarcer, I have never found to be anywhere near as good as their red cousins. I'm sure they must come from the poor side of the family, for they are seedy and completely undistinguished when set side by side with the red raspberries, which have a most delicate and distinctive flavor, whether you eat them picked fresh in the garden, bathe them in sugar and cream, or preserve them in a fine jam.

The gooseberry, alas, seems to be bowing out of the fruit picture, despite the fact that it makes a wonderful jam, fruit tart, and fool.

Next to the strawberry, the juicy blueberry is the berry in most plentiful supply. Here is another fruit you can gather wild, if you live where the high-bush or low-bush blueberries grow. Blueberries, mostly the large cultivated variety you find in the markets in pint and quart containers, are probably eaten more often than any other berry, and in a greater variety of ways. They are superb when served, not chilled but at room temperature, with sugar and heavy cream, even better when covered with maple syrup and either sour cream or yogurt, a combination to dream about. Another partnership to delight the palate is blueberries and peaches. Combine ripe sliced peaches with large ripe blueberries, and give them some brown sugar or maple sugar and heavy cream.

I often take a big bowl of the choicest blueberries, sugar them, and then sprinkle them with kirsch or yellow chartreuse. The liqueur adds great zest to the berries. And have you ever tried peppering blueberries? Sugar them well, give them a few grinds of fresh black pepper and a trifling amount of either Grand Marnier or Cointreau, shake them well to let the pepper sort of mix in, and you'll have something surprisingly good and delightfully restoring—the spiciness of the pepper does the most wonderful thing for the flavor of blueberries, and for strawberries, too.

Blueberries crop up in all kinds of intriguingly named baked dishes, some of them going back to the time of our ancestors. There's blueberry buckle and blueberry slump, blueberry kuchen, blueberry crisp, and blueberry pockets. Canada has an extraordinarily good version of blueberry pie made with three crusts instead of the usual two. You line your pan with pastry, put in blueberries and sugar, another layer of pastry, more blueberries and sugar, and cover with the top crust.

&Of the puddings, *Blueberry Slump* is a typical, fine, old-fashioned dessert, homely and thoroughly pleasing.

Cook 1 quart ripe blueberries in a heavy saucepan with ½ cup water, 1½ cups sugar, and a good ½ teaspoon nutmeg until well blended and slightly cooked down. Add more nutmeg if the berries seem to need it—this spice goes as well with them as it does with peaches.

While the blueberries cook, combine 1 cup flour, 1 teaspoon baking powder, 1 tablespoon sugar, and ½ teaspoon salt, and sift well together. Combine with 1 lightly beaten egg, 3 tablespoons milk, and 2 tablespoons melted butter, and blend very, very well.

When the blueberries have bubbled and boiled until they are thoroughly broken down, drop spoonfuls of the dumpling mixture you have made into the hot sauce. Cover tightly and cook for 10 minutes, then uncover, transfer the cooked dumplings to a serving dish, and spoon the blueberries over them. Serve with heavy cream, whipped cream, or ice cream. And if you cook the same basic mixture of blueberries. sugar, water, and nutmeg down very slowly, a little more than for the slump, until they are well cooked and quite thick, you have a marvelous hot sauce for ice cream.

Fooling with Berries

When raspberries and strawberries, gooseberries, blackberries, and loganberries are in season, my thoughts turn to fools. Fools are relatively unknown in this country (fruit fools, that is), although you will find an abundance of them in England and Canada during the spring and summer. The fool, one of the oldest English desserts, is basically nothing more than a mixture of puréed fruit, sugar, and thick cream, the simplest thing in the world. You find it in seventeenth- and eighteenth-century cookbooks, although it was made rather more elaborately then, according to Elizabeth David, the great English cookbook author, who has written a delightful dissertation on the subject of fools and another equally venerable dessert, the creamy syllabub. She conjectures that the name may have come from the French *foulé*, meaning crushed or pressed.

The Philadelphia Quakers were fools for fools, too. I have a cookbook published in 1855 by Lippincott called *The Philadelphia Housewife* or *A Family Receipt Book by Aunt Mary* that has a recipe for the most famous fool of all, *Gooseberry Fool*. No one seems to make it anymore, which is a great pity, as it is one of the most delicate, refreshing, and tempting of all hot-weather desserts, a delicious swirl of green and white.

    If you can buy gooseberries, or grow them in your yard, here is how to make a fool out of them. Take about 1 pound really hard green gooseberries and about ¾ cup sugar, and just cook them over very low heat until they are quite soft—you may need to add a few drops of water to start the sugar melting. You don't have to stem the berries, as they will be sieved the minute they come off the heat. When they are quite, quite soft, taste to see that you have enough sugar, then put them through a sieve. Let the purée get quite cold before stirring in 1 cup of very thick cream. If it is not really thick, whip it lightly before adding.

    Chill this lovely pale green fool until it is very, very cold. This amount will serve four, so double the recipe for a larger group.

    You don't have to cook the berries for a *Strawberry Fool*. Just hull 1 or 1½ pints ripe strawberries and sieve them. Stir about ½ cup sugar (or to taste) into the purée, and add 1 or 2 tiny drops of lemon juice to accent the flavor. Then whip 1 cup heavy cream and stir it into the purée until nice and smooth. Spoon into a crystal or silver or pottery serving dish, and chill in the coldest part of the refrigerator for several hours.

The strawberry and gooseberry fools can also be turned into a smooth, mousselike ice cream by freezing them in ice trays in the freezer.

For a *Two-Berry Fool*, sieve ¾ pint ripe raspberries and ¾ pint loganberries, and add sugar to taste. Loganberries can be quite tart unless they are dead ripe, when they have a sweetness of their own that needs very little sugaring. Mix the sweetened purée with 1 to 1¼ cups heavy cream, whipped. Pour into your serving bowl and chill in the refrigerator, as before.

A thin crisp cookie or a slice of pound cake (see pages 188–189) or similar dry cake goes very well with any of the fruit fools.

While we're talking about berries, here's another simple summer dessert, a *Strawberry Ice*. Combine 1 to 1¼ cups sugar and ½ cup water, heat until dissolved, and then boil for 5 minutes. Set aside to cool.

Hull and pick over 2 pints ripe strawberries, sieve them, and then add to the purée a few drops of lemon juice and 3 to 4 tablespoons orange juice. Stir the purée into the cold syrup and pour into ice trays. Cover with plastic wrap or foil, and freeze in the freezing compartment for 1 to 1½ hours, until the mixture has begun to firm and form crystals. Remove from the freezer and beat up very well with a fork or whisk. Return to the trays, cover again, and freeze until solid but not frozen hard. For a finer texture, repeat the beating process one more time before the final freezing, being sure to beat thoroughly each time.

If you prefer, you can freeze the ice in an ice cream freezer. This takes only about 10 minutes, either by hand or by electricity, and should be done just before you are ready to serve. A delicate ice like this is far better when eaten fresh and a little bit soft rather than firm and hard and crystallized. Should you want a richer texture, whip about ⅔ cup heavy cream and add just before freezing.

The Strawberry Season

The strawberry, which grows all over the world, is not really a true fruit in the strict botanical sense, but a member of the rose family, the genus *Fragaria*. The cultivated strawberries we see in our markets have a rather fascinating history. They are descendants of an inspired crossbreeding of the Virginia strawberry (*Fragaria virginiana*), the native wild strawberry of the eastern seaboard which was introduced into Europe around 1610, even before the Pilgrim fathers settled in New England, and the Chilean strawberry (*Fragaria chiloensis*), which made the voyage a century later. From their marriage came hybrid strains which were brought back here in the mid-nineteenth century, and the number of varieties that have been developed since then is quite fantastic—especially in California, where strawberries seem to thrive better than anywhere else. Although I will probably be criticized for saying this, I find that the strawberries grown in California, Oregon, and Washington are by far the greatest in this country. Those from Florida do not have the acid quality or the flavor of the others.

We are lucky in never having a shortage of these incomparable berries, for strawberries in their various sizes and shapes have become a year-round crop, with May and June as the peak months. Sometimes we get the very round smallish berries, deliciously sweet, at other times enormous oval berries, some of which are long and pointed. The choicest of these huge berries come with their long stems intact and can be eaten by the stem with powdered sugar and heavy or sour cream, or yogurt, whichever you prefer. Then we have the Marshall strawberry, a great berry for preserves, with a remarkable perfume and taste, which grows best in Oregon and parts of Washington.

There are two distinct types of strawberry. One is the cultivated, the other the tiny wild perpetual or alpine strawberry, which the French call *fraises des bois* or *fraises des quatres saisons*. Europeans favor these little wild berries, which they consider to have a flavor and fragrance superior to the cultivated kind, known in France as *les gros fraises*. Actually, the larger strawberries are extremely good, too, and you will find them in France, in Germany, and in England, where they may be served for tea with clotted cream, one of the most glorious combinations known to man.

The French have come up with some very unusual ways of serving strawberries. I remember some years ago stopping for dinner with three friends at an inn not far from the famous old walled city of Carcassonne, in southern France. We were introduced to a dish called strawberries Carcassonne, which you may think sounds strange and shocking, but I can assure you tastes magnificent if properly prepared. Gorgeous big strawberries in their prime of ripeness were arranged in a deep bowl and sprinkled with just the right amount of sugar (I think one must always taste strawberries before sugaring them, because they take anywhere from no sugar at all to a pretty lavish amount.) Then the berries were given a sprinkling of very coarsely ground black pepper—about twelve to fifteen grinds of the mill, and if that startles you, well it may! About ½ cup of Armagnac, the brandy of the region (for which you could substitute cognac), was poured over the berries, with just a touch of lemon juice. The bowl was gently shaken so that the berries turned over and over and the flavors blended. The trick is not to bruise or break the berries, but just to let them become imbued with the amalgam of flavors. Try this remarkably different approach to ripe strawberries, serve them in individual dishes with a crisp cookie, and I guarantee you'll agree that the pepper does something devastatingly good to them.

In Venice I encountered peppered strawberries again, this time the wild *fraises des bois*. Instead of the usual liqueur, the berries were laved in sugar, pepper, and a little white wine vinegar—a very delicate homemade vinegar with no sharp acidity—all of which blended together to give the tiny berries a most intriguing sweet-sour-spicy taste.

One of the most famous of all strawberry dishes is strawberries Romanoff, which must have come from Russia in the old days. Everyone seems to have a different recipe for it, and I have one of my own which I'm going to share with you.

For four servings of *Strawberries Romanoff*, hull 1 quart fine ripe strawberries, taste them, and sprinkle with sugar to your liking. Then add the grated rind of 1 orange, approximately ⅔ cup orange juice, and ½ cup port wine. Let the berries stand for several hours in the refrigerator, covered with plastic wrap.

Just before serving, remove the berries and place in a serving dish with some of the juice. If they have thrown a good deal of juice, drain some off and put it in a separate bowl. Whip 1½ cups heavy cream, flavor with sugar and vanilla to taste and a few drops of port. Toss the berries with this cream, and serve at once with slices of delicate pound cake or tiny sugar cookies and the extra juice, to be spooned over each serving.

This is a superbly good dessert that does justice to the long and joyous strawberry season.

Cherry Ripe

When I was staying at the beach as a child, one of the things I most looked forward to was the great splitwood baskets of Bing cherries, picked from the trees in our backyard at home, that arrived by mail. The cherries from these enormous trees were as big as a small plum, with a deep black-ish-red color, an exquisite flavor, and an unforgettable texture, the most delicious fruit one ever sank tooth into, completely and utterly soul-satis-fying. From those days on, I have always loved ripe dark cherries.

The Bing is one of the two great varieties we have in this country. Strangely enough, it is one of the few fruits we grow that was named for a Chinese, a gardener called Bing who developed this large, dark, fine-meated cherry by crossing various varieties.

The other variety is the Lambert, a development of the Napoleon cherry, which is deep red and very sweet. The best Bings and Lamberts come from the West Coast. After the California harvest is over, the Oregon and Washington cherries start coming in about the third week in June and last into August, so there is a long period of fruition. Nothing, of course, is more blissful than to stand in a cherry orchard, pick a branch of these cherries, pop them into your mouth, and bite into their luscious juiciness. However, with modern methods of packing and shipping, I find that the cherries remain firm and fresh after being shipped across the country and taste almost as good when we get them on the East Coast as they do when freshly picked on the West Coast.

Cherries have many uses. The less sweet red cherries are much better for pies, but the glorious Bings and Lamberts are excellent in ice creams, puddings, and various kinds of tarts in which you want extreme sweetness. If you have a mind to, you can freeze cherries on the stem and enjoy them all year round. Take fresh cherries, wash them very well, leaving the stems on, then place them in freezer containers (I find the round or square plastic ones are best) and shake the container so the cherries nestle together tightly—don't shake so hard as to crush them, just gently until they slide into place. Cover them tightly without more ado, and put them in the freezer. When you take them out, you'll find they have retained all their beautiful natural color. It's fun to use them as a garnish or as a table decoration—people never expect to see cherries out of season that look as if they had just been picked.

In August, when cherries are at their prime, you have a great opportunity to experiment with Bings and Lamberts. You might like to serve them just chilled, by themselves, eating them from the stem, or to poach them in sugar-and-water syrup, then flame them and spoon them over vanilla ice cream. Or you might try one of the many traditional European dishes made with cherries. Some of these may be new to you, so I am going to suggest one way of using Bings or Lamberts, a French dessert with the unusual name of *Clafouti aux Cerises. Cerises*, of course, are cherries. What *clafouti* means I haven't the faintest idea, but that's the name of the dessert, and see if you don't love it as much as I do. In this country, most people consider it should be made with pitted cherries, but I think part of the fun and tradition is not to pit them. Who minds a few pits if the dish is good?

For *Cherry Clafouti* wash a scant 4 cups Bing or Lambert cherries. Pit them or not, as you wish. I would say not. Toss them with about 2 tablespoons sugar and 2 tablespoons kirsch or cognac, and let them stand for a few minutes while you cream 1 stick (½ cup) butter with about ⅔ cup granulated sugar. Cream the butter very well and work in the sugar until the mixture is light and fluffy. Beat in 3 whole eggs, one at a time. Add 1 tablespoon grated orange rind and 1 cup unsifted flour. Blend very well, then add 1 teaspoon vanilla. Butter and lightly flour a 9-inch cake pan, pie pan, or spring form. Put a few spoonfuls of batter in the pan to cover the bottom, and distribute the cherries well in the batter, then pour the rest of the batter over the fruit. Sprinkle the top with 1 or 2 tablespoons granulated sugar. Bake in a 400-degree oven for 5 minutes, then reduce the heat to 375 degrees and continue baking until the cake tests done, between 40 and 45 minutes. Let it cool to just warm, and serve cut in wedges. Pass sweetened whipped cream with it.

This simple, extraordinarily good summer dessert is even more welcome in winter, made with frozen cherries. If you don't have cherries you can make it with fresh prunes, plums, nectarines, or pears, in the same way.

To me, the cherry season is one of the pleasantest we have, a time to feast on cherries in every possible way—with one exception. I don't like cherries in that awful jellied black cherry salad that you find on so many tables throughout different parts of this country. With all the lovely things you can do with Bings and Lamberts, to trap them in insipid rubbery gelatin is an abomination. So keep your cherries pure and simple, and enjoy them in all their delectable unspoiled ripeness.

Prunes Are No Laughing Matter

People used to make all sorts of jokes about prunes. They were dubbed "boardinghouse food" and not considered to be elegant eating at all, which they really are. I don't know why prunes should strike us as so funny. The French, who have always been great lovers of the fruit (their stuffed prunes are one of the most delicious things you could possibly eat), take them just as seriously as any other food.

The center of prune growing in France is the town of Agen, and dishes that include prunes are called à l'Agenaise. As a matter of fact, it was the French who introduced the prune to California, our own center of prune production. Now, after a hundred years of growing, there are some 100,000 acres of prune orchards in the valleys of California and more in Oregon and Washington. While some people claim that Oregon and Washington prunes are even finer than those of California, it's a matter of opinion, although I do find some of the northern prunes extraordinarily good.

The prune is a variety of purple plum that we buy fresh during the summer and fall to make prune pies and cakes and preserves. In the valleys where the prunes are dried, the ripe fruit is washed, dehydrated, and processed. When prunes were dried in the open air, there was a good deal of variation among them, but nowadays they are given a very scientific warm-air treatment for about 18 hours that dries the fruit very evenly with controlled humidity. After drying they are graded according to size, then steamed to make them soft, moist, and tender, and packaged in various sizes and styles. You can buy very superior, top-quality jumbo pitted prunes at a premium price. These are wonderful to eat as they are or to use in dishes where the appearance of the prune is as important as the taste. The other prunes are packaged in various sizes from small to extra large, averaging from 67 to 43 a pound, depending on size.

Prunes today are really ready to use, and they don't require all the presoaking of yore. Put them in a pan with an equal amount of water, cup for cup, bring them to a boil, and simmer about 10 minutes, then let them cool in the liquid. Or put them in a jar or bowl with an equal quantity of boiling water and let them stand overnight. Either way you will have nicely puffed prunes to which you may or may not add sugar, according to taste.

I have a special trick with prunes. I put large prunes in one jar and smaller ones in another and puff them with the boiling-water treatment. Next day I drain off the water and cover the prunes completely with sherry or port (you can also use vodka, whiskey, or any liquor you like) and let them age in the jar for about two weeks before using them. I keep jars of these "drunken prunes" on the shelf at all times. Being in spirits, they require no refrigeration. For a quick dessert I take them from the jar and serve them topped with whipped cream, or I cook with them—I make a prune cake, stuff baked apples with them, or purée them and mix them into a cake frosting. To make an extremely good hors d'oeuvre, I dry the prunes, put half a walnut, almond, or filbert inside, wrap them in partially cooked bacon, secured with a toothpick, and broil them until the prune is plump and the bacon quite crisp.

Prunes taste marvelous with pork. One of my favorite roasts is a *Loin of Pork Stuffed with Drunken Prunes*. Make an incision through the center of the eye of the loin and stuff the prunes into it. Salt the loin, and roast on a rack in a 325-degree oven, allowing 25 minutes per pound, until the internal temperature reaches 165 degrees on a meat thermometer. Baste with a little of the prune juice during cooking to give a slight glaze.

When the roast is carved, you have a delicious, fruity black core.

When I have to whip up a dessert in a hurry, I take my drunken prunes and make a *Prune Soufflé*, a very different type from the usual one. Rub prunes through a food mill or sieve to yield 1 cup prune purée (you will probably need no sugar, as they are very sweet and sugar is used in the egg whites). Beat 6 egg whites until they form soft peaks, adding a pinch of salt, and ½ teaspoon cream of tartar. At the soft-peak stage, gradually beat in 4 tablespoons sugar, and beat until you have a fairly stiff meringue with firm glossy peaks—not too stiff, or it will break. Fold in the prune purée—be sure it is thoroughly mixed with the whites, but don't overfold. Turn mixture into a buttered and sugared 6-cup (1½-quart) soufflé dish, and bake at 375 degrees for 25 to 30 minutes, or until delicately browned and puffy. Serve with sweetened whipped cream sprinkled with finely chopped pecans or pistachio nuts.

This serves six, and it is an easy, showy, luscious dessert, not very high in calories, and one of the best ways to use the mighty prune that I know.

Upside-down Apple Pie

Apple pie has been a tradition in this country for more than two hundred years, and in England long before that. Lovely fresh apples cooked to juicy tenderness, delicately flavored with sugar, perhaps a little bit of lemon peel, butter, nutmeg, or cloves, harbored in a crisp, flaky crust—that's the kind of apple pie that dreams are made of, but how often do we get it? The type we tend to find in restaurants and at lunch counters nowadays, with a bottom crust as tough as cardboard, filled with badly cooked apples spiced with too much cinnamon, seems to be the norm. It is not very good eating.

The answer, of course, is to make your own. For a few weeks I had fresh firm green apples that cooked beautifully, and I had fun making pies. I tested a couple of recipes that I think should redeem the reputation of the apple pie. The first is borrowed from the French tarte Tatin—and while it is not the authentic recipe I often wonder if anyone can claim that, because every one you find in a French cookbook is completely different. Some are superb and others not so good. Anyway, I decided what I was going to strive for, and the result came out pretty well, even if it does break with tradition.

    Tarte Tatin is baked in a skillet with the bottom crust on top and inverted onto a plate soon after it comes from the oven. You have to handle it quickly and carefully, or the juices will run all over you and the apples with their luscious caramel topping will slide off the crust. To make the pastry for the crust, mix 1 cup flour and 2 tablespoons sugar with ½ cup (1 stick) very cold butter or margarine, cut into small pieces. Add 1 egg yolk and ½ teaspoon salt. Work the fat into the flour and egg mixture very quickly with your fingers or a heavy fork (or do it in a mixer with a paddle attachment), breaking up the fat and mixing it with the flour until it is the size of small peas. At this point, you may or may not need additional liquid. Judge carefully. If you add too much liquid, you'll have to add more flour, and that makes a tough crust. If you do need liquid, add a little ice water, a tablespoon at a time, work it in, then see if you can pull the dough into a ball with your hands. If not, add a touch more water. The idea is to get a light ball of dough that can be rolled out without crumbling or breaking apart. Pat the ball rather flat on waxed paper, wrap it up, and chill in the refrigerator from 30 minutes to 2 hours.

    When you are ready to make the tart, let ½ to ¾ cup sugar melt in a heavy iron or aluminum 8-inch or 9-inch skillet over medium heat until it turns a delicate brown. Remove pan from heat. Arrange on the melted sugar 5 to 8 apples, peeled, cored, and cut in quarters or sixths. The exact number will depend on the size of the apples and the skillet; you need enough to fill the skillet and mound up in the center. Sprinkle them with 2 to 3 tablespoons sugar, and dot with 4 to 6 tablespoons butter, cut in tiny pieces. If you wish, sprinkle with a few grains of nutmeg or cinnamon. Personally, I prefer not to spice the apples for this tart.

Carefully roll out the chilled pastry to a size that will fit inside the skillet. Then, since the exertion of being rolled may make it shrink a bit and you don't want that, let it sit for 5 to 10 minutes to rest (while you are preparing the apples). Lay it over the apples, tucking it down inside the skillet. Make about three holes in the top with a skewer or sharp knife. Bake in a 350-degree oven from 1 to 1½ hours, until the crust is brown and firm to the touch and the apples possibly bubbling up a bit around the edge. Remove from the oven and let it stand 2 minutes, then run a sharp knife around the edge of the tart and invert it onto a plate rather larger than the skillet. Do this quickly and deftly so the apples don't fall off. Should they shift position, push them back into place with a spatula.

Cut into wedges and serve warm or tepid. It's much better that way than cold, and it must be eaten fresh. With it you might have thick heavy cream, sour cream, or whipped cream, perhaps flavored with a little grated nutmeg.

☙ For another, simpler version of this tart, fill a well-buttered ovenproof glass dish with the apples, cut as before. Sprinkle each layer with granulated sugar, little bits of butter, and a few grains of nutmeg or cinnamon. Add ⅓ to ½ cup applejack. Roll out the crust, wet the edge of the dish, and fit the crust over it. Crimp the edge, if you wish, make a couple of steam holes on top, and brush with 1 egg yolk beaten with 2 tablespoons heavy cream. Bake at 450 degrees for 10 to 12 minutes (this is to prevent the crust from sinking), then reduce the heat to 350 and continue baking until the crust is beautifully browned and the apples cooked through. Serve the warm or tepid tart from the baking dish, accompanied by applejack-flavored whipped cream or vanilla ice cream. (If you're going to have ice cream, add a touch more applejack to the apples before cooking so the flavor comes through against the ice cream.)

The combination of apple pie and ice cream is another American custom of long standing, and a delightful one, too.

☙

Ice Cream City

Everyone knows Philadelphia as the city of brotherly love where our independence was declared in 1776, but how many of you are aware that it is the ice cream capital of the country, maybe of the world? This has been going on for a pretty long time. When Philadelphia became the seat of government and George Washington the first president, "iced creams," as they were then called, were often served at the presidential Thursday dinners. We have reason to believe that they were not quite the same as our luscious delights made commercially or at home in an ice cream freezer, but mixtures of cream, sugar, and eggs beaten in metal bowls over ice so that they had more the texture of the soft ice cream sold in certain places today.

By the beginning of the nineteenth century, Philadelphians were ice cream addicts. There is a record of the opening of an early form of ice cream parlor by an Italian who advertised that he purveyed "all kinds of refreshments, as Ice Cream, Syrups, French Cordials, Cakes, Clarets of the best kind, Jellies etc." After the great Exposition of 1876 Philadelphia became known across the country for the excellence of its ice cream, by then a popular American delicacy, and to this day the words "Philadelphia ice cream" connote the highest quality. Philadelphia confectioners were famed for their ice cream. Sauter's was one. I can remember that in Reading, Pennsylvania, theirs was the ice cream served at the most elegant parties. Sauter's is gone, alas, and with it those wonderful ice creams and cakes, but you can still get luxuriously rich ice cream, high in butterfat, from Bassett's, another Philadelphia institution noted for inspired and unusual flavors such as casaba melon and Irish coffee.

Then there is Zendler's, a most extraordinary shop run by Mollie and Fred Zendler, who for more than twenty years have supplied Philadelphia's balls and parties with wondrously shaped and tinted ice cream frozen in a collection of over 300 old ice cream molds of every imaginable design and size. Molding and tinting ice cream is practically a lost art, and if you are in Philadelphia you should visit the Zendlers and see their collection. I have about seventy of these old molds that were left to me by a friend who had cherished them throughout her lifetime, and though from time to time I use them for dinner parties, mostly I just leave them heaped in a big bowl where people can enjoy looking at them.

You can sometimes pick up old ice cream molds in antique shops at a rather exorbitant price, but for general purposes you can use large molds such as melon molds, charlotte molds, and bombe molds sold in kitchen equipment shops. Bombes (not the kind that blow up) are truly spectacular desserts, the kind served at great parties. They consist of various textures and flavors of ice cream, parfait, or sherbet frozen, unmolded, and beautifully decorated or surrounded with spun sugar.

    ☙ Another highly decorative dessert is the frozen pudding, of which probably the most popular is *Nesselrode Pudding*, an indecently delicious confection. To make it, soak ½ cup currants and ½ cup raisins for ½ hour in cognac barely to cover. Drain, reserving the cognac. Beat 5 egg yolks for about 1 minute with a whisk, then add ¾ cup sugar and continue beating, with a whisk or in an electric mixer, until the mixture is very thick, a light lemon color, and forms a ribbon. Heat 2 cups heavy cream in a saucepan just to the boiling point, then beat it into the egg yolk mixture with a whisk or in the mixer. Return to the pan, and cook over medium heat, stirring, until it coats a spoon thickly—on no account let it come to a boil or you'll have sweet scrambled eggs. Remove from the heat and stir in 1 can unsweetened chestnut purée (sold in gourmet shops and some supermarkets) or 1 cup candied chestnuts broken into small pieces. Add the reserved cognac, currants, raisins, and 2 teaspoons vanilla.

Now whip 1 cup heavy cream until it begins to thicken, add 3 tablespoons sugar, and continue beating until quite firm. Fold into the chestnut mixture, making sure they are well combined and thoroughly blended. Lightly oil a 1½-quart melon or charlotte mold and fill with the mixture. Cover securely. Melon molds have a tight-fitting cover with a handle, and so do some charlotte molds, but if yours doesn't you can seal the mold with foil and Scotch tape. Leave the mold in the freezer compartment for about 5 to 6 hours, or until solidly frozen, and about 15 minutes before serving, transfer it to the refrigerator. To serve, unmold it onto a chilled serving dish—you may have to run a towel, wrung out in very hot water, over the mold to loosen the pudding or dip the bottom of the mold in hot water for just a second, not long enough to melt it.

Garnish the frozen pudding with whipped cream piped through a pastry tube or with candied chestnuts stuck into little nests of whipped cream and a few candied cherries.

This beautiful dessert, a joy to look at, with an exquisite flavor, is reminiscent of the glorious heyday of Philadelphia's ice cream desserts, so integral a part of our sweet-tooth history.

☙

The Frost Is on the Sherbet

We call it sherbet, and to the French it is *sorbet* (pronounced sohrbay), a word that I think falls much more pleasantly on the ear. The Oxford Dictionary defines sherbets or sorbets as a variety of frozen sweets (for which, in America, read desserts), and they are probably the earliest known. Originally from the Middle East, sherbet (spelled sharbat in Persia, serbet in Turkey) was a cooling drink with a base of fresh fruit, sweetened, diluted, and chilled—in the far distant past, with snow. The idea was copied later on throughout Europe with sherbet powders, which were used to make drinks and, after freezing was introduced, for water ices made with purées, of fruit and other things, mixed with sugar syrup and frozen.

Nothing could be more delightfully apt than this description of a dinner, from the London *Daily Telegraph* of September 27, 1864, "The menu meandered gracefully through fish, flesh, fowl and truffles and finally melted away into sorbets." Sorbets do indeed melt away, in your mouth, in the most glorious manner, and they make a perfect ending for a good dinner.

When I was last in Paris, I dined at a new and charming restaurant called La Cannelle, at 53 Quai des Grands Augustins. It's a very gay, chic kind of place, frequented by the younger set, where dinner is served quite late and you positively must have a reservation. To me, the outstanding thing about the menu was the number of sorbets on the dessert list, and the extraordinarily interesting flavors and combinations. One was a sorbet of cassis, or black currants. In this country, fresh black currants are not grown or sold, and can only be bought imported in jam, the liqueur called crème de cassis, or a nonalcoholic cassis syrup. You can make a cassis sorbet by combining the puréed jam and the liqueur or syrup.

At La Cannelle the cassis sorbet was served with cassis liqueur poured over it at just the right moment. I was also intrigued by the pineapple sorbet, served on a quarter of fresh pineapple. The flesh had been sliced off, cut in small pieces, and rearranged on the skin with the sorbet on each side so one ate a bite of pineapple and a spoonful of sorbet. One of my friends chose a lemon sorbet, deliciously tart, that had paper-thin slices of fresh lemon, dipped in sugar, pressed into it. The pale yellow sorbet ornamented by the curves of the lemon, skin side up, made a very pretty dessert, and the flavor was accented by Russian vodka, poured over it at the table.

Another exciting flavor combination was the delicate pear sorbet, made with Bartlett pears and a touch of *eau de vie de poire* (pear brandy), served with hot chocolate sauce. Two of the most unusual sorbets on the list were the coconut one, which had a little mound of freshly grated coconut on top, and the marron sorbet, crowned by three perfect marrons glacés, or candied chestnuts. If I were making this, I'd add a little bit of vanilla or cognac to the sorbet mixture to bring out the chestnut flavor.

So now that I've whetted your appetite for these luscious frozen desserts, I'm going to give you the basic method. It's really very simple. The only piece of equipment you need is an ice cream freezer, although in a pinch you can use ice trays, in the freezer. If you have an ice cream attachment for your electric mixer, which is the prize of my kitchen, you can make the sorbet between the main and dessert courses. Sorbets are always best made at the last minute and served soft, not frozen hard. They give off their joyful fruity flavor much more generously. If you make sorbets in ice trays, let them thaw slightly before serving.

For a basic *Fruit Sorbet*, boil 1¾ cups sugar with 1 cup water until dissolved, then boil for 5 minutes more. Allow to cool. Beat this syrup into 2 stiffly beaten egg whites, and then mix in 2 cups fruit purée. For an orange or lemon sorbet, use the grated rind, juice, and puréed pulp of 3 oranges or lemons, and 2 cups of other puréed fruits (if you use raspberries, strain them to remove the seeds). Then freeze the mixture in ice trays. If you make the sorbet in an ice cream freezer or a sorbetière, a gadget specially designed for making sorbets, proceed as you would for ice cream, but be sure to take it out before it is solid as a rock, or you will kill the flavor and texture.

Follow the basic method for any sorbet—the possibilities are endless. You could have a different flavor every night, all summer long. Sorbets are really perfect hot-weather desserts, refreshing to the palate, easy to make, and a wonderful conclusion to any luncheon or dinner.

⚜

Syllabubs

Syllabubs are one of the oldest of all English desserts, and they have been known in this country, especially in Maryland, Virginia, and other parts of the South, since the first American colonies were established. The odd-sounding name itself—sometimes spelled "sillibub"—comes from the early English word "silly," meaning "happy," plus a dialect word, "bub," meaning liquor. As you will see, it is a very happy alcoholic dessert indeed. Essentially fragile, it is a concoction of wine, seasonings, sometimes brandy or cognac, and cream, all of which is whipped to a froth. The froth is skimmed off and served in glasses. This makes one of the most delicious, lightest, and punchiest desserts imaginable, particularly pleasant served along with a good piece of sponge cake or a nice crisp shortbread cookie.

In their heyday syllabubs were as popular as ice cream is today, a featured dessert when entertaining guests and a favorite family sweet. Here is an early American recipe for it, which is now far more picturesque than practicable, but it gives a good idea of what a simple, homely dessert it started out to be. It is aptly called Country Syllabub and comes from a cookbook published in Philadelphia at the beginning of the nineteenth century.

    "For Country Syllabub mix ½ pound of white sugar with a pint of fine, sweet cider or white wine and grate in it a nutmeg. Prepare them in a large bowl just before milking time. Let it be taken to the cow and have about three pints of milk milked into it stirring it occasionally with a spoon. Let it be eaten before the froth subsides. If you use cider a little brandy will improve it."

Well, I don't think very many of us could produce that dessert nowadays. I, for one, do not have a cow in my garden—to say nothing of the inconvenience of having to rush out of doors as the dinner hour approaches. Although people really did make syllabubs in this and equally quaint ways, most recipes are quite easy, like this one, which is also rather old.

    "Take a quart of cream and a pint of Rhenish wine [this was Rhine wine] and the juice of four lemons. Sweeten it to your taste. Put in it some lemon peel and whip it up with a small rod. Put it with a spoon into some syllabub glasses."

That is basically the recipe we use today. I am next going to give you a very simple recipe for a traditional syllabub and then a modern one for a glamorous and delicious raspberry syllabub.

The first of these *Syllabub* recipes must really be started a day before serving. It calls for 1 small glass (½ cup) of white wine or sherry, 2 tablespoons of brandy, 1 lemon, ⅓ to ½ cup sugar to taste, ½ pint of chilled heavy cream, and a few gratings of nutmeg.

Shred or grate the rind of the lemon and extract the juice. Put rind and juice in a bowl with the wine and brandy, and leave it overnight. The next day transfer this to a 2- to 3-quart bowl, add the sugar, and stir until it is dissolved. Add the heavy cream very slowly, stirring it continuously to blend thoroughly with the other ingredients. Grate in a little nutmeg. Beat with a wire whisk until it thickens and holds a soft peak when the whisk is lifted from the bowl. This may take 5 minutes or more, but be patient—it will thicken. The result must not be grainy or curdled. Spoon it into 2 or 3-ounce glasses, add a little lemon zest, and serve cool but not chilled. It is much better if it is not refrigerated and is best when eaten soon after whisking, although it can be kept in a cool spot for a whole day.

Serve with some dry cookies, shortbread cookies, or shortbread fingers. You will find that you have a dessert that is delicious, unusual, and fun, as well as being historical.

The second recipe for *Syllabub* uses fresh or frozen raspberries. If you are using frozen, thaw and drain 1 package, reserving the juice. You won't need any sugar with this, since frozen raspberries are quite sweet as they are. If using fresh berries—you will need 1 pint—place in a bowl, add sugar to taste, and crush lightly. In either case add 1 tablespoon kirsch or a little rose water to the raspberries, or, lacking these, a touch (about ½ teaspoon) vanilla or lemon juice. Let the flavored berries stand while you prepare the cream. Whip ½ pint heavy cream until it is stiff but not stiff enough to hold peaks. Add to this about ¼ cup white wine, or beat in the juice from the raspberries to which you have added a bit of lemon juice. Beat again so that the cream stiffens slightly more. Then, using a spoon, fold in the raspberries so that they streak the cream with red and are distributed throughout. Spoon into chilled glasses and chill for an hour or two before serving.

Serve with ladyfingers, sponge cake fingers, or good sugar cookies. Each of these "happy-liquor" desserts will bring cheer to four people.

Queen of Desserts

One of the greatest desserts in the realm of cooking is called crème brûlée, and despite its name it is not a French dish but a very old English one. No one seems quite to know when or how it became Gallicized, for over a long period of time it was known simply as burnt cream. The earliest recipe I have been able to find was printed in a seventeenth-century cookbook from Dorsetshire. After that it had a rather interesting history and gained considerable renown. Originally, this was a rich custard, a mixture of sugar, egg yolks, and cream cooked over heat, then poured into a dish and cooled. The top was then sprinkled with sugar and the sugar caramelized to a brown glaze with a red-hot salamander, an old type of heavy metal tool which was lowered to the surface of the sugar and moved over it until the intense heat melted and browned the sugar, hence the name burnt cream.

Crème brûlée became a standard dessert at Cambridge University, especially Christ College, where it was made in a special dish designed by the Copeland-Spode Company. This was round, about as wide as a soup plate, an inch deep, and heatproof so that it could withstand the tremendous heat generated by the salamander. It's amusing to read old cookbooks and to discover the many versions of crème brûlée—sometimes it was made with gooseberry or raspberry fool instead of custard.

In various guises, it became the acknowledged queen of British desserts. I can remember having it at a number of places, including the Houses of Parliament. You still are more apt to find it served in England, although in America we went through a great crème brûlée period a number of years ago, and I wish we would again, for to my mind it is without peer—few desserts are more delicious to eat and to look at. There is such a subtle contrast of flavor and texture between the creamy custard and its crisp caramelized topping.

In the years during which the recipe has been used in the United States, the original recipe has been considerably changed, and I'm not sure it is for the better. Many American recipes call for a topping of brown sugar, and although I have used this from time to time, I've never felt the result was all it should be. So much of the brown sugar you get these days does not have the texture it used to. I now use fine granulated sugar instead, and it makes a much more delicious crust.

    Although the dessert sounds simple, there are a couple of tricky points about the preparation, so I'm going to give you my version of *Crème Brûlée*.

    Heat 1 pint heavy cream, the heaviest you can get, to the boiling point. Lightly beat 6 egg yolks with ½ cup sugar and a pinch of salt, and pour the hot cream over them, stirring constantly with a wooden spatula or wire whisk until well blended. Add 2 teaspoons vanilla or a little mace or any other flavoring you desire. Strain the custard into a 1½-quart heatproof baking dish, stand the dish in a pan of warm water, and bake in a 350-degree oven for 25 to 30 minutes, or until the custard is completely set but not overcooked. Do not let the water in the pan boil. Remove from the oven, cool, and then chill thoroughly in the refrigerator.

About 1½ to 2 hours before serving, sprinkle the top evenly with fine granulated sugar to a thickness of about ¼ inch. Put under the broiler (or use a salamander, if you have one) until the sugar is melted and bubbly, watching carefully to see it does not scorch and burn. Remove, cool, and chill again until serving time. You'll have a hard, highly glazed crust on top of an unctuous, voluptuous custard. This will serve about six. If you have more guests, double the recipe, using 12 egg yolks to a quart of cream.

This is the method of making crème brûlée that I prefer. However, after combining the cream with the egg yolks and sugar, you may cook the custard gently until the mixture coats the spoon—stir constantly, and be sure it does not come to a boil. Pour into the baking dish, cool, chill, and glaze the sugared top as above. When the custard is cooked this way, rather than baked, the consistency is less firm, so be sure the chilled custard is completely set before sprinkling it with sugar, or the sugar may sink to the bottom of the dish, which is not what one wants at all.

While you can certainly serve crème brûlée alone, it is sometimes fun to gild the lily a bit. I like a little cream with it, either heavy cream or whipped cream, flavored perhaps with a touch of cognac. Dry, short, sweet cookies are fine with it, and so is a piece of good honest plain cake.

Playing Around with Pound Cake

I remember when I was young, my mother always had a pound cake in the larder. One week it would be a caraway seed cake, with the little pungent flecks pushing through the smooth golden-yellow cake. Another week it might be a citron cake, with thin slivers of citron on the top (never mixed in, lest they sink to the bottom). Sometimes there were chopped walnuts in our cake, or ginger, which gave it an exotic, spicy flavor. Pound cake was our standby. We had it for tea, toasted for breakfast, and as a foundation for fruit desserts, with fresh or poached berries, poached plums or peaches, and slathers of heavy cream poured over everything.

With its fine grain and buttery richness, pound cake is one of the greatest of all our cakes, deserving of a place of honor next to a fine fruit cake and the delicate French génoise. Pound cake must be just about as old as baking. You find recipes for it, under various and sundry names, in England, the United States, Canada, and other countries where the British ruled. Originally, the cake was made with a pound of butter, a pound of flour, a pound of sugar, and a pound of eggs, hence the name, and according to the proficiency and mixing ability of the baker, it was apt to be a pretty heavy cake, for there were no mixers in those days. Some people beat the eggs in whole; others separated them, putting the yolks in with the butter and sugar and then folding in the whites.

It seems to me that in the last twenty-five years, as our tastes have changed and we have learned to appreciate more delicate fare, the old, somewhat heavy pound cake has been reevaluated. We still love its delicious, rather stately quality, but we have found ways to improve on this great standard loaf cake. We have played around with the recipes of our mothers and grandmothers and found that we can improve on them. Why not? I am sure that if the great Carême were alive today he would use modern equipment and methods to improve on his superb pastries. I like to fool around with pound cake, and recently I did some experimenting.

First I made a real old-fashioned one, laboriously beating in every egg by hand. It rose beautifully, but after it had cooled and I sliced it and took a bite, I thought: "Glory be! Is this what I always considered to be the be-all and end-all of cakes? It's not the way it used to taste to me." Actually, it was not the cake, but my palate, that had changed. In my experimentations I came up with a cake that I think is lighter and more delicious and keeps better. This pound cake bakes well in a well-buttered and floured angel-cake or tube pan. Loaf pans work perfectly well, if you prefer that shape.

    One trick for making *Pound Cake* is to sift your flour very well indeed. Sift 3 cups all-purpose flour onto waxed paper, then spoon it gently into a measuring cup. Spoon it back into the sifter, add 1 teaspoon baking powder and a good heavy pinch of salt, and sift twice more, each time spooning it very lightly into the measuring cup. Then, instead of beating all the sugar into the butter, use part of it to make a sort of meringue. Beat the whites of 7 extra-large or 8 large eggs until they hold soft peaks, then very gradually beat in 1 cup sugar, about 2 tablespoons at a time, beating thoroughly.

Put in a large bowl 1 pound very soft butter, and cream with a wooden spoon or your hand until very light and fluffy. Then beat in ¾ cup sugar, using a wooden spoon, a whisk, or the electric mixer with a paddle attachment. Beat in the 7 or 8 egg yolks until light and lemon-colored, and add 2 tablespoons cognac and 1 tablespoon grated lemon rind. Gradually fold the sifted flour mixture into the butter-sugar-egg mixture. Finally, fold in the beaten whites to make a smooth batter, being careful not to overmix.

Pour the batter into your buttered and floured tube or loaf pan, and bake in a preheated 350-degree oven for 1 hour. Test with a cake tester to see that it is thoroughly baked. The edges should break away slightly from the pan sides. Remove from oven, and cool on a rack for at least 12 to 15 minutes. A few more minutes won't hurt. Loosen the sides very, very gently with a spatula and invert the cake on the rack to finish cooling. There you have your beautiful pound cake, which you can vary by flavoring it with caraway seeds, mace, nutmeg, or ground ginger, or by putting thinly sliced citron on top just before baking.

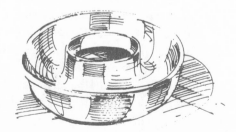

Tea Drinkers, Unite!

One of these days I'm going to start a militant organization of tea lovers, dedicated to improving the standards of the tea served in hotel dining rooms and restaurants. I'm a tea drinker, and I've found that getting a good cup of tea in any public place in this country is virtually an impossibility. It's generally assumed that everyone wants to drink coffee, and the tea drinker is given very short shrift indeed.

I well recall ordering tea one morning in a very famous hotel and being given something that was definitely tap water with a tea bag on the side. When I complained, the waitress retorted, "I knew I was going to have trouble with you. Now I'll have to go downstairs and get some boiling water."

That's the general attitude, yet it is so simple to make a good cup of tea. All you need is boiling water, a pot, preferably of earthenware or porcelain, and tea or tea bags. As the water comes to a boil, rinse the pot to get it well heated, add the tea or tea bags, pour on the freshly boiling water, and let it stand and steep for 3 or 4 minutes. Is this too much trouble? Certainly when you consider the price charged for a pot of tea it shouldn't be. Why, when coffee brewing has been brought to a fine art, should we be forced to accept mediocrity in tea?

At home I prefer to use loose tea, but away from home I've come to accept tea bags. The trouble is that no restaurant gives you more than one, and the amount of tea in a tea bag is totally inadequate for even a small pot—except in Canada, where the tea bags are larger and hold more than ours. You can always ask for two tea bags, but you'll still get the same old routine—a pot of barely warm water with the tea bags on the side.

I'm slightly cheered to notice that there is a growing increase in the types of tea sold throughout the country, with all the great names in tea such as Twinings, Ridgways, and Fortnum & Mason represented on the shelves of grocery stores and supermarkets.

I always have at least four different types of tea on hand. For breakfast I like Darjeeling, an Indian tea that is also a component of the excellent blend called English Breakfast Tea. For afternoon drinking, I keep a selection, for to me there is nothing more comforting than to come home, feeling a bit tired and weary, and make myself a pot of steaming hot tea.

First, there's Formosa Oolong, from an island that produces some of the world's finest teas. It has the wonderful bouquet and slightly exotic flavor characteristic of the true Oolong leaf. Then I have Lapsang Souchong, a smoky Chinese tea cured over peat fires, delicately colored and extremely bracing and pleasurable to the palate and pungent to the nose. I also keep Keemun, another China tea of rather distinctive flavor and bouquet, and that old favorite, Earl Grey, which has an almost orangy aroma, very relaxing and cozy, the kind of tea you like to sip with a toasted muffin or scone or a slice of cake, in the English manner.

I love afternoon tea. I remember, years ago, driving into Westchester to a charming old farmhouse where they served tea and the most delicious cinnamon toast I've ever tasted. They took good bread and toasted it on one side. Then the other side was well spread with butter and sprinkled rather heavily with brown sugar and cinnamon. This was run under the broiler and watched carefully until the sugar melted and mingled with the butter and cinnamon. By the time the almost candied toast had been removed from the oven and cut into strips it was crispy on top and luxuriously rich when you bit into it. I often make this cinnamon toast—it's one of the best contrasts to a good cup of tea you can imagine.

To me, tea should always be drunk from thin, nicely shaped cups, and I prefer mine plain. Although one is often served cream with tea in the United States, milk is preferable. It blends better and has a pleasanter flavor. For sweetening, I think lump sugar is more delicate and fitting than granulated.

On a really cold day—or even on a hot one—you might try what used to be called Russian tea, a boiling hot cup of fairly strong tea to which you add a little rum, a slice of lemon, and, if you like, sugar. It's refreshing, relaxing, and delicious.

Now if all tea lovers got together, surely we could prevail on restaurants and hotels to give us a good, hearty, fairly strong cup of tea to satisfy our thirst with its steaming briskness. And when it comes to iced tea, we should insist on having freshly made tea poured over an ample amount of crushed ice and served at once, rather than the usual horrid brew kept all day in a large container until it is stale, tasteless, and full of tannic acid. Tea is such a precious thing that it is well worth fighting for.

My Historic Cup of Tea

The company whose tea was twice thrown into Boston harbor at the famous tea party, more than two hundred years ago, is still shipping tea to the United States. I discovered this rather startling fact one morning when I was having a cup of remarkably good tea in the offices of the British Travel Association.

Someone brought in a tin of the tea we were drinking, and I noticed that it was called Boston Harbour tea. "What's this?" I asked, and I was told that it came from Davison, Newman, the English company whose tea was dumped overboard in the first and second Boston tea parties, in December 1773 and March 1774.

Davison, Newman is an outgrowth of an old firm that was started about 1650 in a rather remote part of London on the Southwark side of the Thames, near the famous George Tavern, one of the most remarkably preserved old inns in London, where the food is still served in great style. They have moved a couple of times since, but they are still in the same area, so when I was visiting London one time I decided to drop in on Mr. Leslie Simons, the present director of Davison, Newman & Co. Ltd. He took time out to show me some of the old files and records of the petitions the firm made to George III to make good their losses on the tea. George, true to form, never paid up, and there is still a debt outstanding for some of that tea. Mr. Simons told me that some schoolchildren in Massachusetts and, I think, San José, California, read about the money still owing and raised a little bit which they sent as a token gift to Davison, Newman to help recoup some of their losses, which I found a very touching gesture.

I noticed that in the early days Lapsang Souchong, the great Chinese tea, was selling for three shillings a pound, about forty cents at today's rate of exchange, and Pekoe for four shillings and sixpence, or sixty cents, which says something for the inflationary rise. Davison, Newman no longer ships China teas, only the India Ceylon teas, which are more in demand in America at this point. Boston Harbour tea, beautifully packaged in a tin bearing a replica of the petition to George III, has a small distribution, primarily in New England.

Davison, Newman was also one of the first companies to ship Scotch whisky to the United States, and at one point in their history they maintained a huge sugar plantation in Jamaica. Their sign, indicative of their business and status, is a crown and three sugar loaves, and it has hung outside each of the shops in the three moves they've made over the last three hundred years, so the business came to be known as the Three Sugar Loaves and Crown. In the old days, sugar was sold in these moundlike loaves, round at the top and wider at the base. They were cut in pieces, as needed, and broken up in a mortar and pestle to provide fine sugar for baking, sweetening, or sprinkling on fruit. The company was also one of the earliest chocolate merchants, shipping this and sugar to America as well as tea, so they were very much a part of the early beverage habits of this country from the beginning. I'm very sentimental about some things, and this really struck a chord.

Even though we are regarded as a coffee-drinking nation, there are still a lot of tea fanciers in the United States. After I wrote bemoaning the fact that the tea in most restaurants and coffee shops is badly and carelessly made and at times almost undrinkable, I got a stupendous amount of mail from people who agreed with me that we should all unite and try to force restaurants to give us tea made with boiling water and allowed ample time to steep. No more dragging along a tea bag and a cup of warm water and expecting to make tea out of them at the table.

To me there's nothing nicer and more soothing than sitting down in the afternoon to a good cup of tea with a piece of cake or a cookie, or a slice of homemade bread, cut paper-thin and spread with unsalted butter.

When I was a child, my mother used to make for our afternoon tea a pound cake (see page 188) enhanced by 2 tablespoons of spicy. pungent caraway seeds. Usually you associate that almost indescribable flavor of caraway with bread, but try it in this cake for a change.

Tea, English Style

One of the great joys of being in England, as I rediscovered when I spent a few days in London this summer, is being able to sit in the comfortable lounge of a hotel, in a club, or in certain restaurants and have afternoon tea. To me one of life's social pleasures is being able to take tea with friends, to relax and talk, reminisce if you will, letting the stimulus of the steaming tea alleviate any feelings of fatigue from a long day's shopping or sightseeing and warm the cockles of your heart.

When I was a young man studying in London and hadn't much money to spend, I looked forward to the luxury of having tea at that famous old hotel, the Ritz, which in those days cost two shillings and sixpence, then about fifty cents. For this you were given a pot of freshly made tea, wonderful thin sandwiches, toast, and pastries, with the soothing sound of string music in the background. As I couldn't afford to give dinner parties, my way of repaying the hospitality of people who had been nice to me was to invite two or three at a time to tea at the Ritz, which always seemed to delight and entertain them.

So here I was some forty years later, sitting in the Ritz with a friend who had also loved this very English ritual, drinking tea and eating little pastries and sandwiches that weren't quite as good as those we remembered, but we were content. We were recapturing a shared experience in a place that was part of our long friendship and our lives.

Another day I had tea at Brown's, a famous old-time hotel that is typically British in its background and clientele. I remember when tea there was presided over by a maître d'hôtel who looked as if he had spent his life as the head butler in some great country mansion. He was exceedingly forbidding to newcomers until he got to know them or found they tipped well! He is long gone, but Brown's still retains some of that feeling of being a country house, and tea is rather a pompous ceremony, much more so than at the Ritz or the Grosvenor House.

The Grosvenor House is much more cosmopolitan, and in its enormous tea lounge I was fascinated to see Americans, English, Indians, Chinese, Japanese, Italians, and quite a few people in Arab dress having afternoon tea. Afternoon tea is a good time to people-watch, which I find is very important when you travel. Most of us people-watch too little. By watching people and seeing their reactions, you gain new ideas and insights and learn to know them by observation.

The tea sandwiches at the Grosvenor House were extraordinarily good. They were about 5 inches long and 2 inches wide, made from good moist white bread, not the Kleenex type, which had been cut paper-thin and spread with sweet butter. There were sandwiches made from ripe tomatoes that had been quickly scalded, peeled, the seeds squeezed out so the liquid didn't make the bread soggy, then coarsely chopped and seasoned with a little salt and pepper. There were watercress sandwiches, ham sandwiches, chicken sandwiches, and cucumber sandwiches, which with tomato are my favorites among tea sandwiches. These are made with the long European cucumbers, now appearing in our markets as "seedless" cucumbers, which they really aren't although they do have fewer seeds than the ordinary type. If you can't buy them, scrape the seeds from ordinary cucumbers, slice them very thinly, sprinkle them with salt, and let them sit for an hour to draw out the bitter juice. Then dry them on paper towels and put between thin slices of buttered bread with salt, pepper, a tiny squeeze of lemon juice, or just a brush of mayonnaise.

With the tea sandwiches you are given a hot plate of crisp toast with marmalade and jam and tiny little pastries. You choose the tea you prefer, India, Ceylon, Pekoe, the rather smoky Lapsang Souchong from China, the brisk Earl Grey, or a delicate China tea like Oolong or Keemun.

In England, teatime is the time for relaxation and good talk. We in America take for granted that it is the cocktail hour, but I strongly recommend a revival of this civilized custom. If we could only resurrect the pleasure of the tea hour and then move on to cocktails later, we'd be much better fortified and prepared for the evening.

Hot Chocolate

A steaming cup of hot chocolate with buttered toast is surely one of the most heart-warming, body-warming, and taste-satisfying combinations known to man. When I was growing up in Portland, Oregon, my friends and I used to go to a great place called Swetland's where we would sit and sip some of the most luscious thick hot chocolate I have ever tasted.

Later on, when I visited France for the first time as a young man, I found the French breakfasting on enormous cups of hot chocolate with buttery croissants or good rolls and butter, an enchanting marriage of flavors. It wasn't only the taste of the chocolate but also the way it was served in the old days that was so nice—I remember that at Maillard's, on Madison Avenue in New York, you drank it from delightful white porcelain cups that had "hot chocolate" lettered on the sides. Some of those old chocolate cups and mugs were really works of art.

All that seems to have faded away, and it is just too bad. Chocolate now has become something that is tipped out of a little paper bag into a cup, dissolved with hot water, and served with artificial whipped cream or a marshmallow stuck on top. This is not hot chocolate, and it really pains me to think that a whole generation is growing up never knowing the glories of a truly well made cup of hot chocolate.

Chocolate, as you undoubtedly know, was one of the greatest gifts of the New World to the Old. When the Spanish conquistadors arrived in Mexico, they found some of Montezuma's courtiers drinking as many as fifty cups of chocolate a day. In fact, it has been surmised that Montezuma's love of chocolate occasioned the first chocolate ice cream—runners were sent to the mountains to bring back snow over which the whipped chocolate was poured. Personally, I think that is stretching history a bit, but it is an amusing, if apocryphal, story.

Since those days, chocolate has always been popular in Europe, and it is still drunk a lot in France and Vienna and throughout Central Europe, although the British tend to favor its less elegant relative, cocoa. Cocoa and chocolate often get confused, probably because both come from the cacao bean. Chocolate is made from the dried, roasted, and crushed "nibs" of the bean, which yield a thick liquid very high in cocoa fat. This is partially defatted, cooled, and solidified into a block of unsweetened chocolate, the type used for baking (semisweet baking chocolate has some sugar added).

Cocoa is a powdered form of chocolate with practically all the fat removed, so it is much lower in calories.

Hot chocolate can be made with sweet chocolate, unsweetened chocolate, or semisweet chocolate. The French use sweet chocolate, the

Spanish unsweetened chocolate, and the Mexicans and Puerto
packaged sweetened chocolate flavored with cinnamon and
blended with finely ground almonds that is combined with mil
a very rich drink. If you are using unsweetened chocolate, I
honey, rather than sugar, makes a very pleasant sweetening.

For each cup of *Hot Chocolate*, melt a 1-ounce square of
unsweetened chocolate in a heavy saucepan (less of a problem if you
melt it in a warm oven rather than over direct heat), then mix in 1 cup
cold water and honey to taste. Heat over medium heat, beating with a
whisk or rotary beater, until it reaches the boiling point and is good and
foamy. Serve with a dusting of cinnamon on top, or whipped cream if
you like.

The rotary beater is our modern equivalent of the traditional Mexican
molinillo, a little wooden stick with a roughly carved end that is twirled
between the palms to beat the chocolate to a froth. The old chocolate pots
had rounded bottoms and a *molinillo* that stuck through a hole in the top,
and they made a beautifully foamy chocolate. You can still buy *molinillos*,
and they are rather fun to use.

To make chocolate with the Mexican cinnamon-flavored sweet
chocolate, use 1 ounce per cup and heat with cold water or, for a richer
result, warm milk or light cream, beating as before. With semisweet
chocolate, melt 1 ounce per cup, then stir in warm milk and a bit of
cinnamon, vanilla, or vanilla bean, and heat until it comes to a boil. It
is unlikely that you will need further sweetening, but taste and see.

For another delicious chocolate drink, equally good hot or chilled,
for every 4 cups melt 4 ounces semisweet chocolate, then add sugar to
taste and 1 cup hot coffee. Blend the coffee with the melted chocolate,
and then gradually stir in 3 cups warm milk, beating until it reaches the
boiling point and is foamy. Pour into heated cups and serve with
whipped cream dusted with cocoa or cinnamon.

If you let the chocolate cool and then pour it over ice cubes in a tall
glass and top it with whipped cream, you'll have iced mocha, as
refreshing and welcome on a hot day as hot chocolate on a cold day.

CHAPTER 7

Bread, Cheese, and Wine

꙳

... in which we encounter three honest loaves ... trace the tradition of pita . . . try our hand at sandwiches ... flip over pancakes ... meet the big cheeses of America ... uncork the secrets of wine cookery ... sample an American country wine ... enjoy the youthful charms of Beaujolais ... and the infinite varieties of Champagne.

Nothing Beats Homemade Bread

I went to a dinner party the other night where something rather remarkable and heartening happened. After coffee, one of the guests got up and said to his wife, "We must leave now. I have to set my bread." This man had never cooked before in his life. He just had this thing about making his own bread.

When you think about it, bread baking makes more sense than some other forms of culinary endeavor. The disappearance of the neighborhood baker and the pushing of those abominable, tasteless, elastic loaves that fill the supermarket shelves are warnings that the day is coming when we'll be forced to make our own bread or write off one of the greatest and simplest pleasures of the table.

Turning out an honest loaf is less work than you might imagine, and soothing therapy as well. All that kneading and punching down will soon get rid of the day's frustrations. Nor do you have to make a big batch. I bake a single loaf at a time, and it keeps up to a week in a plastic bag in the refrigerator. Or I may make two small loaves and freeze one, against the time I'll need it.

Proper hard-wheat bread flour is not easy to find in this country, but well worth searching for. There are three or four good commercial unbleached flours with enough hard wheat in them to make a fine loaf, and any number of mills that sell by mail excellent flours, some water-ground. I get a flour made from North Dakota winter wheat from a mail-order house in Pennsylvania (they also have that other rarity, soft-wheat pastry flour).

The quality of granular yeast has improved considerably, but if you prefer to use fresh yeast, as I do, that may present a problem too. If you can't find it in the stores, try the bakeries. Ask for it casually, as if it had never occurred to you that buying yeast in a bakery wasn't the most normal thing in the world, or they will act as if they are doing you a big favor in selling it to you.

    For a 1-pound loaf of *Homemade Bread*, weigh a pound of flour or measure 3½ to 3¾ cups of flour. Put it in a 4-quart bowl and add a good tablespoon of salt, preferably coarse or kosher. I like bread to be salty; it makes a much better loaf. Cream a ½-ounce cake of fresh yeast with 1 tablespoon sugar, and then add ½ cup warm water—hot tap water, 90 to 95 degrees. While some say it is not necessary, I like to let the yeast proof (start to bubble) before adding it to the flour. When it has proofed, add another ¾ cup warm water. Make a well in the flour, and pour in the yeast mixture.

Mix the flour and the liquid together with a wooden spoon or your hands until the dough leaves the sides of the bowl pretty well clean (with some flours you may need a small additional amount of liquid). Turn it out onto a lightly floured board and, with floured hands, knead away. Pat out the dough, fold it over, and knead again. Be sure to turn it as you knead. When the dough ceases to be sticky, feels firm and silky, and blisters slightly as you work it, it is ready. Put it in a buttered bowl, cover with a clean towel, and let rise in a warm, draft-free spot. A slightly prewarmed electric oven or a gas oven heated only by the pilot light is a good place.

When it is doubled in bulk, which takes about 1 to 1½ hours, remove to a floured board and punch down, then knead very well for 3 to 4 minutes, really giving it a beating down this time.

Form the dough into a sausage shape and plop it into a well-buttered 9-inch loaf pan. Cover with a towel and let rise for 45 minutes to 1 hour. Then bake in a 400-degree oven for 40 to 45 minutes. Test by rapping the crust with your knuckles—a hollow sound means it is probably done. Turn the loaf out onto a rack and rap the bottom. If it seems soft and doesn't give off a hollow sound, replace in the pan, upside down, and return to the oven for a few more minutes. Then cool, out of the pan, wrap in a towel, and store in a plastic bag.

I doubt you'll find a better loaf anywhere, and you have the satisfaction of knowing you made it yourself.

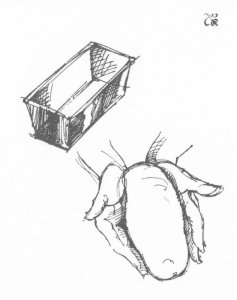

One Man's Bread

I have always maintained that breadmaking is one of the most popular—and one of the most misunderstood—subjects in the culinary realm. Now, after reading the response to a column in which I gave a recipe for a loaf of bread I have been baking and enjoying for fifteen years, I'm convinced of it. Never have I received such a deluge of letters, with the returns running about sixty in favor of and forty against what I called a good, honest loaf.

Perhaps I should have pointed out at the time that this bread is in many respects different from the familiar American type, which tends to be light, fluffy, and spongy. Mine is a typically European bread made with flour, yeast, water, and salt but no shortening or milk, the kind you would find on the table in France, Italy, or Spain. It is firm-textured with a good crust, chewy, flavorful, and well salted, the way I like bread to be. The dough requires more kneading than regular bread dough and takes a good deal longer to rise, both the first and the second time. The ideal flour to use for this kind of bread is hard-wheat flour.

This is not a keeping bread, nor is it intended to be. In most European countries bread is bought every day, sometimes two or three times a day. It is best when eaten fresh or no more than a day or so old, although it will keep for as long as a week if wrapped in a towel and a plastic bag and stored in the refrigerator. It can also, of course, be frozen. You may bake the bread in a loaf pan or shape it into a round loaf and put it on a well-buttered baking sheet. When I bake it in a pan, I usually take it out fifteen minutes or so before the end of the baking time and leave it in the oven, out of the pan, to give a harder, crisper crust.

This is not to say that bread made with milk and shortening isn't excellent also—it's just another loaf entirely, with a texture and flavor of its own. Here's a recipe for a typical, good American white bread, in case you would like to try one against the other.

For *American White Bread*, proof 1 package active dry yeast in ¼ cup warm water (90 to 95 degrees) with 1 tablespoon sugar. If you use a yeast cake instead, cream the sugar and yeast together before adding the warm water. Heat 1 cup milk with 1 tablespoon salt and 3 tablespoons butter until the butter is melted. In a large mixing bowl, combine the yeast and milk mixtures. Mix well. Stir in from 3 to 3½ cups all-purpose flour, just enough to make a stiff dough. Turn the dough out and knead on a floured surface with floured hands until it is no longer sticky, turning the dough often so that it is evenly broken down. Knead for a good 10 minutes, then place it in a buttered bowl, turning it so the top is filmed with butter.

Cover and leave in a warm, draft-free place until doubled in bulk, 1 to 1½ hours or slightly more. Punch the dough down, knead it lightly, and form into one large or two small loaves. Place in a well-greased loaf pan or pans and allow to rise again until light and doubled in bulk, from 45 minutes to 1 hour.

If you want a glazed top, brush with 1 lightly beaten egg white combined with 1 tablespoon water before baking. Bake in a preheated 400-degree oven for 20 minutes, then reduce the heat to 350 degrees and continue baking for another 20 to 30 minutes, or until the bread is well browned and sounds hollow when rapped with the knuckles. Remove from the pan and cool on a rack. If you make this bread with unbleached hard-wheat flour the texture will be more substantial and the flavor better, but you will have to knead it longer and let it rise longer.

So now you have your choice of breads—firm or soft, chewy or fluffy. Either way, you'll have a fine loaf. Good baking!

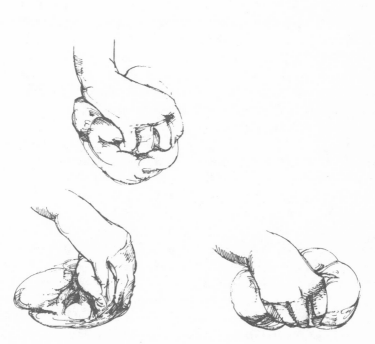

Ireland's Famous Bread

If anything could be considered the national food of Ireland, Irish stew and corned beef and cabbage notwithstanding, it would have to be soda bread. You find it on every table in that enchanting country—in homes, hotels, and restaurants. Wherever you go there is soda bread—freshly baked, packaged, even frozen, made with whole-wheat flour or white flour or oatmeal, sometimes with raisins and sometimes without.

Traditionally, soda bread is baked over a peat fire in a three-legged iron pot that can be raised or lowered over the fire in the old-fashioned way. Glowing peat sods put on top of the pot give an even heat for baking. This all-purpose pot, used for just about everything from stews to cakes, is the origin of the phrase "to take pot-luck," and lucky indeed would anyone be to drop in at an Irish cottage or farmhouse and be given homemade soda bread for tea. For soda bread is very different from any other bread you find anywhere in the world. It's round, with a cross cut in the top, and it has a velvety texture and unusual smoothness quite unlike yeast bread and the most distinctive and delicious taste. Sliced paper-thin and buttered it is one of the best tea or breakfast breads I know, and it makes the most wonderful toast for breakfast or for sandwiches.

After spending a few weeks in Ireland, I have been playing around with soda bread because I discovered that although the recipes you get in Ireland work well if you are using Irish ingredients, when you are working with our flours you have to change the recipe a bit. After about three or four months of experimenting I considered that I had evolved a very satisfactory process, so I gave a little dinner party for three people who are actively engaged in the food business and tried out my latest soda bread achievement on them. I always find this is a good test. I try a recipe for myself, and if it turns out well, I then try it on other people and see their reaction—and I don't always tell them what I'm up to; I just wait and see what they say. If they say nothing, of course I feel quite deflated and strive to do something better. This time I gave my guests both a white and a whole-wheat soda bread, and they were delighted with them, so I think I can safely pass the recipes on to you.

∽When you start to make your *Irish Soda Bread*, set the oven at 375 degrees. This bread doesn't have to rise first like yeast bread. For the whole-wheat loaf, take 3 cups whole-wheat flour and 1 cup all-purpose white flour and mix it with 1 tablespoon sugar, 1 tablespoon salt, 1 very level teaspoon baking soda, and ¾ teaspoon baking powder. The original recipe doesn't include baking powder, but I made this change because I find that in America you get a much better result by adding it. Mix all this very well so that the soda and baking powder are thoroughly distributed, then add enough buttermilk or sour milk (and since sour milk is not easy to come by these days you are better off with commercial buttermilk) to make a soft dough. Most recipes call for 1 cup of buttermilk, but I find the amount varies a good deal and you need closer to 2 cups. You will just have to sense when you have a good soft dough, similar to a biscuit dough. Knead on a lightly floured board for 2 or 3 minutes until it is quite smooth and velvety-looking, and then form it into a round cake. Place it on a well-buttered 8-inch cake pan or well-buttered cookie sheet and cut a cross on the top of the loaf with a very sharp floured knife. Pop it into the 375-degree oven and bake for 35 to 40 minutes, until it has turned a nice brown and sounds hollow when you tap it with your knuckles. The cross on the top will have spread into a sort of deep gash, which is characteristic of Irish soda bread. Let the loaf cool completely before cutting it into paper-thin slices—soda bread must never be cut thickly.

For the white loaf, use 4 cups white flour, preferably unbleached and the same amounts of salt, sugar, and baking powder as before, but decrease the baking soda to ¾ teaspoon. Mix like the whole-wheat loaf, adding just enough buttermilk to make a dough that is soft, but not so soft that it spreads; it should hold its shape. Knead for several minutes, form into a round cake, cut a cross on the top, and bake as before.

 There are all kinds of ways to vary this basic soda bread recipe—you might add to the white loaf 1 tablespoon sugar and ½ cup golden sultana raisins or dark raisins or currants which you flour lightly and stir into the batter at the last minute. Or you can use chopped walnuts and raisins. These are very pleasant tea breads, and the plain raisin bread makes delicious toast, nice and moist. You can experiment and play around with the bread, using maybe half white flour and half whole-wheat, or add other flours such as rye, soy, barley, in the ratio of three parts to one part white.

As far as I'm concerned, I like mine plain and simple, served well buttered with some good preserves and a nice strong cup of tea.

How to Eat a Pita

Pita is a bread that for centuries has been used in the Middle East in place of a plate, or as knife, fork, and plate in one. It has quite a distinctive appearance, round and very flat. To eat it, you tear it across so that it opens into two halves, like an envelope. Often sold as Syrian bread or Middle East bread here, pita is made in two or three different sizes, from small to large. The tradition of pita goes back hundreds of years in the Arab countries, for it was baked and carried with the caravans when cooking was done over open fires. Meat was roasted on spits or skewers, shish-kebab fashion, and people took the spit in one hand and an open piece of pita in the other and slid the pieces of meat into the center. The bread, folded around the meat, made a neat oozeproof package, substituting for both fork and plate.

I find pita great for outdoor parties, so much handier and more versatile than hamburger buns, which are apt to lose their contents when you bite into them. I like to barbecue hamburgers or patties of chopped lamb mixed with pine nuts, garlic, and parsley on skewers (metal, or bamboo ones that have been well soaked in water) and serve them with individual loaves of Arab bread as a novel kind of sandwich. My guests are invariably intrigued to be given food in these edible plates (which have the added advantage of being lower in calories than buns or rolls), and I save on dishwashing afterward! Pita is ideal for almost anything you would put in a sandwich—slices of meat, chicken, ham, or cheese (you can pop it in a hot oven and let the cheese melt inside).

Nowadays, pita is sold in plastic bags all over the United States, even in supermarkets, but in case you would like to try your hand at making it yourself, I'm going to give you the recipe. It's extremely simple, and there's only one thing to make sure of before you start: that your oven, which must be very hot, around 500 degrees, will maintain an even heat so the bread puffs up properly. Check with an oven thermometer to see that the temperature stays exactly on the nose. A good reliable oven will keep a pretty steady temperature, but if yours is questionable, give it a long preheating and check it very well between batches of bread.

 ℂ. To make *Pita*, combine in a bowl ½ cup warm tap water, 2 packages active dry yeast, and ¼ teaspoon sugar. Stir until yeast is thoroughly dissolved and beginning to work a little. (If you use 2 fresh yeast cakes instead, add the sugar and beat with a fork until it melts down—you may need more than ¼ teaspoon with fresh yeast, maybe 1 teaspoon. Then add the ½ cup warm water and let if proof.)

 Sift into a large bowl 6 cups all-purpose flour, bleached or unbleached. I use unbleached myself. Combine with 3 tablespoons olive oil and 1½ to 2 teaspoons salt (or 2½ teaspoons if, like me, you prefer salty bread). Beat in 2 cups warm tap water, using a wooden spoon or electric mixer with a dough hook. When well blended, beat in the yeast mixture until completely blended. Turn the dough out onto a floured board and knead about 10 to 12 minutes, until it is very smooth, satiny, and no longer sticky, as good bread dough should be. Oil a bowl, put in the dough, and turn to coat it with oil on all sides. Let rise in a warm place until double in bulk, about 1½ to 2 hours. Punch the dough down, knead again for 2 or 3 minutes, then roll into a thick sausage about 15 to 16 inches long. Cut this into 15 to 16 equal-size pieces and pat each one into a ball. Roll out on a floured board into circles 6 to 6½ inches in diameter and three-sixteenths of an inch thick. The precise thickness is important, so measure accurately with a ruler. Place the circles on pieces of foil just large enough to take one round. Let stand at room temperature for 1 hour to rise again. Do *not* place in a warm spot to hurry the rising.

Meanwhile, preheat the oven to 500 degrees and put the shelf at the lowest point in the oven. Place the foil pieces right on the shelf, without a pan. Bake until the bread starts to brown and puffs up like a weak balloon. This takes about 5 minutes. Remove and serve hot, or put directly into plastic bags which will keep the loaves moist and pliable until you are ready to serve them (reheat them for a minute or two first). This bread also freezes well. To reheat, wrap stacks of 4 to 6 loaves in foil and put in a 375-degree oven for 10 to 15 minutes.

Super Sandwiches

One of the great American arts, which varies from being a triumph to being a disaster, is the art of sandwichmaking. There's more to this than meets the eye. First, the all-important foundation. You must have good, firm bread and sweet butter. Next, the filling. This should be fresh, tasty, pleasing to the palate, and, above all, of an elegant but not excessive sufficiency, for an overstuffed sandwich is vulgar, messy, and difficult to eat. It doesn't matter if the filling is nothing more than peanut butter and jelly. Provided it is the best peanut butter and the best jelly, it can be just as satisfactory as some magnificent fancy of foie gras, truffles, and breast of pheasant.

I love good sandwiches. They may be the tiny, tempting tea sandwiches the English do so well, made of paper-thin slices of buttered bread, and chicken, ham, paté, cucumber, tomato, or radish; hearty fried-egg sandwiches on thick slabs of bread with salt, pepper, and maybe a bit of bacon, or any of the lusty combinations that have gone down in American gastronomic history, such as the Reuben and the club.

The Reuben, of course, was named for New York's famous delicatessen deluxe, which I first remember when it was at Madison Avenue and 59th Street. It stayed open practically all night and served really extraordinarily good food. You can find the Reuben all over the country, either as a meal-in-itself sandwich or in a miniature cocktail version, and it varies in quality from excellent to awful. I'm not sure who has the right formula. As I recall, the first ones were not toasted. They were made with corned beef, Swiss cheese, cole slaw, and Russian dressing on pumpernickel, and I think sometimes there was a slice of turkey breast, too. Now the standard version seems to be a toasted sandwich of corned beef, sauerkraut, and Swiss cheese. This is an extremely good sandwich combination, but sometime you might try the other version and compare the results.

The club sandwich also used to be rather different. In the last thirty years or so it has evolved into a triple-decker, but as I remember, it was originally made with just two slices of toast, thinly sliced chicken, tomato, and mayonnaise.

Order a club sandwich today, and you'll get chicken or turkey, tomato, bacon, mayonnaise, and lettuce or not, as you wish. Provided the toast and bacon are crisp and hot and the other ingredients of the highest quality, this can be a divine mixture of flavors and textures.

Not long ago I discovered, right around the corner from my house in New York, a most remarkable little delicatessen-type restaurant that had been there for years and somehow I had neglected to explore. One day when my secretary and I were working through the lunch hour she said,

"I'll just run up to Igor's and get us a sandwich," and she brought back from this tiny Arts Food Restaurant, which is run by a couple called Igor and Sonja, a menu that I found startlingly original.

The sandwiches are imaginative, carefully made, and taste as if someone put them together for themselves, not for the assembly line. That day I had a Volga Special #1, thinly sliced smoked salmon, Russian dressing, red caviar, and a tiny touch of onion on pumpernickel, and it was one of the best sandwiches I've had in a long time. Another day I picked the Anne G. Special—a really hearty sandwich of cold rare roast beef, Cheddar cheese, broiled tomato, and bacon—and once I had the Brevoort, a combination of turkey, ham, hard-boiled egg, tomato, and homemade Russian dressing. Each one was outstanding, and rated high on all points. I wish more people used this kind of imagination in making and presenting sandwiches.

One person who does is my friend Teddy Watson. Teddy runs a superb catering business in Portland, Oregon, called Yours Truly, and when she has an order for finger sandwiches for a tea or cocktail party, she scoops out a huge round pumpernickel loaf, fills it with neat layers of the little rye bread sandwiches, puts back the top as a lid, and ties it with a gigantic bow—and the sandwiches stay beautifully moist inside until eaten. You might try this cocktail loaf for your next party.

Another good idea if you are entertaining a lot of people is to have a sandwich buffet. Put out a variety of good rye and pumpernickel breads and crunchy French rolls (plus one or two homemade breads if you like to bake), sweet butter, relishes, cole slaw, homemade mayonnaise, and all kinds of fixings—thinly sliced ham, roast and corned beef, lobster, shrimp, pâtés and meat loaf, and a batch of sliced cheeses. Then let your friends run riot and make their own combinations.

The Pancake Principle

Not long ago, driving in the Northwest, some friends and I stopped for gas and were attracted by the looks of a restaurant we saw across the street. We went in for a cup of coffee and, although we had already breakfasted, found the menu so fascinating that we weakened and ordered griddle cakes, described on the menu as being made from a recipe handed down from a relative of the owner, known as "Sigrid the Great" because she had weighed 298 pounds. If that wasn't enough to sell us, the price was. A stack cost ninety cents, a short stack seventy cents, and a very short stack fifty cents.

Our friendly waitress suggested that, as we weren't particularly hungry, we just split one very short stack between the three of us. When it arrived, it was a dream, a big, tender beautiful pancake which spread over a huge serving plate, accompanied by homemade jam, heated syrup, and whipped butter. After one taste of that pancake, which was light, tender, flavorful, and everything a good pancake should be, had we not already eaten, I'm sure we would all have devoured a stack which was described on the menu as being too much. There was also a pancake sandwich listed, the first time I've ever seen that on a menu, consisting of two of these enormous pancakes with a thick slice of ham tucked in between and a fried egg or two slipped on top. This, with butter and jam, would be a fairly substantial breakfast, don't you think?

It all made me ponder what a tremendous part and heart of our diet pancakes have always been. Of course, they were not originally American. There were the thick fluffy Scots pancakes served cold or warm for tea, and the English pancakes, more like the French crêpes, which are a built-in tradition for Shrove Tuesday feasting, But ours are most closely linked with our heritage, which was sturdily based on wheat cakes, flannel cakes, and stacks of sourdough pancakes, and you can still see in any restaurant or coffee shop in the mornings people devouring great piles of pancakes. There are pancake houses all across the country where pancakes are served in combination with everything from bacon and sausage to steak, chicken, and chili.

There is something very warm and friendly about the smell of pancakes cooking on a griddle, and the sight of that big comforting stack with its accompanying warm butter and warm honey or maple syrup, little crispy sausages and bacon, does the heart good. This is a great meal.

I think we are lucky in the various kinds of pancakes that nourish our lives and spirits—the thick, light, baking powder or soda breakfast pancakes that puff up and get thick; flannel cakes, which are sometimes cooked very thin on a griddle but still retain that soft, tender texture, like the fabric for which they are named; and those plain, wonderful, old-fashioned sour milk pancakes, for which I'm going to give you a traditional recipe. If you make the batter thinner, you will have a more spreading, thinner cake than if you make it thick and drop it on the griddle in little patties (sometimes called "dollar-size" on menus). The large thin ones can be rolled with butter and syrup or preserves and served either for breakfast or for a luncheon dessert.

Getting sour milk is a bit of a problem nowadays, so we'll use buttermilk instead for *Old-Fashioned Pancakes*. Start by beating 2 eggs until light, fluffy, and lemon-colored. Beat in 2 cups buttermilk rather well, then add 1 teaspoon salt, 2 teaspoons sugar, and 1 cup flour which has been sifted with ½ teaspoon baking soda and 1 teaspoon baking powder. Then add enough additional flour (about 1 to 2 cups) to make a batter with the consistency of very heavy cream. Add ⅓ cup melted butter. This makes a good smooth batter that is better if allowed to rest at least 1 hour. If you are making pancakes for breakfast, let the batter sit in the refrigerator overnight—you may have to add a small amount of extra liquid in this case before baking your cakes.

Have a griddle very hot and well buttered, and spoon on your batter to make cakes of the desired size. Watch them until they show tiny bubbles. When the surface is entirely covered with bubbles, turn the cakes with a large spatula and brown on the other side. Serve hot at once, or butter them well and keep them warm in the oven. They will not wait, and become rather dreary when cold.

I think pancakes should always be served with melted butter and warm syrup or honey, and I rather like to serve a little piece of lemon with them because a few drops of lemon juice on the hot syrup or honey gives you a most intriguing and delicious contrast of flavors, adding another dimension to this honest, homely food.

Speaking of Cheese

I'm happy to see that more and more people in this country are becoming addicted to cheese, which, with wine, is such a vital and important part of the good life. New cheese shops spring up every day, and whereas twenty-five years ago there were maybe no more than ten or fifteen well-known cheeses imported, now there must be at least a hundred or a hundred and fifty to choose from. Unfortunately, though, there is no quality control on a great deal of cheese that comes in, and all too often it is carelessly handled and stored.

Cheese, as I'm sure you all know, should be kept cool, but not icy cold, and it should be allowed to come to room temperature before being served. One of the great tragedies of most American restaurants is that they give you cheese straight from the refrigerator, so chilled it is practically inedible, or else they try to pass off on you a cheese that is overripe and past its peak. Soft cheeses, especially the great Brie and Camembert of France, reach a point of perfect ripeness, after which they go rapidly downhill, developing a strong smell of ammonia and a most unpleasant taste. There is an art to selecting and serving cheese. In the restaurants in France one is always aware that the cheeses have been carefully chosen and kept at the proper temperature, but I can think of very few restaurants in New York, and even fewer around the country, where cheese is treated as it should be.

We are not yet accustomed to eating cheese as a course on its own after the entrée, as the French do, with an excellent red wine. I wish more people would adopt this pleasant custom, for cheese and wine are natural and great partners. The best of all ways to finish off the bottle of fine red wine you opened for dinner is with a platter of cheese, and bread or crackers. I like French or Italian bread with Gruyère, Pont l'Evêque, Bel Paese, Roquefort, and Gorgonzola, and I prefer English water biscuits or Bath Olivers with Brie, Camembert, and the softer cheeses, but this is purely and simply a matter of taste.

I happen to love all kinds of cheese, from the simple Cheddars to the great soft cheeses of France, and one of my perennial arguments is with a certain type of cheese snob who, while constantly on the lookout for new and "interesting" imports, claims that there is no American table cheese worth considering. That's a lot of rot. Anyone who takes the trouble to acquaint himself with the best cheese of this country will find that they are often far finer eating than their foreign counterparts, which frequently, through shipping delays and careless handling, are not all they might be by the time they reach the stores.

All very well, you may say, but what are these great American cheeses and where do I find them? Let's start with one of the least familiar, an Iowa cheese called Maytag, for whose creation thanks are due to the appliance manufacturer of the same name. Maytag ranks as one of the best bleu or blue-veined cheeses in the world and is this country's finest example. It is seconded only by the blue-veined cheese from Langlois, Oregon. To the best of my knowledge, Maytag can only be ordered by mail and as a whole cheese, but it keeps well in the refrigerator if tightly covered with plastic wrap and aluminum foil.

You think only France can produce good Brie? Not a bit of it. Illinois can lay claim to a first-rate Brie, made under the name of Kolb [now "Delico"], that is properly aged, creamy, and rich in flavor. Another outstanding American Brie, one I have enjoyed since my youth, comes from the Marin French Cheese Factory in Petaluma, California. Their cheeses, put out under the Rouge & Noir label, also include a decent Camembert and a small cheese similar to Camembert, about 4 inches across, called breakfast cheese. They are mostly available in the western states, but there are occasional shipments to the East Coast, and a real cheese buff will find them well worth tracking down.

Turning to Ohio, we find another domestic Camembert that makes grand fare when properly aged and not overchilled in storage It hails from the locale that gave us one of our truly original creations, Liederkrantz. This soft, runny, pungent native cheese on the order of Brie or Camembert came about by accident. the way so many great cheeses are born. Liederkrantz must be eaten at its rich and creamy peak before the flavor becomes too sharp and an aroma of ammonia sets in, and it needs about three hours out of the refrigerator to come to room temperature and perfection.

Backtracking westward, we have Teleme, a soft, rich creamy California cheese. Then there's the aged, ripely scented, rather strong cream brick cheese made in both Oregon and Wisconsin. This distinctive all-American product can be found in many of the cheese shops that have sprung up around the country. Again, serve at room temperature to draw out its full nuances.

Finally we come to our many and varied Cheddars. Variously referred to as rat cheese, store cheese, or American cheese, they are for the most part true Cheddars and come in both white and red versions, the difference being that the latter are colored when mixed. Some of the Vermont and New York State Cheddars are extremely well aged and therefore much sharper than the younger, milder Cheddars from Wisconsin and Oregon. Blandness may be to the taste of the majority of cheese eaters in this country, but I happen to prefer that strong, characteristic Cheddar bite.

One of my favorite cocktail foods is this *Cheddar-Chili Spread*, tangy and different for a cheese board. Take ½ pound (2 cups) grated sharp Cheddar at room temperature and combine with 2 chopped canned peeled green chilies, ½ canned pimiento, also chopped, a small garlic clove, grated, ½ cup softened butter, 3 to 4 tablespoons of brandy, sherry, or bourbon, a few drops of Tabasco, and salt to taste. Mix in the bowl of an electric mixer or mash with a fork until it has a good spreading texture (if too stiff, add cream or milk, a few teaspoons at a time, until it has the right consistency). Serve in a crock, or form into a large ball or log and roll in chopped toasted nuts or chopped parsley or chives.

Serve with crackers, Melba toast, or sliced French bread and provide a knife to spread it with.

Cooking with Wine

One of my pet abominations is the ersatz liquid sold in supermarkets as "cooking wine." I remember during Prohibition encountering a so-called cooking sherry so heavily laden with salt that you could taste nothing else. I hate to think what would have happened to any recipe to which such a noxious potion was added.

There's only one wine to cook with, and that's the same wine you drink. The old French saying, "The better the wine, the better the dish," sums up the reason for cooking with wine—because it adds flavor. Cooking with wine is not fancy cooking or extravagant cooking, simply good cooking. For the most part only a cup or half a cup of wine goes into the dish, and the rest of the bottle will be left to drink with dinner. The French, who are pretty thrifty folk, pour wine into the pot as readily as we pour stock and that is one reason why their food has gained such a reputation.

However, you shouldn't just fling in any old wine and expect it to work miracles. Wines differ considerably in body and flavor. Some are rich, fruity, and heavy, others light, gay, and flowery. Each contributes its own special quality to the food. So if you want the best of all flavors for a stew or sauce, add the wine you will drink with it—a full-bodied red wine like a Burgundy or Pinot Noir for boeuf en daube or coq au vin; a light dry white for poached fish or coquilles St. Jacques. Naturally, this applies only to table wines, not to the fortified ones like sherry and Madeira. It would be pretty preposterous to drink a bottle of Madeira with beef Wellington just because it had a Madeira sauce.

Similarly, while the rule of thumb about cooking with the wine you are going to drink is a sound one, this certainly doesn't mean that if you were having a bottle of Lafite Rothschild 1953 you'd use half of it to make a Bordelaise sauce. But as the purpose of cooking with wine is to add flavor, the flavor should be that of something eminently drinkable, no matter how simple the food.

ᑛ For instance, when I make *Sausages in Red Wine*, a dish I'm especially fond of, I put 2 Polish sausages or kielbasa in a good-sized skillet with ½ to ⅔ cup finely chopped shallots or green onions, 1 cup water, and enough red wine (a California Zinfandel, perhaps, or a French Beaujolais) just to cover the sausages. Since most kielbasa are already cooked, all they need is to be heated through in the wine. I remove the sausages, cook the wine down a bit, then spoon the lovely winey sauce over the sausages and serve them with a hot potato salad, made with little boiled new potatoes, peeled and dressed with vinegar (or some of the wine from the skillet), olive oil, and a bit of chopped onion and parsley.

This makes a delicious, easy supper or luncheon, with crisp French bread. Drink with it the same wine you used for cooking, and finish the remains of the bottle with some good cheese and maybe a bowl of fruit.

There's one very important point to remember about cooking with wine. The wine must always come to the boiling point and simmer anywhere from a few minutes to an hour or so to burn off the alcohol, If you add wine at the last minute, it can leave a rather strange and strong aftertaste. Cooking removes the alcohol and leaves only the flavor.

In this simple recipe for *Poached Fillets of Fish*, it is wine that gives the sauce its subtle delicacy. For four persons, poach 4 large or 8 small fish fillets in salted water barely to cover, to which you have added ½ cup dry white wine, a sprig of parsley, and a slice of onion, until they are just cooked through, using the timing principle of 10 minutes per inch of fish measured at the thickest point. Remove the fillets to a hot baking dish, strain the liquid, and reduce it to 1 cup by boiling over high heat. Melt 3 tablespoons butter in a pan, blend in 3 tablespoons flour, and cook for 2 to 3 minutes. Stir in the 1 cup reduced fish stock and keep stirring until thickened. Add 2 tablespoons finely chopped parsley, about ½ teaspoon tarragon, and ½ cup heavy cream. Stir and heat thoroughly, and taste for seasoning. Pour this lovely sauce over the fish, sprinkle with grated Parmesan cheese, and run under the broiler for a minute to brown lightly.

Serve with tiny boiled potatoes and perhaps chopped spinach, and drink the rest of the wine. This might be an inexpensive Mountain White from the Napa Valley in California, a fine Alsatian Riesling, or a Pouilly Fuissé from Burgundy district of France, depending on how much you want to spend.

I am all for drinking and cooking with simple wines that don't cost an arm and a leg, and there are enough of these around—from California, New York State, France, Germany, Italy, Spain, and Portugal—for anyone to be able to afford to keep a few bottles on hand. Several vintners produce a light, eminently drinkable Mountain Red, the counterpart of the Mountain White. I recently tasted a Zinfandel from California put out by a company which has not used this grape variety before. It was most pleasing, on the lines of the young, fruity wines of Beaujolais, and very reasonably priced.

One of the joys of wine is tasting. Shop around, try out wines that are new to you, then settle on a good white and a good red inexpensive enough to establish as your "house wine." Wine is a vital part of life and one to be enjoyed to the full, both in the glass and in the food you eat.

An American Country Wine

When American wines are mentioned, what comes to mind first of all are probably the fine varietal wines of California, a state that has earned a reputation as great as any wine district in the world. Next, the wines of New York State and Ohio. If you stop there, then you have missed one of the most fascinating of all stories of American winemaking, the story of Philip and Jocelyn Wagner, who have been great movers in the growth of wine culture in this country.

Outside of California, most of the classic European grapes from which the great wines of France and Germany are made find our climate inhospitable, so the majority of growers in other parts of the country had to depend on wines made from native American grapes. The problem was to find vines that would combine the best of both worlds, the quality of the European and the hardiness of the American. For many years Philip Wagner experimented with a new family of European wine grapes made by crossing European vines with certain American species. These French hybrids, as they are called, could be grown successfully in just about any part of the United States. In 1943 Mr. Wagner established Boordy Vineyards on his home property in Maryland, just north of Baltimore, and began making his own wine from the hybrid grapes. His wine is the kind the French call a *vin de pays*, a country wine. Bottled soon after the harvest, it is put on the market while it is young, fresh and fruity. This isn't a wine to lay down and keep for years before it reaches its peak, but a light, gay wine to open, drink, and enjoy, the kind that plays an important part in the everyday life of any true wine lover.

Until recently Mr. and Mrs. Wagner were forced to hold down their production because of limited acreage, so few people outside the Baltimore-Washington area were lucky enough to be able to buy their wines. Then not too long ago they discovered a section of New York State, near Lake Erie, which was particularly well suited for the French hybrids they had developed, and there they started a new vineyard. Now they can produce a much larger quantity of Boordy Vineyards wine, while still keeping direct supervision over the making, bottling, and quality.

I visited the Wagners one day in early June when they were bottling their most recent vintage. We sat on the tree-shaded lawn and tasted the red, white, and rosé wines of this and the previous year's vintages, comparing, discussing, and nibbling on little bits of cheese and bread to clear our palates.

The current red was a light, fruity, beautifully colored wine reminiscent of a young French Beaujolais, the kind you could drink, at room temperature or slightly chilled, with just about any food. The white, very dry, with a crisp, sprightly freshness, reminded me of a wine from the Loire Valley, such as Muscadet or a Sancerre. It's a refreshing, all-purpose white that would be perfect with seafood, chicken, veal, cold meats and summer foods, or in a kir, that delicious apéritif of chilled white wine delicately flavored and colored by a couple of drops of crème de cassis, the black-currant liqueur. While I'm not a fancier of rosé wines, the Boordy Vineyards Rosé, amber-pink and dry, had a definite and pleasing quality. All of the wines tasted clean, fresh, and fruity, and they reflected the personality and standards of the Wagners, who have devoted their lives to perfecting these delightful and reasonably priced young wines.

The white would be a lovely wine to take on a picnic or have with lunch on a warm day. Your menu might be eggs stuffed with smoked salmon, fresh dill, mayonnaise, and garlic, a freshly roasted chicken, just cooled, and an Alexandre Dumas potato salad, in which you could use some of the same wine. Dumas was not only a great novelist and playwright, but also a great authority on food, and his potato salad is quite different from the usual kind.

To prepare an *Alexandre Dumas Potato Salad*, take 4 to 6 good-sized potatoes, preferably the waxy or new type, and boil them in their jackets until just pierceable. Peel while hot, and slice into a bowl. Season with salt and pepper to taste, and pour over the hot potatoes 8 tablespoons olive oil and ½ cup dry white wine (the one you are going to drink). Let them cool and, just before leaving for your picnic, toss them with 1 tablespoon or more vinegar, ½ cup chopped parsley, and ½ cup chopped chives or green onions. Taste for salt, and pack in a plastic container.

The Endearing Young Charms of Beaujolais

All we wine lovers who enjoy the special delights of that magnificently accommodating red wine, Beaujolais, were rejoicing not long ago at the arrival by plane from France of the Beaujolais Primeur. Beaujolais can only be called Primeur if it is bottled before November 15 of the year in which the grapes were picked and pressed, and the advent of the young wine is as exciting as the first day of bock beer in Germany, or the opening of the hunting season in the West. The wine is rushed by truck to the restaurants of Paris and Lyons and other centers of good eating, where it is hailed with great excitement and anticipation.

I tasted the Beaujolais Primeur the day it arrived in New York. By now I have had more than thirty different ones in various restaurants, and I must say they vary a good deal. At its best, this is a fresh, lovely wine with a full bouquet and a delicious fruity flavor, and it must be drunk very, very young. By French law, it can be sold only before December 15 of the year in which it is made, after which this particular wine is supposed to go through a second fermentation in the bottle and may or may not go bad—very often it does. The Beaujolais Primeur is followed early in the following year by the Beaujolais Nouveau, sometimes called Beaujolais de l'année, which has to be judged for quality and accepted by a jury of tasters from one of the French governmental organizations that supervise and establish the rules for the wine industry.

The wine of Beaujolais is produced in an area just below the Burgundy district and very close to the Rhône River. While a lot of Beaujolais is made, there's not nearly as much as you see for sale, so it behooves you to be very careful when you pick a bottle labeled Beaujolais. A true, typical Beaujolais is never coarse or harsh, but fruity and full-bodied with the flavor of the earth in it. Be sure you buy and drink it young, for after a Beaujolais reaches two and a half or three years old, it is seldom worth drinking. Beaujolais range in price and quality. First there is the wine simply called Beaujolais, then Beaujolais Supérieur, followed by Beaujolais-Villages, which may come from any of thirty-five communes or villages, and finally the Beaujolais worthy of being sold under their own names. Everyone has his preference, but I think Brouilly is one of the finest.

Other names to look for are Chiroubles, Fleurie, Chénas, Juliénas, Morgon, St.-Amour, and Moulin-à-Vent, all exceptional wines to drink with pleasure. I have in the past come across bottles of Juliénas and Fleurie that have remained extraordinarily good for a year or two. If you live in a city or town where there are a number of wine stores selling

Beaujolais, take my advice and have a tasting of several of them until you find the one that seems to be the most honest, fruity, and full-bodied, then buy yourself a goodly amount of it so that for the next few months you can drink it while it is at its peak.

Most red Beaujolais is best served at cellar rather than at room temperature, which means that here it should be slightly cooled, to give it a rounder, pleasanter, more agreeable quality. Because of its light alcoholic content and gay sprightliness, Beaujolais goes wonderfully well with all foods, and since it is served slightly chilled, it's especially good for summer when heavier reds seem inappropriate. In some of the famous restaurants in the district around the Beaujolais, like Paul Bocuse or the great Mère Guy, very often you'll be served a sausage in brioche with the new Beaujolais, or some excellent ham. I find this is one of the few red wines that is really enjoyable with baked or sliced cold ham.

⌘ And should I have a little wine left in the bottle, I use it up in one of my favorite desserts, *Sharlotka*. For this you need a loaf of stale dark bread, preferably Jewish-style pumpernickel. Remove the crusts and crumble the bread into tiny pieces. Melt ¼ pound butter in a skillet and fry the crumbs slightly. Remove from the heat and mix in ½ cup sugar, ½ cup red Beaujolais, 1 teaspoon lemon juice, 1 teaspoon grated orange rind, and a pinch of salt. Mix well and add ½ teaspoon vanilla. Peel and core 10 pippin apples and cut them into eighths. Cook them in a very little water until they are just turning soft. Don't let them get mushy. Butter a mold well, and sprinkle it lightly with the crumb mixture, then alternate layers of crumbs and apples in the mold, sprinkling each apple layer with cinnamon. Cover the last layer of apples with 1 cup tart jelly, then cover that with a last layer of crumbs. Bake in a 350-degree oven for 1 hour. Serve at once.

⌘

Champagne, the Festive Wine

Early in April, while crossing to Cannes on the *S.S. France*, I was struck by the amount of champagne that was consumed aboard—French champagne, naturally. The *France* has probably the most complete stock of this delightfully festive wine you could find anywhere, some seven thousand bottles in sixty-seven varieties from twenty-eight houses, ranging from the famous names—Bollinger, Möet & Chandon, Veuve Clicquot, Krug, Heidsieck, Mercier, and Mumm—to the lesser-known, such as Gauthier, De Venoge, Canard-Duchene. In fact, if you happened to be a champagne fancier, you could spend a month or more on this supremely luxurious ship and never drink the same wine twice.

Champagne was the bon voyage drink, it was the favored apéritif before lunch and dinner with those passengers who knew that this was the best of all preludes to magnificent food and wine, and it was invariably served at most of the parties I attended, from a private luncheon in the captain's quarters to the head purser's cocktail party on Gala Night. Champagne might have been made expressly for shipboard life. One doesn't want to be stupefied by a lot of alcohol, and the bubbling charm and lightness of champagne fits most graciously into the relaxed pattern of one's days, making the trip more glamorous, gay, and elegant.

I imagine this is also the reason why champagne has become the classic tipple for wedding breakfasts and receptions, especially now that they are so much smaller than they used to be, no longer great crushes of six hundred guests, but intimate parties of relatives and close friends.

Champagne is a wine of infinite variety because every house, through skilled blending, produces a wine with definite characteristics that distinguish it from its competitors—marked differences in flavor, lightness, dryness, and body. There are also many degrees of champagne, from the brittle, almost cutting quality of a nature, the driest of all, and the polished crispness of a brut to the soft, caressing brilliance of an extra-dry, or the very special cuvées that have softness without sweetness, gentility without cloying overtones.

These are the true aristocrats of champagne, the greatest wines of the great houses, like the Cuvée Grand Siècle of Laurent Perrier, Moët & Chandon's Dom Perignon, Louis Roederer's Cristal, and of course the most expensive. If I am drinking one of these superb champagnes, I like it unsullied, so I can appreciate the exquisite flavor and balance. I use a large tulip-shaped glass that has been chilled ahead of time, not one of those squat, abominable saucer-type glasses. A tulip-shaped glass or tapering flute is designed so that the tiny bubbles that are the mark of a perfectly made champagne can spiral upward, slowly releasing the natural effervescence of the wine.

For those who like their champagne combined with fruity flavors, or rather more alcoholic, I would suggest that most pleasant and enlivening drink, a champagne kir, which consists of a few drops of crème de cassis, the black-currant liqueur, in a glass of chilled champagne, or the following summer punch, a good choice for an outdoor party.

For *Summer Punch*, wash and slice 2 cucumbers (do not peel unless the skins are waxed heavily, or wash off the wax coating with hot water if you prefer). Put in a large punch bowl with 8 tablespoons sugar, the grated rind of 4 lemons, ½ cup lemon juice, 2 cups orange juice, and 2 fifths of cognac. Let stand for 1 hour. When you are ready to serve, add a large block of ice, and pour over it 2 cups Cointreau liqueur and 4 quarts French champagne. This makes enough for forty 4-ounce servings.

For a punch or mixed drink you naturally would use a less expensive nonvintage brut champagne, not a vintage or the finest cuvée. This also applies if you are using champagne in the kitchen. One of my favorite summer desserts is a refreshing sherbet.

To make this *Champagne Sorbet*, you first cook 1 cup sugar with 4 cups water until it comes to a rolling boil. Boil 6 minutes. Add 1 bottle brut champagne and heat (this volatilizes the alcohol). Remove from heat. Stir in the juice of 1½ oranges and the grated rind of 1 orange. Pour this into an ice cream freezer packed with rock salt and ice, and turn until the sherbet is softly frozen, not hard. Serve immediately. Serves six to eight.

CHAPTER 8

Handwork and Gadgetry

෴

... in which we make friends with a stripper and a zester ... meet the little chief smoker ... turn a mushroom's head . . . sharpen our knowledge of knives ... dissect a chicken ... and invite a robot into the kitchen.

The Gadgets I Love

Two of my best friends are a stripper and a zester. In case that raises some pretty wild visions, let me hasten to say that they are not girls but gadgets, and I couldn't do without them in the kitchen.

The zester is a handy little tool about 4 inches long with a wooden handle and a slightly curved metal end terminating in five sharp little holes. Draw the sharp tip over the colored part—or zest—of an orange or lemon, and presto, you have thin, thin slivers of the aromatic part of the fruit that contains the oil, and a wonderful spicy scent in your nostrils. I find a zester works much better than a grater. With a grater, you inevitably overgrate and get too much of the bitter white pith, whereas the zester is foolproof. My zester not only zips the rind from lemons and oranges for me—it also shreds carrots into lovely long thin strips to toss into a dish at the last minute, or into a sauce or a salad. If you want to add color and texture to a green salad with a mound of shredded carrot or beet, this gadget does the job in no time flat.

So much for the zester. The stripper, its sister under the skin, has a center hole and a sharp-edged groove which cuts a slightly deeper and wider swath. With its aid you can deftly strip long spirals of orange, lemon, or grapefruit zest to drop in a drink, or slice off a smidgen of orange peel to add to a stew. I like to strip off a couple of pieces of lemon peel and pop them into a mélange of sautéed vegetables—this adds a marvelous sharp savor.

&. The stripper simplifies one of my favorite quick desserts, *Oranges Orientale*. You can use a knife or a vegetable peeler instead, but it's quicker with a stripper. Strip the zest from 2 oranges, and cut it into long, very thin pieces (if you use a knife, be sure to slice off only the colored part of the peel and then shred it finely). Bring 2 cups water and 1½ cups sugar to a boil in a saucepan, reduce the heat, and simmer about 5 minutes. Add the orange shreds to this syrup, bring to a boil again, and simmer for about 10 minutes. Meanwhile, remove any remaining rind and the pith from the 2 stripped oranges and carefully peel another 4 oranges, making sure none of the white part is left on the fruit. Halve all the oranges, remove as many seeds as you can, and arrange in a flat heatproof serving dish. Spoon the hot orange-flavored syrup over them, making sure to get some of the orange shreds on each one. Let the syrup cool, then decorate the top of each half-orange with a candied violet. If you can't buy candied violets, use any candied fruits, such as cherries or pineapple, that will give color contrast to the dish. Serve the oranges cold, and provide a fruit knife or fork or a fork and spoon to make it easier to cut and eat them.

These are just a couple of my pet gadgets. Another is a spaghetti lifter with sharp sawline points that resembles a pair of tongs with teeth. It's not only great for fishing slippery spaghetti and noodles out of the pot, but it can also be used to toss a salad or to turn meat on the outdoor grill—the teeth get a really firm grip on a steak. This simple and inexpensive device has more than earned its place in my kitchen.

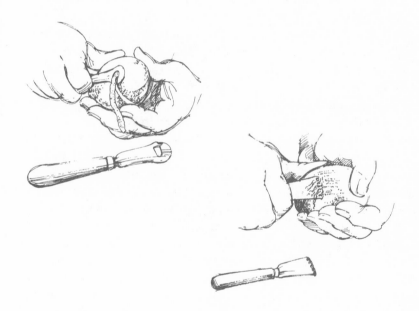

The Knack of Fluting Mushrooms

One of the techniques that most people want to master, once they have learned to cook the more elaborate dishes, is the fluting of mushrooms. You've probably seen in expensive restaurants a beautifully fluted mushroom poised on top of a filet mignon, or garnishing a perfect presentation of fish in white wine sauce. Actually, it's not a terribly hard job to flute a mushroom, and it certainly produces one of the most decorative adjuncts to fine cooking. A dish garnished with fluted mushrooms has a certain flair and finish that you never get any other way. Since mushrooms are so plentiful (and occasionally inexpensive) these days, there is no reason not to invest in a couple of pounds and try your hand. Just keep practicing until you become adept enough to flute with speed and dexterity. You won't waste any mushrooms, either, because there are all kinds of ways to use up those you botch.

Either small or large mushrooms may be fluted, provided they are firm, white, and fresh, with smooth, unblemished caps. Never peel a mushroom that is going to be fluted; you need the skin to get the effect. Actually, you lose a great deal of flavor by peeling, and there is no reason to do it at any time. If the mushrooms are a bit dirty, just wipe them off with damp paper towels, or rinse them very quickly with cold water and pat dry.

The only essential tool for fluting mushrooms is a very sharp paring knife, preferably one with a triangular blade. Unlike peeling an apple or a potato, in fluting mushrooms the knife remains motionless and you turn the mushroom against it. So take your sharp paring knife in your right hand, holding it with the cutting edge turned away from you. Wrap your fingers around the handle, and steady the mushroom cap, which you hold in your left hand, with the thumb of your right hand. Select a spot about halfway down the knife blade as the cutting edge—with a triangular-bladed knife, the point where it begins to thicken in width is just right. Holding the knife motionless, bring the crown of the mushroom against the knife edge. Press the knife very lightly against the mushroom skin, turning the cap away from you as you cut a very thin strip of skin from crown to edge. If you have turned the mushroom correctly, you will have cut a swirling, very shallow groove. Repeat cuts from crown to edge, spacing them evenly and close together, until you have a handsomely fluted cap.

Mushroom fluting takes practice, so experiment whenever you have a free moment or two. Don't wait until guests are coming and try to do it while you prepare a three-course dinner, or you'll be a nervous wreck. Plan on having mushrooms in a dish you're preparing for the family, and get to work. Better yet, buy mushrooms for the recipe I'm going to give you, and keep fluting until you have got the knack. You'll have a great big pile of mushrooms to chop up for a mushroom roll, something that my students learn in one of their cooking lessons. They love it, because it is actually a kind of alien soufflé—a soufflé mixture baked flat in a jelly-roll pan, turned out, filled, and rolled up.

To make a *Mushroom Roll*, first grease an 11-by-15½-inch jelly-roll pan and line it with waxed paper, leaving an overhang of about 1 inch of paper at each end. Grease the paper and sprinkle with dry bread crumbs. Set aside.

Chop 1½ pounds of mushrooms quite finely, put them in a clean dish towel, and twist very hard to squeeze out all the moisture. Put them in a bowl, and mix in 6 tablespoons melted butter, 5 egg yolks, salt, pepper, and nutmeg to taste, and just enough bread crumbs (about ¾ cup) to make the mixture hold together. Beat the 5 egg whites until they hold soft peaks, as for a soufflé, and fold quickly and thoroughly into the mushroom mixture. Turn into the prepared pan and smooth the top evenly with a rubber spatula. Bake in a preheated 350-degree oven for 12 to 16 minutes, or until the center feels barely firm when touched. Put a sheet of buttered waxed paper or foil over the top of the roll, and invert onto a warm platter or long board. With the aid of the overhang of waxed paper, carefully peel away the paper adhering to the roll, gently loosening it with the point of a knife where necessary. It doesn't matter if a little bit of the surface of the roll sticks to the paper, since this is the side you will fill. Fill the roll with scrambled eggs, or with asparagus tips that have been cooked in boiling salted water until just done but still crisp to the bite. Roll up with the aid of the waxed paper or foil and serve to six people as a brunch, luncheon, or supper dish.

If you have some perfectly fluted mushroom caps, use them to garnish the top of the roll. Poach them for a few minutes in salted water and the juice of ½ lemon, and they will come out beautifully white. For meat dishes, you can sauté them in butter the usual way, or brown them under the broiler, basting them well with melted butter.

So now you know the right way to flute a mushroom. You can cheat and use the stripper but it never looks as professional and perfect as the real thing.

A Cook's Best Friends

I defy anyone to cook well without good knives. No piece of kitchen equipment so thoroughly earns its cost and its keep. Buying cheap knives is the worst sort of economy. A good knife, properly cared for, will last a lifetime, which can never be said of the dimestore variety. You'll find the best knives in stores specializing in cooking equipment or housewares sections of the better department stores. Look for those with blades of carbon steel or high-carbon nonstain steel. They can be sharpened to a fine edge, unlike regular stainless steel, and though carbon steel will stain, a bit of abrasive cleanser and steel wool soon removes the marks.

I happen to have a penchant for collecting kitchen knives, and I enjoy using them properly, to do the specific job for which they were designed. I'm always baffled by students in my cooking classes who, after being taught the use of each knife, will start chopping with a boning knife or vice versa. It's so easy to sort out the functions of knives. There are only about four that are essential—a paring knife, a chopping knife, a slicing knife, and a boning knife.

Let's begin with the smallest, the paring knife. The best type to buy is the French carbon steel knife with a comfortable, grippable handle, and a triangular blade, tapering to a point. It comes in three blade sizes—2½-inch 3½-inch, and 4-inch—and will dice, peel, cut, and do other small jobs.

Next and most important of all is its big brother, the chopping knife, often called the chef's or cook's knife. This also has a triangular blade, but it is much larger and heavier, and the thickness of the blade tapers from base to point so that the knife works for you, bringing the weightiest part down on whatever you're chopping and making the process speedy and effortless. Blade sizes range from a whopping 14-inch to an 8-inch. I find the 12-inch is the best all-purpose size, hefty enough for any job, with the 10-inch or 8-inch size as an auxiliary.

The cook's knife will even do a pretty good job of carving, though for this you should really have the slicing knife with its long, flexible blade. The Gerber slicing knives, made in Portland, Oregon, have thin supple blades with a high carbon content and carve extremely well. I've used them for years. In the last ten years slicing knives with scalloped edges have appeared on the market, and although I find them useful, I prefer the straight-edged slicing knife.

The boning knife has a smallish, slim, curving 6-inch blade and a pointed tip, specially designed to work its way between and around bones and meat. It is essential for the finer points of kitchenry like boning chickens and legs of lamb.

Abuse and misuse shortens the lives of knives. Never let your precious knives soak in the sink or put them in the dishwasher—just wipe them off after use with a clean damp cloth and store them in a rack or slotted section of a drawer where they won't bang against each other and blunt their blades. Sharpen them regularly by holding the blade at a 20-degree angle to a sharpening steel and bringing it down in a long sweeping stroke.

A favorite recipe of mine that requires a good deal of knife work is a *Tian Vençoise*. A tian is actually a pottery baking dish which in France has given its name to various concoctions known as a tian of this or that. This is called a tian Vençoise because it comes from Vence, in the south of France.

Take your largest French cook's knife and coarsely chop 2 pounds of fresh spinach that has been well washed and trimmed of the coarser stems. Trim, split, and dice or coarsely chop 5 zucchini. Chop 3 garlic cloves. Peel, slice, and coarsely chop 3 large onions. Heat ½ cup olive oil in a large skillet, add the spinach, cover, and let it just wilt down quickly. Add the garlic, onions, and zucchini, toss together lightly with a wooden spoon, then cook until just crisply tender, stirring occasionally. Season with 1 teaspoon salt, about ½ teaspoon freshly ground black pepper, and 1 tablespoon chopped fresh basil or 1 teaspoon dried basil. While the vegetables are cooking, cook 1 cup rice according to your favorite method. Drain well. Combine with the crisply cooked vegetables and arrange in a buttered baking dish. Bake in a 350-degree oven for about 15 minutes. Meanwhile, beat 4 eggs rather well and combine with ⅔ cup freshly grated Parmesan cheese. Pour over the vegetables and continue baking for another 10 minutes, or until the egg mixture has set. Sprinkle additional grated cheese over the vegetables before baking if you like—I think it improves the finished dish. Let the tian cool before serving. It is best eaten tepid or cold and makes a tasty accompaniment to cold meats in summer, to picnic food or to meat or poultry grilled on the outdoor barbecue.

That Good Old Smoky Flavor

Yet another old-time flavor that is fast disappearing from our food lives is that of hickory, cherry, and applewood smoke. Smokehouses where you can find smoked hams and bacon, smoked turkey, and other goodies are becoming fewer and fewer, and in their place we have an artificial substitute called liquid smoke or smoke flavor, which, as far as this palate is concerned, is absolutely revolting.

If you live in an apartment or city house, you can't build yourself a smokehouse, and not many of us, alas, can afford to put a Chinese smoke oven in our kitchens. So I was delighted when a West Coast friend acquainted me with the Little Chief Smoker, which has since become an indispensable part of my New York kitchen. This portable smoke cooker is very compact, yet capable of holding an ample quantity of meat, or with the inside racks removed, a 10- to 15-pound turkey, or a couple of chickens or ducks. It is clean, simple to operate, and comes in a carton which you are warned not to destroy, as you will need it for insulation if you are cooking in a garden or basement that is colder than the rest of your house.

The smoker has a pan to hold the hickory sawdust supplied by the manufacturer. This goes over an electric unit in the bottom of the smoker, and when that heats up, the smoke begins to permeate the tightly covered container. One pan of sawdust lasts about 45 minutes, and you can remove and refill it during the smoking process. If you want a more intense flavor, or a longer smoking time for certain foods, you can put hickory, cherry, or applewood chips on top of the sawdust.

This little smoker, which is made by the Luhr-Jensen Company of Hood River, Oregon, is one of the most efficient gadgets I have seen in some time. It imparts a good smoked flavor to foods you intend to cook later in the oven, and I have also found that if you put precooked foods in the smoker for a little while they get a really delicious taste. I can think of no drawback, except perhaps that the atmosphere is suffused with an aroma my neighbors claim sharpens their appetites unbearably!

The other evening I smoked two small loins of pork, which I'd had well trimmed, with the chine bone sawed off and just the tiny ribs left. I rubbed the loins well with salt, pepper, rosemary, and a little garlic and let them stand for about an hour before placing them on the two lower racks of the smoker. At the end of the first 45 minutes of smoking, I switched the racks so both the loins would be equally impregnated with the smoke flavor, added another panful of hickory sawdust, and let them stay for a further 45 minutes, so the total time was 1½ hours. Then I switched the electrical unit off and let the pork rest in the smoker until I was ready to roast it.

It was roasted in a 325-degree oven to an internal temperature of 155 degrees, which took about another 1½ hours. I then let the loins sit for 15 minutes before carving them. The pork was sensational, moist inside, with a delicate smoky flavor, and the sawed-off chine bones, which I'd smoked too, were the most deliciously chewy bits you can imagine. This was served with sautéed apples, greenings cored and sliced, cooked in butter, and sprinkled heavily with sugar which caramelized on the slices, and tiny new potatoes baked in the oven with the pork. The pork tasted even better the next night, cold with mustard mayonnaise, tender young ears of corn, and a beet and watercress salad that was a perfect foil for the pork.

For another dinner I rubbed chicken legs and thighs with oil, salt, and pepper and a little tarragon and smoked them for a little over an hour until they were a luscious brown color and gave off a most tantalizing perfume. These I roasted in a pan with a couple of garlic cloves and a little Madeira, and had them piping hot with ripe sliced tomatoes and sautéed shredded zucchini—another glorious feast.

The Little Chief Smoker is a great piece of equipment for your backyard, porch, or kitchen. (If you use it indoors, make sure always to place it under the exhaust fan to draw off the fumes.) You can make your own jerky, smoke sausage or cheese, and experiment with meats—and have lots of good eating into the bargain.

Chicken Anatomy Lesson

I have always preferred the dark meat of chicken. In former days I would always cook chicken so the dark meat would be done to my taste (juicy, with a hint of pink) and then wonder what to do with the light meat, which was invariably overcooked. Well, chicken in parts solved my problem. I can have dark meat to my heart's content. If I want to be very economical, I buy two or three chickens at a time, cut them up, use the dark meat for broiling, and save the light meat for chicken hash or some other dish in which texture and juiciness don't matter that much. Sometimes I bone the breast meat, beat it flat, and treat it as I would veal cutlets.

Everyone who cooks should know how to cut up a chicken. I have discovered that very few people do know, and it's so simple. Here is the cutting process, which needs only a little patience and a good sharp knife.

First, use your finger to locate the joints of the chicken. The major ones are at the point where the thigh joins the body and the point where the wing joins the body. There is also a joint between the leg and thigh, or drumstick and second joint; and there are two joints in the wing. To remove the leg and thigh in one good piece, cut through the skin that connects them to the body, and cut down through the flesh. You will see that the dark meat is separated from the light in this section. Then push away the leg from the body very gently until the "hip" joint appears and begins to divide. The joint can now be severed easily. Remove the other leg and thigh.

You have a choice of severing the wing at the second joint or where it joins the body. I recommend the latter. Again, cut through the skin connecting the wing to the body, and continue cutting through the flesh. Bend away the wing gently until the joint separates. Cut through the joint. Proceed with the other wing. Then cut across the chicken where the lower back and breast divide. It is easy to slice through the little rib bones, and there is just one small joint to sever. You can use poultry shears for this part of the operation. To divide the breast into halves, press it down firmly from the skin side, until you hear a crack. Turn it flesh side up. Remove the breast bone and the small piece of gristle at the end by running your finger along the flesh to loosen it from the bone.

If you are sentimental and want to preserve the wishbone at the end of the breast, you can cut off that piece at the joints, but if you are a realist, you will simply cut right through the wishbone and divide the breast into two pieces. With a sharp pair of scissors trim the rib bones off the breast. Also trim the back and break it into two pieces. In addition to the pieces you have cut you will also have the neck, gizzard, liver, and heart.

If I were cutting up several chickens, I would use the backs and necks for a broth and freeze the breasts for poaching or for chicken cutlets. I might use the gizzards, hearts, and livers, adding extra amounts of each, for a sandwich spread. I often use the legs and thighs to prepare a startling, unusual, and delicious chicken dish. (You can, of course, buy legs and thighs alone for this recipe.)

 Chicken with 40 Cloves of Garlic requires a 3-quart casserole with a good tight cover. Preheat your oven to 375 degrees. Rinse 8 to 10 chicken legs and thighs in cold water, and pat dry with paper towels. Peel 40 cloves of garlic (about 3 bulbs) and leave whole. Cut 4 stalks of celery in thin slices. Dip the chicken in olive oil to thoroughly coat each piece (you will need about ⅔ cup oil altogether) and sprinkle with 2 teaspoons salt, ¼ teaspoon pepper, and a dash of nutmeg. Put the chicken in the casserole along with the residue of oil. Add the garlic, sliced celery, 6 sprigs parsley, 1 tablespoon dried tarragon, and ¼ cup dry vermouth. Seal the top of the casserole with a sheet of foil. and cover tightly with the lid. Bake for 1½ hours. Do not remove the lid during the baking period. Serve directly from the casserole, or transfer the chicken pieces to a serving dish. With this serve hot toast or thin slices of pumpernickel. Invite your guests to spread the softened garlic on the bread. They will find that the strong flavor has disappeared, leaving a wonderful, buttery paste perfumed with garlic. Serves six to eight.

A Robot in Your Kitchen

A few years ago in France I was dining in the restaurant of a good friend of mine, and after dinner he took me back to the kitchen to show me what I consider to be the most wonderful new piece of equipment that has come along in some time. In Europe it is known as the Magimix, and in a matter of seconds it chops, shreds, slices, and grates anything from cubes of raw meat or fish to nuts, vegetables, chocolate, and cheese, makes mayonnaise and even pastry—all rapidly, efficiently, and as if by magic.

There are two versions of this amazing French machine, the Magimix, which is sold here as the Cuisinart Food Processor, and a larger model called the Robot Coupe. It is rather like having a robot in your kitchen, because it does most of the tiring, time-consuming dogwork for you. The Magimix is a neat machine, about 8 by 7 by 14 inches high with a powerful 500-watt motor and two curved steel blades that fit on a center shaft within a large plastic bowl. All you have to do to operate the machine is turn the cover counterclockwise to start the action, clockwise to stop it, until you get the texture you want. I've made an excellent pastry, a pâté brisée, in just 26 seconds. You blend the butter and flour in the machine, add your liquid, turn it on again, and voilá—a solid ball of perfect pastry. You can also make a good thick mayonnaise in nothing flat, and cleaning is a cinch, since the cover, bowl, and blades all lift off the base.

This machine is not inexpensive, but it is a joy to have in your kitchen, and to my mind anyone who really loves to cook will wonder how he ever lived without it. I know I couldn't. It has changed my life completely, and I find I depend on it more and more for many things. For instance, I have always been exceedingly fond of Middle Eastern food, and one of the things I enjoy making is *kibbeh nayé*, a mixture of finely ground raw lamb, onion, bulghur (cracked wheat), and seasonings, which I serve as an hors d'oeuvre or a luncheon dish. I now do the whole thing in the Magimix—grind the lamb, chop the onion, and combine them with the wheat and seasonings. *(See Editor's Note, copyright page.)*

To make *Kibbeh Nayé*, cut away all the fat and tendons from a leg or shoulder of lamb, then cut the meat in cubes and grind until rather fine. Meanwhile, soak 1½ cups washed bulghur (cracked wheat) in water. Grate or finely chop 3 medium-sized onions. Drain the bulghur through cheesecloth, then squeeze out all excess water. Add to the lamb with the onion, 1 or 2 ice cubes, 1½ to 2 teaspoons salt, 1 teaspoon freshly ground black pepper, and ½ teaspoon allspice. Blend the mixture very well and taste for seasoning. If there are any bits of ice left, throw them away.

Spread the kibbeh on a very cold serving platter and decorate with shredded green onions and a few radishes, with perhaps some cherry tomatoes around the edge of the dish to make it look more attractive. Serve it as a spread, with thinly sliced French bread or Syrian pita bread, or if you prefer, wrap the mixture in crisp lettuce leaves. This makes a most delicious, cool, refreshing, and different hors d'oeuvre for your repertoire, and one that is extremely addictive. You just can't stop eating it.

If the idea of eating raw ground lamb upsets you, you can form it into little balls, sauté them in butter over brisk heat, and serve with radishes, scallions, romaine, and endive, with salt, pepper, and cruets of vinegar and oil so everyone can make his own dressing. Or you can put layers of the kibbeh in a baking dish, with some additional, rather fattish minced lamb, pine nuts, and onions and seasonings between the layers and bake it.

That's good, too, but it is the raw kibbeh nayé I most frequently serve, and with the Magimix I can whip it up in minutes.

I also find this magical machine a great aid when I'm grinding almonds or filberts for cookies and cakes and things like that where the ground nuts replace part of the flour—I find if you toast the nuts and grind them freshly they taste immeasurably better.

⁕ CHAPTER 9 ⁕
Holidays, Parties, and Picnics

୬

... in which we de-calorize Christmas ... have sober thoughts about holiday entertaining ... stir up a plum pudding and a batch of mincemeat ... make gifts good enough to eat ... inaugurate le snack de Noël ... cook our goose ... celebrate Christmas in Provence with thirteen desserts ... and in Barcelona with the Three Kings ... spread a Moroccan feast of couscous and a Middle East mezze table ... and indulge a lifelong passion for picnics.

Christmas Remembered

Christmas is the holiday I have always loved the most. Its traditions, foods, and spirit mean a great deal to me. Like most of us, my happiest memories of the season are wrapped up in my childhood. This was the most exciting time of the year. Lovely, tantalizing smells crept from the kitchen, and the doorbell rang constantly as friends dropped by with gifts.

Remembering how Christmas was then, I am disturbed to see how commercial and impersonal it has become now, especially in large cities. Instead of being a time of joy, it is all too often just another giant shopping spree. How weary, frantic, and bad-tempered many of those shoppers look, as they try to cope with lengthy lists, crowded stores and buses, and a haunting sense of spiritual malaise.

I feel very strongly that we are rapidly losing the whole meaning of Christmas and the significance behind the exchanging of gifts. Instead of putting something of ourselves, our love and our skills, into a gift, we are all too apt to rely on a store to provide the idea, the sentiment, the wrapping—even the delivery.

We could recapture some of the happiness of Christmas past if we just took the trouble to make, rather than to buy, a few of the presents we give each year. My mother believed in making all her own Christmas foods. She prepared Christmas puddings, fruit cakes, and mincemeat a year ahead of time and ladled generous libations of brandy into them for the next twelve months until they were aged to a ripe, dark mellowness. Come next Christmas, some of these were earmarked for friends, many of whom planned their holiday menus in the expectation of getting one of Mother's mincemeat puddings or cakes.

Everyone in the house had to stir the pudding for luck during the mixing and, while so doing, make a wish. The puddings were so well lubricated with cognac during the twelve months of periodic dousings that by the time they were reheated and served for Christmas and New Year celebrations they had acquired an extraordinary flavor, texture, and quality. I once kept a pudding for two years, and by then it was so saturated with cognac that after eating just a little bit with hard sauce it was hardly possible to move from the table.

Here is another Christmas pudding recipe that was my mother's, a fruity and spirituous concoction which needn't marinate for month, and I love it. She used to make great batches, boil them in two-pound baking powder tins and give them as presents. I prefer to make mine in English pudding basins, tapering pottery bowls with a deep rim under which the pudding cloth is tied. You can often find these in the better kitchen shops. Or you can use stainless steel bowls or molds with simple shapes and designs. I sometimes use a melon mold with a tight-fitting cover. Anything will work as long as you keep in mind the way the pudding will look when unmolded and served.

For your *Christmas Pudding*, buy 2 pounds of seeded raisins—the large ones with big fat seeds. Seed them by hand—a tiresome chore, but it makes a better pudding. You will also need 2 pounds sultana raisins (these are made from seedless grapes, whereas the seeded are from muscat grapes and have a different flavor). The raisins sold in health food stores are very good, incidentally. Add 2 pounds currants to make up your 6 pounds of dried fruit.

Add 4 tart apples, finely chopped, ¾ pound mixed citron, lemon, and orange peel, a little bit of angelica for its beautiful green color, and ½ pound chopped blanched almonds. Now for another tough job—finely chop 2 pounds of beef suet. Combine all this with 3 cups flour and 3 to 4 cups fine bread crumbs, freshly made, not packaged. For spice, add 1 teaspoon cinnamon, 1 teaspoon mace, 1 teaspoon nutmeg, ½ teaspoon ground cloves, ½ teaspoon ground ginger, ½ teaspoon ground allspice, and 2 teaspoons salt. Mix very thoroughly with your hands, then add the juice and grated rind of 3 lemons, 1 cup cognac, 1 cup Grand Marnier or Cointreau and 12 well-beaten eggs. You will notice there is no sugar in this recipe—you don't need it with the sweetness in the other ingredients. Mix very well with your hands, and if there is not enough liquid, add more cognac or Grand Marnier or even beer. It must be well bound together and thoroughly mixed, but not a tight dough. Cover with foil and let stand to mellow for a day or two or even three, before cooking. Then taste and see if it lacks salt, spice, or spirits.

Fill your pudding basins or molds with the mixture, leaving some room for expansion. Put on the lids if you are using covered molds, or tie around the basins or bowls cloths that have been wrung out in hot water and dusted with flour. Tie foil over the cloths. Stand on a rack in a deep saucepan, add water to come halfway up the molds or basins, cover the pan, bring to a boil, and boil from 6 to 8 hours, depending on size, adding more water if it boils away.

Remove from the heat and let the puddings cool in the pans. Keep the puddings in a cool place for several weeks or months (not necessarily in the refrigerator, although this is a good place to store them if you have the room). Add more cognac or other spirits to the puddings while they are ripening.

Plum pudding must be reheated for 2 to 3 hours on a rack in a pan of boiling water before being served. Unmold it on a warm serving dish and garnish with candied fruits or whatever you like. Some people stick a sprig of holly or mistletoe in the top, which is a pretty custom but apt to cause a conflagration if you flame it inadvertently along with the pudding. Pour warmed cognac, rum, or whiskey on the pudding, ignite, and serve the pudding flaming at table, either with the traditional hard sauce or the following brandy sauce.

~ For *Brandy Sauce* cream 6 tablespoons butter very lightly. Add ⅔ cup powdered sugar and beat in 2 egg yolks. Put in the top of a double boiler over hot water, blend in ¾ cup heavy cream, and cook, stirring constantly with a wooden spoon, until the sauce coats the spoon. Pour into a bowl, flavor with brandy (or rum) and serve hot.

Now comes the test, for, as we all know, the proof of the pudding is in the eating. I think you are going to approve of this one.

Let's Make Mincemeat

Mince pies have been part of my gastronomic life from way back. I can remember really fantastic ones made in a deep 10- or 12-inch pie tin lined with rich pastry and filled to the brim with heavily brandied mincemeat mixed at the last minute with finely chopped apple—for in our household there were no apples in the mincemeat. They were added when the pies were made, which I have found gives a much better result. Over the filling went the rich, flaky crust decorated with cut-out pastry leaves and flowers and painted with egg yolk and cream so it baked to a beautiful glossy brown. This noble holiday offering to the delights of the season was quite unforgettable. We would reheat the baked pie slightly, cut into the deliciously flaky crust and breathe in the overpowering bouquet, then eat it in tiny bites, savoring every bit of flavor. Some people put hard sauce on theirs, or cream, or Cheddar cheese, and my father liked both cream and Roquefort cheese on his, but I have always considered that a sacrilege. I have a great deal of respect for a good mince pie, and to me it should be eaten pure and simple.

∜ This *Mincemeat* recipe has been in my family for ever and a day, and I consider it is just about the best I've ever tasted. First, take 3 pounds brisket or lean rump of beef and 1 fresh beef tongue weighing about 3 pounds. Boil them in water until they are very tender, cool them in the broth, and skim off the fat. Remove all fat from the meat, and either grind coarsely or chop very finely by hand.

Chop 1½ pounds beef suet very, very finely, and prepare 2 pounds seeded raisins, 2 pounds sultana raisins, 2 pounds currants, ½ pound citron, shredded and diced, ¼ pound orange peel, shredded, ¼ pound lemon peel, shredded, and ½ to 1 pound dried figs and dates, cut into small pieces.

Put the meats, suet, fruits, and peels in a deep crock. Add 2 cups sugar, 1 pint strawberry or raspberry preserves, 1 tablespoon salt, 2 teaspoons nutmeg or 2½ teaspoons cinnamon, 1 teaspoon allspice, 1 teaspoon mace, and a dash of ground cloves.

Add a fifth of good sherry and enough cognac to make a rather loose mixture of the meats and fruits—it will take 2 bottles. If you don't want to use cognac, you can substitute Irish or bourbon whiskey or even gin or vodka. Mix very well, cover the crock, and let it stand for a month before you use it. Check it each week and add more liquor if it has all been absorbed. Then put it in sterilized jars and seal. This makes a most wonderful Christmas gift for any of your friends who love good mincemeat.

Mincemeat will keep for a long, long time, provided you give it plenty to drink. If you keep on adding a bit more booze to it every year, it will keep in the refrigerator for as long as five years—I know, because I've done it.

Apart from the traditional mince pie, you can make a deep-dish pie with layers of sliced apple and mincemeat covered with a streusel topping—a crumbly mixture of butter, sugar, flour, and nutmeats. Or make tiny mince pies by cutting out small circles of rich pastry, putting 2 or 3 spoonfuls of mincemeat on them, sealing them very well, and baking them in a 375-degree oven until they are nicely browned and crisp. Add these to your gifts of Christmas cookies or have them, reheated a bit, with a cup of coffee or tea. Another trick is to get the mincemeat very hot, flame it with warmed cognac, and spoon it blazing over vanilla, eggnog, or coffee ice cream. For a frozen dessert, make a mousse by combining 1 to 1½ cups mincemeat with 1 pint heavy cream, whipped, and an Italian meringue made by beating 2 egg whites until stiff and then beating them until cold with a heavy syrup made with ½ cup sugar and 2 tablespoons water. Put this in a mold or soufflé dish and freeze.

Or make a *Mincemeat and Apple Flan*, one of my favorite recipes. For this you'll need a flan case, which is a bottomless round, rectangular, or square metal form which you put on a cookie sheet and line with pastry. After baking, the case can be lifted off, leaving the flan to stand alone.

So take a 9-inch round or 14-by-5-by-2-inch rectangular flan case and line it with rich tart pastry. Peel and core 6 tart cooking apples, and cut them into sixths. Steam them, covered, in a heavy skillet over medium heat with 4 tablespoons butter and 1 teaspoon vanilla until tender and easily breakable, but not soft and mushy. Cool slightly, then arrange in the pastry shell. Top with a thickish layer of mincemeat, about 2½ to 3 cups. Dot with butter, and bake at 375 degrees for 35 to 40 minutes, or until the pastry is cooked through and the apple and mincemeat flavors well mingled.

Cool and brush with an apricot glaze, made by melting a 1 pound jar pure apricot preserves (the kind without any added pectin) in a saucepan, letting it come to a boil, adding a few drops of cognac, and then straining it through a fine sieve. Sprinkle the glazed flan with thinly sliced toasted almonds, and serve warm with cognac-flavored whipped cream.

You'll have one of the best cold-weather desserts you have ever tasted.

Gifts They'll Eat Up

When I was young, we always had our big gathering of family and friends on Christmas Eve, and a gay, jolly, wonderful time it was, with a great buffet supper, much good will, and exchanging of gifts and toasts to the holiday season. In our family, Christmas Day was a much more personal celebration. My mother, my father, and I all liked to do things that didn't include the whole family, which I feel was a very good idea. We managed to see a lot more people that way, and if any one of us was invited out for Christmas dinner and wanted to go, we did. Unlike many families, we didn't feel any sense of "duty" to each other or to our relatives on Christmas Day.

I discovered that the time I really liked to entertain the most was Christmas breakfast. By that I don't mean the crack of dawn, but around the civilized hour of noon. Whenever I'm in New York at Christmas time I start planning how many people I can squeeze into my house for Christmas breakfast. It's such a nice time to have people in. You don't encroach on the rest of the day's festivities, you give your friends a break from being in their own houses, and you can serve such good, simple dishes. I like at Christmas to give foods that I have made in my own kitchen, which ties in very well with a breakfast party. The homemade goodies you wrap and present to your guests can be things they'll be able to use for their Christmas dinner or supper, or have the next day or week. I very often make pâtés, loaves of bread, and mincemeat and plum puddings, and I enjoy dreaming up imaginative and attractive ways to package them. People, I've found, are delighted and touched to get foods you have made yourself.

Homemade bread is much in favor these days. Those of you who have seen my book *Beard on Bread* will find in there a number of breads that make excellent gifts. Some keep well, some should be eaten almost immediately, and still others can almost be compared to fruitcakes for their lasting quality.

A good pâté always comes in handy for Christmas eating and gifts. Every year I make a variety of pâtés, some to give away, some to keep in the refrigerator. The following recipe for my favorite pâté makes quite a lot. If you like, you can bake it in small loaf pans, molds, or baking dishes, then keep one and give the others away.

⮞ For *My Favorite Pâté*, trim 1 pound chicken livers, cutting away the little tendons. Sauté lightly in a heavy skillet in 4 tablespoons butter until just firm. Whirl in the blender with 2 eggs, 6 garlic cloves, 1 medium onion, peeled and cut in small pieces, and ½ cup cognac (substitute California brandy, if you wish—or whiskey will do just as well). Put in a large bowl, and add 2 pounds ground veal (if unobtainable, or too expensive, ground chicken or turkey will do), 2 pounds not-too-lean ground pork, 2 tablespoons salt, and ½ teaspoon freshly ground black pepper. Blend well with your hands, then add another ⅔ cup cognac or brandy, 1 teaspoon thyme, ½ teaspoon summer savory, a pinch of nutmeg, and a small pinch of cloves. Blend thoroughly. Check the seasoning, but on no account taste the raw texture—sauté 2 teaspoons of it in a little butter, turning well until cooked through, then taste. Add whatever additional seasoning the mixture needs before baking. It's much better to take that extra time than to have a badly seasoned pâté.

Cut 1 pound boiled tongue into long strips, ⅜ inch thick, and 1 pound fresh pork fat into strips about ¼ inch thick. Line a 2½-quart baking dish with bacon strips. (If you want to make small pâtés, use two or three small baking dishes, molds, or aluminum-foil loaf pans.) Put one-third of the ground mixture in the lined dish (or divide equally between small pans), and top with strips of tongue and pork fat, then add another layer of the ground mixture, more tongue and pork strips, and cover with a final layer of the ground mixture. Top with more bacon slices and bake in a 325-degree oven, allowing 3 to 3½ hours for 1 large pâté, 2 to 2½ hours for small ones. Remove and cool. This pâté does not need weighting. When cool, wrap in foil or plastic wrap and refrigerate until ready to use.

To make a more rustic-looking pâté, very easy to slice, form the full recipe into a loaf and bake on a bed of bacon slices in a baking pan. This is a delicious, perfect pâté for any season of the year. I love it for lunch with a good salad, spicy pickles, maybe a thin slice of ham, and a glass of wine. For a Christmas buffet, you might follow the pâté with a big bowl of chicken salad, rolls, and perhaps a mincemeat soufflé or pie.

I also like to make *rillettes de Tours*, that French country pâté that might be described as the essence of the pig. It is simply pork cooked down with plenty of fat until it is meltingly tender, then shredded, seasoned, and packed into little pots. It makes a rich and luscious Christmas food.

Because of the work involved, it is a bit tedious to make all by yourself. I usually ask a friend to come and help and share the results. We pass a winter afternoon very pleasantly, sitting around my kitchen table, shredding away and talking. I find it a kind of therapy in the midst of the Christmas rush.

⮑ Long, slow cooking is essential for the *Rillettes*. First heat 3 pounds of leaf lard (pork kidney fat) in a very large pot until it has all melted down. Then add 3 pounds of fresh pork shoulder, loin, or leg, cut into small pieces, and 1 cup of water. Cook this very slowly on top of the stove or in a 250- to 300-degree oven until the meat is so tender that it almost falls apart—this will take about 4 hours.

Remove the pork from the fat, shred it finely with two forks, then season it to taste with salt and freshly ground black pepper. Now mash it with enough of the fat to make a smooth paste. Pack the shredded pork mixture into small crocks, jars, or terrines, mashing it so that it absorbs plenty of fat. This is essential to give it a smooth texture and rich flavor. Ladle enough clear melted pork fat on top to cover the pork and make an airtight seal, then cover the pots with the lids, or tie aluminum foil tightly over them if they have no lids, and store in the refrigerator.

This will keep well for weeks, provided the sealing layer of fat is not broken. Serve with thin toast or French bread as a first course, or for friends who drop in during the holiday season, bring out your *rillettes* and your pâté with plenty of thin toast and plenty of chilled champagne.

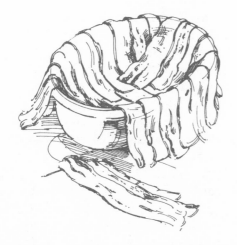

Let's Keep Christmas Simple

Why do so many people seem to feel that at Christmas every meal they serve their guests must be a feast? They may entertain simply and sensibly all year, but come the festive season they offer much too much rich food, far beyond what anyone could possibly want. Sooner or later in the round of entertaining I find myself longing for something simple and good to eat.

I've found many of my friends feel as I do, so on many Christmases I've given the kind of party that everyone can enjoy. It's easy, it's unassuming, it's guaranteed not to upset the delicate balance of anyone's digestion, and it is a great contrast to the traditional Christmas celebration.

First, I give my guests a well-chilled dry sherry. This may be one of the bone-dry Spanish sherries like Tio Pepe or La Ina or one of the extremely pleasant California cocktail sherries from Almadén or Louis Martini or any of the other well-known American wineries. Then I bring on good healthy servings of oyster stew and continue pouring the chilled sherry because sherry and seafood things go well together. Oyster stew might have been made especially for a Christmas or New Year party—it's a most reviving, nourishing, and delectable dish, and I like to accompany it with piles of hot buttered toast.

After the oyster stew I put out a big board of various slicing sausages—salami, Polish sausage, bologna, whatever I find in the market that looks good. I provide sharp knives so everyone can cut off what he wants, and an assortment of mustards. I also like to have another board of cheeses—Swiss Gruyère cheese, a fine Cheddar, and maybe a Brie—and with the cheeses, thinly sliced rye bread and crackers of some kind and a bowl of fruit. I have plenty of iced beer and a bottle or two of red wine for those who prefer it.

This, to my mind, makes the best of all Christmas parties because you haven't loaded your guests down with Christmas cheer and Christmas richness and lots of cakes and pies and sweet things. It's novel, it's a perfect combination of food and drink, and each person can take as much or as little as he pleases.

My recipe for *Oyster Stew* will make 4 very generous servings or 6 medium-sized ones. You can increase or decrease the recipe, depending on how many servings you need and how lavish you make them.

The first important thing is to heat the 4 or 6 individual bowls in which you will serve the stew and, when they are quite hot, put a large dab of butter in each one. Keep them warm while you do the cooking, which takes only minutes. Heat to the boiling point 1 pint cream, 1 pint milk, and the liquor from 1½ to 2 pints shucked oysters—2 pints is a safer amount: it will give you quite a bit of liquor if you buy the oysters in bulk. Season to taste with salt and freshly ground black pepper, and add a good dash of Tabasco and ½ to 1 teaspoon Worcestershire sauce. Now add the oysters and let them just come to the boiling point, so that the edges curl slightly. Don't overcook them—they are awful if you do. Ladle the stew into the hot bowls and serve with hot buttered toast.

If, on the other hand, you're just having a few friends in for a drink, there's the problem of what to give them. Most traditional Christmas drinks tend to be pretty sticky and gooey and sweet, and, to my taste, quite revolting.

I like to do something different—*Hot Spiced Wine*. Stick whole cloves into 4 oranges, making a pattern if you like. Bake the oranges in a 350-degree oven for 15 to 20 minutes, or until they are heated through and the cloves begin to show a little white dust, which looks very attractive. Put the oranges in a large heatproof bowl of silver or pottery with the cut rind of 1 lemon and 2 bay leaves. Heat ⅔ to ¾ cup cognac, brandy, or bourbon, pour it over the oranges, set it alight, and let it burn down. While it is burning, pour over the oranges 2 to 3 fifths or ¾ of a gallon jug of a good dry red wine, such as a California Pinot Noir or Cabernet Sauvignon, heated until very hot, but *not* boiling. Add about ½ cup sugar and stir it in well—the amount of sugar is up to you; you can sweeten to taste. I like a minimum or none at all, if the wine is good. Stir well and serve warm in mugs or glasses with a little twist of orange peel. With this very pleasant hot drink serve some small dry cookies or cakes or tiny ham, cheese or roast beef sandwiches, or just have cheeses and bread.

Where's the Turkey?
In the Lettuce.

In the days when we all led a closely knit family life, there were definite traditions about holidays that were strictly observed. Now it seems that, except for a very few families, the old traditions have flown to the winds and everyone is off hither and yon pursuing his own thing. For most of us, Christmas will begin with everyone gathering around the tree in the early morning for an exchange of presents, followed by a family breakfast, maybe calls on friends and relatives, and then the climax of it all, the noble Christmas dinner with turkey and all the trimmings, mince pies, and the pudding borne in flaming on a platter, garnished with holly sprigs. There was a pattern, almost an unbreakable rule, of what the Christmas menu should be. I used to think that a formal sit-down affair like this was an absolute necessity, but lately my thinking has changed.

While Christmas—or Christmas Eve—is still, to me, the time to entertain one's nearest and dearest, be they family or close friends, few of us can cope with an enormous meal for twelve to fourteen people without help. Present circumstances call for an extremely different kind of entertaining, so last year I dreamed up a casual, almost snack type of Christmas menu that while festive and fun requires very little preparation or last-minute attention in the kitchen. Although it may not be the feast I grew up with, it does have many of my favorite bits and pieces in it, and it bows to tradition in that the main course is based on turkey. I like it, and so do the friends who come to my house, so I'm passing it on to you as a new idea.

Last year I invited twelve friends for six o'clock on Christmas Day, and we sat around the fire and had magnums of French champagne, which made it all very festive and special, and I set out a big platter of charcuterie—thin slices of Smithfield ham, Polish kielbasa (a sausage you can buy all over the country), salami, pepperoni, homemade pâté—with several different kinds of bread: homemade white bread, rye bread, and the wafer-thin Norwegian flatbread, which I adore with charcuterie, sweet butter, olives, cornichons (the tiny French pickles), and American bread-and-butter pickles. We sat and chatted happily, with no feeling that we had to face a huge dinner, drinking champagne and munching for a couple of hours. When I felt everyone was ready for the main course, I brought on a casserole of a turkey mixture which I'd cooked earlier in the day and warmed up at the last minute in a large decorative casserole.

This was the fun part of the meal, because the hot turkey was eaten in icy-cold lettuce leaves, which I brought in on a large platter, separated from the head and arranged in piles like an overblown rose. The guests spooned some of the hot filling on the chilled leaves, rolled them up and ate the whole thing like a taco, so there was no need to set a table or provide knives and forks—only some big lap-covering linen napkins were necessary.

To make the filling for *Turkey in Lettuce Leaves*, melt 6 tablespoons butter in a large skillet and sauté 2 cups finely chopped onion and ¾ cup finely chopped green pepper until wilted. Add a 4-ounce can of green chili peppers, drained and chopped, 1 to 2 tablespoons fresh hot chili pepper, finely chopped, and 4 cups finely diced cooked turkey (you could roast a turkey breast or one of those boneless turkey rolls), and toss well. Cover and simmer 5 minutes. Add 2 tablespoons chopped fresh basil or 1½ teaspoons dried basil, 1 teaspoon salt, or to taste, ½ teaspoon freshly ground black pepper, and ⅓ cup cognac. If the mixture seems too dry, you can add ½ cup turkey or chicken broth. Taste, and adjust the seasoning. Arrange in a large heated bowl or casserole, and garnish with ¼ cup chopped parsley and ¾ cup shaved toasted almonds. To eat, spoon onto the leaves of 2 to 3 heads of well-chilled iceberg lettuce and roll up. This will serve ten to twelve, and the contrast between the crisp, icy lettuce and the hot, spicy filling is unbelievably delicious.

With this as a main course, all you need are some hot rolls and, rather than a salad, either cold vegetables à la Grecque (see page 64) or a hot vegetable mixture of some kind that would go with the turkey and could be reheated at the last minute. Drink your Christmas champagne with this, or switch to a light red wine such as a Beaujolais or a California Zinfandel.

If you're like me, you always wonder what to do with the candies and cookies and fruit that pour in as gifts at the holiday season. Well, here is the perfect time to use them. After your casual dinner around the fire, have a platter of the Christmas goodies, a bowl of fruit, maybe some cheese and crackers, and coffee with a selection of liqueurs and port or Madeira.

I can recommend this kind of meal (shall we call it le snack de Noël?) as an ideal kind of Christmas dinner if you don't want to do the whole traditional bit. People eat as much as they please. No one goes home with that horrible feeling that he is stuffed beyond belief or comfort. You save yourself a lot of stewing and slaving, and you're free to relax and enjoy Christmas as it should be, a time of closeness and warm, friendly hospitality.

A Golden Goose for Holiday Feasting

Why is it that whenever the Christmas bird is mentioned it is invariably turkey, not goose? Roast goose must surely be one of the most neglected and misunderstood of all fowl in this country, yet in Europe, since Roman times, it has been regarded as the tenderest and most succulent of all the birds that come to the kitchen. The English have a great tradition of goose for the holiday feast, and it has had a long run of popularity in Germany, too. In France, the force-fed goose produces that marvelous delicacy known as foie gras (literally, fat liver), and the well-fattened bird itself is roasted or made into confit d'oie, goose cut into pieces, simmered long in its own fat, then put down in crocks with an airtight covering layer of fat so it can be served all through the year. You can buy canned confit d'oie here to serve with white beans or in that famous French mélange of meats and beans, cassoulet.

In the early history of this country, the goose was a very important bird. Our New England forefathers kept flocks of geese as watchbirds, for they would vociferously sound an alert the minute animal or human prowlers came around. Then, of course, the feathers yielded down for their beds and the larger ones quills for their pens. The goose supplied meat in the winter, and the grease was used as a preventative or balm for chest colds and similar ailments.

Perhaps the reason why goose has been so long neglected is because the quality that could be procured in our city markets was not of the finest. Now, however, we are blessed with a golden goose brought forth by the National Goose Council, raised with an eye to tenderness and flavor and then quick-frozen. These golden geese are available in sizes from 6 to 14 pounds, with the majority in the 8- to 10-pound range, which means they fit easily into a modern oven and make good sense for a small family. I can testify, as one who has served a couple of them for Thanksgiving, that they are extraordinarily fine eating, tender, succulent, and tasty.

The frozen geese should be thoroughly thawed before roasting, either in the refrigerator, which will take 1½ to 2 days for the very large ones; in cool water for 4 to 5 hours; or at room temperature, which takes 6 to 10 hours for the medium size. For refrigerator or room-temperature thawing, leave them in the original wrap, and after room-temperature thawing, put the goose in the refrigerator until you are ready to cook it.

Naturally, you will remove the neck and giblets from the cavity and make them into a delicious broth for sauce for the goose. It is also a good idea to remove the excess fat from the body cavity, render it, and use it for cooking, for this is one of the most delicate, pure, and flavorful fats we get. Nothing tastes better than potatoes or meat browned in goose fat, and it makes very good pastry, too.

So now for a *Stuffing for Your Golden Christmas Goose* that I think enhances the rich meat marvelously well. Sauté ½ cup finely chopped onion in 6 tablespoons butter, add 5 to 6 cups bread crumbs, moistening them in the butter, and blend with 2 teaspoons salt and 1 cup cooked peeled chestnuts or canned chestnuts, 2 cups peeled and chopped apples, and 1 cup coarsely chopped prunes which have been puffed in hot water, or steeped in Madeira for a couple of days (or you may use 1 cup apples and 2 cups prunes, which I prefer). Season with ½ teaspoon nutmeg and 1 teaspoon thyme, and blend well together. Stuff an 8- to 10-pound goose with this mixture, truss, sew up, or skewer the cavity, and tie the legs together. Place the goose breast side up on a rack in a roasting pan.

Roast for 1 hour at 400 degrees, then reduce the temperature to 350 degrees and roast for another hour, without basting. As the fat renders from the goose, remove it to a jar for future use. After the second hour, reduce the heat to 325 degrees and continue roasting until nicely browned and done. The leg meat should be soft when pressed, and the juices, when the thigh is pricked, should run beigey-pink. Total roasting time for a 6- to 8-pound bird will be 1½ to 2 hours, for the 8- to 10-pound size from 2 to 2¾ hours, and 2¾ to 3¼ hours for a 10- to 12-pound bird.

To serve with goose, I favor either mashed potatoes or a chickpea purée (see page 106) and something tart and fruity, like more prunes in Madeira or applesauce to cut the fat and balance the richness. As a green vegetable, I like broccoli or spinach. You can thicken the goose broth with flour, arrowroot, or cornstarch to make the sauce.

There's nothing quite as satisfying as a goose well cooked. If there is any left, serve it the next day with white beans, cooked until tender and dressed with a little of the goose fat, salt, pepper, and chopped parsley.

So let's drink a toast in French champagne (the perfect wine for this bird) to the golden goose and its long overdue renaissance as a great and glorious specialty for our holiday feasting.

The Thirteen Desserts
of Christmas

Although I've been lucky enough to celebrate Christmas in many parts of the world and to discover the lore, traditions, and foods of the season in different countries, I think that by far the most affecting, the most delightfully Christmas-like Christmases were those I spent in Provence. In this southern region of France the centuries-old traditions seem to have survived unchanged. They are still observed by many families, especially those in the countryside.

The first great feast is the Gros Souper, or big supper, which takes place on Christmas Eve, a feast day. The Gros Souper is an elaborate evening meal that takes in all manner of very special Provençal dishes. First there is a huge bowl of aïoli, the wonderful garlicky mayonnaise called by some "the butter of Provence" (see page 291). On Christmas Eve this is served with snails, salt cod fish either sautéed in olive oil with little onions and garlic and olives or simply boiled and served in one piece, and all kinds of vegetables—artichokes, zucchini, carrots, celery, and potatoes. This is the main part of the meal, and after it comes the dessert that is absolutely typical of Provence and of the season, not one dessert, but really thirteen in all.

Les Treize Desserts, the thirteen desserts, consist of a selection of sweet things arranged on a tray, traditionally served all through that area of France. It makes a perfectly beautiful presentation, and it's customary to taste a little bit of everything for luck.

In the thirteen desserts you might find candied or dried figs, raisins, glacé fruits, shelled and sometimes toasted almonds, toasted hazelnuts, and several different candies—the dark, rich nougat of the area, marzipan fruits, sometimes chocolates, and dates, either plain or stuffed with nuts or fondant. The stuffed dates, rolled in sugar, are exquisite both to look at and to eat. Then there are fruits—small oranges, mandarin oranges, and sometimes winter pears, and either little fruit tarts or a fascinating big tart that is one of the gastronomic wonders of Provence. It has a filling of spiced and sweetened spinach mixed with a rich custard, masked with the glistening gold of an apricot glaze, and crisscrossed with pastry strips.

For the final touch, there are crispy, crunchy cakes of fried dough which in many ways resemble the Christmas desserts one finds in Italy, Mexico, and certain other countries. If you'd like to try these wonderful Christmas cakes—and they're great fun to make—here is the recipe.

    ❧ For *Pompe à l'Huile*: sift together 1 teaspoon salt, 1 teaspoon baking powder, 2 tablespoons sugar, and 4 cups flour. Beat 2 eggs very, very well, and beat into them 1 cup milk. Gradually combine the dry and the liquid mixtures, and then add ¼ cup melted butter. Turn out onto a floured board and knead for about 5 or 6 minutes, or until the dough is very smooth and elastic.

Divide the dough into 28 or 36 balls, and roll them out from 4 to 6 inches in diameter. Have ready a pan of deep fat heated to 370 degrees. Drop the circles into it, and let them brown delicately on both sides. Remove carefully and drain on absorbent paper, then sprinkle them with powdered sugar. Some people like cinnamon, but I much prefer them simply sprinkled with sugar. It's a matter of your own taste.

These crispy cakes should be served very fresh and almost warm, because they don't keep very well. They're short, crunchy, delicious, and quite different from anything we have at this time of year, and I think you'll find your guests will gobble them up. Arrange them on a tray with a selection of the thirteen desserts, and you have a most unusual Christmas collation to serve with coffee, perhaps for a Christmas Eve open house or a tree-trimming party.

After the Gros Souper, the Provençaux will go to midnight mass, and then they rush home to eat another stalwart meal—a Christmas Eve supper-breakfast which can go on well into the dawn. At this you find things like pâtés and blood sausage and capon or turkey, all washed down with either the local country wines or another Provençal specialty called "cooked wine." This is actually a mixture of sweet grape juice mixed with marc, the sharp, acrid brandy that is made from the residue left after the grapes are pressed. The combination of the rather bitter brandy and the sweet juice has an extremely exciting quality, but a robust red or white wine would be equally good with this Christmas meal.

Spain's Great Day for Gifts

In Spain, gifts do not come at Christmas but on January 6, Twelfth Night, or Kings' Day as it is called there, the time when we take the tree down and consider the Christmas season at an end. The Kings were, of course, the Three Kings or Wise Men who brought gifts to the Christ child in Bethlehem, and to the Spanish and their children they take the place of Father Christmas.

I happened to be in Barcelona for this holiday not long ago, and I was fascinated by the legends and traditions surrounding it. Between five and six on the afternoon of January 5 the Kings appear in the harbor on a beautiful ship, are rowed to shore, and parade through the city in full regalia with their retinue, much to the delight of the children, who are looking forward to the gifts that will be distributed through the windows that evening. Up until midnight the streets of Barcelona were thronged with people buying gifts and visiting the special gift and candy and sweet-meat shops that are set up only for this occasion.

Certain traditional foods are made just for this holiday. One is a form of Twelfth Night cake, like the galette du rois of France. It is decorated with green angelica and red cherries that resemble the holly leaves and berries of our Christmas cakes, and a crown of icing or gold paper. Baked inside are tiny, tiny charms which, if you are not terribly careful, you can miss and swallow. Each has a particular meaning—they bode good luck or money or poverty or whatever may be in store for the year ahead.

The candy shops are a picture. One of the Kings' Day traditions is to give marzipan candies, and as I wandered through Barcelona on January 5 I saw marzipan in just about every shape you can imagine. There were long braided strings of marzipan garlic and onions, every sort of known vegetable and fruit, and marvelous little marzipan plates of olives, orange sections, fried eggs, anchovies—all fashioned of tinted marzipan. If you had wanted, you could have reconstructed a whole hors d'oeuvre tray with these pretty little marzipan fruits, vegetables, fish, and meats.

I don't think I've ever seen more of the real spirit of giving and fun than in Barcelona. From the smallest bookstores and boutiques to the big department stores, the shops were packed with people and their excited, eager children.

Except for two or three pre-Christmas Saturdays in New York, I have never known such a rush to buy and to have the things bought beautifully wrapped—there must have been millions of yards of gorgeous wrapping papers. It made you long to be buying for and giving to a large family your-self. Some of the better shops have for years had a tradition that I think will astound you as it did me. They not only wrap gifts but have a special delivery service of men dressed as the Three Kings who go around after nightfall leaving packages on the windows and sometimes entering houses through the windows to distribute the gifts and candies.

On January 6, all the children get gifts from their parents, grandparents, aunts, and uncles, and taxis are at a premium as people go from house to house leaving and receiving presents. It's all very gay and jolly. The weather was mild, so a friend and I sat in an outdoor cafe and watched the promenade of parents with children sporting their new treasures. We were amused to see that in Spain cowboy and Indian outfits seem to have taken over completely from the traditional matador costume.

Eating comes second only to giving on Kings' Day. We made luncheon reservations at one of the oldest restaurants in Barcelona, the Antica Casa Solla, which is in Barcelonette, the ancient part of the city near the docks. Thank goodness we did. When we arrived at about one thirty, early for lunch in Spain, there was only one vacant table—all the rest were occupied or reserved—and when we left at three fifteen there was a long line of people waiting to get in. We ate a delicious suckling pig with aïoli, a Kings' Day specialty that is a particular favorite in this part of Spain. In the restaurant there was much gaiety and exchange of greetings and eating and drinking. By the time we had finished lunch the long round of gift giving and feasting had begun to tell, and all around us children were falling asleep on their chairs.

Kings' Day in Barcelona was a most exhilarating experience. The streets were magnificently decorated, and in the Town Hall there was a great crèche with figures made of tiles and enamel, very beautiful and startlingly modern, something I'm sure no American city would ever countenance. At noon there was a big reception at the Town Hall and the House of Deputies. The buildings were illuminated with spotlights, tapestries had been thrown over the balconies, and the army was out in full dress in honor of this happiest of all celebrations.

Couscous—A Taste of the Exotic

People often ask me to suggest a different but not too expensive dish to serve at a big party. Lately, I have been recommending couscous, the national dish of the North African countries of Morocco, Tunisia, and Algeria. You may have seen, in the better kitchen equipment shops, a couscousier, the traditional pot in which couscous is cooked. It looks like an enormous double boiler with a deep bottom and a perforated top in which the couscous grain, a fairly coarse ground wheat, is steamed over an aromatic spicy stew. There are two types of couscous to be found in gourmet specialty shops and groceries selling Middle East foods—the instant and the long-cooking. I find the latter gives the best results.

I accompany my favorite Moroccan version of couscous with a fiery sauce piquante and a subtly flavored Moroccan chicken dish that is served with pickled lemons.

As these have to be made ahead of time, first I'm going to give you the recipe for *Pickled Lemons*. Slice 6 lemons just over ¼ inch thick, put in a colander, and sprinkle heavily with coarse salt. Cover with plastic wrap, and drain over a bowl for 24 hours. Wash off salt, pack the lemons into quart jars with coarse salt (about 2 tablespoons per jar), and fill the jars with vegetable oil. Cover jars with lids and let stand from 5 days to 3 weeks, by which time the lemons will be soft, mellow, and not at all bitter.

Start the *Couscous* about 2 hours before your party. To serve twelve to sixteen, put in the bottom of the couscousier (if you don't have one, use an 8-quart cooking pot over which you can fit a colander) 1 pound neck or shoulder of lamb cut in 1½-inch cubes, 2 large onions, thinly sliced, 1 teaspoon each of ginger and turmeric, 2 teaspoons freshly ground black pepper, ½ cup vegetable oil, 2 ounces butter, a pinch of saffron, and enough water to come 2 inches above the ingredients. Bring this to a rapid boil.

Line the colander or steamer top of the couscousier with cheesecloth to prevent the grains from falling through, add 2 pounds long-cooking couscous, and put over the boiling stew. Cover with the couscousier lid or wrap aluminum foil tightly over the colander, and put more foil around the point where colander and pot meet to keep the steam from escaping. Steam 1 hour, then remove the steamer top and run cold water over the puffed-up couscous for 2 or 3 minutes, breaking up the lumps with your fingers. Set aside to drain.

To the stew in the pot, add 6 scraped and quartered carrots, 4 peeled and quartered turnips, and 4 peeled and quartered potatoes. Cover and cook 20 minutes. Meanwhile, turn the drained couscous into a big bowl and mix in thoroughly, by hand, ¼ cup vegetable oil and 3 teaspoons salt. Replace in steamer. Add to stew 3 thickly sliced zucchini, 1 can drained and rinsed chickpeas, and ¼ cup seedless raisins. Put steamer over stew, cover, and steam for another 20 minutes.

≈ Start the Moroccan chicken dish, *Djaj M'Kalli*, the night before. Remove all fat from three 3-pound chickens, and rub them well with 2 tablespoons coarse salt mixed with 3 chopped garlic cloves. Let stand 1 hour. Wipe off salt. Rub chickens with a mixture of 1 cup vegetable oil, 2 teaspoons ginger, 1 teaspoon turmeric, 1 teaspoon black pepper, and a good pinch of saffron. Put in a large bowl with any remaining oil mixture, cover, and refrigerate overnight.

Next day, while the couscous steams, put the chickens in a very large pot with 3 large onions, grated, ¼-pound butter, 3 finely chopped garlic cloves, 2 cups water, and 2 cups chicken stock. Bring to a boil, reduce heat, and simmer until chickens are tender, 40 to 45 minutes. Remove chickens and rapidly boil broth down to a thick, rich sauce, stirring often. Add 1 pound soft ripe olives and a few slices of pickled lemon. Carve chickens and return to simmering sauce to reheat.

≈ Now make the *Sauce Piquante*. Whirl in a blender 2 or 3 hot red peppers with 3 tablespoons olive oil, 1 crushed garlic clove, 1 teaspoon Tabasco, and ¼ cup finely ground walnuts.

Now you are ready to assemble everything. Transfer the steamed couscous to a bowl, and mix in 4 tablespoons butter. Mound the couscous on a very large platter. Drain stewed meat and vegetables and arrange on one side, with carved chicken and olives on the other. Put the stock from the stew in one bowl, the sauce from the chicken in another. Have the sauce piquante and drained pickled lemons in separate bowls. Serve each guest some couscous as a base, a piece of chicken, some lamb and vegetables, and spoon stock over the couscous, sauce over the chicken. Let them help themselves to the lemons and a judicious dab of the blistering-hot sauce piquante.

With the couscous I serve pita, the flat Middle East bread (see page 206), and a good, chilled rosé wine. Dessert can be a cool, refreshing apricot sherbet.

This Moroccan feast is a beautiful, exciting combination of colors, textures, and flavors, an exotic tour de force that will earn you full marks as an imaginative cook, and it will serve twelve to sixteen people easily. You can serve it buffet style or Moroccan fashion, with the dishes on a low table and the guests seated on cushions around it. ≈

Introducing Mezze

I've always been a devotee of hors d'oeuvre, and ever since I visited Iran and other parts of the Near and Middle East, I've become utterly addicted to mezze, the type of hors d'oeuvre you find there. In one particular section of the great bazaars of Teheran are little shops that specialize in mezze, where for almost no money you can feast on a staggering variety of tastes and textures, from savory pastries to tiny bites of fried liver.

Now I'm not talking about the cocktail appetizers we know, but the little platters of different foods you are served in Provence, Greece, Iran, Egypt, and other places as a beautifully presented first course or snack. I remember starting lunch with a table of mezze in a small restaurant in Isfahan, that magic city of exquisite mosques and marvelous architecture. The thing that struck me most was a bowl heaped with tiny sprigs of crisp, freshly washed herbs—tarragon, thyme, basil, mint, parsley, coriander, everything you could possibly imagine—which one munched on along with the bread and other mezze. It was a memorable beginning to the meal, and if you grow herbs in the summer and don't know what to do with them all, there's your answer.

I'm going to mention a few mezze so you will get an idea of what they are like. There are eggplant dishes: eggplant purée made with oil, garlic, parsley, and lemon juice, sometimes called poor man's caviar; another very old version which includes yogurt and sometimes highly seasoned meatballs; fried eggplant with yogurt and mint. Many other mezze are fried—fried mussels, fried cheese, fried brains served cold with parsley and lemon, fried minced chicken balls flavored with turmeric, the fried patties of ground and spiced white broad beans called ta'amia, one of Egypt's national dishes. Then, of course, that wonderful tahini, the sesame-seed paste we buy canned in Greek and health food stores and delicatessens, combined with chickpeas in hummus bi tahini (see page 106), with salt fish, or in a cream salad (which we would call a dip) with yogurt, lemon, garlic, and parsley—and the divine taramasalata of Greece and Turkey, a "cream salad" of smoked cod's roe, garlic, oil, lemon, and milk-soaked bread.

Lately, since avocados have been introduced to the Middle East, the Israelis have contributed a new mezze—avocado purées mixed with cream cheese, or tuna and mayonnaise, very different from guacamole or the avocado dips we know.

One of the mezze most people have heard of, and invariably love, is stuffed vine leaves. These, naturally, are grape leaves, which we buy in jars or cans, preserved in brine. Before using them you should get rid of the brine by putting them in a bowl and pouring hot water over them, making sure it penetrates between the leaves. Let them soak for 20 minutes, drain, soak in cold water, drain again, then repeat the whole process one more time.

Middle East cuisine enchants me. The flavors and combinations of foods are so unusual and delicious. For the last couple of years I've been cooking dishes from *A Book of Middle Eastern Food* by my good friend Claudia Roden, who was born and raised in Cairo and now lives in London.

I'm going to give you her recipe for *Cold Stuffed Vine Leaves*, because it is traditional, honest, and extraordinarily good. Drain a 1-pound jar or can of vine leaves (40 to 50 leaves), and wash off the brine. For the filling, cook ¾ cup long-grain rice by your favorite method, drain thoroughly and mix with 2 to 3 ripe tomatoes, peeled and chopped, 1 large onion, finely chopped, or 12 green onions, finely cut (include some of the green part), 2½ tablespoons finely chopped parsley, 2 to 2 ½ tablespoons crushed dried mint. ¼ teaspoon ground cinnamon, ¼ teaspoon allspice, and salt and freshly ground black pepper to taste. Mix this filling well.

Place the leaves on a plate, vein side up, and put a heaping teaspoon of filling in the center, near the stem edge. Fold the stem end up over the filling, then fold both sides toward the middle and roll up like a small cigar. Squeeze lightly in the palm of your hand. You'll get the knack after doing a few. Pack the rolls tightly in a pan lined with slices of tomato (this prevents the leaves from sticking to the pan and burning), and slip 3 to 4 cloves of garlic in between them. Mix together ½ cup olive oil, ½ cup water, ¼ teaspoon powdered saffron (this is optional), 1 teaspoon sugar, and the juice of 1 or more lemons.

Pour this over the rolls, then put a small plate on top to prevent their unwinding. Cover the pan and simmer very, very gently for at least 2 hours, until thoroughly cooked. Add water occasionally, about half a cup at a time, as the liquid becomes absorbed. Let the rolls cool in the pan before turning out. Serve cold, with drinks or as part of a table of mezze.

Portable Feasts

Ever since I was a child in the Pacific Northwest, I've had a passion for picnics. I can remember picnics at the beach or in the woods when the salty tang of the sea breeze or the fresh sharp scent of the pines seemed like nature's spice for the food we were eating. A picnic can be anything you make it—great baskets of luxurious delicacies served on fine linen with your best glass and china, or just a half-hour halt at some picturesque spot to munch on a sandwich, a piece of Swiss Gruyère or Emmenthaler cheese, a tomato or crisp raw vegetables, and some fruit, with a bottle of wine to wash everything down.

Sandwiches might have been invented for this kind of portable feast, and they don't have to be as dull as some people make them—a slice of dried-out chicken or limp roast beef between two pieces of flabby bread is hardly worth the trip. There is a tremendous repertory of really exciting and interesting sandwiches to draw on, all easy to prepare.

One of my favorites is the Italian *Pan Bagna*. For this you take the large roll known as a hero roll, or a small loaf of French bread, or a hard round roll, split it, and brush the bottom part lightly with olive or salad oil (olive oil gives the most flavor). Let it stand for a little to let the oil sink in, then cover with very thin slices of red or white onion. Top these with green pepper strips, tomato slices, and a few anchovy fillets or, if you prefer, pieces of tuna. Slice a few pitted black olives, strew these on top, and season to taste with salt and pepper. Brush the top half of the roll with oil (if you are a garlic lover, rub it with a garlic clove first to give a little more zing), put the halves together, press down firmly, wrap in foil, waxed paper, or plastic wrap, and take it along with you. The longer it sits, the better it tastes because the delicious flavors have a chance to get together.

Or you might make *Egg and Onion Sandwiches*. Sauté ½ cup finely chopped onion or green onion in 1 tablespoon butter for a few minutes, until just wilted and soft. Toss in about ½ cup finely chopped mushrooms, if you have them, and cook down with the onions for 2 or 3 minutes. Salt and pepper the mixture, let it cool, then toss with 4 finely chopped hard-boiled eggs and, if it needs binding, a tiny bit of mayonnaise. Spread this on whole-wheat or rye bread, and there's your sandwich.

I'm also very fond of tongue sandwiches with horseradish butter, for which this delicate meat seems to have a great affinity. Get your butter quite soft, cream it, and beat in grated fresh horseradish to taste and a touch of prepared mustard. Spread a layer of this on a slice of bread, cover with very thin slices of cooked fresh tongue or smoked tongue, and top with another slice of bread for an unusual, piquant combination.

~ Then, of course, there is our old friend the onion sandwich. For this I've found nothing is better than oatmeal bread. Spread it with butter, top with paper-thin onion slices, salt, clap the other slice of bread on top, and press down tightly. Take a deviled egg, some cold chicken, or a ripe tomato to eat with your onion sandwiches, have a bottle of wine or beer, and you've got a great picnic.

~ To make the *Oatmeal Bread*, first dissolve 2 packages active dry yeast and 2 teaspoons sugar in 1 cup lukewarm water—110 to 115 degrees. Let stand for 10 minutes, then stir very well. Cream ⅓ cup butter in a large mixing bowl, add 1 cup boiling water, and stir until completely melted. Add 1 cup rolled oats, ⅓ cup molasses, and 1 tablespoon salt. Blend thoroughly and cool to lukewarm. Add the yeast, then fold in 5½ cups sifted flour. Add 1 egg and beat well. Put the dough in a buttered mixing bowl, turning it so it is well greased on all sides, then refrigerate for at least 2 hours—you can leave it for 3 or 4 hours and it won't hurt. Turn out the chilled dough on a floured board and shape into two loaves. Place in well-buttered 9-by-5-inch loaf pans, and let rise in a warm, draft-free spot until double in bulk, about 2 hours.

Bake in a 350-degree oven for approximately 1 hour, or until the loaves are nicely browned and sound hollow when you rap the bottom with your knuckles. Remove from the pans and cool on a rack. This makes excellent sandwiches and the best toast ever.

Supermarket Picnics

Any place where there are a few blades of grass and a place to sit down is picnic ground for me. I love eating in the outdoors, and I love a casual picnic just as much as, or even more than, an elaborate gastronomic delight with wines and a great variety of hot and cold foods that has taken hours of preparation. I've enjoyed just about every imaginable kind of picnic, from a small and elegant feast of champagne and caviar to a big homely affair of cold fried chicken, potato salad, baked beans, homemade bread, and chocolate cake, with lots of beer and loads of coffee to wash it all down.

My favorite summertime picnic is the impromptu one that just happens. You are driving along and suddenly you say, "Goodness, wouldn't it be fun to have a picnic?" So you stop and buy some food and just do it.

A few years ago I was taking a long tour through the western states with friends, and one night we had dinner at a place in Idaho where the specialty was chicken, and very good chicken it was. They had an hors d'oeuvre of giblets, so we asked for a double order, kept some overnight in a small refrigerator, and had them for our picnic next day along with a loaf of freshly baked bread we bought on the road.

Recently I have been doing some trekking along the Oregon coast, and I've had several impromptu picnics that I thought you might like to hear about, if you are a picnic buff, too. These are the kind of picnics that are great fun and very easy because you don't have to prepare and pack any food—you just pick it up en route. If you keep in the car a little basket with knives, forks, spoons, napkins, and a can opener and buy plastic or paper plates and plastic glasses at a dime store, you have no waste and no worries.

One of our most successful picnics was completely unplanned. On that particular day we had driven farther than we had intended and we were hungry, so we stopped at the nearest big supermarket.

First we bought a half-gallon jug of California red wine. Then I shopped the cheese counter and found a nice-looking Swiss cheese, some Cheddar and Monterey Jack, and, being the adventurous type, I took a chance on a canned Camembert. The meat section came up with an acceptable Polish sausage and a salami, so I headed for the mustard shelf and picked out a jar of mustard.

The bread situation wasn't very satisfactory, so I bought some interesting crackers and English water biscuits and a stick of butter. With a basket of cherry tomatoes and some nice ripe plums (there were beautiful strawberries, but I decided on the plums) this turned out to be a most gratifying repast. The sausages, crackers, and wine were good, the cheeses pleasant although not startling, and we sat and looked at the ocean, chatting and having a perfectly delightful time, and there were no dirty dishes, no debris, only the knives to wash when we got home.

Another day we knew we were going to picnic but we didn't want to make a big production out of it, so we just took along a couple of bottles of white wine in a cooler and some hard-boiled eggs, and once more investigated the supermarket. Supermarkets in the West have marvelous produce, and we bought bunches of beautiful big radishes, scallions, tomatoes, a jar of herring tidbits, canned Norwegian sardines, the kind that have such a delicate smoked flavor, and lemon to squeeze on them, rye bread and butter, and Norwegian flatbread. Rye bread goes so well with any kind of smoked fish—be it sardines, smoked salmon, or kippered sturgeon. With nectarines for dessert we had a perfect picnic, with no trouble, no leftovers, everything disposable and delicious.

Perhaps if there were really good wayside inns in this country, as there are in Europe, the urge to picnic would not be quite as strong, although as far as I'm concerned, I will swap a wayside inn for a picnic any day—unless it happens to be a three-star restaurant with impeccable food and wine. But no matter how famous it was, I don't think it would be half as much fun as hunting a cozy spot to have a supermarket picnic.

CHAPTER 10

Memorable Meals, Places, and People

☙

... in which we are entertained by a fearless host ... an artist with a fine Italian hand for cooking ... and an American in Provence ... find a welcome in Ireland ... and in Maryland ... stoke up with a smörgåsbord break-fast ... delight in a delicacy in Lyon ... take a chance on cullen skink in Scotland .... come out for common mar-kets ... are seduced by socca in Nice ... glory in garlic in Catalonia ... are surprised by bleeding mushrooms in Majorca ... and have a field day of fish at Prunier's.

The Perfect Dinner Party

I often have people say to me, "I would be afraid to ask *you* to dinner." Well, why? Everyone has some specialty he does extraordinarily well, be it bacon and eggs or chili or chef's salad or filet of beef en croûte, so why should entertaining be such a problem? The thing is to entertain within your scope and not get yourself in an uproar by feeling you have to attempt something beyond it. Even if you serve the simplest of meals—just one course with a bottle of wine and some cheese—that's true hospitality. Hospitality is enjoying a meal with your friends, and enjoyment is the key word.

I'm sure we've all suffered through the nerve-racking experience of dining at a house where the host or hostess, who is doing the cooking, keeps on twitching and nervously getting up and rushing to the kitchen. By the time you sit down to dinner you feel it can't possibly be worth all that effort.

The perfect dinner party is the kind I attended the other evening. It was given by Maurice Moore-Betty, a man of great charm and distinction who happens to be a well-known cooking teacher and cookbook author. Apart from the fact that the meal was extremely well planned, well cooked, and well presented, what impressed me most was that there was no visible display of dinner being prepared, no air of unease. Our host excused himself twice, briefly, about ten minutes in all, came back, replenished someone's drink, chatted, and then asked us in to the dining room, which makes one enormous open-plan room with the kitchen where he gives classes. The table was beautifully set with silver, glasses, candles, plates for the first course, and two small terrines. As we sat down he brought in the first course, hot asparagus which he had drained and put on a napkin in a silver dish. With this we had our choice from the terrines of hollandaise sauce, which he had made ahead and put on the table while he was away from his guests, and vinaigrette sauce. I didn't try the hollandaise, but the vinaigrette was extremely good with a plenitude of fresh herbs—chives, parsley, and a tiny touch of mint.

When we had finished the asparagus, Maurice went on talking with us as he removed the plates and popped them right in the dishwasher. He then brought the wine to the table and took from the oven a large casserole of potatoes boulangère (for which I'll give you the recipe later) and a double rack of lamb, timed to the minute. Without any lull in the conversation, he carved, served us, and we continued our meal.

After the main course, he again cleared the table and brought from the refrigerator two desserts, baked pears delicately spiced with cloves and a frozen chocolate mousse, unmolded on a plate, which he took straight from the freezer and cut on a serving table. At the last minute he poured water on the coffee, so right after dessert we had coffee and liqueurs.

By actual timing, we had been at table just an hour and a half, enjoying good talk, excellent food, and the personal service of our host. A dinner like this, perfectly planned, perfectly cooked, and perfectly simple—no bread, no relishes, no salad, no fuss, no rush—is all one needs. This is the way to entertain; otherwise give it up.

Potatoes boulangère, which means "potatoes from the baker," is something that originated years ago, when people in rural France didn't have ovens, as they do now. They put the Sunday roast of lamb in a dish, surrounded it with sliced onions and potatoes, and took it to the baker, to be cooked in his oven while the family went to church. Afterward, they picked it up, done to a turn, and took it home for lunch.

To prepare *Maurice Moore-Betty's Potatoes Boulangère* to serve four, peel and very thinly slice 4 medium-large potatoes—the slices should be paper-thin. Heat 3 tablespoons butter and 2 tablespoons oil in a skillet, add 2 medium onions, thinly sliced, and cook until golden and soft (not brown), shaking the pan occasionally. Liberally butter a 2-quart baking dish. Put in a layer of potatoes. Drain the cooked onions, saving the liquid from the pan, and put a layer of onion on top of the potatoes. Season with salt and pepper. Continue to make layers of potatoes and onions, seasoning the layers, and end with a top layer of potatoes. Season with more salt and pepper, dot with butter and pour on the liquid from the onions and just enough water to reach the top of the potatoes. Bake in a 375-degree oven until the liquid has been absorbed and the potatoes test tender with a fork, about 30 or 40 minutes. You don't need an elaborate meat dish to complement the good taste of these baker's potatoes, just plain roast lamb or beef, steak, meat loaf, or braised lamb shanks. You can vary the recipe by adding a touch of thyme or rosemary to the seasonings or dotting more butter between the layers.

Potatoes boulangère with their crusty brown top and luscious flavor of onion look marvelously appetizing, make very good eating, and take a minimum of preparation and no watching. These are all factors to take into account if you and your guests are going to enjoy a perfect, well-planned dinner.

An Artist in the Kitchen

Every once in a while you go to someone's house for lunch or dinner and have a meal that is so utterly satisfying in every way that you leave thinking: "That was exactly what I wanted to eat today!"

Granted, these occasions don't come too often, so when they do they are all the more to be savored. Recently I had an experience like that, one that was completely unexpected, for I was invited to lunch by someone I had never met. I left well fed and well entertained, feeling that I had found new food and new friends all in one day.

My new friends are Ed and Ellie Giobbi, a genuine, charming young couple who live with their three children in a rambling country house in Katonah, New York. Ed Giobbi is a well-known artist whose paintings hang in many museums and private collections, and his other passion, next to art, is cooking—the honest, simple, nourishing, and flavorful Italian country cooking he learned from his family and friends here and in Italy. To him, cooking is a joy, a celebration of life, as absorbing and rewarding a pursuit as painting, to which he feels it is closely allied. In fact, he says, if he hadn't been able to cook cheap, nutritious meals for himself when he was a struggling art student he might never have survived the poverty and hardships an artist experiences in his early years.

One of the remarkable things about the Giobbis is that they grow or prepare about 80 percent of the food they eat. They raise squab, rabbits, ducks, and chickens, grow vegetables, herbs, and fruit, and in summer, when they go to their house on Cape Cod, Ed buys a whole 165-pound tuna which he cans in olive oil. He also cans his own tomatoes, makes pesto, that sublime green sauce for pasta, from the basil flourishing in the herb garden, and even presses grapes and makes wine, an art he learned from his father.

A carafe of Ed's wine was on the table when we sat down on the porch for lunch, and a loaf of bread freshly baked by Ellie. The food Ed had cooked was so unusual and delicious that I'm going to give you recipes for two of the dishes. One used breast of veal, an economical cut which is usually cooked with the bone left in and a pocket cut in it for the stuffing.

&This *Stuffed Breast of Veal with Marsala* had been completely boned, so he started with one large flat piece of meat that was spread with the stuffing and rolled up like a jelly roll.

For the stuffing, mix 1½ cups fresh ricotta cheese (if unavailable, put cottage cheese through a rather fine sieve to get the same texture as ricotta), 2 tablespoons chopped parsley (preferably the broad-leafed Italian parsley), 3 tablespoons grated Parmesan cheese, 1 lightly beaten egg, ¼ teaspoon nutmeg, ¼ pound chopped boiled ham, 1 teaspoon salt, and ½ teaspoon freshly ground black pepper. Blend well. Lay the veal flat and spread the stuffing over the surface, being careful not to get it too close to the edges of the meat. Gently roll as for a jelly roll, tie the roll with string, and sew the ends together to prevent the stuffing, which expands as it cooks, from oozing out. Rub the roll with salt, pepper, and 2 tablespoons butter or olive oil, place in a baking pan, and sprinkle the roll with 1 teaspoon rosemary. Bake in a 450-degree oven, uncovered, for 1 hour, basting often with the pan juices. Add ¾ cup Marsala wine, cover, and cook for 30 minutes more, basting frequently. The roll tastes best cold or tepid, so when you take it from the oven let it rest for at least 3 hours before serving. It is even better the next day. To serve, cut into ½-inch slices. You'll have a most attractive effect of layers of stuffing meat, and enough to serve four easily.

You could serve noodles or cornmeal polenta with the roll, or the unusual vegetable dish we had, *Verdura Mista*, a really delicate blend of flavors.

Peel and dice 1 very large potato, and cut 1 stalk celery into 1-inch pieces. Wash and chop 1 pound fresh spinach, ½ pound escarole, and ½ pound Savoy cabbage or ordinary cabbage. Put all the vegetables in a deep pot and pour boiling water over them. Let the water return to the boil, then drain the vegetables, saving ½ cup of the water. Heat 3 tablespoons olive oil in a big skillet, sauté 2 finely chopped garlic cloves until they begin to brown, then add the blanched vegetables and salt and pepper to taste. Cover and cook over low heat until vegetables are tender, adding some of the reserved water if the mixture gets too dry.

This was one of the most enjoyable luncheons I have had in a long time, cooked as Ed believes food should be—with a free hand, creatively, using the freshest ingredients you can get.

An American in Provence

It isn't often you find an American who has made a reputation as a culinary authority in a country as supercritical about food as France, but Richard Olney has—and rightly. Richard was born in Iowa, but he has lived in France for more than twenty years and is the only regular American contributor to the leading French gastronomic review, *Cuisine et Vins de France*.

Like me, Richard is in love with the light, the landscape, and the odors of Provence. He has a tiny house in Solliès-Toucas, a village in the south of France. To reach his house, which is far away from other houses of the village, perched on a crag of rock overlooking the stupendously beautiful countryside and hills of Provence, you must drive up a steep, steep incline. The struggle of getting all the provisions, wine, and fuel up that precipitous hill must be tremendous, but despite the difficulties, some wonderfully good food comes out of Richard's kitchen, which is dominated by a huge stone fireplace where he does a great deal of open-fire cookery and spit roasting.

When I was in Provence recently, some friends and I were invited to luncheon by Richard, and after a two-hour drive, we arrived with keen appetites. The remarkable thing about the meal, apart from the excellence of the food, was the way it was cooked—with love and care, but totally without fanfare or any great show of performance.

We started with a mousseline of merlan and oursins (whiting and sea urchins), a very light fine mousse of the fish and the orange roe of the sea urchins which had been put through a fine sieve, mixed with egg whites and heavy cream, beaten well over ice, then poached in a mold well in advance and finally coated with a natural jelly. Sliced, it was a most delicate coral pink with an unforgettably good combination of fish flavors, herbs, and a touch of Sauternes.

Just before we sat down to the mousseline, Richard put a pheasant on a spit in front of the fire to turn and roast while we took our leisurely time eating the first course and drinking a delicious white Burgundy. When the pheasant was done just to the right point, it was carved and served with shoestring potatoes, sautéed very quickly in butter in a heavy pan until they were almost a pancake, with a crisp brown crust contrasting with the soft white inside.

Another extremely interesting dish, served as a separate course, was a ragoût printanier, a kind of vegetable stew that is one of Richard's specialties. The basic idea is so simple that anyone can follow it, and it's fun to play around with because you can use your imagination in putting together all kinds of combinations of vegetables, adding any herb you prefer.

Our *Ragoût Printanier* started with tiny artichokes, so young the choke was undeveloped and didn't have to be removed. Only the stems and tough outer leaves were trimmed away. (These baby artichokes, so tender they can be eaten whole, are usually sold in Italian markets and occasionally in supermarkets, but if you can't find them you could substitute frozen artichoke hearts.) These went into a big sauté pan with a large chunk of butter, 4 or 5 unpeeled garlic cloves, some tiny white onions, skinned young broad beans (the Italian fava), salt, pepper, and a pinch or two of summer savory. The pan was covered and shaken often while the vegetables cooked over fairly moderate heat, with an occasional testing, until they reached just the right crisp tenderness. At the last minute, they were given a sprinkling of chopped parsley.

The habit of serving vegetables like this as a separate course is very typical of Provence. They may come between the first and main courses, or after the main course, which I think is a most civilized idea. If you have a good entrée with potatoes or rice, it is so intelligent to feature the veg-etables on their own, giving them a chance to shine in their own spotlight, so to speak. You can vary your vegetables according to whatever is in the market—spring carrots, baby zucchini, broccoli, celery hearts, flowerets of cauliflower, tender young peas—taking into account that some will need more, or less, cooking time than others.

We'd had two beautiful wines with our mousseline and pheasant, and we ended our meal with yet another wine, accompanying a platter of cheeses, as is the custom among wine lovers. It was a perfect luncheon, and as we sat and gazed over the countryside, warmed by the great fire in front of which the pheasant had roasted, I felt blissfully relaxed. This, to me, is true entertaining—simple, gracious, and wonderful.

An Irish Welcome

Ireland is a country full of unexpected delights, and not the least of these is finding in remote places extraordinarily good food, cooked with love and care.

One glorious day in April, when the hedges blazed with the golden blossoms of broom and every little front garden flaunted tulips, azaleas, and all the lovely spring flowers, I drove down from Dublin to one of the most interesting inns I have ever stayed in. It's called Ballymaloe House, and it lies in the rolling farmland of east Cork, near the tiny village of Shanagarry on the Ballycotton road, not far from the town of Midleton. The house is on a 400-acre working farm where owners Ivan and Myrtle Allen raise sheep, cows, pigs, and chickens, fruits, and vegetables. Under 200 acres of glass are grown mushrooms, tomatoes, cucumbers, and straw-berries, all of which appear regularly on the inn's menus.

The house is great fun. It started as a Geraldine castle, and the four-teenth-century keep still stands in its original form, but the main building has been rebuilt, added to, and modernized over the centuries, and it ram-bles all over the place, with tucked-away rooms and stairways. There are thirteen rooms in the main house, more in the coachyard buildings and gate lodge, and, for passing the time in true country style, there's a swim-ming pool, tennis courts, a nine-hole golf course, horses to ride, and trout ponds to fish in. What makes Ballymaloe so distinctive, though, is the feeling you get the minute you walk in of being in a private country house. There's no desk where you are obliged to register. You are welcomed warmly and shown to your room, where you find little nosegays of fresh flowers. If the night is cool, there's a comforting surprise—a hot-water bottle in your bed.

The dining room, called the Yeats Room because the walls are hung with genre paintings by one of Ireland's best-known artists, Jack B. Yeats, brother of the poet, is also open to the public for dinner, Tuesday through Thursday. It has earned high praise and awards in Europe and America for the quality of the food, and small wonder. Mrs. Allen, who does all the cooking herself with the help of four local girls in the kitchen, is an imag-inative, creative cook who seeks out the best-quality materials that she can find. Hers is good, honest, flavorful country food, lovingly prepared and well served. She is a follower of my writings and flattered me by telling me that the night I arrived (and she hadn't known I was coming) she had one of my recipes on the menu.

That evening for dinner I first chose from a two-tiered hors d'oeuvre cart laden with vegetable salads, a finely textured chicken liver pâté, and lots of dishes made from the seafood for which Ireland is famous—cockles and mussels from County Kerry in rémoulade sauce, lobster and crab from the west, fresh salmon from the Shannon, and a very good scallop and rice salad. Passing up the soups, I found it hard to decide which of the main dishes to have and finally picked the pork with garlic. The skin had been left on and scored in the English and Irish manner so it roasted to a lovely crisp crackling, and the meat had been rubbed with garlic and then roasted with more garlic cloves in the pan, which gave the pork an unusual, lively flavor. With this there were vegetables from the farm. Finally, another cart arrived with a most tempting selection of desserts, from tiny tarts filled with poached rhubarb to a delicious cream-filled nutted meringue.

Next morning I breakfasted on good Irish bacon, freshly gathered eggs with rich yellow yolks, and a wonderful whole-wheat bread Mrs. Allen had made, not the usual soda bread, but a bread made with yeast, coarse whole meal, and a touch of molasses. It was dark, nutty, chewy, the very soul of bread, and I got the recipe so you could try it.

To prepare *Myrtle Allen's Brown Bread*, put 3¾ cups whole-wheat flour (preferably the stone-ground flour sold in health-food stores) in a large mixing bowl, and place in a warm oven—a gas oven with the pilot light on or an electric oven set as low as possible. Both flour and bowl should be warm when you make the bread.

Dissolve 1½ packages granular yeast in ½ cup hot water (105 to 110 degrees). Blend 2 tablespoons unsulfured molasses with ½ cup water of the same temperature. Combine the flour, proofed yeast, molasses, and 1 tablespoon salt. Add enough hot water to make a wet sticky dough (about 1 cup or more according to the flour). Put directly into a buttered 9-by-5-by-3-inch bread tin and allow to rise by one-third its original size. Bake in a 450-degree oven for 50 minutes, or until the crust is nicely browned and the loaf sounds hollow when tapped. Remove from the pan and leave on the rack in the turned-off oven for 20 minutes more to give a crustier exterior.

As I drove away after breakfast down a driveway banked with huge bushes of rhododendrons in brilliant bloom, past soft green fields where sheep grazed, like a scene from an eighteenth-century print, I thought what a delightful way and place this would be to live. I shall carry the memory of peaceful Ballymaloe and its wonderful Irish food and welcome for a long, long time.

Crab Galore

I don't think I could ever have my fill of crab, which is my all-time favorite shellfish, but I came pretty close to it one summer in Maryland, where for five straight days I ate crab—I must have had it eight or nine times. It was in Maryland that I came across Phillips Crab House, a restaurant in Ocean City, on the Atlantic, that I consider to be unique and one of the best seafood houses in this country. There are so many things that make it different and distinctive and good.

It's a family operation, run by Shirley and Brice Phillips with their sons Steven and Jeffery, Steven's wife Olivia, and Shirley's mother, Mrs. Lily Flowers, who is famous for her crab cakes. The Crab House started in the smallest way in 1956 when Mr. and Mrs. Phillips, who operated a seafood packing plant, had such a surplus of crabs that they looked around for a retail outlet and found a tiny shack on Philadelphia Avenue in Ocean City where they opened a four-table restaurant and take-out service.

As the boys grew up, they brought their friends to help in the kitchen, which led to the Phillipses' practice of hiring mainly college kids whom they could train the way they wanted. The Crab House has now expanded through constant building to a rambling, enormous place seating 1,200 people. During the height of the season, between 7,000 and 8,000 meals are served a day—by the happiest, smartest, most adorable bunch of young girls you've ever seen.

Every year the Phillipses take on 350 college boys and girls from all over the country (many are repeaters; their present chef came to them when he was sixteen). Of these, 175 are waitresses, handpicked from 2,000 applicants by Shirley Phillips, an enchanting, bright-eyed, slim woman who looks hardly older than a college girl herself. She and her husband love and look after the young people, taking them out in groups of thirty every Tuesday for a day at the beach and dinner afterward so they get to know each other. "The kids are what made this place—they deserve all the credit for its success," Shirley told me.

That's partly true, but it is undeniably the Phillipses' loving, understanding approach to youth that gives the service at the Crab House such a rare and wonderful warmth and friendliness. The waitresses are told to think of the restaurant as their home and the diners as their guests. They introduce themselves and then write their names on the paper tablecloths so anyone who wants another cup of coffee or the check knows whom to ask for, which I think is a perfectly delightful custom.

Everything about the Crab House is just as personal and pleasant. The dining rooms were decorated by Shirley with stained glass and Tiffany lampshades she collected in the years when they were a drug on the market (she never paid more than two dollars for any of the shades), old trolley-car seats as benches in one room, sewing-machine bases for the wood tabletops, and all kinds of offbeat bits of decor that blend together beautifully in a causal, uncontrived way.

The Crab House has no beer, wine, or liquor license, but it's easy enough to pick up cold beer or a bottle of wine at the Pub in the shopping plaza across the way to go with your seafood dinner. The menu is medium large, with shrimp, lobster, clams, flounder, chicken, ham, and, naturally, crab galore, served in every way imaginable. You can start with cream of crab or vegetable crab soup, then go on to a claw finger cocktail, tiny, tasty little nibbles that you dip in a spicy sauce. There's crab salad, fried softshell crabs, crab Imperial, crab Newburg, crab Thermidor, crab cakes, and that dish so typical of Maryland and Virginia, hot spiced steamed crabs. These are the local blue crabs cooked with a lot of pepper, salt, and spices and served hot or cold, in the shell, with a mallet and pick for you to crack the claws and winkle out the meat, a lovely messy job. It's basically a rather primitive form of the West Coast's cracked Dungeness crab with mayonnaise. That's a much more elegant presentation, but either fashion this is one of the most absorbing and rewarding forms of eating crab.

Another Crab House specialty is *Sautéed Crab Lumps*, a simple and delicious marriage of the flavors of Maryland crab and Virginia ham. For each serving, cook in an individual lidded skillet about ⅓ pound backfin crabmeat in 4 tablespoons butter with a squeeze of lemon juice and seasonings to taste. The Phillipses have their own packaged seafood seasoning, a blend of many spices, but you might use salt, pepper, a touch of onion, a dash of Tabasco, and just a little chopped fresh thyme or savory. Sauté briefly, until the crab is just heated through, then cover it with paper-thin slices of Smithfield ham, put the lid on, and simmer for 2 or 3 minutes until the ham is lightly curled at the edges and the flavors blended. This is awfully good served as it is, or on toast.

Crab dishes like this can, of course, be made with Dungeness crab as well as Maryland crab, but if you happen to be traveling on the eastern seaboard during the summer, do make a stop at the Crab House not only to sample their excellent food but also to enjoy the very special atmosphere of this happiest of restaurants.

Smörgåsbord Breakfast

Perhaps more than any other meal, breakfast is an expression of a country's personality and manner of living. The average American grabs some orange juice, coffee, and maybe a Danish at a drugstore counter on the way to work. The westerner often takes time for bacon, eggs, hash brown potatoes, toast, and coffee. The British dearly love their bacon, tomato, and mushrooms, or sausage and eggs. Breakfast in France is fleeting—café au lait, a croissant, a hard roll with butter and marmalade.

Breakfast in Norway is as staid and unbending as the life pattern of that beautiful but serious-minded Scandinavian country, a firm and formal foundation for the activities of the day. Here breakfast is a cold table or smörgåsbord, very similar to the lunchtime smörgåsbords of Sweden or Denmark, but without certain things one finds at lunch. It is the Norwegian chance to prepare for the day and ignore lunch, as it is known in other countries. Look in the briefcase of a Norwegian businessman, it is said, and you will find papers and one or two smørrebrød, or open-face sandwiches, on which he will lunch while working.

Although I know this statement may well revolt those who can barely open an eye and down a cup of coffee first thing in the morning, I think a cold table with a variety of things to snack on is a great breakfast idea. To me, cold meats, cold chicken, and a little bit of salad are fascinating variations from the usual fare that really intrigue and please my palate.

If you have never walked into a hotel dining room in Norway, you don't know the excitement of looking at a cold table, sometimes 14 or 16 feet long, beautifully arranged with a tremendous selection of foods, starting with the black breads, crisp breads, and other breads for which this country is renowned. The average loaf of bread in Norway is far ahead of that in most countries, for the people demand good baking and so maintain a high standard of flour.

In a hotel dining room where a lot of people are breakfasting you may find five or six different kinds of perfectly sliced cold meats—ham, roast and salt beef, lamb, chicken—cold salmon, cured herring with various sauces, and the eternal Norwegian sardines in two or three guises. There will be cheeses with those fascinating Scandinavian scrapers which shave off paper-thin slices, perfect for putting on bread or a roll. Then there is usually a huge basket of boiled eggs (not always boiled to your order), scrambled eggs, and maybe a hot section with grilled sausage, fish balls, perhaps sautéed small fish and salmon.

Then, of course, marmalade and jams, weinerbrød, which we would call a Danish, orange juice, a big bowl of prunes, and, as a bow to modern civilization, cornflakes and other cereals, and sometimes hot porridge.

The Norwegians, realizing it takes eye appeal to awaken good appetites first thing in the morning, make their spreads a visual feast. Unfortunately, a great many visitors, especially British and American tourists, are not prepared for this kind of breakfast and don't know they are expected to use a number of plates—a different one for fruit and cereal, for meat, for fish, for bread, butter, and marmalade. I have watched people who came upon a Norwegian cold table for the first time stop, stare, walk around it in wonder, look around to see what others are doing, and then dive in, with some often calamitous results. I once saw a couple put prunes and cereal on their plates, add a slice of cheese, some cold ham, a helping of roast beef, then herring with sauce and two or three sardines, also with oil and sauce. By this time their plates were filled. So what did they do? They sprinkled sugar on the cornflakes and poured cream over the prunes and cereal, which oozed into the cheese and meat and fish. Naturally, their breakfast went back to the kitchen uneaten. It reminded me of our buffets at which I've seen guests do this very thing in an equally horrendous way, never stopping to think that even if the hostess does not provide plates, they can still take just one or two things and bring their plate back for the next go-round.

As a matter of fact, if you are thinking of giving a weekend brunch or lunch, you might well have a buffet based on the Norwegian breakfast. You can buy many of the foods, like herring and cold meats, from the delicatessen, and you might make a herring salad, which is a beautiful buffet dish. A proper herring salad is rather involved, but I often make a shortcut version, usually if I've had roast veal or turkey the night before.

To make enough *Shortcut Herring Salad* for four to six, combine a 12-ounce jar of herring tidbits, cut in tiny julienne strips, 1 cup cold tongue (it may be canned), cut in little julienne strips, 1 cup diced cooked veal or cooked breast of turkey or chicken, 1 crisp unpeeled apple, cored and finely diced, half a medium onion, diced, and 1 cup diced cooked potatoes. Add 1 to 2 tablespoons finely chopped fresh dill or 1 teaspoon dried dill, then bind your salad with equal parts of mayonnaise and sour cream, enough to make a pleasantly moist mixture. Arrange on a bed of greens, garnish with quartered hard-cooked eggs, plenty of chopped parsley, and more chopped dill, and, finally, surround it with tiny canned beets, which add flavor and color to your herring salad.

A French Country Dessert

One of the great delights of travel—in this country and abroad—is being able to sample on their own ground some of the superb regional specialties that make eating away from home a continuous adventure. For instance, if you travel through the Burgundian and Beaujolais districts of France you will be staggered by the wealth of distinctive foods, an incredible largess. There are the superlative chickens of Bresse, famous all over France, properly fed until their flesh has an exquisite tenderness and always cooked here to perfection. You will also encounter fine hams and sausages. One sausage in particular, called a rosette, is very similar in appearance to a salami, but it has a definite, spicy flavoring all its own. Here, too, you are near the part of the country where Charolais cattle are raised. Charolais beef is regarded as the choicest in France, and if you eat it in its own bailiwick, perhaps as an entrecôte Béarnaise, steak with a Béarnaise sauce, I think you'll agree that it is extraordinarily fine.

Go to the city of Lyon, and you are deep in the gastronomic heart of France. I believe it can claim more famous restaurants and famous foods than any other single city. Near Lyon there is a charming old hill town, Pérouges, with one or two extremely pleasant restaurants, and there, as in other parts of this district, they make a special dessert that is wonderfully simple and wonderfully good—galette Pérougienne. It is made from a yeast dough rolled very thin and baked very quickly, and it is usually eaten with *crème fraîche*, the French version of heavy cream. Although we don't have *crème fraîche*, I've found there is a way to approximate it with heavy cream. You put 1 pint heavy or whipping cream and 5 tablespoons buttermilk in a screw-topped jar and shake it steadily, as if you were shaking a cocktail, for a full minute. Let it stand at room temperature for 5 or 6 hours, until the buttermilk has clotted the cream to a thick rich texture with an intriguing flavor somewhere between sweet cream and sour cream, and then refrigerate it. If you can't get buttermilk, you can also whip ½ cup heavy cream with ½ cup sour cream to get much the same result.

Now for the recipe for *Galette Pérougienne*, with some of the variations I have worked out on the classic theme. First, make a yeast dough. Dissolve 1 package active dry yeast in ½ cup warm water (105 to 110 degrees) and add 2 tablespoons sugar. Let this proof while you combine in a large bowl 1 cup all-purpose flour, ½ teaspoon salt, the grated rind of ½ lemon, 1 lightly beaten egg, and 1 tablespoon softened butter.

Add the yeast mixture to the flour mixture and blend together very well. When blended, work in another cup of flour, mixing thoroughly. The dough should be quite firm, but not sticky. It does not have to be kneaded, just mixed well with your hands. Or you can make it in an electric mixer that has a dough hook or paddle attachment.

Let the dough stand in a warm place in a greased bowl covered with a cloth until it doubles in bulk, about 1 hour, then divide it in half and roll each half on a lightly floured board into a circle 9 inches in diameter and less than ¼ inch thick. Put each circle in a well-buttered 9-inch cake pan or pie pan, and dot the top of each with ¼ cup butter, cut in small bits. Sprinkle ¼ cup granulated sugar over each circle, and bake in a preheated 450-degree oven for about 6 to 8 minutes, or until just golden in color. While the galettes are still warm and fresh, cut them in small wedges and serve with *crème fraîche*. Or spoon sugared strawberries, raspberries, blueberries, or blackberries over the wedges and top with the cream. You can also sprinkle thinly sliced blanched almonds over the buttered and sugared dough before baking. Any of these versions makes an exciting change from the usual dessert.

Sometimes I roll the dough into an oblong that will fit into a well-buttered 11-by-14-inch jelly-roll pan, sprinkle it lightly with about ¼ cup sugar and arrange on it rows of peeled and quartered peaches or halved and pitted Italian purple prunes, sprinkle the fruit with about ¼ to ½ cup sugar, dot lavishly with butter, and add perhaps a sprinkling of cinnamon, nutmeg, or mace. This I bake at 450 degrees for 5 to 10 minutes, then reduce the heat to 350 degrees and bake about another 20 to 25 minutes, or until the fruit is cooked through (test for tenderness with a fork). I serve this warm, cut in squares, with *crème fraîche*, or with sweetened whipped cream flavored with a touch of bourbon for peaches, cognac for plums. You can, of course, use other fruits, and you'll find the fruit flavor combines with the tender yeastiness of the dough in a most delightful way.

My final version of the galette comes from the south of France. Roll the dough into 9-inch circles and place in buttered 9-inch pans. Sprinkle each one with about ½ cup sifted light or dark brown sugar. For each circle, beat 2 egg yolks well with ½ cup heavy cream, add a pinch of nutmeg or mace, pour this over the brown sugar, and bake in a 375-degree oven until the custardy topping is just set, about 12 to 15 minutes. Serve warm.

The galette is a useful dessert with all the virtues of French country cooking—it is simple, inexpensive, and thoroughly delicious eating, and I think you'll enjoy making it and working out your own variations.

A Great Scottish Soup

I recently had one of the best soups I've had in a long time—Cullen Skink—on a trip to Scotland organized by the British Tourist Association. We stayed at one of the world's most luxurious hotels, the Gleneagles, some 60 miles north of Edinburgh. You have probably heard about it, because of the famous golf courses in the vicinity. The hotel is like an enormous country house, with vast bedrooms, even vaster bathrooms, and a ravishing view of lawns, flowers, and trees.

Dinner on the night of our arrival had been specially planned, and it was very Scottish indeed. We tasted the famed haggis with bashed neeps (mashed yellow turnips), and we had bashed potatoes, too, I might add, and whiskey with the haggis, but it was the cullen skink that really won my heart. This wonderful Scottish soup is a very good and subtle mixture of puréed potato and leek combined with smoked haddock or finnan haddie (originally, Findon haddock) that had been poached in the potato water and partly puréed as well. A bit of the haddock was kept out, crumbled, and added to the soup at the last minute, so there were nice tender little chunks to munch on as you devoured it—and devour it I did.

Finnan haddie is one of the great joys of Scotland and England. I don't think it ever tastes as good here as it does there. I always look forward to having this lightly cured and smoked fish for breakfast, poached in milk in the Scottish way, with a big slather of butter tossed on just before it comes to the table. With good hot toast, tea, and marmalade, it makes a memorable breakfast.

I also like it cut in small pieces and heated in heavy cream with a couple of cherry tomatoes—rich, but delicious. You can heat the flaked poached haddock with melted butter, cream, and a dash of Tabasco and serve it on hot buttered toast with a sprinkling of chopped parsley, or for lunch, bake potatoes, scoop out and mash the pulp, mix it with flaked finnan haddie, milk, butter, salt, and pepper, stuff the shells, and put in a 375-degree oven for 20 minutes until hot and lightly browned.

Poached, chilled finnan haddie tossed with potatoes, onion, and mayonnaise makes an excellent salad, too. All in all, this is a very useful and varied fish, with a superbly smoky flavor.

     To get back to *Cullen Skink*. I have worked out my own version of the Gleneagles recipe, so you don't have to go to Scotland to taste it. Peel 3 medium to large potatoes (preferably the type that come out floury and dry when cooked) and boil until tender in 1½ quarts water with just a touch of salt (not much, as the fish is salty) and 2 or 3 leeks, which you have cut in half lengthwise, rinsed well to remove the sand, halved again, and then cut into small pieces. Remove the cooked potatoes and put them through a food mill or potato ricer. Add to the pot ½ to ¾ pound finnan haddie (sometimes called smoked fillet in our markets) and poach very gently until soft, about 10 to 15 minutes. It should flake extremely easily with a fork. Remove the haddock and put two-thirds of it through the food mill with the little pieces of leek. Combine this purée with the potatoes, mix into the cooking liquid, and blend well. Bring slowly to a boil, stirring so the potato thickens the soup. Taste for seasoning and add salt if needed, freshly ground black pepper, and a tiny bit of grated nutmeg. Stir in 4 or 5 tablespoons butter (more if you want a richer soup), and serve in large soup cups or plates. Crumble the remaining haddock and add just before serving, with some chopped parsley. This will serve six.

For a richer, creamier soup, stir in ½ to 1 cup heavy cream after thickening with the potatoes, and let it come to a boil. Or, if you would like to serve the soup cold, purée all the finnan haddie, chill the soup overnight, and the next day stir in heavy cream to taste. Garnish with finely chopped chives and parsley.

This makes a beautiful cold soup, with great body, flavor, and flair, something quite out of the ordinary.

They say you can't judge a book by its cover. You can't judge a recipe by its name, either. If you should go to Scotland and run across cullen skink on the menu, or partan bree (crab soup), cockaleeky (chicken and leek soup), Forfar bridles (little meat pies), black bun (fruitcake in a pastry crust), or rumbledethumps (a cabbage and potato dish, similar to colcannon), don't turn up your nose at them.

Found, A Woman Chef

For years and years I have been plied with questions as to why there have been no great women chefs. Somehow it never seems to occur to anyone that the reason we have had no female Escoffiers or Montagnés was not lack of talent, but lack of strength and stamina. In the past, embryo chefs started a long period of apprenticeship at the age of eight or nine, spending the first two or three years lifting and polishing heavy copper pots, hauling in coal, and carrying baskets heaped with vegetables, all tasks that a young lady of the same age would find it rather difficult to perform.

However, there have always been, in this country and England, women who made their mark in the world of food. We have been blessed with such accomplished cooks as Eliza Leslie, Sarah Tyson Rorer, Mary Lincoln, Fanny Merritt Farmer, and Irma Rombauer, and, more recently, Dione Lucas and Julia Child. France can claim the great Mère Brazier, who reigned over two restaurants in Lyon and earned her three stars.

Recently, I came across another fine cook when I spent two wonderful days at Inverlochy Castle in Scotland, a most attractive Victorian castle, perhaps more of a hunting lodge. Mr. and Mrs. Hobbs, who keep this as a second home and run it as an inn for part of the year, inherited from Mr. Hobbs's father not only the castle, but also Miss Shaw. Miss Shaw calls herself a self-trained cook, because she does everything by sensing it, but I call her as good a chef as most men. She has a great storehouse of her own dishes, which she makes when the right materials are available, for much of the food is raised on the property. For instance, we had delicious, freshly caught crayfish from Loch Lenny, a lake on the estate. Miss Shaw cooked the crayfish very simply in butter with lemon juice, white wine, and a touch of garlic. The sirloin of beef, from the castle's own Aberdeen Angus cattle, was perfectly pink from the point where the fat ended to where the bone would begin. The beef had been properly raised and hung, so the fat had great flavor and texture. One of my companions remarked that this was the first time in ages he had eaten fat with relish. With the beef we had a beautiful crisp Yorkshire pudding and tiny Brussels sprouts dressed with local butter. Dinner ended with Miss Shaw's luscious unmolded soufflés, sent in on silver platters.

Miss Shaw is not above eating other people's food. Indeed, in the three or four months after the inn closes, she often vacations in such far-flung spots as San Francisco, Spain, France, and Italy, not so much to pick up recipes as to compare cuisines. It's a joy to find a woman chef who really takes a delight in what she does, whether it be a simple roast of beef or delicate little new potatoes cooked to perfection, or a more elaborate salmon mousse, made with fresh salmon brought in that morning, or perhaps a filet of beef en croûte.

As if Miss Shaw was not talent enough for one inn, Mrs. Hobbs, a charming Danish woman, is herself no mean cook, although naturally her achievements lean more to the Danish kitchen. She supervises the running of the inn and had a hand in the decoration of the rooms and the installation of bathrooms—my bathroom had the largest fireplace you ever saw, and a shower, too, rather a rarity in Scotland.

Queen Victoria once stayed at Inverlochy Castle and pronounced it one of the loveliest houses in the land. Had she been there to taste Miss Shaw's delicious food, she would have been even more complimentary. I have told you how I love poached smoked haddock for breakfast, and that is what Miss Shaw served us, along with hot oven scones and exquisitely good marmalade, also made by her own hand.

   Since I don't have Miss Shaw's recipe for *Scones*, I am going to give you one that was a specialty of my mother's. Sift 2 cups all-purpose flour, 1 tablespoon baking powder, ½ teaspoon salt, and 1 tablespoon sugar into a bowl. Add ¾ to 1 cup heavy cream and stir quickly until the dough holds together. Turn out on a floured board and pat or roll out to ½-inch thickness. Cut in squares. Place on a buttered cookie sheet or in a buttered 9-by-9 inch pan. Bake in a 450-degree oven for 12 to 15 minutes, or until light and brown.

To make the scones even richer, melt 4 tablespoons butter in a small skillet and dip each square in the melted butter before placing on the sheet or pan. Serve these delicious scones hot, split and buttered, and have them with good marmalade or raspberry preserves for breakfast or tea.

Then close your eyes and imagine you are at Inverlochy Castle.

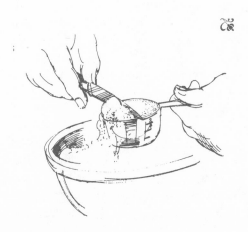

Let's Have More Common Markets

Whenever I am in Los Angeles, I always make a point of visiting the Farmer's Market. I know that most of my friends who live in this vast, sprawling city are apt to take it for granted and look on it as perhaps rather contrived and touristy, but that is not so. A combination of a country fair, a European marketplace, and an eating festival of foods from around the world, the Los Angeles Farmer's Market is unique in America. Not all of it is great, some things are pure corn, but beyond a doubt you can find there some of the most magnificent marketing in this country.

Not long ago I took a long, leisurely stroll through the market, looking at food people were buying to eat from the various stands—Mexican food, of course, Chinese food, blintzes, sandwiches. One woman was making aebleskiver, which is a sort of Danish fritter or pancake. There was every imaginable kind of food, some good, some mediocre, and, frankly, some pretty awful. I wasn't really as interested in the ready-made foods as in the tremendous variety of fresh things for sale. You'd expect to find good meat markets, and you aren't disappointed. I noticed some of the most beautiful veal I have seen west of the Rockies, extraordinarily fine prime beef, and good lamb. The profusion of fresh seafood from the Pacific is absolutely staggering—petrale sole; the little sand dabs that are so good when sautéed in butter just for a minute or two with seasonings, lemon, and some parsley; red snapper; fresh salmon; tiny shrimp and the superb Dungeness crab—and all beautifully presented. Sometimes you can even find abalone, which is becoming rather a rarity nowadays.

Then the piles of vegetables—practically anything you could possibly want. I was there in the asparagus season, and there must have been five or six different kinds of asparagus, greens of every type, all the different varieties of cucumber, artichokes minuscule and enormous, peas, every sort of bean, and leeks, which used to be very hard to find in Los Angeles but now are there all the time.

This must be one of the last places where you can buy unborn chicken eggs, the kind you once got in the big fat mature hens you cooked in a fricassee, using the eggs to enrich the sauce. That was a great treat that seems to have disappeared from our lives.

I could lose myself for hours in the specialty shops. There's a bakery shop with every bread you can imagine and at least five or six nut shops.

In one shop I saw bitter almonds, which you almost never find nowadays, although they are still called for in certain recipes. There are regular almonds any way you could want them—blanched and in their skins, salted, slivered, chopped, and thinly sliced both in the skin and without it, all these versions of just one nut. There were filberts, whole, chopped, toasted; walnuts and pecans; huge piles of macadamia nuts; raw peanuts, toasted peanuts, and the tiny red peanuts; pine nuts; pistachio nuts—the whole gamut of nuts. It's the same with dried fruits; there's just about nothing you could name that can't be had here. Spices like poppy and sesame seed are sold by the pound, and fresh horseradish is ground to your order.

To watch people eat, to stand in a butcher's shop or by a fruit stall and observe what they buy, is an education in itself, endlessly fascinating. I love the alive, throbbing excitement of the market, the busy movement of the shoppers, the common denominator of food that brings people together from all sections of Los Angeles and other parts of the country, too. How I wish that other American cities would establish this kind of big common market filled with good things to eat and take home, like a huge united nations of supermarkets and specialty markets under one roof. It is my dream to see the continent spanned, from coast to coast, with markets like this. What a great advance for the American table it would be.

The market makes you just itch to buy and to cook. I happened to be staying with a friend in Pasadena, Philip Brown, who writes cookbooks and gives classes in cooking at California State College, and I thought I'd like to try an Algerian recipe for almond cookies he'd demonstrated in one of his classes. They're just about the best cookies I've ever tasted.

෴ I bought some almonds and tried them out so I could pass on to you *Philip Brown's Soft Almond Cookies.* In a bowl stir 1¼ pounds blanched almonds, pulverized in the blender, 1 cup sugar, and 1 tablespoon grated lemon peel until thoroughly mixed. Make a well in the center, drop in 2 eggs, and stir until smooth. Divide batter in half, and roll each half on a well-floured surface into a cylinder about 18 inches long and 1½ inches in diameter. Flour your hands frequently as you roll the dough. Flatten cylinders into oblongs about 2 inches wide and cut into diagonal 1½-inch slices. Dust with flour and place about an inch apart on ungreased baking sheets. Bake in a 350-degree oven for about 15 minutes. Cool on wire racks. Make a syrup with ½ cup sugar and ½ cup water, let cool, then add 1 tablespoon orange-flower water. Dip cookies into syrup, then roll in confectioner's sugar.

෴

The Marvel of Markets

When I'm abroad, I always seek out the local markets. It's the best way I know to get a feeling of the region, the foods, and the people. To walk through the great markets in Cannes, Nice, and Grasse is a wondrous experience.

The Cannes market is covered and about the size of a city block. Leading to it is the Meynardier, a narrow street full of food shops and closed to traffic during the peak market hours. There is one very famous shop called Ernest that makes a bread, rich with butter and eggs, known as *pain de mie*. It has an extraordinarily good texture and is delicious toasted. According to the season, you can buy all kinds of prepared dishes there—picnic foods in summer, the first sauerkraut in September, foie gras at Christmas.

The fresh produce in the Cannes market, brought in by local growers and from other parts of France, is a constant delight. One day I bought the tiniest of *haricots verts*, the string beans so beloved by the French, that were no more than 3 inches long. There were tree-ripened peaches, easy to peel and glorious to eat, strawberries, raspberries, and the first little yellow prunes called *mirabelles*. One whole section is devoted to herbs—practically every herb you can think of—and another to flowers. One Saturday I bought a bouquet of about five dozen magnificent red carnations for just over a dollar. Long-stemmed roses from the greenhouses around Cannes and Antibes were to be had for a song, so all summer long I kept the house where I was living filled with the fragrance of flowers.

The Nice market is held in a picturesque square that used to blossom with huge parasols that shielded the market people and their wares. Now, alas, it is mostly filled with cars belonging to the shoppers. This is the only place I know where you can buy a type of galette or cake known as *socca*, about as thick as a pancake and with a most unusual and intriguing flavor. *Socca* is made from a mixture of chickpea flour, oil, and various ingredients spread in round tins about 30 inches across and baked in huge wood ovens. You buy it at stalls where the owner cuts little strips with a spoon, puts them in a piece of paper, and sprinkles them with pepper. A slice costs half a franc, about ten cents, and even if I've just had a big meal I can't resist stopping at a socca stand and buying a slice to munch on.

The Grasse market, a real farmer's market, takes place in the Place des Aires, a beautiful square lined with food shops. There's a man in the market who makes fine charcuterie—products made from the pig. One morning he was selling slices of suckling pig that had been boned, filled with a pâté of pork and pork liver, reshaped, roasted, and glazed. To one who loves pork as I do, it was irresistible. I bought a big slice and ate it on the spot. If one markets intelligently in France, life becomes very simple. In addition to the superb fresh vegetables and fruits and the bake shops with their astounding variety of breads, there are so many shops where, if you're feeling lazy, you can buy ready-made dishes that are really good eating. I always carry a string bag and a canvas bag, and an hour or so of pleasurable shopping nets me two days of even more of pleasurable eating.

In the Grasse market I also came across a remarkable service for the cook I wish American markets would copy. The ingredients for a ratatouille, the superb French vegetable stew—onion, eggplant, zucchini, peppers, tomatoes, and garlic—were sold packaged in a plastic bag for the equivalent of 75 cents. You could also buy in a package the greens and vegetables for salade Niçoise, to which you only needed to add the tuna, eggs, olives, and anchovies.

✿ *Salade Niçoise* is one of the best luncheon salads you could have. What is especially good about it is that you can vary it to taste by adding different vegetables, whatever happens to take your fancy. The only constants are the tuna, anchovies, hard-boiled eggs, tomatoes, and the famous black olives of Provence.

✿ For a basic *Salade Niçoise*, cover a large platter or line a shallow salad bowl with crisp fresh greens. Place in the center one or two 7-ounce cans of tuna in olive oil, well drained. The amount depends on how many people you are serving and how hungry you are. Two cans will usually serve four to six. Surround the tuna with 20 or 30 anchovy fillets, drained on paper towels. Arrange around the edge of the greens 4 to 6 ripe tomatoes, quartered, or 12 to 18 cherry tomatoes, and 4 to 6 hard-boiled eggs, quartered, and add a sprinkling of small black olives (the tiny Niçoise olives, if you can find them).

Now arrange on top of these basic ingredients vegetables of your choice: rings of sliced red onion or ½ cup finely chopped yellow onion; tiny boiled new potatoes, or boiled sliced potatoes; green pepper rings; green beans cooked just until bitey-crisp; artichoke hearts; pimiento strips. Add a sprinkling of 1 tablespoon fresh chopped basil, if available. Pour over this wonderful mélange a dressing made with ¾ cup olive oil, ¼ cup wine vinegar, and salt and pepper to taste, and toss lightly. Serve as a main course, with a loaf of crusty French bread.

This is one of the most inspired salads I know, and I never seem to tire of it.

✿

The Flavor of Catalonia

The breath of Catalonia, like the breath of Provence, is garlic. Catalonia is the province that takes in the Mediterranean coast of northeast Spain from below Barcelona to the French border. Stretching it, you might also include the Balearic islands of Majorca and Minorca, which have a great deal in common with Catalonia—a taste for garlic being part of it. When I say garlic is the breath of Catalonia, it is because most of the famous dishes of the region are not spicy or herby but highly garlicky.

On my latest trip to Barcelona, I dined with a Catalan of great distinction, a man who collects and restores antique cars and is also a very fine cook. We discussed the unique relationship of garlic to the various dishes of Catalonia, Provence, and other parts of the Mediterranean where it is so much a part of the eating pattern, and my friend told me that according to one of the foremost chefs of Catalonia, garlic, not onion, should be used with fish, for onion smothers the natural flavor of fish, whereas garlic enhances it.

This was a new idea for me, but I'm not sure he isn't right. Certainly the two or three fish dishes we ate, in which garlic was the main seasoning, tended to support this theory. One was that singular Spanish delicacy, angulas. These are infinitesimal baby eels, white in color and no bigger around that a strand of spaghetti—in fact, when served they look very much like a bowl of spaghetti. They were cooked with oil, garlic, and a touch of pepper, and the garlic perfectly complemented the delicate little fish and gave them a most distinctive taste. To eat them we were given a special wooden fork that held them securely so they didn't slide off on the way from plate to mouth. After we had finished, the waiter came with a napkin and broke the forks in two in front of us to show that they were thrown away after one use, a nicety that particularly impressed me.

Garlic is also the very soul of ailloli, the Catalan version of the French aïoli. While both the Catalans and the Provençals claim this rich, garlicky mayonnaise, they make it very differently.

In Provence you take a mortar and pestle (preferably of white marble) and at least a clove of garlic per person and pound it very thoroughly, then grind egg yolks into the garlic and work in olive oil, drop by drop, until you have a garlic-perfumed sauce, like a thick mayonnaise. Salt is added, perhaps a touch of lemon juice. Bread crumbs are sometimes worked in as well. Aïoli, often called "the butter of Provence," is an integral part of the Marseille fish specialty, bourride, and the star of the Grand Aïoli, a tremendous spread of poached fish, salt cod, hard-boiled eggs, snails, and all manner of cooked vegetables such as potatoes, carrots, onions, green beans, artichokes, and zucchini, all arranged around the huge mortar of sauce.

If you would like to make a typical *Aïoli,* you don't have to grind away with a pestle and mortar, it can be done in a blender. Put 3 garlic cloves and 2 egg yolks in the blender container with 1 teaspoon salt, and run at high speed for about 30 seconds. Measure 1½ cups of good fruity olive oil, turn on the blender, and pour the oil in slowly until the sauce is thick and thoroughly blended. If by any chance it should curdle, remove the mixture to a bowl, start with another egg yolk and a tiny bit of oil in the blender, then slowly pour in the curdled mixture. *(See Editor's Note, copyright page.)*

It will emerge as a dense, mayonnaise-like mass, highly fragrant and flavored with garlic, a change from anything you have ever tasted. It makes a magnificent sauce for hot or cold poached fish, cold vegetables, cold fowl, or hot or cold meats such as boiled beef or lamb.

The Spanish ailloli is even more varied in its preparation and uses. When I had it in Barcelona with grilled rabbit and grilled chicken, there were noticeable chunks of garlic in the sauce, and it was extremely hot to the tongue, with great pungency. I encountered yet another version at a friend's house in Majorca. This one had crushed baked potatoes worked in with the egg yolks and oil, which gave it a different, more solid consistency, and we ate it with tender little snails from the garden, freshly prepared and delicious.

The Wonders of Majorca

Majorca is full of surprises. Did you ever see mushrooms that bleed? I never did until I went there. I was invited to lunch in a home where the cook was a local man, imbued with island lore. He found and cooked the wild herbs, fruits, and vegetables, including mushrooms of all the different seasons. As it had been raining a lot when I was there—unusual in winter—he went to one of his secret spots to hunt for the *seta de sangre*, or bleeding mushroom, which flourishes after rain. It is a rather large mushroom with an upturned cap, dark in color, and when it is cut a red fluid flows out, not as thick and dark as blood, more like a light red wine. We had the mushrooms sliced and sautéed in olive oil with a little garlic and parsley, and the fluid, mingling with the oil, made a reddish sauce for the meaty, extraordinary texture of the *seta de sangre* and kept it deliciously moist.

With its rocky hills, sea, and unbelievable variety of landscape, Majorca has some great and unusual food traditions. The markets are full of vegetables, fruits, game, and other things native to the island, including some little birds about the size of a robin that were plentiful and apparently popular. I bought a 10-pound suckling pig that my host and I roasted on an eighteenth-century spit (with a battery-powered twentieth-century motor) until the skin had a rich walnut glaze and the meat was meltingly tender—the best pig I've ever eaten.

The markets, especially in Palma, sell exquisitely hand-woven baskets in all shapes from flat trays to oval baskets, in which the women carry finished ironing, and huge baskets and panniers of woven grass to hold everything from firewood to clothing. The local pottery, deep brown and ovenproof, is beautiful and cheap but hardly durable enough to survive the rigors of travel. It is best used on the spot. Another specialty and a major export is *ensaimada*, made from a light coffee-cake dough which is rolled into a strip, stuffed with a candied fruit mixture called "angel's hair," shaped into a ring, baked, and dusted with sugar. It keeps remarkably well, and you see the Spanish tourists from the mainland taking home four or five boxes of it.

For dinner one night we had a version of the Spanish *ropa vieja* that was new to me. (The name of this stew translates literally as "old clothes," a Spanish joke.) The Majorcan *ropa vieja* was made with roast lamb, thinly sliced and recooked in a sauce with onions, garlic, peppers, and other vegetables. At the last moment, deep-fried potatoes were tossed in—they retained their crispness and made a most exciting contrast to the very soft meat.

One of the most famous island dishes is *sopa mallorquin*, actually more a vegetable stew than a soup. In the old days it was the mainstay of life on the island and was stretched with cheese, eggs, or, on Sunday, rabbit or chicken—whatever could be had.

To prepare *Sopa Mallorquin* for six, toast 12 pieces of thinly sliced bread (dark or protein bread is best), and after toasting dry it in a 300-degree oven for 10 to 12 minutes. Sauté 2 thinly sliced onions and 3 sliced garlic cloves in a little olive oil in a 12-inch skillet, then on top arrange layers of thinly sliced or cut vegetables—carrots, zucchini, broccoli, cabbage, celery, spinach, cauliflower, whatever you like; the onions and garlic are the only two essentials. Salt the layers. When the skillet is about two-thirds full, add stock barely to cover and simmer until just crisply tender, no more; the vegetables must not be overcooked. Put the toast in an ovenproof serving dish, spoon the vegetables on top, and bake in a 375-degree oven for 4 to 5 minutes, then serve. You can grate a little cheese on top, before or after baking, if you like, or serve the dish with pancake-style omelets.

It's a very variable feast.

My ultimate surprise in Majorca was a restaurant called El Gato. The menu is Majorcan, French, and international, but whoever wrote it was not strong on spelling. Quiche Lorraine came out Kiche Loran, cassoulet appeared as casula, and crêpes Suzette as creps susett! Imagine, though, a restaurant in a major city where you can get good service, a linen napkin, a big plateful of fresh hors d'oeuvre, a beautifully grilled piece of dentón, one of the scarcest and most expensive of Mediterranean fish, two vegetables, caramel custard, bread, butter, and wine, all for about one-third of what you would pay here. That really is a pleasant surprise.

Prunier the Great and Other Greats

There used to be a tradition of restaurants run by and named for one family. Delmonico was the great name in New York. In Paris and London it is Prunier. Delmonico's is long since gone, but the Prunier establishments, of which there are three, are alive and flourishing. The original restaurant, founded by Emile Prunier in 1872 on the rue Duphot in Paris, is managed by Jean Barnagaud, who married Simone Prunier, daughter of the founder. She herself runs the London Prunier on St. James's Street, while their son is in charge of the fledgling Prunier-Traktir on the Avenue Victor-Hugo in Paris.

The specialty of this great house is fish, and the whole family has made it their life. You can find just about everything that swims on their menus, and they have a reputation in each capital for being sticklers about the fish they buy; only the freshest will do.

Oyster lovers can have a field day at Prunier's. In London they serve the finest Colchesters and sometimes the Galway Bay oysters from Ireland, extraordinarily delicious because of the cold, clean water they inhabit. In Paris there are the three chief varieties of French oysters—Belons, Marennes, and Portugaises—all graded, as is the French custom, according to size. The smallest are usually considered the choicest, and they are listed on the menu in zeros, double, triple, quadruple, down to the tiniest specimens. Oysters are always opened to order and served on trays with a little bit of seaweed and crushed ice to give the impression that they have just been taken from their beds. The French, much heartier oyster eaters than we, think nothing of devouring eighteen or two dozen of these babies at a time.

The rue Duphot Prunier also has a small retail shop on the premises that sells oysters from heaped bins facing the street, all manner of fresh, salted, and smoked fish, and other superb French shellfish—mussels, clams, lobster, écrevisses or small crayfish, and langouste, the spiny or rock lobster. They sell caviar, too, and thereby hangs a tale told me by my old friend Simone Prunier.

Contrary to what many people think, caviar comes not only from Russia and Iran but from many places in the world that harbor the sturgeon with its precious load of eggs. Astoria, at the mouth of the Columbia River in our own Pacific Northwest, produces some very good caviar, although very little ever reaches the retail market.

Connoisseurs consider caviar from sturgeon caught in the Gironde, the river that skirts the vineyards of Bordeaux in southern France, to be on a par with that of Russia or Iran. The egg is not as large, but the flavor is delicious. Emile Prunier recognized this many years ago and made it one of the specialties of his restaurant. As a result, Prunier's has an exclusive on the small supply of Gironde caviar.

Madame Prunier, as she is always known, rather than Madame Barnagaud, is the inspiration for the family restaurants. It is she who travels and tastes and brings back recipes to be tried out in London and passed on to her husband and son. The fish chowder she found in Bermuda is served in all three restaurants, and each interpretation is slightly different but equally good. Then there are her versions of those two famous Provençal dishes, bourride and bouillabaisse, also completely individual and exciting.

There are meat dishes on the menu at Prunier's as well as fish, but the gamut of seafood is so great and the wines so carefully chosen to complement it that it would be the sheerest folly to order anything else. At the French Prunier's I would recommend starting with the caviar, or oysters in season, or something we seldom see here, oursins (sea urchins), spiny spherical little monsters that contain the most delicately flavored morsels of flesh. Then choose one of the great French fish, daurade or bar or loup de mer, poached and served with a beurre blanc sauce. The Paris Prunier's prides itself on serving the best cheeses and finest fruits of the season, which make a perfect conclusion to a luncheon or dinner of fish.

In the London Prunier the first course might be oysters or, in summer, dressed crab, a typically English dish in which the crabmeat and roe are seasoned and dressed and served on the back shell with a garnishing of lettuce and capers. After this, a turbot soufflé or grilled Dover sole.

  Whether or not you are going to Europe, you can always capture the flavor of Prunier's with *Crab Diable* from *Madame Prunier's Fish Cook Book*, a classic compendium of fish and shellfish recipes. For four servings, finely chop 1 small onion and 2 shallots, and sauté in 4 tablespoons butter until limp and golden. Remove. Rinse the pan with ¼ cup brandy. Stir in 2 teaspoons Dijon mustard and 1½ cups rich white sauce. Mix in 1 pound crabmeat, and season to taste. Put in crab shells or individual ovenproof dishes, sprinkle the top with buttered crumbs and chopped parsley, and put in a 425-degree oven for just long enough to brown the crumbs.

In my travels, I have been fortunate enough to eat some superb meals at restaurants both here and abroad. Though space does not permit my telling you about every place. I have gathered together a sampling of a few of the dishes I have enjoyed most.

The Berkeley is one of London's truly luxurious hotels—possibly the most luxurious now that the old Berkeley of my youth, which stood on the corner of Piccadilly and Berkeley Street for more than a hundred years, has been replaced by a new deluxe hotel at Wilton Place, in Knightsbridge. Many of the old staff, including the maître chef des cuisines, Marcel Auduc, are back on the job, keeping up the high standards of food and service for which the Berkeley has always been noted.

One of M. Auduc's special dishes, named for the Marquis de Lafayette, is *Escalopes de Veau Lafayette*. To make this dish for four, season 4 large veal scallops with salt and pepper, dust them lightly with flour, and sauté them quickly on both sides in 4 tablespoons butter until golden brown. Remove to a hot ovenproof serving dish.

Peel and seed 2 ripe tomatoes, and cut in neat slices. Peel and seed 1 small avocado, then cut in crosswise slices. Arrange four rows of the tomato and avocado slices on a baking sheet, overlapping them alternately, season with salt and pepper and sprinkle liberally with grated Parmesan cheese. Put under the broiler just until the cheese colors. Arrange a row of slices lengthwise down the center of each veal scallop, dust with a little more Parmesan, and brown lightly under the broiler.

Meanwhile, take the butter from the cooking pan. Add to the pan ¼ cup port wine and ½ cup veal, beef, or chicken stock, and bring to a boil over high heat, scraping with a wooden spoon to remove the brown glaze from the bottom of the pan. Let this sauce cook down and reduce, then blend in 1 to 2 tablespoons butter and pour the sauce around the veal.

The combination of flavors and textures is wonderfully good, and the whole dish couldn't be simpler and quicker to make.

If the Berkeley is the most luxurious hotel in London, Brenner's Park in Baden-Baden must be one of the most luxurious in all Europe. Baden-Baden is a very old spa on the edge of the Black Forest in Germany, and the hotel's grill room, appropriately called the Black Forest Grill, always has local foods on the menu. The Black Forest Fruit Dessert is a delicate, aromatic mingling of liqueur-flavored whipped cream and all kinds of berries, including wild strawberries and blackberries from the forest. You can use any seasonal berries for this—strawberries, raspberries, blueberries, and blackberries.

To make four servings, of this *Black Forest Fruit Dessert*, first put in a bowl 2 pints of seasonal berries, one kind or a mixture, as you prefer. Sprinkle with 2 tablespoons sugar, the juice of ½ lemon, and 2 tablespoons Grand Marnier, and let stand for a few minutes to absorb the flavors, shaking the bowl now and then so they are well mixed.

Whip 1½ cups heavy cream until stiff, but not too stiff, then whip in 1 tablespoon sugar. Put in a flat bowl or soup plate, and add 2 tablespoons Grand Marnier and 1 tablespoon kirsch or framboise. (If you don't have either of these white fruit brandies, substitute the same amount of cognac or bourbon.) Mix into the cream, stirring briskly, and serve by tossing the cream lightly with the berries and heaping the mixture in 4 dishes. Sprinkle with a few chopped almonds or pistachio nuts or crumbled almond macaroons, and serve with thin sugar cookies, macaroons, or a slice of pound or sponge cake.

This simple dessert has an intoxicating perfume and a ravishing taste, and if you do the flavoring and stirring in front of your guests, it makes a tremendous impression.

One of the great standards of German cuisine is Lady Curzon soup which has all kinds of stories attached to it. Some say Lady Curzon, an American married to Lord Curzon, later Viceroy of India, created the soup, others that it was created for her. Strangely enough, we seldom see the soup here or in England, but in Germany it is almost universal. At Hamburg's Vier Jahreszeiten, a beautiful, privately owned hotel that is renowned all over Europe for its superb restaurants, the soup is served in tiny cups, so you have just enough to savor the delicious flavor before the next course arrives.

⬿ For six servings of *Lady Curzon Soup*, take 4 cups canned turtle soup, the kind with turtle meat in it. The quality varies a great deal, so get the best brand you can. Heat the soup to boiling. Meanwhile combine 2 egg yolks with ⅓ cup heavy cream and ½ teaspoon or more of good curry powder. Very gradually stir 1 cup of the boiling soup into the egg mixture. Remove the soup from the heat and stir the egg-cream mixture into it with ¼ cup Madeira, sherry, or cognac—any one works well. Stir and reheat gently without letting the soup boil. It won't thicken, but will become light and creamy. Pour into hot cups, float a little lightly whipped cream on top, then, if your cups are ovenproof, put them under the broiler for a second to glaze the cream. Otherwise just dust it with minced parsley.

You can vary the amount of curry powder and cream to taste in this delicate and unusual soup, always remembering that no one flavor should overpower the other.

Some of the best food in France today is coming from intimate mini-restaurants run by owners who are their own chefs. This fruit dessert, so easy and quick that you'll never believe how good it is until you taste it, is typical of the original approach to food that has made Jean Senderens's small restaurant, L'Archestrate, one of the most talked-about places in Paris.

⬿ For *Bananes à l'Archestrate*, slice 6 ripe bananas very thinly. Melt 6 tablespoons butter in a heavy iron pan, and when hot, add the bananas. Sauté, sprinkling them with 6 tablespoons sugar, until they brown and caramelize a little and get really crispy. Flame them with ⅓ cup warmed cognac, and spoon over vanilla ice cream.

The London Chop House is a Detroit institution, and one of the greatest restaurants in the United States. When I'm there, I often order for a late supper spaghetti with oyster sauce, a dish that has always intrigued and pleased me. Clam sauce has become rather a cliché, but this oyster sauce is something else again.

🐟 For *Chop House Spaghetti with Oyster Sauce*, take 1 dozen large or 2 dozen small oysters, fresh or canned. Chop them or not, as you wish. I think they are rather better chopped. Save any liquor from the oysters.

Melt 2 tablespoons butter and 2 tablespoons olive oil in a small skillet, add 2 finely chopped garlic cloves and 2 tablespoons chopped onion, and sauté until wilted and just beginning to turn golden. Add the oyster liquor plus enough clam juice or white wine to make 1 cup liquid. (If you don't have any oyster liquor, use ½ cup clam juice and ½ cup white wine.) Cook this down, then add ¼ cup finely chopped parsley and salt and pepper to taste.

Meanwhile, have ready a large pan of rapidly boiling salted water to cook your pasta. For four persons you will need ¾ pound spaghetti, or 1 pound if your guests are pasta lovers. Add 2 tablespoons olive oil to the water to prevent the strands from sticking together, and boil the spaghetti rapidly until it reaches the stage of tenderness you like. I like mine *al dente*. While draining the pasta well, toss the oysters in the sauce just enough to heat them through. Add more chopped parsley and a touch of chopped fresh basil or a little dried basil. Divide the pasta among 4 plates, spoon the oyster sauce over it, and serve at once.

Drink a good white wine with this. I usually order a Muscadet from the Loire Valley, which is light and brisk and goes well with seafood.

Quo Vadis is to me a paragon among New York restaurants, a place of beauty, quiet, and comfort. I have known the owners, Gino and Bruno, for many years, and when I eat there or take friends from out of town, I feel almost as if I'm in my own home.

Every Saturday during the winter months, Quo Vadis serves for lunch one of my all-time favorite dishes, bollito misto, which sounds more glamorous in Italian than in translation—mixed boil. When this comes rolling out of the kitchen on a cart, it is a dramatic sight. First, there is a fine piece of boiled beef flavored with pot vegetables and herbs, and very often some veal or a veal tongue, or a calf's head or feet for contrast. There is always a large Italian sausage—a cotechino or zampone (a sausage stuffed in a boned pig's foot), and usually a chicken or capon. This is not a dish in which everything is thrown into a pot and then served up; it needs to be prepared with great care, patience, and style. While it bears some resemblance to the French pot-au-feu or the New England boiled dinner, it has certain distinct variations which make it, to my mind, infinitely more interesting.

To make *Bollito Misto*, combine in a very large pot (at least an 8-quart size) 4 pounds beef brisket, 2 or 3 onions, one stuck with 2 cloves, 3 carrots, several leeks, 2 garlic cloves, 2 tablespoons salt, a bay leaf, 1 teaspoon thyme, and ½ teaspoon freshly ground pepper, with an ample amount of water. Bring to a boil, skim off the scum, and simmer for 1½ hours.

Add 2 veal tongues to the pot, and continue cooking for 1½ hours, then add a 4-pound roasting chicken or capon and 1 or 2 cotechino sausages. Continue cooking until the meats are tender, removing the chicken if it is cooked first and keeping it warm. Taste the broth for seasoning. Meanwhile, boil additional carrots, leeks, onions and 12 medium potatoes separately in salted water, timing them so they are done at the same time as the meats.

When everything is cooked, arrange the meats and vegetables on a large hot platter, and have a carving board handy for slicing. Give each person a slice or two of each meat, some vegetables, and, if you like, a small cup of the broth.

As accompaniments, have coarse salt, horseradish sauce, and the traditional sauce verte, a vinaigrette sauce made with 3 parts oil to 1 part wine vinegar, salt, pepper, and finely chopped parsley, chives, and thyme—it should be really thick with herbs. Also traditional are Italian mustard fruits (fruits preserved in a mustard syrup, sold in specialty food shops); their sharp flavor goes well with the meats.

To do justice to the bounty of a bollito misto, you need at least twelve people, so plan on serving it for a buffet party—it makes a wonderful meal, spectacular, impressive, and something quite out of the ordinary.

CHAPTER 11

Gastronomic Musings

❧

... in which we play the menu game ... count the invisible calorie ... call French dressing by its true name ... lose our fear of hollandaise ... and take a mouthful of midnight and a bite of heaven and earth.

The Making of a Menu

Planning menus seems to plunge so many people into the doldrums. It must be because they haven't really developed an intelligent approach to their entertaining. Their pattern is always the same—the soup or first course, a hot main dish, vegetable, salad, and dessert, and so on and so on, ad infinitum. First of all, I think you should consider all the relevant factors when you are having guests for luncheon or dinner—the season, the weather, the balance of hot dishes against cold; creamy foods against sharp flavors. Certainly, if you are serving wines, you should plan dishes that will be suited to them.

Menu making is a great game. I think it is a good idea to try out new dishes you find in a cookbook or a newspaper, or eat in a restaurant or at a friend's house. Jot them down in a little menu memorandum book, and make a note that this would be a good dish to go with so-and-so, or follow such-and-such.

Recently, at the home of some Florida friends, I had a dinner that was memorably good because there was a great deal of thought and planning behind it. First we had small portions of a very hot, very concentrated mushroom soup, next a lovely mousse of fish with crabmeat around it, and then a platter of cold fillet of beef with foie gras, exquisite to look at, wonderfully satisfying to eat, and a most intelligent choice on the part of our hostess because the beef had been glazed with aspic, arranged on the platter, decorated with glistening chopped aspic, and left in the refrigerator, covered with plastic wrap, well ahead, so there was no fuss or stew.

So often we forget that cold food is not just for summer, and that a good cold entrée or first course is always welcome. Also, it is foolish to plan meals in which everything takes last-minute attention—a roast to come out of the oven or tournedos to be sautéed, vegetables to be tossed in butter—it becomes a great chore. How much easier to plan a hot soup, a baked dish, or stuffed and rolled crêpes for a first course, and then have a beautiful cold main course with vegetables vinaigrette or mayonnaise, or a tossed salad, perhaps cheese, and either a hot or a cold dessert, depending on your mood.

It is wonderful to be able to have practically your whole dinner ready before your guests come and relax, knowing things will go smoothly. If you make a great soup, it can be reheated at the last minute. If you have a quiche, you can prebake the shell and then fill it and put it in the oven after the guests arrive. There are so many things in the field of entertaining that are simple and spectacular and good to eat.

A favorite dish of mine, one I serve over and over, is cold roast pork. Sometimes I do it with pork loin; sometimes, if I have a large number of guests, with a fresh ham or uncured pork leg, which I usually have the butcher bone and tie, although I have also made it with the bone in.

To prepare *Cold Roast Pork*, let's say you have bought a fresh ham weighing about 8 or 9 pounds, and had it boned. Make a smooth paste with 2 cups toasted ground almonds and hazelnuts (toast for 5 minutes in a 350-degree oven before grinding), ½ cup dried figs, cut into tiny pieces, ½ cup chopped seedless raisins, 1 or 2 cloves garlic, 1 teaspoon thyme, 2 tablespoons chopped parsley, and ¼ to ½ cup cognac. I either grind this very fine or pound it in a mortar and pestle. With a larding needle or a knife with a long thin blade, make long deep crisscross incisions in the pork, down, up, and through the meat, and push the paste into these holes very tightly, so there will be a marvelous marbleized look to the meat when it is sliced. Rub the fresh ham well with olive oil, salt, pepper, dried thyme, and 1 or 2 crushed garlic cloves. Really give it a good massage. Place on a rack in a roasting pan, and roast at 325 degrees for approximately 20 minutes per pound, or until the internal temperature registers 165 degrees on a meat thermometer. Remove from the oven, and let it stand and cool gradually to room temperature before serving. This takes about 4 or 5 hours, but it is much better than refrigerating the pork. Carve into nice even slices so you get a mosaic effect with the stuffing.

With this delicious and extremely attractive main course, for a summer supper party you might have steaming hot corn, cooked at the very last minute, crisp bread, and perhaps a green salad, accompanied by a light, fruity Alsatian white wine. Follow this with a dessert of fresh peaches poached in simple syrup to which you have added a good slug of bourbon—serve with whipped or heavy cream and some crisp wafers or cookies. If you feel you should have a first course, there are many you could choose from, but frankly, I don't feel you need it with this thoroughly satisfying cold roast pork.

Calories Do Count

Calorie counting seems to have become one of our great indoor sports. Today practically everyone you meet is doing the diet thing in one form or another, and so am I. I've counted calories faithfully, and it has really worked. Of course, it is provoking to find that so many of the foods one likes are high in calories, but there are plenty that you can eat with impunity, and often they taste all the better for being left in their unalloyed state, without all the sauces and gobs of butter and cream that put the calorie count up. Vegetables, for instance. A plain boiled or baked potato without butter or sour cream, just some coarse salt and a grind of pepper, is perfect in itself—and only 100 calories. Practically any vegetable has enough natural flavor to need nothing more than salt, pepper, and perhaps a squeeze of lemon juice. I no longer put butter or hollandaise on asparagus. I just enjoy eating it in all its lovely crisp green freshness, hot with salt and pepper or cold with lemon juice and maybe some crumbled hard-boiled egg.

You can diet without really denying yourself if you know how. Let's take a look at some of the foods we all like and see how they add up. A 3-ounce piece of broiled boneless steak with a little bit of fat on it is 330 calories. If you don't know how big a 3-ounce piece is, it's about an inch thick and 5 inches long by 2 inches wide—not a lot but still a satisfying serving. A 3-ounce broiled lamb chop is 305 calories, and 3 ounces of roast loin of pork, which I just adore, is 310. Or you can have two small pork chops for only 230 calories, provided you trim off every trace of fat, for it's the fat that counts. Now anyone can exist on that. Seafood is even better. A whole cup of crabmeat—and that's quite a big serving—is only 170 calories, and a cup of shrimp about the same. You can have quite a lot of shrimp as a main course without increasing your calorie count very much.

Ah, you may say, but what about sweet things? I just have to have something sweet. Well, take melon. Half a cantaloupe is 60 calories, a 7-inch wedge of honeydew is 50, and a 2-inch wedge of Cranshaw just 40. Half a grapefruit is about the same. A whole cup of strawberries or blueberries totals 55, and even a banana is only about 35.

If you were having guests for dinner, you could combine a cup of strawberries, a cup of melon balls, ½ cup blueberries, and a sliced banana, and you'd have a pretty, delicious dessert. Serve it in separate bowls and let your guests put sugar and kirsch on theirs while you have a little artificial sweetener or maybe a drop or two of sherry.

Salads are great diet material, unless you load them with dressing. If you can't eat a salad without dressing, here are two that are good and tasty, but low in calories because they don't use any oil.

For *Low-Calorie Dressing Number 1*, whirl in the blender 2 cloves garlic, a 6-ounce can of tomato sauce, ¼ teaspoon Tabasco, 1 tablespoon soy sauce, 1 teaspoon each of salt and basil and 1½ teaspoons freshly ground pepper.

For *Dressing Number 2*, whirl in the blender 1 cup tomato juice, 1 hard-boiled egg, ½ cup skim-milk cottage cheese, 1 small onion, cut up, 1 tablespoon soy sauce, 1 teaspoon salt, and 1 teaspoon tarragon.

Now for things to shun—like chocolate-fudge topping. Two table-spoons add up to 135 calories. A wedge of yellow cake with chocolate frosting is 366 calories, a piece of apple pie 306, one little brownie is 95—and who could be satisfied with just one? Sometimes there comes a day when you just have to sit down and gobble up five or six brownies, and that plays havoc with your calorie count, but if you are careful and eat very little else that day you may not gain an ounce and you'll have given yourself the emotional release of eating something you crave, which can be worthwhile. The other night I succumbed to a particularly luscious custard which was one of the best things I ever tasted. My conscience hurt a bit, but I didn't have anything else, and next day I ate sparingly. For breakfast, melon, a slice of unbuttered toast, and plain tea, then for lunch a nice slice of cold roast beef with mustard and two ripe, locally grown tomatoes with salt and pepper, just about 265 calories in all. I had all I wanted to eat, and I'd made up for the 303 calories of custard the night before, which I was glad I'd had because we all have to be a tiny bit indulgent once in a while.

The secret of staying on a diet, I find, is to keep counting, and fix in your mind the end result—the svelteness and vigor we all want to recapture and maintain, especially difficult as we grow older. You may have to go without foods you love, but you've had enough of them in the past and you can do without now—just live on your food memories.

෴

Why Call It French Dressing?

One of the great misnomers in our gastronomic world is "French dressing." It's not French, it's not Italian, it's not English, it's not American—it's simply a universal mixture of oil, vinegar, and seasonings for salad. Not only is French dressing a misnomer; in many of its manifestations it is a misconception. Some French dressings take on a ghastly red hue, and others look as if someone had spilled the parsley bin into them. Some have great milky streaks of poor cheese in them, while yet others reek of garlic powder.

What we are really talking about is a vinaigrette sauce, and a true vinaigrette is as simple as one, two, three. First, good oil, preferably olive, and that very rich and fruity. Second, good vinegar or lemon juice, but usually vinegar, and that should be either a fine cider vinegar or an excellent red or white wine vinegar. Third, salt and pepper. There is your basic vinaigrette sauce for salad.

Now there's much to be said for proportions in a vinaigrette. You often get one so acid with vinegar you can barely manage to choke down the greens. Other times it will be drowned with a very fruity oil, and that is all you taste. Neither is right. There should be a balance. After years of experimenting, I find that for the most part I want 3 to 4 parts of oil to 1 part of vinegar.

    To make a *Vinaigrette Sauce* to dress a salad for four, I take 6 tablespoons of very fruity olive oil and 1½ tablespoons of vinegar, 1 teaspoon of salt and about ½ teaspoon freshly ground black pepper. I blend that together and taste to see whether I want an additional dollop of vinegar in it or not.

This basic dressing needs no ketchup or Worcestershire sauce or anything else to enhance it, save perhaps one of the few permissible things that do vary a dressing. Garlic, for instance. This should be a fresh clove, and it should be crushed and either rubbed into the salt for the dressing or into a little nubbin of dry bread (called a *chapon)* which is then popped into the salad bowl. Personally, I don't like wooden salad bowls, only those of glass or china, so I never rub my bowl with garlic as many people do.

You can also impale the crushed garlic clove on a toothpick, put it in the dressing, and remove it before you toss the salad, unless you like to eat garlic—it's very good if you don't mind carrying around a little garlic breath with you afterward.

There are times when mustard—either dry mustard or the rather hot French-style Dijon mustard that you serve with meat—goes into a vinaigrette sauce. Adjust the amount of mustard to the type of salad. Celery salad, for instance, will take more mustard than a green salad.

Then herbs. I find those that are most agreeable for salads are tarragon, chervil, parsley, chives, and, if you are using tomatoes in your salad, basil. These are the outstanding salad herbs and should be used to your own discretion, either chopped fresh herbs or the dried herbs, crushed well in your hand. There is one other herb that goes very nicely with certain salads, notably cucumber and sometimes tomato, and that is dill. While tarragon is universal, dill is rather limited as a regular salad herb, but it does have its place. Mind you, I don't think you should have a bouquet of herbs in a salad. One, with the possible exception of some parsley as an addition, is ample.

Vinaigrette sauce for salad is so quickly made that there is no need to concoct great jars of it, shake it like mad, and keep it in the refrigerator, as some people do. It only gets stale and tastes unpleasant, especially if there is garlic in it.

The possibilities of a vinaigrette don't end with salad. Marinate cold cooked vegetables in it for a first course, or use leftover beef and make *Beef Salad Parisienne* for a luncheon or supper main dish. Cut 2 pounds lean cold boiled or pot-roasted beef into slices and then into bite-size squares or strips. Combine on salad greens in a bowl or deep platter with 6 boiled, sliced potatoes, ½ pound cooked green beans, 1 peeled, sliced cucumber, 4 peeled tomatoes, cut in sixths, 2 cups celery, finely sliced, and 1 sliced green pepper. Dress with ⅔ cup vinaigrette heavily flavored with 1 tablespoon chopped fresh tarragon or 1 teaspoon dried tarragon and 2 tablespoons chopped parsley. Garnish with 6 halved hard-boiled eggs, 1 red onion, sliced, and a dozen cornichons (small sour pickles), and serve to six.

Who's Afraid of Hollandaise?

One sauce that people love to order in a restaurant but seldom attempt to make at home is hollandaise. Somehow the impression has got around that making hollandaise, like making mayonnaise by hand, is a difficult and arduous process, fraught with disaster. Actually, that isn't true. This rich, elegant butter and egg sauce is tricky to make, admittedly (unless you do it in a blender, which won't give you quite as good a result as the hand-made version), but all it takes is a little patience, care, and a knowledge of what you're doing. Once you've got the knack of it, you'll never be afraid of hollandaise.

Hollandaise and mayonnaise are known classically as emulsified sauces, which means that one ingredient (egg yolks) absorbs another (butter or olive oil) and holds it in suspension, giving you a very thick and creamy mixture. The trick is to coax the egg yolks to absorb the butter or oil without curdling or separating. This takes time, constant stirring or whisking, and, in the case of hollandaise, keeping a sharp watch to see that the sauce doesn't overheat and the eggs scramble.

While there are many members of the hollandaise family—Béarnaise, Maltaise, paloise, and mousseline are some of the other sauces—they all start with a perfect hollandaise.

✎ Make *Sauce Hollandaise* in the top of a double boiler or in a glass or pottery bowl, over water that should remain hot, but never be allowed to boil, during the whole procedure. For 1½ cups sauce, put 3 egg yolks into a bowl and add ½ teaspoon salt, a pinch of pepper or a dash of Tabasco, and 1 tablespoon lemon juice or wine vinegar. Work this with a wooden spatula or wire whisk over the hot water until the eggs and seasonings are well blended and the warmth of the water and the steady stirring have caused the egg yolks to thicken slightly. Have at your elbow on a warm plate 8 tablespoons (1 stick) butter, cut into small pieces. Drop one piece of butter into the egg mixture and stir until the eggs have absorbed it and started to thicken, then quickly add another piece of butter and stir again until it is completely blended into the sauce. Continue to add butter, one piece at a time, until you have a sauce of a thickish consistency that coats the spatula or whisk quite heavily. If by any chance you feel the sauce is thickening too fast, add a tablespoon of cold water, which will slow down the process.

Should your sauce get overheated because you've let the water become too hot, it will break and curdle, giving you rather fancy scrambled eggs. If it is just slightly curdled, there are ways to bring it back. Some people recommend stirring in a tablespoon of heavy cream or a tablespoon of very hot water. Others start all over again with a clean bowl and a fresh egg yolk, stirring the curdled sauce into it gradually, over the hot water, which is the method I happen to favor.

Once the sauce is made, don't let it cool and then try to warm it up in another pan. Leave it in the bowl over lukewarm water and reheat it slowly, covered, letting the water get warm but nowhere near boiling. However, it is my contention that hollandaise should be eaten as soon as it is made and not reheated, because there is always the chance that if it is held, it will develop bacteria, and it's much better to be safe than sorry. So use your hollandaise lavishly and don't try to keep it. You've probably had it on asparagus, artichokes, and eggs Benedict, but try it sometime on poached fish, especially salmon, striped bass, and halibut—it's really delicious.

After you have mastered hollandaise, you can move on to the other members of the family. Sauce Béarnaise, hollandaise with a seasoning of finely chopped shallots, parsley, tarragon, and wine vinegar or white wine and lemon juice that has been cooked down until it is almost a glaze, is superb with steak, broiled liver, or fish such as halibut. Sauce paloise, a variation of Béarnaise with finely chopped fresh mint in place of tarragon and a touch of finely chopped anchovy, tastes absolutely glorious with roast leg of lamb, grilled butterflied leg of lamb, or roast venison.

Then there's garlic hollandaise, with a little finely minced or crushed garlic added to the sauce, which gives it a wonderful pungency; mustard hollandaise, sharpened with ¼ teaspoon dry mustard; and sauce mousseline, for which you whip 4 tablespoons heavy cream and fold it into the sauce just before serving to give it a light ethereal texture that is just perfect with delicate foods like fish, poached chicken, or even soufflés. One of the most intriguing spinoffs is sauce Maltaise, made like a regular hollandaise but without the lemon juice or vinegar—orange juice and grated orange rind are mixed in instead, giving the sauce a deeper color and an orangy overtone that makes asparagus or broccoli seem like quite another vegetable.

So there you have the hollandaise family, a rich bunch, calorically speaking, but definitely the aristocrats of the sauce world.

What's in a Name?

Things are not always what they seem, especially in the world of food. As I travel around I always seem to be encountering national dishes or snacks that are nothing like the names they go under. For instance, in Florida and around New York, wherever there has been an influx of Cubans, you'll find a snack called *medianoche*, or "midnight." So what is *medianoche*? It's a very special sandwich with a most unusual and delicious combination of flavors. I love it, because I love roast pork, especially the Cuban and Puerto Rican version. You take a long sort of hero-shaped soft roll, split and butter it, and put on the lower half a good portion of nicely seasoned cold roast pork. On top of that you place an equally healthy portion of a cheese that melts well, such as Swiss cheese (Emmenthaler or Gruyère) or Monterey Jack or even what is known as American Munster, if that's all you can get. Slap on the top of the roll, and put the whole thing in the oven or on a griddle, with a weight on top, so the cheese melts all over the pork. This takes its place alongside the "poor boy" and the "hero" and all those other honest, hearty sandwiches that are so satisfying.

Cologne, in Germany, is a city with all kinds of funny food names. When I was last there, a friend and I went into a bar for a pre-opera snack and he ordered "two half a hen." I thought: "My heavens, what are we getting?" A half a hen, or *halve Hahn*, turned out to be a slice of local cheese with a hard roll, butter, and a glass of beer, a far remove from any chicken I've ever eaten, but a fine snack nevertheless.

In another restaurant I found a dish called *Kölnische Kaviar*, or Cologne caviar, that wasn't caviar at all, but a portion of cold, highly spiced blood sausage, the kind sold in many German delicatessens and even more supermarkets, served with mustard, a roll, and a couple of tiny dill pickles. How that ever got the name of caviar I'll never know. It's like the Mexican *mantequilla de pobre*, or "poor man's butter" (see page 87), a flavored purée of avocado that in this country would certainly be more a rich man's than a poor man's daily spread.

Another German menu baffler is *Himmel und Erde*—heaven and earth. That's actually mashed potatoes with a little cooked apple beaten in, served with fried blood sausage or fried liver sausage, a very nice combination, especially if there's a slice of onion with the sausage. I suppose this has a symbolic significance because there is an old saying that there must be heaven and earth or man cannot thrive, so "heaven and earth" means that man can survive.

Then there's the English "bubble and squeak," which doesn't bubble, except perhaps in the frying pan, and has never been heard to squeak.

Bubble and squeak is one of those ingenious British ways of using up the leftovers from Sunday's roast beef dinner, cabbage and potatoes and some-times parsnips. These are chopped up and cooked together in some of the beef drippings. There are all kinds of versions. I've had it with little pieces of cold roast beef thrown in at the last minute, and mighty good it is. So good, in fact, that you might cook extra vegetables for dinner just in order to have bubble and squeak next day for lunch.

A British recipe you'll sometimes find here, too, is almost bound to be misunderstood by people who've never had it before, and if they see it on a menu and order it, they are liable to be furious at what they get. It's called Scotch woodcock, and that must be some kind of Scottish joke, because nary a woodcock is there in this dish. In England it is usually served as a savory at the end of a meal, after dessert, or as an evening snack.

There are two ways to make *Scotch Woodcock*; theirs and ours. The Scottish way is to take a slice of well-buttered toast for each person and spread it with 4 finely chopped or pounded anchovy fillets. Then, to serve four, 6 egg yolks, 1 cup heavy cream, and a dash of pepper (no salt—the anchovies are salty enough) are stirred together over hot water in the top of a double boiler until thickened. This rich sauce is then spooned over the toast, sprinkled with chopped parsley, and served at once.

For the American version, an adaptation of the original, put on the buttered toast anchovy fillets to taste—if you like them a lot, 8 or 10 on a slice; if you're not so fond of them, 3 or 4. Then, instead of making a sauce, beat 6 or 7 eggs with 3 or 4 tablespoons heavy cream and freshly ground pepper, melt 3 or 4 tablespoons butter in a pan, and make very light, creamy scrambled eggs. Spoon these over the anchovies, and top with a little chopped parsley.

Either version is extremely pleasant provided you like anchovies. I happen to love the combination of flavors, and I often have Scotch wood-cock for breakfast or Sunday brunch, or I'll serve it with a glass of beer or white wine if friends drop in unexpectedly in the late evening.

A Subject Guide
to the Recipes

Frijoles, page 111
Frijoles Refritos, page 112
Frijoles con Queso, page 112
Spaghettini Estivi, page 23
Risotto alla Milanese, page 125
Myrna Davis' Potato Gnocchi, page 94
Sautéed Hominy with Cream, page 7

SALADS AND SALAD DRESSINGS
Radish and Orange Salad, page 78
Salade Niçoise, page 289
Scandinavian Cucumber Salad, page 82
Scandinavian Salad, page 99
Cannellini Bean and Tuna Salad, page 109
White Bean Salad, page 109
Lentil Salad, page 108
Waldorf Salad, page 114
Potato and Sardine Salad, page 47
Greased Pig Salad, page 116
Shortcut Herring Salad, page 279
Cheese and Olive Salad, page 140
Rice Salad, page 163
Salade Orientale, page 164
Beef-and-Rice Salad, page 164
Alexandre Dumas Potato Salad, page 219
Max Dekking's Beef Salad, page 117
Beef Salad Parisienne, page 307
Sweet Peppers with Anchovies, page 69
Vegetables à la Grecque, page 64
Ranch Salad, page 105
Peppers Stuffed with Anchovies and Raisins,
    page 70
Broccoli Rabe, page 100
Brussels Sprouts, page 101
Guacamole, page 86
Vinaigrette Sauce, page 306
Low-Calorie Dressings, page 305

SAUCES, MARINADES, PICKLES, AND PRESERVES
Sauce Diable, page 8
Tartar Sauce, page 41
Mustard Sauce (for Gravlax), page 43
Tomato Sauce, page 62
Caper Sauce, page 127
Sauce Hollandaise, page 308
Aïoli, page 291
Duxelles, page 88
Sauce Piquante (for Couscous), page 259
Butter Sauce, page 76
Ragú Bolognese (for Pasta), page 153
Snail Butter, page 60
Dill Butter, page 129
Horseradish Cream, page 39
Teriyaki Marinade, page 9
Oil Pickles, page 141

Pickled Lemons, page 258
Tomato Preserve, page 84
Mincemeat, page 243
Brandy Sauce, page 242

BREADS, SNACKS, AND SANDWICHES
Homemade Bread, page 200
American White Bread, page 202
Irish Soda Bread, page 204
Oatmeal Bread, page 263
Myrtle Allen's Brown Bread, page 275
Pita, page 206
Scones, page 285
Croque Monsieur, page 28
Wined Sardines on Toast, page 46
Scotch Woodcock, page 311
Egg and Onion Sandwiches, page 262

DESSERTS, CAKES, AND COOKIES
Baked Rhubarb, page 166
Rhubarb Fool, page 167
Gooseberry Fool, page 170
Strawberry Fool, page 170
Two-Berry Fool, page 171
Rhubarb Pie, page 167
Blueberry Slump, page 169
Strawberry Ice, page 171
Strawberries Romanoff, page 173
Cherry Clafouti, page 175
Black Forest Fruit Dessert, page 297
Bananes à l'Archestrate, page 298
Oranges Orientale, page 226
Tarte Tatin, page 178
Mincemeat and Apple Flan, page 244
Fruit Sorbet, page 183
Champagne Sorbet, page 223
Prune Soufflé, page 177
Vanilla Soufflé, page 143
Nesselrode Pudding, page 181
Syllabub, page 185
Crème Brûlée, page 186
Sharlotka, page 221
Christmas Pudding, page 241
Tomato Preserve, page 84
Galette Perougienne, page 280
Pompe à l'Huile, page 254
Pound Cake, page 188
Philip Brown's Soft Almond Cookies,
    page 287
Country Syllabub, page 184

HOT AND COLD DRINKS
Hot Chocolate, page 197
Hot Spiced Wine, page 249
Summer Punch, page 223

Index

bananas, 304
  bananes à l'Archestrate, 298
  with blueberries, strawberries, and melon, 304
barbecuing
  meat, 20–21
  vegetables, 64–68
Barcelona: Kings' Day (Twelfth Night), 256–257
basil, 120, 129
  pesto, 120, 153
Bassett's (Philadelphia), 180–181
bay leaves, 120
beans, broad, see fava beans
beans, dried, 106, 109–112
beans, green
  à la Grecque, 64
  with bacon and nuts, 9, 164
  tomatoes stuffed with, 116
beans, kidney, see cannellini; kidney beans, red
beans, pea, see pea beans
beans, pinto, see pinto beans
Beard on Bread, 245
Béarnaise sauce, 41, 121, 309
Beaujolais, 218–219
  sharlotka, 221
béchamel sauce, 154
  with capers, 127
  with mustard, 135
Beck, Simone: Simca's Cuisine, quiche, 158
beef
  cuts, 9–10, 14–15
  boiled beef: aïoli, 291
    bollito misto, 300
    caper sauce, 127
    hash, 17
    mincemeat, 243
    pot-au-feu, 16
    salads, 17, 100, 164, 307
  braised beef, see pot roasts below
  deviled beef bones, 11
  hamburger, 2–3, 16
    à cheval, 2
    au poivre, 4
    cheeseburger with bacon, 28
    with duxelles, 89
    with guacamole, 86
  oxtail, 12
    ragout, 12–13
  pot-au-feu, 16
  pot roasts, 14–15, 123
    baked, with ratatouille, 72
    braised beef, 15
    salad Parisienne, 307
    sandwich, 15
  roast, 14

beef (cont.)
  "bubble and squeak," 310–311
  deviled beef bones, 11
  hash, 30
  salads, 110, 117–118
  sandwich, 207
  salads, 17
    Max Dekking's, 117–118
    Parisienne, 307
    with red kidney beans, 110
    with rice, 164
    Scandinavian, 99
  steak, 14, 120
    au poivre, 3, 132
    braised, 9
    broiled, 9, 304
    grilled, 21
    London broil, 8–9
    with rosemary and brandy, 120
    sandwich, 110
    sauce diable, 8
    teriyaki marinade, 9
    steak tartare, 4–5, 126
beef, corned, 148
  hash, 30
    quick, with eggs, 148–149
  sandwich, with cheese and sauerkraut, 209
beets, 98–99
  shredder for, 226
  boiled, 98
    with orange juice and rind, 98
    with sour cream, 73, 98
    with spinach, 98
  pickled, 99
    in rhubarb wine, 166
  salads: with bitter greens, 98, 137
    with herring and meat, 99
    with onion, 98
Bennett, John, 50
Berkeley Hotel (London), 296
blackberries
  Black Forest fruit dessert, 297
  with galette Perougienne, 280
Black Forest fruit dessert, 297
blueberries, 168–169, 304–305
  Black Forest fruit dessert, 297
  with galette Perougienne, 280
  with liqueur, 168
    and pepper, 168
  with maple syrup and sour cream, 168
  with peaches, 168
  sauce, 169
  slump, 169
  with strawberries, melon, and banana, 304
Bocuse, Paul, 221
bollito misto, 300
Boordy Vineyards (Baltimore, Md.), 218

soup *(cont.)*
  garlic, 146
  Lady Curzon, 298
    lentil, 107
  pesto in, 120, 153
  seafood Mediterranée, 56
  sopa mallorquin, 292
sour cream
  with baked potato, 130
  with beets, 73, 98
  with berries, 172
    and maple syrup, 168
  with cottage cheese and sardines, 47
  with horseradish, 39
  with mayonnaise, 33, 98
    and dill, 23
spaghetti (spaghettini), 148
  with chickpeas, 105
  lifter for, 227
  sauces: butter and cheese, 153
    clam, 149, 153
    garlic and oil, 137, 153
    meat (ragú Bolognese), 153
    oyster, 299
    pesto, 120, 153
    tomato, 62, 123, 153
    truffles, 153
  with tomato salad, mixed, 23
Spencer, Evelyn, 38
spices, 122–123
spinach, 123
  with beets, 98
  Lacy's Irish stew, 18
  quiche, 158
  roll, 54
  tian Vençoise, 231
  verdure mista, 271
  wilted, 158
squash
  spit-roasted, 67
  see also zucchini
steak tartare, 5
stews
  bouillabaisse, 55–56
  cioppino, 56
  clam chowder, 57–58
  Irish stew, Lacy's, 18
  oxtail ragoût, 12
  oyster, 248
  ragoût printanier, 272–273
  ropa vieja, 292
  seafood Mediterranée, 56
strawberries, 172–173
  with blueberries, melon, and banana, 304
  Carcassonne, 172
  fool, 170
  ice, 171

strawberries *(cont.)*
  with liqueur and pepper, 172
  Romanoff, 173
stripper, 226–227
sweet peppers with anchovies, 69–70
sweet-sour dressing, 82
syllabubs, 184–185
Syrian cucumber salad, 82

tahini (sesame-seed paste), 106, 260
  hummus bi tahini, 106, 260
  taramasalata, 260
  with yogurt, 260
taramasalata, 260
tarragon, 120, 121, 130, 131
tartar sauce, 41
tea, 190–195
  in England, 193–194
  iced, 191
  kinds, 190, 191, 195
  to make, 190
  Russian, 191
Teleme cheese, 213
tempura, 77
teriyaki marinade, 9
thyme, 15, 120, 130, 131
  with cream cheese, 120
tian Vençoise, 231
toast
  cinnamon, 191
  fried, 60
tomatoes, 55, 62–63, 83–85, 115–116
  baked, 84
  broiled or fried, with bacon, 28
  chopped and sautéed, 62
  with cream and finnan haddie, 282
  grilled in foil, 68
  ice cream, 83
  preserve, 84–85
  ratatouille, 68, 71 137
  salad, 66, 115–116, 307
    with cucumber, 82
    greased pig, 116
    with hot spaghettini, 23
    with onion, 66, 97, 115
  sandwiches, 194–195
    with bacon, 28, 83
    with beef, cheese, and bacon, 209
    cheese dream,28
    club, 28, 83, 208
  sauce, 62–63,
  steamed, 84
  stuffed: with green beans, 116
    with tuna, 115–116
tongue
  mincemeat, 243

About the Author

Born in Portland, Oregon, in 1903, James Beard was destined to find his calling in the food profession. He acquired a sophisticated palate while still a boy, thanks to the good example of his mother, who had run a small residence hotel with a fine kitchen, but he first aspired to be a singer and then an actor. He failed to make his mark as either, and in the late 1930s joined two friends in a catering service in New York. It was called Hors d'Oeuvre, Inc. and led to the publication in 1940 of his first book, *Hors d'Oeuvre and Canapés*, which remained in print for nearly sixty years and has become a classic. More than twenty cookbooks followed, including the best-selling *James Beard Cookbook*, *James Beard's American Cookery*, *James Beard's Theory and Practice of Good Cooking* and *Beard on Bread*. In 1946 Beard appeared on television's first cooking program, and in the 1950s he started the classes that grew into his renowned cooking school. Throughout his career he was sought after as a consultant by restaurants and food producers. On behalf of the latter he toured the country continuously, giving lectures and food demonstrations. He was an exponent of simple, honest cooking, using the best ingredients, and an early believer in the existence of genuine American cuisine. By the time he died, in 1985, he was generally acknowledged to be the country's most influential food authority.